Why Do You Need this New Edition?

American media are going through an unprecedented period of change. Newspaper circulation is dwindling. Television viewership of local news is declining, and audiences are becoming more and more fragmented. Magazines face rising printing and distribution costs, and radio stations must contend with declining audience share. The result is a level of angst in media boardrooms seldom, if ever, seen in the history of modern media.

The ninth edition of *The Art of Editing* focuses on the major changes revolutionizing the media industry and addresses how these changes impact the roles of editors. As media companies embrace convergence—the melding of print, broadcast and online operations—the demand increases for a new type of editor trained in cross-media operations. *The Art of Editing* provides you with the techniques and guiding principles for navigating the challenges and opportunities. What follows are just some of the changes you will find only in the ninth edition.

- An increased emphasis on editing for multimedia formats better prepares you to work in converged media environments.

- A focus on visual journalism helps you understand what it is, how it's done and its growing importance in the field.

- New discussions of the impact of citizen-produced media (i.e., YouTube) on traditional media provide you with an understanding of the real challenges and opportunities facing journalists, editors and news media organizations.

- Updates to media law cases affecting the industry inform you of the new laws and regulations governing the practice of journalism.

- An analysis of the shifts in media consumption helps you identify the major impact of those shifts on journalists and editors.

- An examination of school newspaper censorship identifies the new challenges for editorial staff working in school newsrooms across the country.

THE ART OF EDITING
IN THE AGE
OF CONVERGENCE
Ninth Edition

Brian S. Brooks

Missouri School of Journalism

James L. Pinson

Eastern Michigan University

PEARSON

Boston   New York   San Francisco
Mexico City   Montreal   Toronto   London   Madrid   Munich   Paris
Hong Kong   Singapore   Tokyo   Cape Town   Sydney

Acquitions Editor: *Jeanne Zalesky*
Project Manager: *Lisa Sussman*
Editorial Assistant: *Megan Lentz*
Marketing Manager: *Suzan Czajkowski*
Production Editor: *Karen Mason*
Editorial Production Service: *Publishers' Design and Production Services, Inc.*
Manufacturing Buyer: *JoAnne Sweeney*
Electronic Composition: *Publishers' Design and Production Services, Inc.*
Interior Design: *Publishers' Design and Production Services, Inc.*
Cover Administrator: *Joel Gendron*

For related titles and support materials, visit our online catalog at www.ablongman.com.

Between the time Website information is gathered and then published, it is not unusual for some sites to have closed. Also, the transcription of URLs can result in typographical errors. The publisher would appreciate notification where these errors occur so that they may be corrected in subsequent editions.

Library of Congress Cataloging-in-Publication Data

ISBN-13: 978-0-205-56964-9
ISBN-10: 0-205-56964-1

Printed in the United States of America.

10 9 8 7 6 5 4 3 2 1   HAM   12 11 10 09 08

CONTENTS

Preface   **xiii**

 PART 1   EDITING IN THE AGE OF CONVERGENCE   **1**

Chapter 1   **Editing for Today's Changing Media**   **1**

The Editor's Changing Role   1
Democratization of the Media   2
The Changing Media Environment   3
*The Media Begin to Converge   5   •   The Changing Nature
of News   7*
The Role of the Editor   8
Jobs for Editors   9   •   The Art of Editing   11
Suggested Web Sites   12
Suggested Readings   12

Chapter 2   **The Editor and the Audience**   **13**

The Disconnected Audience   13
Advertising Prompts Change   14   •   Media in Turmoil   15
Interaction with Consumers   16
The Contrary View   17
Evaluating the Media Mix   19
Responding to Change   20
Understanding U.S. Audiences   21
*Credibility and the Media   23   •   Changing Needs of
Changing Consumers   26*
Suggested Web Sites   27
Suggested Readings   27

PART 2   THE FUNDAMENTALS OF EDITING   28

Chapter 3   The Editing Process   28

The Editor's Role   28
The Value of the Copy Editor   29
What Makes a Good Copy Editor?   30
Understanding the Newsroom and What Editors Do   32
Understanding the Flow of Copy   37
Editing the Story   38
The Three R's of Copy Editing   43
   Is the Story Reader-Centered?   43   •   Is the Story Readable?   44
   •   Is the Story Right?   46
Copy-Editing and Proofreading Symbols   48
Proofreading   52
   The Difference Between Proofreading and Copy Editing   53   •   What
   Do You Do When Told to Read Proofs?   54   •   What If a Story is
   Too Long?   54
Suggested Web Sites   55

Chapter 4   Macro Editing for the Big Picture   56

Making Sure Stories Are Worth Running   56
Making Sure Stories Have Good Leads   58
   Hard News   58   •   Features   59   •   Rules for Both Hard-News
   and Feature Leads   63
Making Sure Stories Are Organized and Flow Well   66
Making Sure Stories Don't Leave Unanswered Questions   68
Making Sure Stories Are Accurate   69
   Common Kinds of Inaccuracies   70   •   Where Editors Create Mistakes   80
Making Sure Stories Are Objective   82
Suggested Web Sites   84
Suggested Readings   84

Chapter 5   Macro Editing for Legality, Ethics and Propriety   85

Freedom of the Press   86
   What Does "Freedom of the Press" Mean?   87
Legal Problems   95
   Libel   95   •   Should We Print a Correction?   104   •   Negligence   105   •
   Invasion of Privacy   106   •   Anonymous Sources   108   •   Obscenity   109
   •   Raffles   109   •   Intellectual Property   109   •   Censorship of School
   Newspapers   111   •   Regulation of Electronic Media   113
Ethical Issues   119
   Confessions   120   •   Printing Names and Addresses   120   •   Ethical
   Flashing Lights   120   •   Finding Ethical Answers   125   •   SPJ Code
   of Ethics   127

Propriety   129
  Being Sensitive   130
Suggested Web Sites   134
Suggested Readings   134

Chapter 6   **Micro Editing for Precision in Language   135**

Grammar   135
  *Sentence Problems   136   •   Nouns and Pronouns   139   •   Verbs   144
  •   Modifiers   151   •   Interjections   153   •   Connecting Words   154*
Usage   157
  Confused Words   157   •   Misused Idioms   163
Style   164
  *Abbreviations and Symbols   164   •   Capitalization   165
  •   Numbers   166   •   Punctuation   166   •   Quotations   168
  •   Miscellaneous   171   •   Spelling   173*
Tightening   176
Suggested Web Sites   183
Suggested Readings   183

Chapter 7   **Holistic Editing: Integrating the Macro and the Micro   184**

Accident and Disaster Stories   185
Advance Pieces   187
Analysis Pieces   188
Boating and Shipping Stories   188
Business Stories   189
Calendar Items   191
Celebrity News   192
Chronological Stories   193
Color Pieces   193
Columns   193
Court Stories   194
Crime Stories   197
Education Stories   199
Entertainment Stories   200
First-Person Stories   200
Focus Pieces   200
Follows   201
  Follow-Up Features   202
Food Features   202
History Pieces   203
How-to Articles or Service Journalism   203
Human-Interest Stories   203
Labor Disputes   204
Medical News   205

Meeting Stories   206
    Government News   207
Obituaries   207
    Feature Obituaries   209
Personality Profiles   210
Political Stories   211
Press-Release Stories   212
    *Calendar Items   212   •   Personnel: Appointments, Promotions,
Training, Retirement   213   •   Personal: Weddings, Engagements,
Anniversaries, Reunions   214   •   Cause-Promoting Releases   214
•   Image-Building Releases   215*
Question-and-Answer Interviews   215
Religion Stories   215
Reviews   216
Science and Health Stories   216
Seasonal Features   217
Speech Stories   217
Sports Stories   219
Travel Pieces   221
War Stories   222
Weather Stories   222
Suggested Web Sites   225
Suggested Readings   225

PART 3   THE VISUAL SIDE OF EDITING   226

Chapter 8   Writing Headlines, Titles, Captions and Blurbs   226

Getting People to Read   226
Some Thoughts on Headlines   226
    *The Laws of Newspaper Readership   227   •   Assume the Reader
Won't Read the Story   228   •   The Reader's Favorite Newspaper   233
•   Shorter Stories—And More of Them   234*
The Headline-Writing Process   234
    *Understanding Headline Orders   236   •   Headline Terminology   237
•   Headline Mechanics   238*
How to Write the Headline   240
    *Headlines That Tell   240   •   Headlines That Smell   242   •   Headlines
That Sell   249   •   What to Do If You're Stuck   251*
Title Heads in Magazines   252
Blurbs and Captions   254
    Blurbs   254   •   Captions   255
Headlines and Titles for the Internet   256
Suggested Web Sites   258
Suggested Readings   258

Chapter 9   Using Photos, Graphics and Type   259

Editing for Graphic Appeal   260
Using Photos   261
    Photographer–Editor Relationships   263 • *Editing Decisions   264*
    • *Pictures as Copy   269* • *Changing Photo Technology   271*
    • *Taste in Picture Editing   272* • *Caption Guidelines   272*
Using Information Graphics   278
Types of Information Graphics   279
Using Type   282
    How Type is Measured   283 • *Differentiating Typefaces (Fonts)   283*
    • *How to Measure Type from a Printed Page   289* • *An Introduction to
Leading   290* • *The Typography of Headlines   291*
Suggested Web Sites   292
Suggested Readings   292

PART 4   EDITING FOR DIFFERENT MEDIA   293

Chapter 10   Editing Newspapers   293

Editing the Wires   296
    Sources of Wire News   297 • *How the Wires Operate   298* • *Budgets
and Priorities   299* • *Sorting the Pieces   303* • *Selecting Wire
Stories   304*
Designing the Newspaper   308
    How to Recognize a Well-Designed Newspaper   308 • *Objectives of
Newspaper Design   310* • *Newspapers and the Principles of Artistic
Design   311* • *Visualizing Total Page Structure   316*
Suggested Web Sites   317
Suggested Readings   317

Chapter 11   Editing Magazines and Newsletters   318

What is a Magazine?   318
    Magazine Staffing   322 • *How Magazine Editing Differs From
Newspaper Editing   323*
Magazine Design   324
    Goals of Page Designers   329
Graphic Styling Alternatives   329
    Body and Headline Typeface Styles   330 • *Initial Caps As
Ornamentation   330* • *Line Spacing or Leading   330* • *Blurbs or Type
Inserts   333* • *Rules   333* • *Sidebars or Boxes   333* • *Background
Screens or Tint Blocks   334* • *Picture Styles and Uses   334*
    • *Color   335* • *Placement of Advertising   335*
What is a Newsletter?   336
    Newsletters Then and Now   337 • *What is the Key to a Newsletter's
Success?   338*

How to Make Money with a Newsletter   339
Newsletter Design   340
Suggested Web Sites   344
Suggested Readings   344

Chapter 12   Editing for the Web   345

Layers and Links   348
Online Journalism and Credibility   349
Types of New Media   350
Sources of Information   351
The Online Editor   352
The Web's Importance   353
Designing for the Web   355
Online Media and the Future   357
Suggested Web Sites   359
Suggested Readings   359

Chapter 13   Editing for the Broadcast Media   360

Sources of Copy   363
Preparation of Copy   364
Broadcast Style   366
Taste   369
Soundbites   370
Television News   370
Copy Formats   373
Suggested Web Sites   375
Suggested Readings   375

Chapter 14   Editing in Other Fields   376

Job Opportunities in Public Relations and Advertising   376
Public Relations   378
Print Advertising   380
Broadcast Advertising   382
Jobs in Book Publishing   382
Suggested Web Sites   385
Suggested Readings   385

PART 5   EDITORS' OTHER HATS   386

Chapter 15   The Editor As Coach   386

The Assignment Editor and the Reporter   386
The Assignment Editor As Coach and Fixer   387 • *The Assignment Editor
As Coach and Mentor   388*
The Assignment Editor and the Production Editors   389

The Production Editors and the Supervisor   390
Editors Coaching Junior Editors   391
Some Advice for Beginners   392
Suggested Web Sites   393
Suggested Readings   393

Chapter 16   **The Editor As Manager and Leader**   **394**

Manage or Lead?   395
Managers: What They Do   395   •   Leaders: What They Do   398
Suggested Web Sites   399
Suggested Readings   399

Glossary   401

Index   411

As we publish the ninth edition of *The Art of Editing,* the media industry is changing more rapidly than ever. Significant layoffs have rocked the editorial staffs of newspapers, television has felt the effects of ever-increasing competition, and new methods of receiving news, particularly over mobile phones, promise to change the industry in ways heretofore unimagined.

Convergence is fundamental to what's happening in the industry, as the subtitle of this book would suggest. *Convergence* means many things to many people, but we define it here as cooperative ventures among print media, radio, television and the Web. There is a growing demand for multimedia editors who can edit print, audio and video, and cope with the nuances of the Web. Therefore, in this edition we place more emphasis than ever before on editing for the Web.

Also inevitable is the continued march toward greater ownership concentration in the media. Rupert Murdoch's News Corp. now owns the venerable *Wall Street Journal*, a reality that would have been unfathomable a decade ago. In the lower end of the market, chain operations are buying up every remaining independently owned newspaper in sight. Indeed, while metro newspapers suffer declines in circulation and advertising revenue, small newspapers thrive.

Through all the turmoil and change, one constant remains: Those who can edit, and edit well, have no trouble finding jobs. If the market for reporters is stressed, the market for editors is not. Good editors are hard to find, and they are in great demand. This book is designed to help students find their first jobs as editors and perform well when they do. It also is designed as a refresher and update for professional editors.

As in past editions, we stress the importance of editing as an art. We say that because in editing, unlike in the sciences, there often is no one right way to do things. The best editors learn the principles of editing and then adapt them to the story at hand. In this edition, readers will find an increased emphasis on the Web, more on editing for magazines and broadcast, extensive revisions that build on the concepts of micro and macro editing, and expanded coverage of legal and ethical issues.

In this ninth edition, as in earlier ones, we have included numerous examples of editors' successes and failures as illustrations of how to edit and how not to edit. We have taken examples, both good and bad, from newspapers, magazines, radio and television stations, and Web sites from coast to coast. Through them, we learn.

Journalism is an interesting, stimulating and exciting profession. Editing, in turn, is a vital part of journalism, whether delivered in print, through broadcast or on the Web. Newspapers, magazines, radio and television stations, and Web sites would not be nearly as good without editors as they are with them. They can be superb with top-flight editors. We hope this book inspires many of you to become just that.

The excitement of producing the news is universal, and it is a process in which editors are full partners. Still, it is difficult for any book to capture the excitement of editing because the beginner must first master the intricacies of the editor's art. Attention to detail is of primary importance to the editor, and we believe this book attends to that detail more thoroughly than any other.

Those of you who are attentive to detail will note a deviation from Associated Press style, which the book generally follows. We have adopted the book publisher's convention of italicizing newspaper, magazine and book titles.

We thank the reviewers who took time to provide detailed suggestions for this revision. They are Elizabeth W. Cook, College of Charleston; Margaret A. Finucane, Hofstra University; and Robert K. Hays, Northampton Community College.

We also thank our managing editor at Allyn and Bacon, Lisa Sussman, who provided the inspiration and careful editing that all authors need. Thank you, too, to Lynda Griffiths for overseeing all the details and to Publisher's Design and Production Services for their full-service production of this ninth edition.

So, we have updated the entire text. Through it all, one axiom holds true: Editing is an art no matter where or by whom it is practiced. To those who will accept the challenge of careful and thoughtful editing, this volume is dedicated.

—Brian S. Brooks (brooksbs@missouri.edu)
—James L. Pinson (jpinson@emich.edu)

CHAPTER 1

EDITING FOR TODAY'S CHANGING MEDIA

 ## THE EDITOR'S CHANGING ROLE

For generations, news was produced and distributed in assembly-line fashion. Reporters gathered and wrote it, editors edited it, and publishers produced and distributed it in print or broadcast form to mass audiences. It was a one-to-many model born in the Industrial Revolution.

Editors in that environment served as **gatekeepers.** They decided when to open the gate, allowing information to flow to the public. Editors had total control over what was published or broadcast. They determined which stories were *newsworthy*—those they deemed useful, relevant or interesting to their audiences. Editors controlled the gate, and consumers got only what editors gave them.

Editors also controlled the **play** a story received. Was it newsworthy enough for Page One, where almost everyone would notice it, or should it be relegated to a brief on Page 37, where few would read it? Did it make the cover of *Time,* or did it not make the magazine at all? Did it warrant top billing on the evening newscast, or was it left to the local newspaper?

Editors were powerful. They called all the shots.

Today, all that is changing. The Internet and wireless devices (cell phones and personal digital assistants) allow users to *choose* what news they want to consume from multiple providers—some traditional and some not—and from digital databases of information vastly larger than the content of the nation's largest newspaper or even the capacity of a 24-hour-a-day cable-television news channel. In this environment, the one-to-many model disappears, and the user takes control.

Consumers now have almost unlimited access to millions of daily news items on the Internet. Sophisticated software allows them to program computers or wireless devices to receive only the news they want. That software, not an editor, serves as the gatekeeper. The consumer, not the editor, has control of the flow of information.

Obviously, not everyone consumes news this way. Editors still serve as gate-keepers at newspapers and magazines, and in radio and television newsrooms. Editors still choose what to put on the front page of news Web sites. Editors still edit newsletters, corporate magazines and even advertisements. But an ever-increasing percentage of the world's population is discovering that it doesn't need editors to get information.

Editors, for their part, lament the erosion of their power. One veteran editor said at a recent meeting of newspaper editors: "We have historically performed a great service to society by setting the public agenda. When people consume only news that they want or like to read, they miss out on reading about important public issues they *need* to know about. Not many people want to read about garbage collection or sewer plants, but they need to know about the city's problems with those things."

The editor's point is well-taken. Newspapers, magazines, radio and television have performed an important public function in setting the public agenda. Editors must continue to find ways to serve that function in an era when the audience is no longer a captive one. That will happen only if editors produce compelling publications, newscasts and online sites that are perceived to be accurate and truthful.

Editors, then, are faced with a changing environment. No longer are their roles as gatekeepers and **agenda setters** guaranteed. In today's changing media environment, these roles must be earned. Consumers must trust editors to give them what they need to know to be productive citizens. Consumers must perceive value in the editor as gatekeeper and agenda setter. Consumers must perceive a need to have editors help them sort through the sea of information now at their disposal.

Earning that trust won't be easy. Each time a newspaper makes a mistake or a television station ignores real news in favor of the sensational, public confidence in the media erodes. Each time a cable news network passes off editorializing as news, the credibility of that medium among thoughtful consumers erodes a bit more.

Editors cannot afford to be arrogant. They must earn the public's trust by making good judgments and presenting the news fairly and accurately. If they fail to do that, their influence will continue to diminish.

Thus, the best path editors can follow is this one: Practice good journalism grounded in the fundamentals of truth and accuracy. In the end, this is the only way to earn the public's trust.

DEMOCRATIZATION OF THE MEDIA

The one-to-many model big media employed exclusively in the past still exists, but it exists alongside a new form of media known as **citizen journalism.** Modern technology lowers the cost of entry into the media business. Desktop-publishing programs such as Adobe InDesign have made typesetting and design a snap, which in turn lowers the cost of starting a printed publication. The Web makes it simple for anyone with Internet access to create a site. **Podcasting** makes it easy to create a radio or television program and distribute it worldwide. The result? Anyone and everyone can publish a newspaper, newsletter or magazine. Anyone and everyone can be a broadcaster.

These easily accessible media provide ample opportunities for the public to avoid big media if it so desires. Think *The New York Times* has a liberal bias? Avoid it by going to any number of conservative Web sites. Think your local newspaper does a poor job of covering recruiting for your favorite college football team? Avoid it by going to a Web site that covers nothing but what you want.

The problem with the old one-to-many model is that readers don't get to talk back or discuss the issues except in limited ways. Sure, you can write a letter to the editor about a story you dislike, but it may or may not be published. What readers and viewers want is a chance to *discuss* the news with those who report it. Readers and viewers want to read about or see things the traditional media seldom cover. They want to be part of the news-gathering and reporting process. They want their views heard.

Some editors are embracing the concept. Increasingly, blogs on the sites of traditional media provide a forum for readers to criticize a newspaper column or blast a television station for gory coverage of a crime. Some have gone even further. The *Columbia Missourian* devotes several pages of its Sunday paper to reader-produced news. Local citizens write stories and take photographs. Newspaper editors work with them to do minor editing and design the pages. The result? Readers who write for the paper feel a connection to it that never existed before. And for the stuff that won't fit in the printed product, there's also an outlet—a Web site called MyMissourian.com produced by the newspaper's staff.

Editors around the country, like those in Columbia, are embracing citizen-produced news as a welcome extension of what they do. After all, reporters can't be everywhere and can't cover every story. Citizen journalism allows editors to extend their coverage in ways never before possible.

THE CHANGING MEDIA ENVIRONMENT

While the role of the editor is changing, it is doing so in consort with the changing nature of the media. Consider these realities:

- Newspapers continue to reach a smaller segment of the general population each year. While the population continues to grow, newspaper circulation remains flat. Most newspapers are still profitable, but often, that's true only because of a virtual print monopoly in a given community. In almost every city across the nation, circulation is declining.

- Broadcast television audiences have been fragmented by the growth of competition. New networks such as Fox and The CW have added local stations in many markets, and the proliferation of cable-television channels—particularly 24-hour news channels such as CNBC, MSNBC, Fox News Channel and CNN—have added to audience erosion.

- Except for public broadcasting and all-news stations in a few major markets, radio isn't much of a player in news in North America. Many stations air network news or read news items from local newspapers, but few local stations employ news reporters. Arguably the best news found on American broadcast radio is produced by National Public Radio, which has affiliates nationwide. Satellite radio has also allowed subscribers to listen not only to public radio news but also to the audio of 24-hour cable-TV news channels, as well as to foreign news services such as the BBC and CBC, and channels devoted to 24-hour coverage of traffic and weather for the nation's main metro areas.

- Magazines, for the most part, reach targeted audiences that are widely dispersed, often making them unsuitable for local advertising. Production costs are high, and postal rates, on which many depend for distribution, inch ever higher.

Thus, the traditional media, while still quite profitable, often find their profit margins challenged by forces largely beyond their control. But make no mistake about it: The existing media, while challenged, are certainly not dying. To illustrate:

- Newspapers typically operate on profit margins around 15 percent of gross income. That's a remarkably healthy margin, far surpassing those in many other industries, which are typically only about a third of that and often less. Even extraordinarily profitable industries such as oil have lower margins. ExxonMobil in 2006 earned 10 percent.

- Most magazines, while not necessarily news oriented in the traditional sense, attract advertisers in droves because of the appealing demographics of their audiences. If an advertiser wants to reach computer users, *PC Magazine* or *Macworld* will do the job.

- Most local broadcast stations are thriving, even as the traditional networks—NBC, CBS and ABC—have been hurt by audience fragmentation. And cable-television outlets such as The Food Channel and ESPN do a great job of delivering the target audiences advertisers crave.

- All-news radio stations, found mostly in large metropolitan areas, are doing well financially.

The traditional media, then, are far from dead, even if they are not quite as profitable as they once were. Newspapers, magazines, radio and television are with us to stay, even in the face of new challenges such as Web publications and wireless devices.

The Media Begin to Converge

Indeed, traditional media are finding news ways to compete. The buzzword in the media industry these days is **convergence,** and traditional media are exploring many forms of it. So what is convergence? It's defined in many ways, but possibly the best definition yet offered is this:

> Convergence is the practice of sharing and cross-promoting content from a variety of media through newsroom collaborations and outside partnerships.

Perhaps the best-known convergence experiment to date is one that involves the *Tampa Tribune,* WFLA and Tampa Bay Online (www.tbo.com), all owned by Media General and based in Tampa, Fla. Media General took the unusual step in 2000 of constructing a new building to house all three operations. Management then pushed the three media outlets to overcome competitive distrust of each other.

Gil Thelen, former senior vice president and executive editor of the *Tribune,* confesses that the process of converging operations wasn't easy. Some workers quit rather than learn new ways of doing things. Others stayed, complained and ultimately made the process work.

Today, crossover reporting in Tampa is increasingly common:

- A *Tribune* story about a passenger who landed a plane after the pilot became ill carried the bylines of both a *Tribune* reporter and the WFLA anchor.
- A report on dog bites ran as a two-part WFLA series, a front-page *Tribune* story and a Tampa Bay Online package.
- A *Tribune* story on the removal of a statue from a shopping center included a picture by the photo editor, who also shot video for WFLA.

Cultural differences among the media can cause problems when media converge. When television first came along, many of its early newscasters came from the newspaper industry. Edward R. Murrow and Walter Cronkite brought with them the demanding ethical and reporting standards of the newspaper industry. But over the years, television developed a new set of standards driven more by what is visually pleasing than by traditional news values as practiced by newspapers. Now, as convergence occurs, these disparate cultures must begin to meld again.

Cultural differences aside, convergence makes sense, and it is happening nationwide. Television is the unquestioned leader in providing the American public with today's news headlines. Newspapers and magazines can provide more depth and understanding. The Internet can offer even greater depth than newspapers and interactivity unmatched by either print or television. The merging of these disparate media makes sense for a changing world in which the consumer sets the terms for the consumption of news. The goal of forward-thinking media companies is to give consumers the news and information they want in whatever form they prefer.

Convergence isn't happening only at large operations in big cities. The *Lawrence* (Kan.) *Journal-World* still prints a newspaper, but it also operates Web sites, including one focused on University of Kansas basketball, and a cable-television operation complete with local newscasts. Indeed, many newspaper companies are adopting a print-second model in which news is posted on Web sites or broadcast stations before it appears in the newspaper.

The federal government is attempting to provide impetus for this change. In 2003, the Federal Communications Commission voted to ease restrictions on media cross-ownership, making it easier for companies to own television stations and newspapers in the same market. Fearing too much concentration of media ownership, Congress blocked the move, but each year, there are efforts to reverse that decision.

Whatever the outcome, one thing is evident: Convergence is here to stay, and it is not necessarily dependent on common ownership. A separately owned newspaper can pair with a local television station for cross-promotional purposes. And both are quite likely to operate Web sites, possibly collaborating, as well.

In converged newsrooms such as the one in Tampa, journalists are finding they must learn about a medium other than the one in which they were trained. A television reporter might be asked to write a newspaper story, and he or she must be able to do so. A newspaper reporter might be asked to take along a recorder to get a sound bite of a news event for a Web site or radio station. And many, while not required to cross quite so dramatically into a new field, must have at least enough knowledge of the strengths of various media to know how best to tell a story in a multimedia environment. This is the world of the editor in the era of convergence.

Increasingly, journalists may train in one medium, go to work upon graduation in another, and at some point change to a third or fourth career, depending on job opportunities at the time. As a result, today's journalists should view themselves not as television reporters or newspaper editors but as news specialists comfortable with working in a variety of settings—on the Internet, at a magazine, in television and perhaps even in the related fields of public relations and advertising.

Media companies realize the importance of giving consumers news and advertising information whenever and however it's wanted. That, in the end, is what convergence is all about.

The Changing Nature of News

If the media are changing, so is the nature of news itself. Editors no longer are the sole arbiters of what news is and what it isn't. Today, consumers increasingly decide that for themselves.

Traditionally, editors defined news as information having one or more (usually more) of these qualities:

- *Audience.* Readers of *The New York Times* are more likely to be interested in urban renewal than those of a local paper in Cedar City, Utah.

- *Impact.* The number of people involved in or affected by an event, as well as the emotional depth of an audience's reaction, helps to determine whether it is news.

- *Proximity.* Things that happen close by are often more interesting than things that happen far away.

- *Timeliness.* Something that just happened is likely more interesting than something that happened last week or last year.

- *Prominence.* People like to read about famous, wealthy or powerful people, so entertainer Jennifer Lopez is more interesting than someone of whom few people have heard.

- *Novelty.* Something that is unusual or the first, the largest or the greatest is news.

- *Conflict.* People are drawn to read about conflict between people, states and nations.

Another way editors have defined news is to evaluate how *relevant* it is to readers or viewers—that is, how *useful* or *interesting*.

Today, however, consumers are defining news for themselves. If a Web site has appealing content, some viewers will find their news there, no matter how reliable or unreliable that site may be. And Web entrepreneurs are carving out niche markets to take advantage of this reality.

Traditional media have done little, for example, to cover the recruiting of high school athletes for college football and basketball teams. Today, two national Web sites, The Insiders (www.theinsiders.com) and Rivals (www.rivals.com), provide reporters who collect that information and distribute it online to an audience with a seemingly insatiable appetite for sports. The related forums on these networks help spread both news and rumor.

The reality is that much of the information provided by these specialized Internet services is timely and reliable. On the reader forums, however, much of it is not. Consumers don't seem to care. Whether fact or rumor, to them it is news.

Another challenge to credibility is Web sites that support a cause. When people surf the Internet for information about a topic, it's often difficult to determine whether a site is objective or supporting one side of a controversial topic. Again, much of the public doesn't seem to care.

This could help explain the proliferation of cable-television news networks, where solid news coverage is interspersed, often without any warning, with commentators who editorialize rather than objectively report the news. Cable-news networks with a political bias—either to the left or right—are easy to find, and people who share their biases gravitate toward one or the other, based on political preference. Seemingly, many in the public are comforted to find a news channel that reinforces their biases.

Is the stuff these channels produce really news? By traditional definition, much of it certainly is not. But perhaps that is not important. This tells us that many consumers don't value the traditional media's penchant for objectivity. Nor do they perceive any real value in the traditional news brands, those media companies with a long history of providing quality news. Given the freedom they have to roam the Web, many consumers will get information wherever they can find it from whatever source.

Although critics often accuse the mainstream media of unconscious bias in stories, intentional political bias once played a central role in American journalism. During the party press era of 1781 to 1833, writers were certainly colorful in their invective against political opponents, but few would argue that readers were better served 200 years ago when it came to getting fair coverage and accurate information.

Regardless, consumers are voting with their feet. They are going to media outlets that provide the information they want. For many, if the information they want is politically tilted, that's not a problem if the political tilt agrees with their own views. Convincing these people that this isn't the best idea is perhaps the single biggest problem facing the editors of tomorrow.

If all this is discouraging, it's important to keep one thing in mind: Most thoughtful citizens still *want* someone to help them sort through the news. Most *want* editors who are reliable and who work at branded publications and television outlets they trust.

THE ROLE OF THE EDITOR

The changing nature of news is the reason the role of the editor will remain important, even as society embraces nontraditional media. Because anyone can become a reporter or publisher on the Web, there will be an increasing need to separate fact from fiction, to know the source of information and to determine its credibility. Editors are trained to do just that.

Editors, however, will have more competition than in the past. Consumers will look to other sources of information to help guide them in their decision

A New Source of News

The growing popularity of **blogs,** sometimes called *Web logs* or *Weblogs,* illustrates the rapidly changing patterns of news consumption in the United States. Blogs are Internet Web sites on which users exchange information, personal thoughts and Web links, and they are increasingly popular.

Some blogs focus on the media and are frequent stops for journalists. Others cover almost any imaginable topic. Some offer useful information. Some are totally useless. But a good blog gives people with common interests a place to exchange ideas.

For some interesting examples of blogs, see the list of links on K. Paul Mallasch's Web site: www.mallasch.com. Mallasch also has created a blog on grassroots journalism called Journalism Hope: www.journalismhope.com/.

Sites such as Blogger (www.blogger.com) offer automated publishing systems to permit the easy creation of blogs.

Nationwide, newspapers and television stations are creating blogs, often moderated by their own reporters and editors. Such blogs allow readers, viewers and editors to connect.

---

making. One such source will be the Web, with its **chat rooms** and discussion forums. These digital conversation rooms, in which users interact with each other, serve much the same purpose as town-hall meetings or call-in talk shows on radio and television. They provide a forum for a variety of views, which in turn enables the consumer to form an opinion about an issue.

But information provided in town-hall meetings or on talk shows is not always accurate. That's where editors can help. With their training in fact checking and their ability to separate fact from fiction, they can continue to play a major role in agenda setting, if not gatekeeping.

Indeed, good editors can help consumers sort through the mass of information now readily available and make sense of it. Good editors can help the public define what's credible and what's not. Good editors can have a significant impact on the audiences they serve.

The public may play a greater role than ever before in defining news, but editors are far from obsolete. Indeed, they are needed more today than ever before.

Jobs for Editors

Those who write well are in demand, and those who edit well are in even greater demand. That's because writing jobs are common entry points for those graduating with a degree in journalism or communications. The glamour of the byline seems irresistible for many.

Those who eagerly pursue editing careers, however, are fewer in number. As a result, the media industry scrambles to find qualified editors. That explains the existence of a program such as the Dow Jones Newspaper Fund editing intern program, which for almost 50 years has offered lucrative internships at big newspapers in an effort to entice young journalists to consider newspaper copy editing careers.

But newspaper copy editing is merely one of many options for those trained as editors. Newspapers need editors at every level—copy editor, city editor, graphics editor, photo editor, design editor, Web editor, news editor, editorial page editor, managing editor and executive editor. Magazines have similar needs but sometimes give their employees different titles—researcher, editorial assistant, contributing editor and senior editor.

Similarly, broadcast newsrooms require a raft of editors—news director, executive producer, show producers and desk assistants. The notion that nothing but video is edited in a television newsroom is far from true.

Web sites often are staffed almost entirely with editors who rely on freelance writers and others for content. Most Web site news operations are like big newspaper copy desks with multiple editors to handle content.

The companies that advertise also have editors. Someone must edit the text in advertisements. And many other types of companies require editors in their corporate communications department, where they work on employee magazines and newsletters, annual reports, technical manuals and industry newsletters.

And, of course, there is the matter of convergence. Convergence is creating a demand for a new type of editor, one as capable of handling a magazine or newspaper story as editing video and the words that accompany it. The demand for those cross-trained in various media is growing daily. This, too, adds to the demand for editors.

Editing jobs are so plentiful, in fact, that companies are often willing to pay editors a higher salary than writers. Some of the nation's largest newspapers pay a differential to copy editors as a means of enticing journalists to work at the copy desk. The difference in pay between copy editors and reporters is sometimes considerable.

The variety of skills editors must master and the large range of news with which they must be up-to-date keep their work varied and interesting. Rather than being specialists on a narrow beat, they are generalists. And the skills good editors must have make them prime candidates for advancement either to better, larger newspapers or into management. Since their job brings them into daily contact with other departments of the newspaper, they quickly become familiar with how each departments works, as well as how the business as a whole fits together.

The shortage of editors exists not because people don't like being editors. Instead, it exists because more people think of writing as a first choice.

The Art of Editing

In the first edition of this book, published in 1971, editing was described as an art, no matter where or by whom it is practiced. That axiom remains true today. Although media may change, the role of the editor remains clear: Provide timely and accurate information in the best form possible.

This edition of *The Art of Editing* has been extensively revised to reflect the dramatic changes occurring in the media industry. It's worth remembering that despite the unsettled nature of the industry, there is no chance that editing jobs will disappear. Indeed, the number of career opportunities for talented editors seems to grow each year.

The skills that can be acquired from this text will help you edit, no matter which medium you enter. Not everyone is an artist, and not everyone can be an editor. Those who learn here can be both.

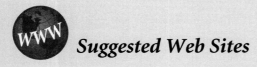

Suggested Web Sites

American Copy Editors Society **www.copydesk.org**
American Society of Newspaper Editors **www.asne.org**
Dow Jones Newspaper Fund **djnewspaperfund.dowjones.com**
Lawrence (Kan.) Journal-World **www2.ljworld.com/**
MyMissourian (citizen journalism) **www.mymissourian.com/**
Newsletter & Electronic Publishers Association **www.newsletters.org**
Radio-Television News Directors Association & Foundation **www.rtndf.org**
Tampa Bay Online **www.tbo.com/**

Suggested Readings

Gant, Scott. *We're All Journalists Now*. New York: Free Press, 2007.
Hewitt, Hugh. *Blog: Understanding the Information Reformation That's Changing Our World*. Nashville, Tenn.: Thomas Nelson, 2005.
Jenkins, Henry. *Convergence Culture: Where Old and New Media Collide*. New York: New York University Press, 2006.
Keen, Andrew. *The Cult of the Amateur: How Today's Internet Is Killing Our Culture*. New York: Doubleday, 2007.
The Missouri Group: Brian S. Brooks, George Kennedy, Don Ranly and Daryl R. Moen. *Telling the Story: The Convergence of Print, Broadcast and Online Media*. New York: Bedford/St. Martin's, 2007.

CHAPTER 2

THE EDITOR AND THE AUDIENCE

 THE DISCONNECTED AUDIENCE

Editors and their audiences are too often disconnected. Consider these indications of that reality:

- Weekday circulation of newspapers continues its steady decline, while the population continues to increase dramatically.
- According to the Newspaper Association of America, about 78 percent of the nation's adult population read newspapers daily in 1970, but by 2006, that percentage had declined to 49.9.

These are damning figures for newspapers, and the situation may be even worse than it appears. Further examination of newspaper circulation trends indicates that declines are most prevalent among people 35 and younger. That's bad news because young people are on the advertisers' most-wanted list. People in their late 20s and early 30s are in the process of setting up households and making major expenditures. Advertisers covet their attention.

Recent statistics from the Newspaper Association of America show that only 34.6 percent of Americans 25 to 34 read newspapers daily. The percentage is 36.1 percent for those 18 to 24.

Perhaps the biggest problem for newspapers is that there's little hope of reversing this trend. Study after study shows that if the newspaper reading habit is not acquired early in life, it probably never will be. As a result, newspaper readers are increasingly older. Worse, as older readers die, younger readers are not taking their place.

One anecdotal incident vividly illustrates the problem: After being exposed to an **electronic newspaper** used in a University of Missouri research project, one junior high student was asked what he thought of the new medium.

"Cool," he responded.

"Cool or way cool?" asked the researcher.

"It can't be way cool," responded the student. "It's a newspaper."

13

For those fond of newspapers and the significant role they have played in winning and maintaining democracy in the United States, that comment hurts deeply. For the editor or publisher trying to ensure a newspaper's future, it is equally devastating. But it is a view shared by many school-age children. Newspapers, they believe, are boring, written for older people and simply not relevant to their lives.

That same study, however, showed that the online media have a chance to turn that attitude around. After a two-year study of elementary and junior-high school students, researchers concluded that computer-based media could convert young people into news consumers if not into newspaper readers.

"Children would stay in from recess to read the [digital newspaper]," one teacher reported. "I've never seen anything like it." And researchers confirmed that the students weren't just looking at comics and reading horoscopes. News ranked high on the list of items consumed. Clearly, young people are more willing—and more eager—to consume information from a computer screen than from the printed page.

Perhaps that's because the younger generation was weaned on television and computers. But television has never managed to attract young viewers to its news—they are entertainment consumers almost exclusively. Computer-based media may well be the last great hope for reaching this generation, which needs news information if it is to make well-informed decisions in the voting booths of America.

If young people are disconnected from the media, so, too, are many adults. Study after study shows that the public views journalists with disgust. Journalists, as a whole, are ranked among the least popular of professional groups—often below politicians and used-car vendors. Those dismal and declining newspaper readership figures are further confirmation of dissatisfaction with the media.

Television also has problems. The decline of network and local news operations is an often-discussed topic among broadcast journalists. The consensus seems to be that budget cutbacks and pandering to ratings has led to a marked decline in the quality of broadcast news. Today's television news, it is said, revolves around "talking heads" who look good on the screen but have limited journalistic talent and ability. Gone are respected figures like Walter Cronkite, the former CBS news anchorman who once ranked as the most trusted person in America.

The fragmentation of audiences also has hurt. The three big networks—ABC, CBS and NBC—once dominated network news, and their affiliates dominated the local news scene. Today, the networks compete with MSNBC, CNN, Fox News Channel and others, and cable has made local stations' audience shares increasingly smaller. No longer are the local stations the only thing to watch.

Advertising Prompts Change

Newspaper editors and broadcast news executives have done plenty of self-examination in an effort to arrest some of these alarming trends. In reality, they can do little about most of the problems by changing editorial content. That's because the big mass-media outlets of the past are giving way to smaller media designed to reach specific segments of the audience. All this is driven by advertising, not news.

Audience fragmentation is fed by advertisers' desires to reach targeted segments of the reading, listening or viewing audience—teenagers, young adults, even cyclists and exercise addicts. A few products (soap, for example) can and should be mass-marketed items. Other products are marketed most efficiently and at the lowest cost by reaching those who are more likely to be interested in buying. Why advertise Maseratis to a mass audience when only the elite have the money to buy them? **Target marketing** goes after those who can afford to buy or those who need the product.

Radio lures certain audiences with station formats (country and Western, oldies and rock, for example). Magazines increasingly are aimed at targeted audiences with titles like *Skiing, Boating* and *Popular Mechanics,* while the number of general-interest magazines (*Life, Look* and *Saturday Evening Post*) has dwindled dramatically. Radio stations and magazines efficiently deliver target audiences, and television (with targeted cable channels on subjects as diverse as sports, health and fitness, and cooking) isn't far behind. Newspapers, on the other hand, are poor vehicles for targeting audiences because they are, by nature, a mass medium aimed at a general, not specialized, audience. It's difficult enough to print special editions for one part of the city and almost impossible to target specific socioeconomic groups. Why place an ad in a newspaper (with a high cost per thousand consumers reached) when radio (with a much more cost-effective pricing plan) will get the same results?

As if these shifts in the existing media aren't enough food for thought, just consider the likely impact of advertising in the online media. Computer-based media are able to tell advertisers exactly how many people read (or watch) an ad for how long. Even more significant, they are able to tell that advertiser the demographic profile of the potential customer or customers and—with the consumer's permission—generate a firm sales lead. Advertisers are willing to pay a lot for that capability.

An advertising director for Microsoft's Internet sites asked executives of one large automobile company what they would be willing to pay for such information. The answer? "Name your price." This means the existing media face formidable competition from the Web as the newer medium grows and matures.

Media in Turmoil

If all this makes it seem as if media industries are in turmoil, they are. Not only are great shifts taking place in the impact of one medium versus another, but the arrival of new media forms has complicated the situation. All this has led to an increased emphasis on the packaging and marketing of media products.

Newspapers are a great example. In the 1980s, many newspapers launched massive redesign projects to improve their appearance. Many also created marketing committees made up of executives from various departments—circulation, advertising and news among them—who tried to settle on joint approaches to improving and selling the product. In prior years, such cooperation was frowned on for fear the news department would be influenced by market considerations to cover stories that advertisers wanted and ignore those they wanted to hide. Most of these barriers broke down as editors and publishers decided that something had to be done. Said Gregory Favre while editor of *The Sacramento Bee,* "I think we have to quit putting out newspapers for [older] editors like me."

Newspaper editors' eagerness to reconnect with youthful readers, in particular, led to some rather questionable pandering. In New York, the *Syracuse Herald-Journal* tried youth-page articles that addressed readers as, "Hey you, yeah you," or, on occasion, "You knuckleheads," or even, "Yo, buttheads." Explained the youth-page editor, "We decided we would give [our readers] things they wanted to read, not only things we think they should read."

Critics charged that newspapers were guilty of doing what they perceived television had done: pandering to the market concept of simply giving people what they want. The media, critics argued, are a public trust and should be above the pressures of marketing. But the reality is that media operations in free societies produce products that must be marketed. There is no government subsidy to keep most of them running, and as competition increases, marketing pressures grow accordingly. The reality is that broadcast programs and newspapers are products that must be marketed and sold if they are to survive.

Good marketing requires a bit of research. Traditionally, newspapers have done that with readership studies, and television has relied on Nielsen Ratings to determine who's watching and in what numbers. In today's competitive media marketplace, however, efforts of that sort simply aren't adequate.

INTERACTION WITH CONSUMERS

Editors at traditional media outlets often fail to understand that an increasing percentage of today's media consumers want to interact with editors about the events occurring around them. Getting information with no opportunity for feedback is simply not satisfying.

As we noted in Chapter 1, in the media environment of most of the last century, the only way news consumers could participate was to write a letter to the editor or call the local television station news desk to comment or complain. At the end of the 20th century, that began to change as **talk radio,** blogs and other forms of interactivity allowed consumers to join the dialog.

Editors who hope to stay in touch with their audiences—and retain those audiences—must realize that the media landscape has changed. Today, some media show signs of trying to adjust. One such effort is being made on the Web site of the *St. Louis Post-Dispatch,* where editors and reporters engage in regular dialog with readers in a number of forums. On that site, it's not unusual for lead sports columnist Bernie Miklasz to defend himself from reader assaults on a position taken in his latest offering.

Miklasz is not alone. Similar interaction takes place on the Web sites of other newspapers, magazines and broadcast stations nationwide. That's a sign that the traditional media are trying harder than ever to gauge reader reaction and to be responsive to criticism.

Still, it would be foolish to suggest that the traditional media fully grasp the import of the changing media landscape. Most Web sites of the traditional media hold firmly to old models of simply regurgitating information found in the printed or broadcast medium of old. Few have truly been creative when taking advantage of the Internet's power.

For example, it would be relatively easy for a local broadcast station or newspaper to create a user-friendly interface to the local property tax records or to a voter registration database. These public records would provide fascinating reading for citizens interested in how much a neighbor paid for his or her house or how much the mayor's house is worth.

Surprisingly, most traditional media Web sites haven't figured out that interactivity is the current rage and that such content would likely drive users to their sites in droves. It is, perhaps, another great example of media managers just not "getting it."

Good editors recognize there are ways to connect with audiences, even in the face of corporate reluctance to move rapidly in that direction. Many newspapers now print the e-mail addresses of reporters. Internet site forums and chat rooms provide a good opportunity to engage in dialog with readers and viewers. And Web site records that show page-click data at least let editors know which pages interest readers and which do not.

In the past, there were few ways for editors to listen to their readers and viewers. Today, there are many more. Good editors listen.

THE CONTRARY VIEW

If all this sounds depressing for someone who aspires to enter the media industry, it's important to remember that plenty of positives still surround the traditional media. For example:

- While newspaper daily circulation declined from about 62 million in 1970 to 52 million in 2006, newspapers still reach 49.9 percent of U.S. adults each day, a figure higher than prime-time television (39.4 percent), morning drive-time radio (22.1 percent) and prime-time cable (13.9 percent). (See Figure 2–1.)

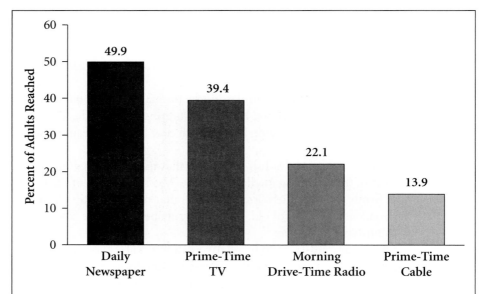

Figure 2–1   The percentage of U.S. adults reached daily by mainstream media, 2006.
Note: Radio drive times reflect Monday through Friday average quarter hour.
Source: Scarborough Research and Newspaper Association of American Research Department.

- While the Internet grows rapidly, most Americans still say they get most of their news from television. Newspapers are a close second.

- Revenues of the traditional media dwarf those of the Internet. In 2005, newspapers brought in $49.4 billion in advertising revenue, while broadcast television produced $44.3 billion, magazines $12.8 billion and the Internet a mere $7.8 billion. (See Figure 2–2.)

One who thinks the traditional media, particularly newspapers, are relatively healthy is Ben Bradlee, former executive editor of *The Washington Post*. "I don't see any point in shutting down now and saying it's too hard [to publish a newspaper]," Bradlee says. "If we could lick the ink [rub-off] problem, I think we could do very well."

The reality of newspapers' profitability is sometimes lost among all the talk about declining readership, flat circulation, the disappearance of afternoon dailies and the decline in the number of newspapers. Most industries would be thrilled with profit margins of 15 percent, and newspapers still enjoy such a rate.

The broadcast industry is doing quite well, too. Local stations are doing extremely well, and the networks are making a comeback after some lean times in the 1990s. The magazine industry thrives, and even local radio is in most cases profitable. Online media are only beginning to make a dent in the profitability of traditional media.

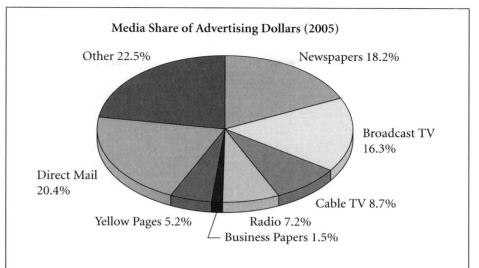

Media Share of Advertising Dollars (2005)

Other 22.5%

Newspapers 18.2%

Broadcast TV
16.3%

Direct Mail
20.4%

Cable TV 8.7%

Yellow Pages 5.2%   Radio 7.2%
└─ Business Papers 1.5%

*Figure 2–2   Daily newspapers capture a large share of U.S. advertising dollars,
exceeding the share of broadcast television and trailing only direct mail.*
Source: Universal McCann Inc. and the Newspaper Association of America.

EVALUATING THE MEDIA MIX

In an age widely heralded as the Information Age, no one suggests that the desire
for information will wane. Instead, the main question is how that information
will be consumed. One can make a persuasive argument that no medium is doing
a good job of satisfying the public's thirst for information. Perhaps that's because
no one medium has all the technological advantages.

Radio has immediacy of delivery on its side, but so does television, which
adds the appeal of color and moving pictures. Conversely, newspapers are far better suited than either of the broadcast media to carry large amounts of information and to provide the space necessary for analysis. Newspapers also have the
advantage of portability and selective consumption—you choose what you want
to read when you want to read it. With radio and television, you take what you are
given when it is being offered unless you record a program and replay it later. The
Internet allows editors to overcome all those limitations and adopt all those good
traits, which is why many consider it the medium of the future.

These realities may help explain why the arrival of television did not spell
doom for newspapers, as many predicted in the 1950s. They also may explain the
overall confusion in the information marketplace. As the technology continues to
evolve, editors are bringing new delivery mechanisms to consumers.

More than 5,000 newspapers, magazines and television stations now have sites on the Internet, and companies are scrambling to figure out how to make a Web profit. A sure sign that the Internet plays a major role in the media mix is the rush of media companies hiring students well-versed in Web site creation, including HTML (hypertext markup language).

Newspapers, television and the Internet are evolving into a new **infomedium** that combines the best attributes of them all. Wise young journalists of today should therefore view themselves not as print journalists, online journalists or broadcasters but as information providers equipped to provide news and other messages in whatever form the audience desires. After all, what is more important: the message or the way it is delivered?

RESPONDING TO CHANGE

Newspapers make an excellent study on the inevitability of change. As newspapers increasingly moved to a marketing approach in the 1980s and 1990s, newsrooms were forced to change their relationships with other departments. There was a time not so long ago when newspaper editors had the luxury of working almost independently of the other managers of their newspapers. Newsrooms were sacred, and no one in advertising or circulation departments presumed to tell editors how to edit their newspapers.

Now, editors meet regularly with top management executives and the heads of other departments to develop marketing strategies. There is a realization that news departments must work with other departments to develop marketing plans for their products. Sometimes, this results in decisions to change the content of newspapers. Usually, the final decisions about such changes are left to editors, but today the heads of other departments are more likely to make suggestions. Most editors are inclined to listen. Advertising and circulation people have extensive contact with the public, and often they hear compliments and complaints about their newspapers that editors never hear. Good editors appreciate hearing these things.

The danger, of course, is that the editor may go too far in an attempt to accommodate others. A newspaper full of nothing but what the public wants to read would be a poor one in most editors' judgment. Editors must balance what the public *wants* to read with what it *needs* to read. Only then will the newspaper fulfill its role as guardian of the public's welfare.

Today's editors know that the key to a newspaper's integrity—not to mention its existence—lies in its ability to remain financially sound. A marginally solvent newspaper may be more susceptible to advertiser influence on editorial decisions. Attention to the demands of the marketplace is important, but it also is important to remember that the press is the only private institution mentioned in the U.S.

Constitution. That is tacit recognition that the media, while competing in the marketplace, also have a special mission in U.S. society.

The fact that editors are now active participants in marketing the newspaper should not be viewed negatively. A newspaper is a manufactured product, a commodity, and like other products it must be marketed aggressively. A newspaper's marketing strategy probably will work best if all departments—including the news department—are working to accomplish the same goals.

Already, the changing realities of the marketplace are forcing newspapers to reexamine their future. Most are increasing resources for their Web sites in hopes of giving consumers more targeted content delivered as news breaks. Some are even committing to Web-first strategies in which stories go straight to the Web before the newspaper is published. Still others are programming local news channels on cable television or for the Web.

One such site is Roanoke.com, published by the *Roanoke* (Va.) *Times*. Its TimesCast is produced by staff reporters and posted regularly to the Web site. It is, in effect, a local newscast delivered over the Internet. Most newspaper companies with such successful experiments are marketing them aggressively and trying to increase the proportion of the company's revenue that comes from the online site.

Editors of the new century know that successful market strategies are a plus: Their newspapers will be stronger, and more people will read the work of their staffs. Magazines, radio stations and television stations have been forced to make similar changes as an awareness of increased competition became widespread. Almost invariably, the self-examination that resulted has improved the media's responsiveness to their audiences. Understanding these audiences is the key to success in the marketplace.

↗ UNDERSTANDING U.S. AUDIENCES

Research tells editors much about how their audiences consume news. Here are some highlights from recent research studies:

- Readers expect news in their newspapers, whether it's national, state, regional or local. What editors call *hard news*, or *late-breaking developments*, is most important.

- Readers want information about health, science, technology, diet, nutrition and similar subjects but will figure out for themselves how to cope with these problems. Newspapers don't need to tell them.

- Overall, readers like their newspapers. Most think they are indispensable, although younger readers aren't so sure. Most agree that newspapers are here to stay, regardless of the potential that television and computer screens may have for disseminating information.

Measuring Audience Reaction

Media companies know that gaining and maintaining an audience of acceptable size is important to their bottom line. For that reason, they go to great lengths to measure audience reaction.

Newspapers and magazines do that with **readership studies**, which measure the relative popularity of articles, photos, graphics and other features. Such studies often lead to changes in content, as when an editor drops an unpopular column or comic strip.

Focus groups also are increasingly popular. Representative groups of readers are brought together to discuss what they like and don't like about the publication. Editors often are present or watch videos of the sessions. It's one more way for them to keep in touch with readers.

Radio and television depend on **Nielsen Ratings** to determine the relative popularity of programs, including news shows. Nielsen Media Research uses sample families and measures what they are watching at certain hours. Low ratings often lead to shake-ups in the station, including the replacement of lead newscasters.

Certain "sweeps" periods, when critical ratings measurements are done, prompt broadcasters to prepare special series with high audience appeal for the evening newscasts. They do so to wring out every possible point in the ratings.

The online media have a distinct advantage in this area: It is possible to measure the exact number of times an item is accessed and the duration of that access. As the online media refine that technique, they should have a competitive advantage over the traditional media, which depend on audience estimates, not actual data. Online media audience estimates tend to be more reliable.

- Readers sometimes feel manipulated by editors and question whether they are fair and unbiased in covering and allocating space to various constituencies.
- Give readers a complete, balanced paper with solid reporting of national and international news but equal quality in coverage of local news.
- Strike a balance between bad news and other important news readers need to know. Don't sensationalize or attempt to manipulate public opinion.
- Provide the important details readers don't get from television news, but remember—readers are short of time.
- Do a better job of covering the new subjects of major interest—business news, health, consumerism, science, technology, schools and education, family, children and religion.
- Recognize that women's interests have expanded to the sports and business pages that used to be read almost exclusively by male readers. Of course, food, fashion and other traditional subjects are still appealing and interesting features for women as well as men.
- Readers want to feel that they belong. Newspapers must widen their focus if they are to win more regular readers among young people, working women and members of minority groups.
- Readers would like to know more about the newspaper's editors and reporters.

Public Journalism: Connecting with the Audience

Editors trying to find ways to connect better with the public have engaged in a new form of journalism called **public journalism** (sometimes also called **civic journalism**). It should not be confused with *citizen journalism* (see Chapter 1), also called *participatory journalism*. Public journalism seeks to find new and better ways to listen to the public, to focus attention on key public issues and to help citizens think through major decisions on public policy.

One public journalism project involved collaborative efforts by a local newspaper, radio station and television station. Together, they focused the public's attention on key issues—such as the quality of trade education in the local school system for students not going on to college—by timing high-profile stories on the topic to run in all three media at the same time. Surveys showed that, compared to citizens who consumed other local news media, those who gained their information from the participating media knew more, grew more interested in the issue and felt more positive toward the media.

This activist brand of journalism is not without its critics. Traditionalists argue that the media should merely measure public opinion, not manage it. In fact, the media have long tried to manage public opinion for the good of the community. Public journalism merely formalizes the process.

The strong pro-community motivation of public journalism clearly places it on a higher plane than other attempts to improve communication between the media and the public. Television's infamous "happy talk," in which newscasters engage in mindless chitchat on the air, is one example of pandering to the public for the purpose of merely improving ratings, not content.

- Include readers in on the fight to preserve the First Amendment. Readers are ready to support their right to know.
- Readers today are a far more serious, concerned, interested and demanding audience than the readers served in the past.

Credibility and the Media

The most important factor in the relationship between media and consumers is credibility. Concerned about study after study that showed declining levels of credibility, the American Society of Newspaper Editors decided to study the phenomenon in depth as the first step toward improvement.

The landmark 1998 study, based on telephone interviews with 3,000 Americans, was conducted by Urban & Associates of Sharon, Mass., under the direction of the company's president, Christine Urban. Sixteen focus groups followed.

"Throughout the survey, the public expresses constant and consistent appeals for fairness and even-handedness in news coverage," Urban said. "They see the editorial page as the only home for opinion or suggestion. The public believes that the reporter's job is to report the facts—completely, insightfully and without spin, and clean of any intent to sway or convince."

Major findings of the study are:

- The public sees too many factual errors and spelling or grammar mistakes in newspapers.
- The public perceives that newspapers don't consistently demonstrate respect for, and knowledge of, their readers and their communities.
- The public suspects that the points of view and biases of journalists influence what stories are covered and how they are covered.
- The public believes that newspapers chase and overcover sensational stories because they're exciting and sell papers. The public doesn't believe these stories deserve the attention and play they get.
- The public believes its priorities and those of newspapers are sometimes in conflict.
- Members of the public who have had actual experience with the news process are the most critical of media credibility.

At the forefront of the criticism is inaccuracy and the increasing number of spelling and grammar mistakes. More than a third of readers said they see mistakes more than once a week, and 21 percent reported seeing them almost daily. "It seems like the paper's gotten sloppier in the last 10 years," said one focus group respondent.

More than 80 percent of Americans believe that sensational stories get lots of news coverage simply because they are exciting, not because they are important. Further, 78 percent believe the media are biased. The same percentage believes powerful figures in society are able to influence a newspaper to "spike or spin" a story.

When asked which medium was the worst offender in the realm of bias, 42 percent said television and 23 percent said newspapers. Television is overwhelmingly seen as the dominant source of national and world news, while a majority (54 percent) of readers sees newspapers as the primary source of local news.

Results of the study sparked eight newspapers to start the Joint Credibility Project, an attempt to devise strategies to improve the public's perception of the media.

Skepticism about the veracity of the media is not new. Unfortunately, the media reinforce doubts about their credibility when they refuse to admit errors, when the names of people and places are misspelled, when grammatical mistakes abound and when hoaxes of one type or another are uncovered.

Unfortunately, scandals involving prominent media personalities are all too frequent, and many of them involve fabrication of information, sloppy reporting and disregard for the publics they serve. Reporter Stephen Glass was fired from the *New Republic* for fabricating articles, quotations and sources. Anchor Dan Rather left CBS with a cloud over his head after reporting that President George W. Bush used family influence, while a young man, to avoid being sent to Vietnam. Much of Rather's report was based on records that proved to be fabricated. Several newspaper columnists have been fired or disciplined in recent years for ethical lapses in their reporting.

The New York Times, arguably the most respected newspaper in the world, was engulfed in turmoil in 2003 when one of its reporters, Jayson Blair, was fired after editors determined he had regularly fabricated information for his stories. Another highly regarded publication, *The Washington Post*, also was involved in one of the most celebrated scandals in U.S. journalism history. In 1981, Janet Cooke, a reporter for the *Post*, won a Pulitzer Prize for a story about a child named Jimmy who became a heroin addict. Subsequently, it was learned that Jimmy didn't exist and that Cooke had invented the fictional youngster as a composite of situations involving children she had learned about while doing research for her story. The resulting publicity in both cases damaged the credibility of the media nationwide.

The Washington Post also was involved in one of the most noted scandals in the political history of the United States—the Watergate affair, which eventually led to the resignation of President Richard Nixon. Through a series of stories featuring anonymous sources, the *Post* and reporters Carl Bernstein and Bob Woodward unraveled the involvement of Nixon and his aides in the burglary of the Democratic Party headquarters in the Watergate complex in Washington. The service the newspaper performed in that investigation probably is unparalleled in U.S. newspaper history, but along the way, the many stories with anonymous sources raised serious questions about the credibility of the media. Editors today are reluctant to use anonymous sources without compelling reasons to do so.

Editors concerned about their credibility have tried to find ways to convince the public that newspapers are in fact reliable. These range from simple steps, such as the attempt to reduce annoying typographical errors, to elaborate schemes designed to check the accuracy of reporters' work.

To enhance the image of newspapers, today's editors readily admit errors. Some papers run a daily notice, prominently displayed, inviting and encouraging readers to call attention to errors in the paper. A well-known editor regularly conducts an accuracy check of his newspaper's locally written news stories. A clipping of the story is mailed to the source along with a brief query on the accuracy of facts in the story and headline. Another editor invites people involved in controversy to present amplifying statements when they believe their positions have not been fully or fairly represented.

More corrections are being printed, even though this practice is distasteful to editors. When the old *Minneapolis Star* had to print four corrections on one day, the editor warned the staff, "Let's hope it is a record that is never equaled—or something besides the sky will fall."

More balance in opinion is evident in the use of syndicated columnists whose opinions differ from those of the newspaper and in expanded letters-to-the-editor columns. Some newspapers are using ombudsmen to hear readers' complaints. More are providing reader-service columns to identify newspapers with readers' personal concerns. More attention is also being given to internal criticism in employee publications or at staff conferences. There's even a blog devoted to holding journalists accountable for corrections: www.regrettheerror.org.

Broadcast stations are making similar efforts to increase their credibility. Many stations now have e-mail addresses for their news directors. Listeners and viewers are encouraged to write with questions or complaints. Still, some studies show that the public considers broadcast news more credible than print news. The reason? It's easier to believe what you can see and hear.

Changing Needs of Changing Consumers

If the media industries are changing, so are the lives of media consumers. The U.S. Census and other data reveal much about changing lifestyles:

- Both spouses are working in more families, and there are more single-parent households.
- The number of people choosing to remain single also is increasing, contributing to a rapid increase in households. (That, by the way, makes those newspaper circulation numbers even worse. Market penetration, a key measure of media effectiveness, is measured by dividing the number of households in a given market area by circulation.)
- Leisure time is shrinking, and media use is a leisure-time activity.
- More players—direct mail, special-interest magazines and an increasing number of television channels—are competing for that decreasing amount of time.

All this puts pressure on editors to know and understand their audiences. They do so by reading everything they can find about their communities. They also keep an open ear to topics of discussion at the local health club, at parties and anywhere else people gather. An editor who knows what people are talking about has a good idea which stories would interest them.

Some editors have tried other means of taking the pulse of the community, including formal readership studies, open forums or focus groups (representative samples of media consumers assembled into small discussion groups). Such sessions often are recorded for the benefit of editors. Whatever the technique employed, there is no substitute for learning the community, even if that is an inexact science. The editor who is part of the community—who participates actively in it—is in the best position to be connected to the audience.

 *Web First*

As newspaper companies attempt to reinvent themselves and move to the Web, more and more are moving to a Web-first model. As news breaks, it goes on the Web site immediately. Then, as the deadline for the print edition nears, that same news is packaged—or repackaged—for the newspaper.

Some newspapers are institutionalizing this approach by appointing what they call *immediacy editors,* those responsible for ensuring that spot news gets to the Web site as soon as possible.

Moving to Web-first publication is difficult for some old-timers in the newspaper business, who still see the printed edition as the heart and soul of the operation. But while the printed edition still produces 90 percent of the income at the typical U.S. daily, Web advertising income is increasingly important to newspaper companies. Furthermore, as print circulations shrink and as young people flock to the Web, online publication clearly is the business of the future.

The idea is to give news consumers the product in the medium they prefer. Increasingly, that means the Web.

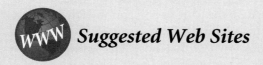 *Suggested Web Sites*

American Journalism Review **www.ajr.org**
Columbia Journalism Review (Media Criticism) **www.cjr.org**
Newspaper Association of America **www.naa.org**
Nielsen Media Research **www.nielsenmedia.com**
Pew Center for Civic Journalism **www.pewcenter.org**
The Poynter Institute **www.pointer.org**
Roanoke (Va.) Times **www.roanoke.com/wb/xp-index**

Suggested Readings

American Journalism Review
Columbia Journalism Review
Anderson, Brian. *South Park Conservatives: The Revolt Against Liberal Media Bias*. Washington: Regnery, 2005.
Kennedy, George, and Daryl Moen, Eds. *What Good Is Journalism?* Columbia, Mo.: University of Missouri Press, 2007.
Meyer, Phillip. *The Vanishing Newspaper: Saving Journalism in the Information Age*. Columbia, Mo.: University of Missouri Press, 2004.
Mindich, David T. Z. *Tuned Out: Why Americans Under 40 Don't Follow the News*. New York: Oxford University Press, 2005.

CHAPTER 3

THE EDITING PROCESS

THE EDITOR'S ROLE

Every editor edits. That is, every editor determines to some extent what will and will not be published or broadcast based on the editor's perception of the mission and philosophy of the publication or broadcast station.

This book stresses the skills of editing, but learning those skills without a thorough understanding of the philosophy of editing would be like learning to hit a baseball without knowing why hitting is important. Why bother to hit if you don't know to run to first base? In editing, it is important to know not only *when* a change in copy should be made but also *why* that change should be made.

Good editing depends on the exercise of good judgment. For that reason, it is an art, not a science. To be sure, in some aspects of editing—accuracy, grammar and spelling, for example—there are right and wrong answers, as often is the case in science. But editing also involves discretion: knowing when to use which word, when to change a word or two for clarity and when to leave a passage as the writer has written it. Making the right decisions in such cases is clearly an art.

The editing skills taught here are those used at newspapers in general and at newspaper copy desks in particular. These same skills, however, apply directly to magazine editing, Web editing and broadcast editing. Editing for those media differs slightly from newspaper editing because of special requirements, so separate chapters highlight those differences.

Still, the skills required of all editors are much the same as those required of newspaper copy editors, the valuable members of a newspaper's staff who have the final crack at copy before it appears in print. Copy editors are the last line of defense before a newspaper goes to press. As such, they are considered indispensable by top editors but remain anonymous to the public. Unlike reporters, who often receive bylines, copy editors' names seldom appear in print.

Some believe that absence of recognition accounts for the scarcity of journalism graduates who profess interest in copy-desk work. Editing is regarded as not so glamorous or exciting as reporting. But those who view desk work as boring clearly have never experienced it. To the copy desk come the major news stories of the day—war, the eruption of a volcano, the election of a president, the rescue of a lost child. The copy desk is the heart of the newspaper, and it throbs with all the news from near and far. Someone must shape that news, size it, display it and send it to the reader.

The copy editor is a diamond cutter who refines and polishes, removes the flaws and shapes the stone into a gem. The editor searches for errors and inaccuracies, and prunes the useless, the unnecessary qualifiers and the redundancies. He or she adds movement to the story by substituting active verbs for passive ones, specifics for generalities. The editor keeps sentences short so readers can grasp one idea at a time and still not suffer from writing that reads like a first-grade text.

Ah, but editing isn't so much fun as writing, some say. Why learn editing skills if you want to write? Columnist James J. Kilpatrick knows. Although noted as a writer, he bemoans the demise of *editing* skills:

> To read almost any American daily today is to conclude that copy editors have vanished as completely from our city rooms as the ivory-billed woodpecker has vanished from the southern woodlands. We appear to have reared a generation of young reporters whose mastery of spelling, to put the matter mildly, is something less than nil. . . . Once there was a white-haired geezer in an eyeshade to intercept a reporter's copy, and to explain gently but firmly to the author that *phase* and *faze* are different words, and that *affect* and *effect* ought not to be confused. The old geezer has gone and literacy with him.

Kilpatrick's fond memories of the good old days probably are enhanced by the passage of time. The fact is that newspapers always have made errors, and the newspapers edited by crotchety old copy editors wearing green eyeshades were no exception. Still, few would disagree with Kilpatrick that language skills in general have deteriorated. Newspapers, without a doubt, have been affected.

Too many reporters and editors at today's newspapers are products of an educational system with misguided priorities. That abandonment of the basics is commonly acknowledged today as one of the great tragedies of modern education. Now, a back-to-basics movement has swept the country, and there is evidence that teachers in today's elementary and secondary schools—some of whom were victims of the errors of the past—are at least attempting to stress language skills. Unfortunately, this won't help those who failed to learn, including many reporters and editors now on the job.

THE VALUE OF THE COPY EDITOR

No position on the newspaper offers greater opportunity for growth than that of copy editor. Work as a copy editor provides the chance to continue an education and an incentive to climb to the top of the newspaper's hierarchy. Copy editors must of necessity accumulate a warehouse full of facts they have gleaned from the thousands of stories they have read and edited and from the references they have had to consult to verify information.

Copy editors are detectives who incessantly search stories for clues about how to transform mediocre articles into epics. The legendary Carr Van Anda of *The New York Times* studied ocean charts and astronomical formulas to find missing links in a story. Few editors today would correct an Einstein formula, as Van Anda did, but if they are willing, they can probe, question, authenticate and exercise their powers of deduction.

Historically, a stint on the copy desk has been considered important to professional advancement at newspapers. The desk serves as an important spawning ground for administrative editors because those who serve there have a more complete picture of how the newspaper operates than those who do not. Reporters have little feel for copy flow and production requirements, but copy editors develop that in the normal course of their duties.

There are encouraging signs that the lot of the copy editor is improving. Many newspapers pay copy editors more than reporters as an incentive for the best and brightest to work at the desk. Journalism schools and departments have awakened to the reality that copy editors are more difficult to find than reporters and have responded by improving course offerings in editing. This, in turn, encourages more good students to pursue careers in editing.

No longer do editors require that newcomers work as reporters before becoming copy editors. Many now realize that wanting to be a copy editor is more important than having experience as a reporter. Many of the best newspapers in the United States and Canada now have editors who never worked as reporters.

Furthermore, the artificial barriers that once prevented women from becoming copy editors have been torn down. No longer is the copy desk a man's domain. Women with editing skills have risen to important positions at most newspapers, large and small.

All this indicates that new life may yet be breathed into the profession of editing. If, as Kilpatrick and others suggest, there is a serious problem with the quality of editing, many journalists have hope that things will improve. They have hope that the art of editing is not a lost art.

WHAT MAKES A GOOD COPY EDITOR?

The best copy editors typically have:

- A passion for, and detailed knowledge of, grammar, spelling, style, punctuation, usage and tightening.

- A love of good writing and the ability to see the potential in a piece, then the skill to help bring it out—or the good sense to know when to leave it alone.

- Knowledge of graphics processes and typefaces; the creativity to see photo, illustration and graphics possibilities; knowledge of good design.

- An interest in everything and a broad grasp of news. One wouldn't want to play a game of trivia against a good copy editor.

- Knowledge of enough mathematics and accounting to calculate percentages and to read budgets and see whether they add up.

- A grasp of legal, ethical and taste considerations.

- Skepticism that raises doubt in everything and fortitude to check it. They also need a librarian's ability to find the best sources in print or on the Internet to check facts.

- A mind that lets them see embarrassing double meanings before they are published. Evidently, a "nice" person missed this headline in the *Richmond* (Va.) *Times-Dispatch:* "Elliott's size no obstacle for Trojans."

- Enough self-confidence to know how to improve even veteran reporters' copy but enough maturity not to rewrite everything into the editor's own style.

- The ability to handle people—whether stringers or staff, sources or subscribers.

- Sound business and management skills.

- A clear vision of the publication's purpose, its personality, and the audience and advertisers to whom it appeals, as well as expertise, if possible, in the publication's specialty.

- A strong sense of responsibility. "The buck stops here," read President Harry Truman's desk sign.

- A willingness to work anonymously behind a desk for eight hours a day. For many journalists, this is the toughest hurdle.

Here are some suggestions for developing as a copy editor:

- Stay informed. Read your paper and others. Read newsmagazines and books on history, politics and economics. Listen to National Public Radio's news or talk-radio programs while you commute. Watch local and network TV news, Sunday-morning news talk shows, and cable news programming, such as CNN, CNBC, MSNBC and Fox News Channel.

- Join the American Copy Editors Society (www.copydesk.org).

- Compare your headlines with those in other papers. Look for fresh approaches. Keep an eye open for useful headline synonyms.

- Notice what information typically needs to be in particular kinds of stories, what order that information generally takes and which errors usually crop up.
- Keep notes on things you have to look up or useful tips you learn from the copy-desk chief, staff attorney or other staff members.
- Ask your supervisor to give you feedback about your strengths and weaknesses, and what you can do to improve.
- Every so often, organize what you learn.

UNDERSTANDING THE NEWSROOM AND WHAT EDITORS DO

It's not easy to describe the typical organizational structure of a newspaper news department because no two are organized alike. Still, most metropolitan newsrooms have editors with fairly common job descriptions and titles, as summarized here and as portrayed in Figure 3–1. Smaller papers have simplified versions of the same basic organization.

PUBLISHER

The **publisher** tops the organizational ladder and is ultimately responsible for the overall operation of a newspaper, including both the journalistic and business operations. At a large paper, the publisher typically is appointed by the owner, often a newspaper chain. At a smaller paper, the publisher may be the owner.

EDITOR

The **editor**—also sometimes called the **editor in chief** or the **executive editor**—is responsible for all editorial content of the newspaper. This includes everything from local to international news in categories ranging from sports to business to entertainment. The editor's responsibilities even include the comics. Today, these responsibilities may extend to editorial content in the newspaper's online service.

MANAGING EDITOR

The **managing editor** is typically the person directly in charge of the newsroom, managing its news operation and budget.

The managing editor hires and fires heads of the various newsroom departments, which might include the city desk (main department for local reporters), the copy desk, the sports desk and the lifestyles desk. The **editorial-page editor** (and staff) is the one part of the newsroom that may be under the direct supervision of the editor or publisher rather than the managing editor.

Typically, the managing editor reports to the publisher at smaller newspapers, but at larger ones, there often are editors between them with titles such as

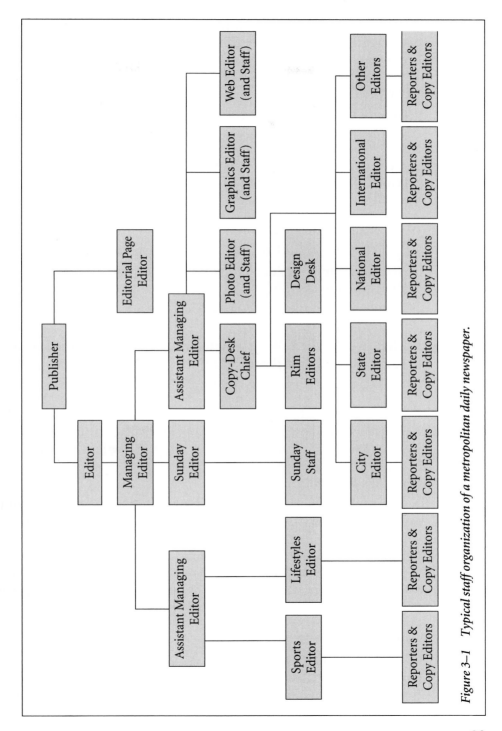

Figure 3–1   Typical staff organization of a metropolitan daily newspaper.

editor in chief or *executive editor*. In addition, at larger newspapers, there may be one or more *assistant managing editors,* who often are responsible for specific areas of coverage—AME-News, AME-Graphics and AME-Features, for example.

CITY EDITOR

A **city editor** (sometimes called a **metropolitan or metro editor**) supervises the staff of local reporters and may also direct reporters located in remote bureaus. At all but the smallest papers, there may be two or more *assistant city editors.*

The city editor plays an important role in setting the newspaper's agenda because he or she decides which local stories are covered. The city editor also does the preliminary story editing, looking primarily for big things like:

- Making sure stories are worth running.
- Making sure stories have good leads, are organized and flow well.
- Making sure stories don't leave unanswered questions. Is any information missing or unclear?
- Making sure stories are accurate. That may mean checking facts, figures and names.
- Making sure stories are as objective as possible. For example, are there other sources with whom the reporter should talk?
- Making sure stories are legal, ethical, tasteful and sensitive to the audience.

If the city editor has done his or her job well, the copy desk will be able to concentrate more on the details: spelling, grammar and AP style. The copy editor will then cut the story to fit the space allocated to it and write a headline.

SECTION EDITORS

A large newsroom is divided into departments, with a **section editor**—or **assignment editor**—in charge of each department of reporters. Some common departments include sports, lifestyles, business, state news, national news and international news. The duties of assignment editors typically include those of the copy desk—stories for the sports section, for example, may be read by only the sports editor before being set in type. Depending on the size of the paper, a section editor may have his or her own staff of copy editors.

COPY-DESK CHIEF

The **copy-desk chief** is in charge of the **copy desk**. Sometimes the copy-desk chief is called the **news editor** or the **slot person**. The name *slot person*, or *slot*, comes from the pre-computer days when copy desks were arranged like a horseshoe, with the copy-desk chief sitting in the slot of the horseshoe and the other editors (sometimes called *rim editors*) around the rim of the horseshoe.

Editing in Teams

More and more large newspapers are reorganizing their newsrooms to create teams of reporters, assignment editors, copy editors, photographers and graphic artists. In the traditional system, copy flows from the reporter to the city editor, then to the copy desk, where a copy editor shapes the story into final form and writes a headline. Photos and graphics in the traditional system are handled separately, then paired with the story at the copy desk or design desk.

In a team environment, a team leader directs reporters, copy editors, photographers and graphic artists, who follow the story from its inception to publication. Typically, teams are organized by content area (education, business, sports, health). Copy editors often remain with the same team for extended periods, allowing them to develop expertise in a given area rather than forcing them to become generalists.

Proponents of the team system insist that it improves story content because more people are involved in the story from the outset. That means more individuals have opportunities to suggest possible approaches to the story and its accompanying photos and graphics. Other advantages of such a system include:

- More editing is done earlier in the process, which improves quality.
- Copy editors get more respect because they are no longer faceless editors who enter late in the process.
- More sets of eyes lead to more questioning of what the story says, ultimately improving it.

But the team system is not without critics. Those who argue against it insist that:

- Workloads are distributed more unevenly, increasing the likelihood of sub-par quality.
- Style errors increase sharply because over time different teams start doing things differently.
- Copy editors no longer have the slot editors who once served as their mentors.
- The copy desk disappears, scattering copy editors throughout the newsroom and harming their professional interaction.

Despite these criticisms, the team concept seems likely to become more popular. At newspapers where teams have been implemented, the overwhelming reaction of all, including copy editors, seems to be positive.

The tasks of the copy-desk chief include:

- Hiring, firing and scheduling work for the other copy editors on the desk.
- Coordinating with other newspaper departments—with advertising for page dummies, with circulation on deadlines, with photography and graphics for art, with the rest of the newsroom for stories and, of course, with production for getting pages laid out and printed.
- Deciding what news will go where in the newspaper—in consultation with the managing editor and other newsroom department heads for the big stories but alone for most of the paper.
- Laying out pages—deciding where each story will be displayed on a page, how long it will run, how large the headline will be and whether any graphics will accompany it. At some newspapers, especially larger ones, the layout and design duties may fall on a separate layout and graphics editor. At many other

newspapers, the copy-desk chief may share some of the layout duties with the rim editors, sometimes assigning responsibility to them for various pages.

- Assigning stories to the other copy editors to edit and write headlines.
- Looking over all the editing and headlines of other copy editors before sending the stories to the production department.

COPY DESK'S COPY EDITORS

The **copy editors,** also called the **rim editors,** carry out the assignments given to them by the copy-desk chief, including the following tasks:

- Editing stories for spelling, grammar, usage and style, including proper treatment of abbreviations, capitalization, numbers and punctuation.
- Tightening or combining stories as necessary.
- Writing headlines, captions and blurbs.
- Backing up the assignment editor by looking for any big things that might have been missed—perhaps a possible problem with libel or important information that should be moved up in the story.
- Proofreading pages that have been set in type.

PHOTO EDITOR

The **photo editor** supervises the photographers who take pictures for the newspaper. In addition to news photos, the photo department produces photo illustrations and studio shots to complement food and fashion stories. At some small papers, the photo editor also is in charge of producing graphics.

GRAPHICS EDITOR

The **graphics editor** is in charge of the **graphic designers** who produce charts, maps and other nonphotographic illustrations for the newspaper. The importance of information graphics in telling the news has made this an increasingly common position at U.S. newspapers. At small papers, one person may handle all these chores, or they may be handled by the copy desk or photography staff.

WEB EDITOR

The Web editor is in charge of the design and content of the news outlet's Web page like an assignment editor in charge of a section of the newspaper. The Web editor at a newspaper typically reports now to the managing editor, but as time goes on, the Web editor may increasingly be seen as comparable in rank to the managing editor of the print publication.

✦ UNDERSTANDING THE FLOW OF COPY

After a reporter turns in a story, the reporter's boss—usually the city editor or an assistant city editor—edits it first. Figure 3–2 shows an example of **copy flow** through a newspaper news department.

If the story originated at the city desk, the story is then typically sent to the copy desk, where the copy-desk chief decides where it will go on the page to which it has been assigned by the managing editor at the daily editors' meeting.

Individual	Action
Reporter	Gathers facts, writes story, verifies its accuracy, forwards to city editor.
City Editor (or assistant)	Edits story, returns to reporter for changes or additional detail (if necessary), forwards story to copy-desk chief.
Copy-Desk Chief	Decides on placement of story in newspaper, prepares page dummy that determines story's length, setting and headline size. (At some large newspapers, a separate design desk may play this role.) Forwards to copy editor.
Copy Editor	Polishes writing of story, checks for missing or inaccurate detail, writes headline, returns to copy-desk chief for final check.
Copy-Desk Chief	Verifies that story is trimmed as necessary and that correct headline is written, transmits story to page output device.

Figure 3–2   How copy flows through a newspaper news department.

After laying out the page on which the story will appear, the copy-desk chief sends the story to a rim editor to edit it and write a headline. When the rim's work is done, the copy-desk chief checks it, and if everything is OK, the story is fit into its place on the page using a page-layout computer program like InDesign or QuarkXPress (see Figure 3–3).

The **backshop** then pulls a proof for the copy desk to check. After the proof is OK'd, the page is sent to the camera room, where a plate is made to put on the press.

If the story was assigned by one of the section editors—at the sports desk, for example—the section editor might handle the jobs of the copy-desk chief and the rim editor, or copy editors may be assigned to the section editor to handle some of these jobs.

EDITING THE STORY

Now that we have discussed the editor's role and what that editor is expected to do and not do, let's examine the editing process itself. Most experienced editors suggest that the process be divided into three distinct steps:

1. Read the story.
2. Edit it thoroughly.
3. Reread the story.

Figure 3–3   At smaller newspapers, the copy desk also is the design desk.
Photo by Philip Holman.

Editors often skip the first step or abbreviate it by scanning the story for the gist of the news. To do so may be a mistake because intelligent editing decisions cannot be made unless the editor understands the purpose of the story and the style in which it is written. That understanding is developed with a quick but thorough reading.

Some editors try to skip the third step, too. They do so at the risk of missing errors they should have detected the first time or those they introduced during editing. Few sins are greater than to introduce an error during editing. The more times a story is read, the more likely errors will be detected.

Unfortunately, deadline pressure sometimes dictates that steps 1 or 3, or both, be skipped. When this is done, it becomes increasingly important for the editor to do a thorough job the first time through the story.

To illustrate the editing process, let's see how one copy editor edited the story shown in Figure 3–4 (on Page 40) on the defeat of a bill in the Missouri General Assembly. This alert copy editor recognized immediately that although the lead was well-written, it also was inaccurate. The state's streets and stores are not deserted on Sundays. The reporter, reaching for a bright lead, overstated the case.

Because the story is from the newspaper's state capital bureau, it needs a dateline, or place of origin, which the editor inserted. The second paragraph became the lead, and the third paragraph was tightened and combined with the second. Note that the editor struck the phrase "with two members present but not voting." In many states, there is a difference between *present but not voting* and *abstaining*. An abstention allows the legislator to change his or her vote later, whereas present but not voting does not. The editor decided that in this case it wasn't important, so the phrase was deleted.

The story is confusing as written, probably because the reporter was too close to the subject to realize that readers would have difficulty following its meaning. The editor clarified fuzzy passages, tightened the story and distinguished between the amendments that were adopted and defeated before the bill itself was defeated.

The editor deleted the next-to-last paragraph because the legislator quoted used a colloquialism that may have been offensive to some readers. It added nothing to the story, so it was deleted.

The last paragraph illustrates how important it is to use common sense when editing. Conformity to the stylebook would have called for the identification of each legislator by party affiliation and district number. Because there are five legislators, the paragraph would have been difficult to read. The editor decided that the legislators' hometowns gave more information to the reader than the district number, and grouping by party affiliation made the paragraph less awkward than it would have been if the editor had followed stylebook practice. Such editing helps the reader make sense of the story. As a result, it is good editing.

BLUE LAW

]state capital bureau[

Missouri's city streets and stores will continue to be deserted
on Sundays, at least for another year.

JEFFERSON CITY, Mo. — The House Tuesday afternoon rejected a bill that would have submitted the repeal of the state's blue laws to the voters in November.

The measure was soundly defeated 97-53, with two members present but not voting.

The state's blue laws, or Sunday closing laws, prohibit the Sunday sales of nonessential chosen merchandise, goods, including automobiles, clothing, jewelry and hardware, items.

During a lengthy debate that lasted four hours, the original bill was amended twice. One amendment would have placed the issue on this November ballot, and another would have required

The bill also was amended to require that counties and cities decide whether to exercise local option to approve repeal of blue laws within their jurisdictions, locally if the measure was approved by voters in Nov.

Several amendments were defeated. One that would have required employers to pay increase wages for as much as twice the wages per hour to employees working on Sundays. Another would have set a

Rep. James Russell, a Florissant Democrat, included in one amendment the proviso that employers be fined $1,000 fine for each violation of the wage requirements. His amendment lost.

Yet Another amendment defeated introduced by Rep. Jerry McBride, St. Louis, would have levied a 1-cent excise tax on retail businesses open on Sundays. Proceeds seeds from this were to have gone to city and county treasuries.

The McBride amendment also was defeated.

During debate much of the support for blue law repeal came from urban representatives whose constituents districts include large retail chain stores and businesses that supported repeal of the existing law during committee hearings.

In the end, the majority of the house agreed with Rep. Walter Meyer D. Bellefontaine Neighbors, that "this bill is all screwed up."

Area local Democratic Reps Ray Hamlett of Ladonia, Joe Holt of Fulton and John Rollins of Columbia, and Republican Reps Larry Mead and Harold Reisch all voted in favor of putting repeal on the ballot.

Figure 3–4   Good editing helps readers make sense of a story.

That story needed plenty of attention. More typical are stories that need only a bit of polish and clarification. Figure 3–5 shows unedited and edited versions of the same story. Look carefully to see the changes the editor made.

The editor first sought to trim the article's length under instructions from a higher-ranking editor. The lead, or opening paragraph, was both punchy and to

UNEDITED

LOS ANGELES (AP)—A little girl born with a perpetually grumpy look underwent surgery Friday that could literally bring a smile to her face.

"I'm fine, and excited," 7-year-old Chelsey Thomas, clutching a favorite doll, said as she walked with her parents into Kaiser Permanente Medical Center in Woodland Hills.

The corners of the blond, blue-eyed girl's mouth sag because she was born without a key nerve in her face, a condition called Moebius Syndrome that afflicts up to 1,000 people nationwide. The nerve transmits commands to facial muscles that control smiling, frowning and pouting.

In an eight-hour operation that began at mid-morning, doctors planned to remove muscle and nerve from Chelsey's leg and transplant it to one side of her face. If the transplant succeeds—something that won't be known for at least three months—the other side will be done in about six months.

"She'll be able to smile for the first time, and that's something every parent waits for. Usually it happens in the first few weeks of their life, but we've had to wait a little bit longer," said Lori Thomas, her mother.

The $70,000 two-step operation is covered by the family's health insurer, Kaiser Permanente, because it is not considered cosmetic.

"Just being unable to smile has numerous problems associated with it, social and psychological," said Dr. Avron Daniller, one of Chelsey's surgeons.

Her mother said: "It's been hard for her because people think she's unfriendly or ignoring them or bored. It's been hard. Kids stare at her. Adults are pretty understanding, but she has a worse time with kids."

Kaiser flew renowned Canadian surgeon Dr. Ronald Zuker, who pioneered the procedure, to Los Angeles to lead the surgery. Chelsey was expected to be hospitalized five days.

Last month, Chelsey said she was eager to have the operation: "After the surgery, I'm going to smile at all my friends and have a party."

EDITED

LOS ANGELES (AP)—A little girl born with a perpetually grumpy look underwent surgery Friday that could literally bring a smile to her face.

"I'm fine and excited," 7-year-old Chelsey Thomas said as she walked with her parents into Kaiser Permanente Medical Center in suburban Woodland Hills.

The corners of the blond, blue-eyed girl's mouth sag because she was born without a key nerve in her face. It is a condition called Moebius syndrome that afflicts up to 1,000 people nationwide. The nerve transmits commands to facial muscles that control smiling, frowning and pouting.

In an eight-hour operation, doctors removed muscle and nerve from Chelsey's leg and transplanted it to one side of her face. If the transplant succeeds—something that won't be known for at least three months—doctors will do the other side in about six months.

"She'll be able to smile for the first time, and that's something every parent waits for," said Lori Thomas, her mother. "Usually, it happens in the first few weeks of their life, but we've had to wait a little bit longer."

The $70,000 two-step operation is covered by the family's health insurer, Kaiser Permanente, because it is not considered cosmetic.

Kaiser flew renowned Canadian surgeon Dr. Ronald Zuker, who pioneered the procedure, to Los Angeles to lead the surgery. Chelsey was expected to be hospitalized five days.

Chelsey's mother said: "It's been hard for her because people think she's unfriendly or ignoring them or bored. It's been hard. Kids stare at her. Adults are pretty understanding, but she has a worse time with kids."

Figure 3–5   Example of a typical story edit.

Overediting

The quality of writing depends on the reporter, but the editor can do much to help. Good editing invariably complements good writing. Occasionally, good editing can save mediocre writing. Poor editing can make writing worse or destroy it.

Most copy can be tightened. Even if only a few words in a paragraph are removed, the total savings in space will be considerable. Some stories, notably material from the wires and syndicates, can be trimmed sharply. But the editor should not overedit.

If a story is so poorly organized it has to be rewritten, the story should be returned to the originating editor. Rewriting is not a copy editor's job. Nor should the editor make unnecessary minor changes. Indiscreet butchering of local copy is a sure way to damage morale in the newsroom. Good editors know when to take their fingers off the keyboard as well as when to click the keys.

One of the greatest dangers facing the editor is that of overediting. One editor who became a journalism professor after 40 years in the business, the last part of it as a high-ranking editor with United Press International, writes:

During this time, it became clear that the biggest problem we had with our editors scattered around the world was their inability to keep their blue pencils off a well-written story.

Too many editors think they are better writers than those submitting copy to the desk. They often make unnecessary changes in clear, accurate copy just to put it in a form they believe is superior. Most of the time they disrupt the rhythm and continuity of the copy. Frequently, these changes cloud and distort the copy as well.

Today, that editor urges his students to avoid changing copy for the sake of change. Indeed, each change in copy must be well-justified. "I would have done it another way" is no such justification.

Here's a good rule to use when you are editing: *Unless you can demonstrate that a change improves the accuracy or clarity of a story, leave it alone.* In other words, let the writer write the story. The editor's job is to edit, not rewrite.

the point, so the editor left it alone. In the second paragraph, the editor chose to eliminate "clutching a favorite doll" because the doll was never again mentioned in the story and because the sentence was awkward and cluttered. Removing that phrase seemed to help. The editor inserted "suburban" in front of Woodland Hills to show that the city is a suburb of Los Angeles, where the story is datelined.

In the third paragraph, the editor broke a long sentence in half. In the fourth, the editor eliminated "that began at midmorning" on grounds that the story would be dated with its inclusion. Also, notice that the reporter used the incorrect tense ("planned to remove . . . and transplant"), considering the operation has been performed.

The mother's quote in the fifth paragraph of the original was not identified until too late in the paragraph. The editor chose to move the attribution to the end of the first sentence. That way, the editor explained, the reader would not have to guess who was speaking. Another option would be to introduce the two-sentence quote with something like this:

Lori Thomas, Chelsey's mother, said:

The editor also moved together two paragraphs about Kaiser Permanente's role in the surgery. That enabled the editor to avoid excessive shifting back and forth among sources within the story. The editor also deleted a dated quote from the child and ended with a quotation from the mother.

Along the way, the editor deleted a comma in the second paragraph and added one in the fifth. The first comma came out because the conjunction *and* did not introduce an independent clause. The second comma was added to follow the introductory word *usually* before an independent clause.

Were all these decisions the right ones? That, of course, is a matter of judgment, and each editor's judgment is different. Arguably, though, this editor's decisions were good, and the story is better as a result.

➤ THE THREE R's OF COPY EDITING

Over the years, journalism teachers have come up with various useful outlines for describing what editors look for in copy. In this book, we've used one common convention of dividing editors' text-editing duties into the *macro* and *micro*.

Another useful approach has been suggested by Don Ranly, a professor emeritus at the Missouri School of Journalism and a widely sought speaker in professional-editing circles. He refers to "The Seven C's Plus One"—that's eight, but Ranly argues most people can't remember more than seven things at once. Ranly says writers and editors should make sure copy is *correct, concise, consistent, complete, clear, coherent, creative* and *concrete.*

Here, we offer another approach, one focusing on the Three R's of Editing: making sure writing is *reader-centered, readable* and *right.*

Is the Story Reader-Centered?

Editors have to approach their job as though they are the readers' advocates, making sure stories serve the readers' interests, needs and time.

Is the story focused on what the audience wants and needs?

1. Has the writer kept foremost in mind what the audience wants and needs? People's time is limited. If the story isn't interesting—if it isn't informative and fresh—then what's the point of running it? Do I care 20 inches (or however long it is) about it? If not, how much? Then that's how long the story should be.

2. Is the topic important to our readers? Does it clearly show the reader why he or she should care? If the story could have an *impact* on the audience, does the writer take that angle instead of something else? If there doesn't seem to be any major impact, does the writer at least focus on whatever in the story would be of *most* interest to the audience? Does the story answer the question, "So what?"

3. News is people acting and reacting, as the late Jessica Savitch, a former anchor of NBC News, once said. Does the story focus on how the news affects the *people* involved, or does it focus on a thing?

4. Is the tone appropriate for this story?

Did the writer make the story new for the reader?

1. Does the writer apply relevant news formulas—intelligently as opposed to slavishly?

2. Does the writer focus on the latest news rather than on old news? If this is a second-day story, does it have a second-day lead, or did the reporter lead with yesterday's news?

3. Does the writer take a fresh, creative approach to the story? Does the reader learn something new? Or will the reader think this sounds like a story read many times before? Does the lead grab you? Are the lead and story angle fresh or hackneyed? Does the writing sound honest?

4. Does the writer offer original, concrete details, quotations, examples and comparisons that lend color, authenticity and clarity? Does the story appeal to the senses or just seem abstract? Is the overuse of adjectives and adverbs avoided? Are specific nouns and verbs used instead? Are the details concrete? Or does the story contain clichés of wording or of vision that make it seem tired and dishonest?

5. If the story is a feature, does the writer use an appealing, personal voice but one that does not detract focus from the subject and inappropriately draw too much attention to itself? If this is a hard-news story, was the writer careful not to editorialize or intrude his or her own personality and value judgments?

Is the Story Readable?

Editors need to make sure readers will be able to understand what's being said.

Is the story clear?

1. Is the main point of the story clear? Does every sentence grow from the main point and point back to it? Are the words and sentences simple to understand? Would it sound natural and conversational if read aloud? Do I understand the world better after reading the story, or am I left confused or apathetic? (If anything is unclear to you, ask the reporter or city editor—don't guess.)

2. Does the story answer any questions and concerns the audience would likely have? (Examples: What does the story mean by a "sizable crowd"? One hundred people? A thousand? If there's a community blood shortage, where can

you go to give blood, and what types are needed most? If a jogger had a heart attack while running, how hot was it that day? Did the jogger have a history of heart disease?)

3. Have loose ends been tied up? Are any intriguing angles introduced then dropped without explanation? Are all first references to someone or something complete?

4. Is it clear who is saying each quotation or paraphrase in the story?

5. Are all unfamiliar terms explained? Has jargon been avoided wherever possible and defined where unavoidable? Are all words used precisely and correctly? (*Admitted, anxious, bureaucrat, claimed* and *refuted* all have specific meanings that may not be intended by the writer who uses them but are likely to be inferred by a reader.)

6. Is the story arranged in the most logical manner? Does it seem well-organized? Does it flow well? Are the transitions between sentences and ideas smooth? Is the pacing good? Do sentence lengths vary?

7. Are rhetorical techniques such as metaphors, analogies and images used to illustrate the meaning? Are examples given? Are comparisons made?

8. Are there possibilities here to tell the story better with graphics so it will be more appealing and understandable to the reader? Would the reader benefit from a photo, illustration, chart, summary box, blurb or second deck to make the meaning clearer and the story more interesting?

Is the story concise?

1. Does the story need to be this long? Is its news value worth this many inches in a tight newspaper?

2. Is anything in the story irrelevant?

3. Has the writer avoided redundancies, clichés, unnecessary use of passive voice and other windy phrases that add uninformative bulk to a story?

4. Can any paragraph be said in a sentence, any sentence in a clause, any clause in a phrase, any phrase in a word, or any word in a shorter, simpler word? (For more specific hints on tightening, see Chapter 6.)

5. Are too many examples or quotations used?

6. Does each quotation say something either unique or important enough to quote?

7. Can quotations be shortened? Can partial quotes be used? Can quotations be succinctly paraphrased, without loss of impact?

8. If the story goes off on a lengthy tangent, can that part be turned into a sidebar?

Is the Story Right?

Editors need to make sure stories are right in all ways, big and small—all the way from being accurate, ethical and legally safe to being correct in spelling, grammar and punctuation.

Is the story accurate, objective, legal, ethical, tasteful and sensitive?

1. Are there any inconsistencies within the story, in matters of facts, style, viewpoint, verb tense or tone?

2. Is anything inconsistent between this story and previous stories?

3. Have you checked that facts and quotations are accurate?

4. Have you checked the math? (Examples: ages with birth and death dates in obits, percentages and totals in budget stories, vote ratios in election stories.)

5. Have you checked names and addresses of local people?

6. Have you checked when a story says *today* whether it means the day it was written or the day of publication?

7. Does the writing sound honest, or is its credibility undercut with refutable logic, sloppy writing or clichés (such as with a lead that says "Christmas came early for . . . .")?

8. Is the story objective? Is it factual, neutral, fair and, if hard news, impersonal in style?

9. Does the story avoid any statements that might bring a lawsuit?

10. Is the story ethical and in good taste? If someone is accused of or criticized for something, does he or she get a chance to reply? Are all sides given? Were enough people interviewed?

11. Is the story or picture in good taste? Or is there, for example, gore or nudity the audience might find offensive?

12. Has the writer avoided saying anything that may unnecessarily disparage or offend someone on the basis of age, race, sex, religion, sexual orientation or ethnic background?

Are the mechanics in the story correct?

1. Have you checked for typos? Have you checked the spelling of all unfamiliar words, especially proper nouns? Have you checked all compound words to see whether they should be written as one word, two words or hyphenated?

2. Are there any grammar or usage problems? Has the writer correctly distinguished between *if* and *whether, while* and *although, who* and *whom, which* and *that?*

Tips for Getting the Most Out of a Copy-Editing Internship

Some Things to Find Out Early on the Job

- Names of people with whom you'll work.
- The newsroom organization and chain of command (papers differ).
- How to use the computers and other equipment.
- Local style—identify the differences from AP style and the additions to it.
- Local ethics policies.
- Protocol on consulting with reporters about their stories. (Some papers frown on this; others encourage it when you have questions.)
- The pace of work—about how fast, in minutes, copy editors are expected to finish editing stories and writing headlines (often about 15).
- What you can do on your own when you get caught up. Should you inform the slot, read proofs, just look through the news wires, or what?
- Dress-style expectations.
- And, of course, the location of restrooms, snack machines and the best nearby places to eat.

When to Talk With the Copy-Desk Chief

- Before making major changes in story structure, such as changing a lead, reorganizing a story or doing a major rewrite.
- If you spot legal, ethical or fairness problems.
- Before changing head sizes.
- If you have suggestions for a second deck, blurb or graphic.
- Before reducing a story by more than an inch or two beyond any requested cuts (can mess up the design).
- Depending on local policy, before talking with the reporter, city desk, photographer or artist about problems with a story or art.

If you're stuck on a headline, it's probably better to ask another copy editor for suggestions rather than bothering the copy-desk chief or sitting too long on the story.

How Professional Editing Differs From Work on the School Paper

Because you'll be working with professionally written copy, editing should involve far less work fixing easy mistakes. This could leave you more time to work on better headlines, captions and blurbs.

But don't think professionally written copy is perfect. It's not. The mistakes, however, tend to be more sophisticated. So you may need extra time to deal with trickier problems about which you may be unsure, such as more difficult issues of grammar and usage, style and spelling, legality and ethics.

For example:

- Reporters aren't likely to write *don't* when they mean *doesn't,* but they are likely to confuse *comprise, compose* and *constitute.* You've probably done well knowing the easy rules many of your classmates didn't, but now you'll be expected to fix the more advanced mistakes of professionals.
- Reporters will generally know the 10 percent of the style rules that are most common, so their mistakes will often be in the other 90 percent that send you to the stylebook. For example, which air carriers serving the local market spell *airlines* in their name as one word and which as two?
- There should be fewer easy-to-fix spelling problems, but you will still have to look up harder-to-intuit compound words to find out whether they're one word, two words or hyphenated. No matter how good you are, these words are so unpredictable that you'll have to look them up to be sure.
- Sitting in a media law or ethics class discussing cases is one thing, but knowing what to do to protect your paper legally is another story. The more stories you edit involving potential legal or ethical problems, the more questions you will have. Ask your copy-desk chief, and learn from each situation.

3. Is the story punctuated correctly? (Comma placement in compound versus complex sentences is especially a problem, even for the wire services.)

4. Does the story conform to wire-service (typically, Associated Press) and local style? Remember to change wire copy to fit local style.

COPY-EDITING AND PROOFREADING SYMBOLS

Today's editors do most of their work on computers, so the editing of paper manuscripts, or *copy* (see Figure 3–6), is increasingly rare. A few small newspapers and magazines, however, still use manual methods of production, and some book publishers still do so. In such cases, knowing the long-established copy-editing symbols is essential. Even at large newspapers and magazines, editors pass printouts of articles to publishers, attorneys and others, and those individuals use copy-editing symbols to make suggested changes. Therefore, it's a good idea to know the standard symbols and how to use them, even if you usually edit with a computer.

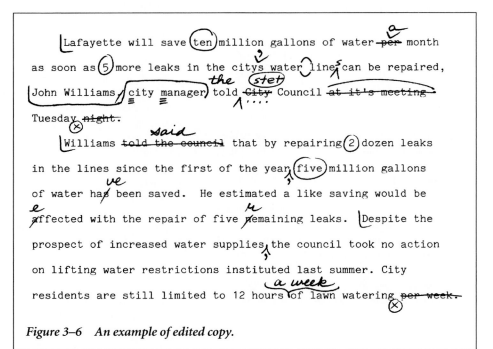

Figure 3–6   An example of edited copy.

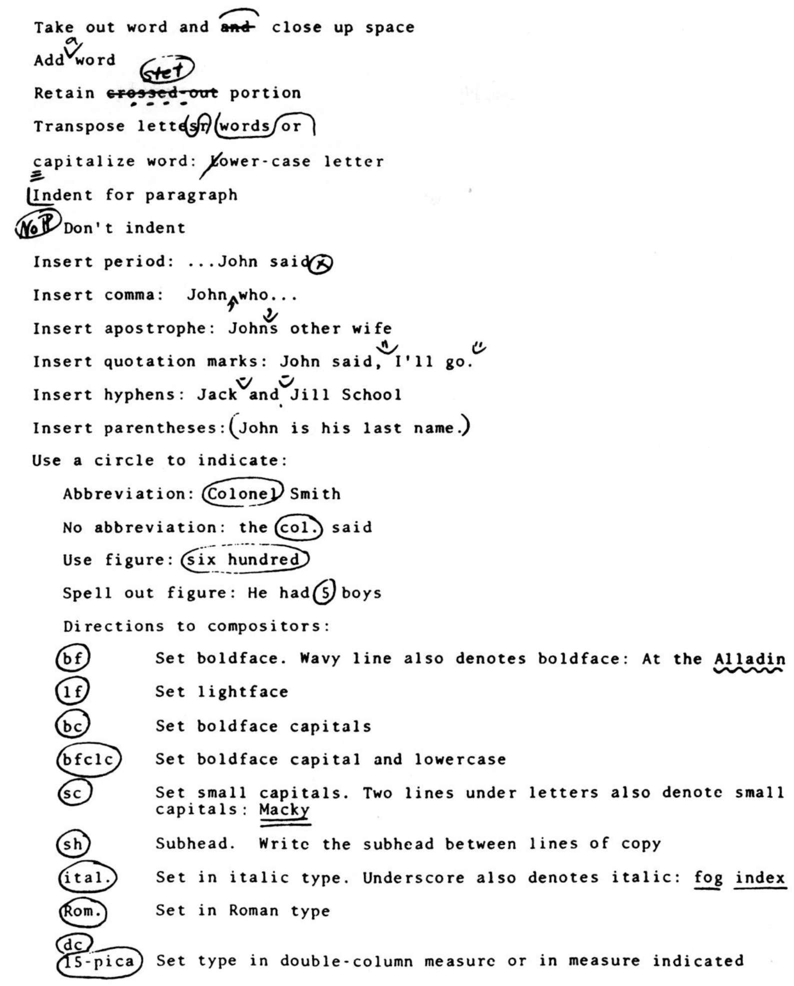

```
Take out word and and͡ close up space
Add͜word  ͡stet͡
Retain crossed-out portion
Transpose lett͡ers (words or
capitalize word: /ower-case letter
‗Indent for paragraph
No¶ Don't indent
Insert period: ...John said⊗
Insert comma:  John͜who...
Insert apostrophe: John's other wife
Insert quotation marks: John said, I'll go.
Insert hyphens: Jack͜and͜Jill School
Insert parentheses:(John is his last name.)
Use a circle to indicate:
    Abbreviation: Colonel Smith
    No abbreviation: the col. said
    Use figure: six hundred
    Spell out figure: He had 5 boys
    Directions to compositors:
    bf      Set boldface. Wavy line also denotes boldface: At the Alladin
    lf      Set lightface
    bc      Set boldface capitals
    bfclc   Set boldface capital and lowercase
    sc      Set small capitals. Two lines under letters also denote small
            capitals: Macky
    sh      Subhead.  Write the subhead between lines of copy
    ital.   Set in italic type. Underscore also denotes italic: fog index
    Rom.    Set in Roman type
    dc
    15-pica Set type in double-column measure or in measure indicated
```

Figure 3–7   Copy-editing symbols.

Copy-editing symbols (see Figure 3–7), which are universally understood in the business, are used to make changes in paper manuscripts or on printouts of stories that reside in computers. In modern newsrooms, these changes usually are transferred to the computerized version of the story before the story is typeset. Few newspapers and magazines still have compositors who set type directly from the manuscript.

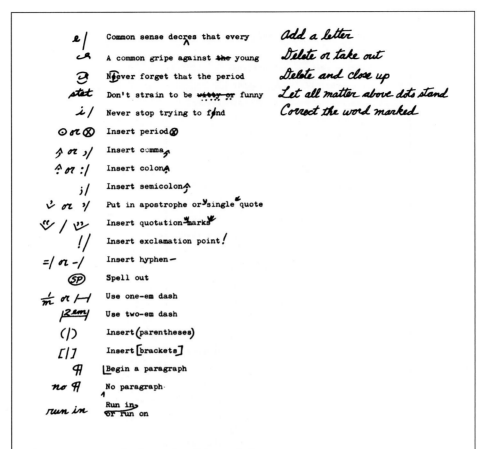

Figure 3–8 Standard proofreading symbols.

Proofreading symbols (see Figure 3–8), which differ from copy-editing symbols somewhat, are used to make corrections after the copy has been typeset. In the newspaper and magazine businesses, editors often use proofreading symbols to mark minor changes on page proofs before those pages are sent to the platemaking department. Newspaper editors also use page proofs to make minor changes in pages between editions. Newspapers and magazines use the informal method of marking proofs, where as book publishers use a more formalized version (see Figures 3–9 and 3–10).

Joyce on Film-Gal 2
Adv for Sunday, Nov. 6

"I'm afraid the essence of this picture must challenge him — if it's done honestly."

He made one of his long pauses again. *I*

"All I can do is to say I think this is a fair approximation of what Joyce intended. I think it would almost be fairer to call the film 'Homage to Joyce,' or 'Homage to Ulysses,' than to call it 'Ulysses.'

"I've gotten what I consider is the main line of the story. I want to give the audience a special thing that relates to Joyce's vision. If I can do that, then I'll be in great shape. We hope" — he emphasized the word — "to have the cooperation of the censor in Britain."

Strick must get "Ulysses" past the British censor, John Trevelyan. To get the $840,000 necessary to make the movie in Dublin — using Joyce's actual locations — he had to promise to get the censor's O.K.

"There are only two general territories in the United States, I believe, that require pre-censorship. They are Chicago and the state of Maryland.

"The only viable censorship in America rests in the hands of the police who are entitled to terminate the performance of any show or screen exhibit. But they've got to say, 'This is deleterious to the public and we're going to end it.'

The more than 700-page book, first published in a limited edition in 1921, is about one day in the life of a Dublin Jew, Leopold Bloom. *K*

"It is, I believe," said Stric, "the central literary work of the century, concerning itself with the affirmation of life, the search of a father for a son, and of a son for a father.

Strick looks on Bloom as the most ully developed character in fiction. He wanted an actor of stature to play such a part and he says he is sure he found

Figure 3–9 Informal or newspaper method of marking proofs.

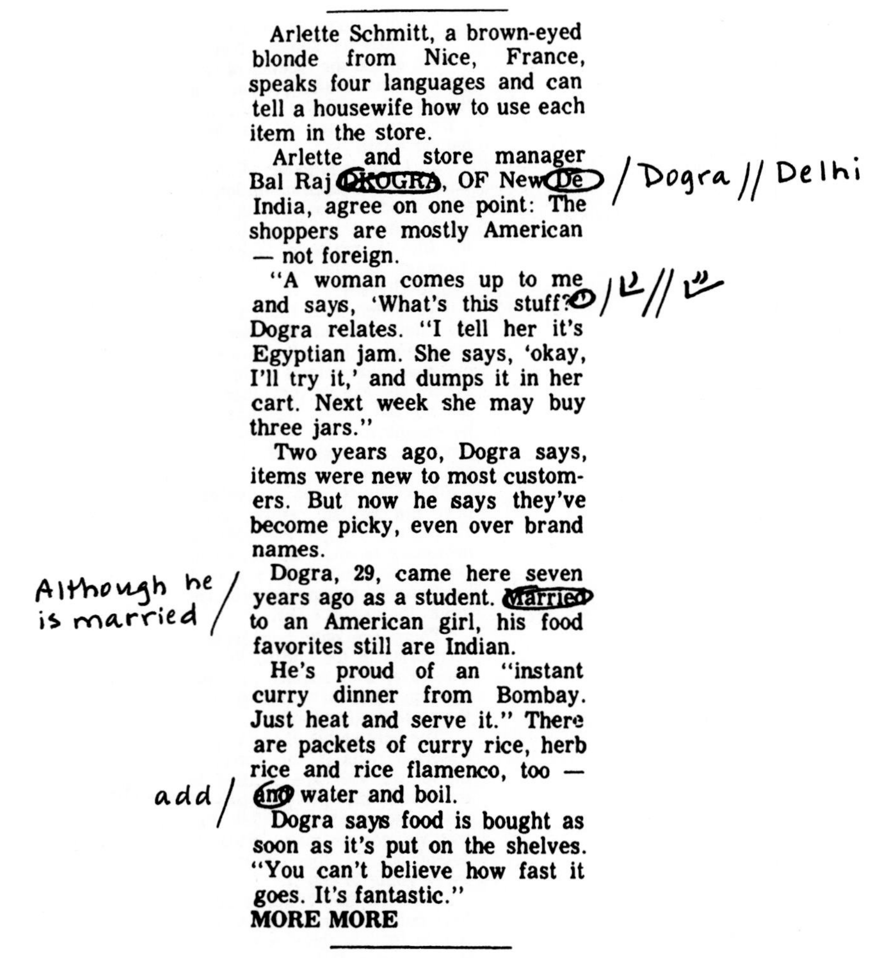

Arlette Schmitt, a brown-eyed blonde from Nice, France, speaks four languages and can tell a housewife how to use each item in the store.

Arlette and store manager Bal Raj ~~DKOGRA~~, OF New ~~De~~ India, agree on one point: The shoppers are mostly American — not foreign.   / Dogra // Delhi

"A woman comes up to me and says, 'What's this stuff?~~,~~○ Dogra relates. "I tell her it's Egyptian jam. She says, 'okay, I'll try it,' and dumps it in her cart. Next week she may buy three jars."   / レ // レ

Two years ago, Dogra says, items were new to most customers. But now he says they've become picky, even over brand names.

Although he is married /   Dogra, 29, came here seven years ago as a student. ~~Married~~ to an American girl, his food favorites still are Indian.

He's proud of an "instant curry dinner from Bombay. Just heat and serve it." There are packets of curry rice, herb rice and rice flamenco, too —

add /   ~~and~~ water and boil.

Dogra says food is bought as soon as it's put on the shelves. "You can't believe how fast it goes. It's fantastic."

MORE MORE

Figure 3–10   Formal method of marking proofs.

PROOFREADING

After the copy desk has laid out the pages, edited the stories, written the headlines and other big type and set them all in print, the editors are called on to check over the pages one last time before sending them off to the prepress department. In this **proofreading** stage, the editors just check over the pages for any glaring mistakes.

A **proof** is a copy of the completed page, ready to print except for any last-minute corrections you may be able to make. If the newspaper digitally paginates,

A Proofreading Checklist

Headlines or Titles

- Are style, spelling and grammar correct?
- Does it make sense?
- Is it accurate?
- Does it fit?
- If there's a second deck or blurb, is it in lighter type?
- Have repeated words been avoided in big type on the spread?
- Is it in good taste?
- If there's a photo, does the headline go well with it?

Layout

- Are there any design problems?
- Are any heads bumping?
- If stories are too long, cut them.
- If stories are too short, then suggest a blurb, second deck or extra copy.

Captions

- Are style, spelling and grammar correct?
- Are names spelled the same as in the copy?
- Make sure the caption doesn't repeat what's in the title or headline.

- If there's more than one **leg** (column of type), there must be an even number of lines.
- Make sure there aren't any *widows*—a single word or part of one on a line by itself.
- Is the caption set on the correct measurement?
- If there's a **catchline**, is it a clever one?
- Make sure identification of people is from left.

Blurbs

- If the blurb contains a quote, have single quote marks been used?
- Is attribution set flush right with a dash in front of the name and a comma after the name if a title follows on the next line? (Or follow your publication's style.)

Text

- Is anything libelous?
- Is everything clear?
- Are there no deleted first references?
- Is there consistency in spelling of names?
- Are the ages correct in obits?
- Check other style, spelling and grammar as time permits.

proofs will be laser printouts or photocopies of pages. If the newspaper still pastes up pages, no actual proof may be pulled. Instead, the proofreader will read the pasted-up camera-ready page.

The Difference Between Proofreading and Copy Editing

Copy editing and proofreading used to be separate careers, but now most copy editors also do the proofreading. The main difference is that the proofreading stage is not the time to continue editing or rewriting—except in case of emergency.

Determining which mistakes should be corrected depends on how close you are to deadline and how serious the errors are. When there's plenty of time, fix anything that's incorrect in fact or grammar, inconsistent or obviously unclear. Closer to deadline, minor errors tend to be overlooked so the paper will come out on time.

Most of the symbols are similar in proofreading and copy editing, but because of the limited space between lines in a proof, the corrections are brought out to the margin and connected by lines to where they are to be made in the text.

If you're reading an actual proof, you may make your corrections in pencil or pen because it's just a copy of the page. But if you're reading the original pasteup, only mark on the page with a photo-blue pen that will not show up when the page is shot (photographed to make a printing plate).

What Do You Do When Told to Read Proofs?

Look mainly for mistakes that have slipped through, especially in large type. Also, make sure everything fits the space given it—cut stories if they're too long and rewrite headlines if they don't fit.

When you look at a page, first check the heads and the blurbs (the biggest type on the page) because people are more likely to see errors at this size. Then check the captions and folio lines. Make sure these fit and are accurate. If any names are present, do they agree with the spelling in the story?

Next, look for holes caused by stories that are too short. For these, you will need to add a blurb or some sort of filler art.

Finally, check all stories that jump from one page to another. Are the page numbers in the continued lines accurate? Is the rest of the story where the continued line says it will be?

What If a Story is Too Long?

Newspaper stories are generally written in the inverted-pyramid style (most important information first, least important information last) and should be cut from the end. But this is not true of magazine articles or newspaper features, which should be tightened within rather than chopped from the end.

- Cut either the number of lines that won't fit or up to three extra lines—the story can be spaced out.

- If the paper still uses pasteups (few do anymore), don't cut in the middle of paragraphs if you can help it. Such a cut means resetting the paragraphing and waiting for it to come out of the typesetter. If you instead cut whole paragraphs or sentences from the ends of paragraphs, the change can be done with a knife. If a story is both too long and has errors, try to cut the sentences that have the errors and thus save time waiting for a fix.

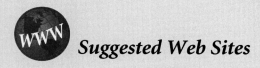 **Suggested Web Sites**

American Copy Editors Society **www.copydesk.org**
American Press Institute **www.americanpressinstitute.org**
The Poynter Institute **www.poynter.org**
The Slot: A Spot for Copy Editors **www.theslot.com**

MACRO EDITING FOR THE BIG PICTURE

Editors often speak of *macro editing* and *micro editing,* borrowing the terms *macro* and *micro* from economics.

Macro editing is big-picture editing and include:

- Making sure stories are worth running.
- Making sure stories have good leads, are organized and flow well.
- Making sure stories don't leave unanswered questions.
- Making sure stories are accurate.
- Making sure stories are objective.
- Making sure stories are legal, ethical, tasteful and sensitive to the audience.

In this chapter, we'll look at all of these except the last item, then devote Chapter 5 to matters of law, ethics, taste and sensitivity.

Micro editing is editing with an eye toward the details and includes:

- Making sure the grammar and usage are correct.
- Making sure words are spelled correctly and that there aren't any typos.
- Making sure abbreviations, capitalization, numbers and punctuation conform to the publication's or station's stylebook.
- Making sure the copy is tightly written so that it doesn't waste the audience's time and it conforms to space or time limits.

We'll look at these matters in Chapter 6. Then, in Chapter 7 we'll show how to combine macro and micro editing into a holistic-editing approach.

 MAKING SURE STORIES ARE WORTH RUNNING

As explained in Chapter 3, the first of the Three R's of copy editing is to make sure the story is reader-centered—viewer- or listener-centered if you're editing broadcast stories. To be worth the time, a story should focus on something your audience either wants to know or needs to know. It should also be told in a way that makes it new, that comes across as fresh rather than stale. To know whether a story contains information that's wanted or needed by your audience, you first should get to know your audience, as described in Chapter 2.

The stories that mean the most to media consumers usually directly affect their lives in some way. Examples include money-related items, such as tax cuts or college-tuition increases; information that has an impact on daily life, like road closings and weather; and stories that have an emotional effect, such as human-interest features or obituaries of close friends or family members.

Of course, not all stories have a direct impact on your audience, so the next best thing is a story about a topic that interests them. A brief, humorous story about a ventriloquist, placed in the bottom corner of Page One, or a science-page story about a new theory concerning dinosaurs may not have much impact on the way readers live, but both will be well-read items in the paper that day.

If the story seems to have neither the potential for audience impact nor interest, before killing it the editor should check whether the reporter focused the story on people. Former television news anchor Jessica Savitch once defined news as people interacting and reacting, and when reporters forget the broadcast maxim that "News is *people*," it's easy to make a potentially good story boring. If the story is focused on a *thing*—say, the widening of a street—ask the reporter to refocus it on the reactions of people who live there and will now have bedrooms 10 feet from the traffic.

But sometimes, reporters turn in a nonstory—a story that seems pointless and not worth running. Perhaps the story has been written from a press release about something that would better be handled by an advertisement. Perhaps the story is out of date, or it advances an event too far in the future to run at this time. Sometimes, a story is handed in that just plain leaves you asking: "So what? Why would anyone care?"

That was the case with a food-page story that explained how to pack a sack lunch. There was nothing in the story anyone wouldn't already know. It explained how to pack a lunch in either a sack or a lunch box, and advised the reader to include a sandwich (perhaps lunch meat or peanut butter and jelly), a piece of fruit (an apple, orange or banana is good), maybe a dessert (but watch those unhealthy calories!) and some kind of drink (a juice carton, a Thermos of milk or coffee, or a canned drink) if a vending machine is unavailable.

In such a case, if you're the **assignment editor**—the city editor, sports editor, features editor or other editor to whom the reporter answers directly—the solution is to *kill* or *spike* the story. Of course, if you think the point of the story is unclear and that you might have missed something newsworthy, check with the reporter. If you're a copy editor, point out the problem to the copy-desk chief, who may want to speak with the assigning editor about it.

If you decide the story is worthwhile, as most are, how long should the story be? Both the assigning editor and the editor laying out the section should ask themselves two questions:

1. How much will our audience care about this story?
2. How much of the available space is this story worth compared to the other stories we want to run?

Try to answer these questions in terms of inches in a publication, or seconds or minutes in broadcast. For example, at a particular newspaper, briefs might be 3 inches, short stories typically 8, medium stories 12 to 18, and longer stories typically no more than 30. Likewise, at a broadcast station, brief items might be 10 seconds, medium ones 30 and longer ones two to three minutes.

Answering these questions will help give the reporter guidance as to how much to write, then determine trimming, first at the assignment desk and later at the copy desk as the story is fit into the page. A rule of thumb for copy editors, though, is that when even good stories must be trimmed, cut wire-service stories first, allowing local stories to run as completely as possible.

MAKING SURE STORIES HAVE GOOD LEADS

Editing hard-news stories is a little different from editing feature stories—their **leads** are different, and so is the structure of the rest of the story. The two types will be examined separately before looking at organization and **flow** issues they have in common.

Hard News

A **hard-news story** is an article that focuses on presenting the news in a no-nonsense, straightforward, get-to-the-gist-right-away manner. Often called an **inverted-pyramid story**, hard news is written in the order of most to least important, and usually has a **bottom-line lead** that tells the main news in the first paragraph.

THE HARD-NEWS LEAD

The hard-news lead sentence is typically in the order of first *who,* then *what*—although sometimes these are reversed, especially when covering speeches and public meetings.

There are two ways of writing the *who:*

1. If the person is well-known to your audience or appears often in the news, then an **immediate-ID lead** is used. The person's name appears in the first paragraph, sometimes after a descriptive title. Examples:

> City Council President James Smith. . . .
> Rap singer Eminem. . . .

2. If the person is not well-known to your audience, a **delayed-ID lead** is used. A brief label for the person is used in the lead, with the person's name stated, usually at the start of the second paragraph. Example:

> A Columbia man was in critical condition Tuesday after he was knocked off his bicycle by a truck.
> Paul Rodriquez was riding . . . .

The lead next tells *what* the who did or *what happened* to the who. The *what* could be one thing or several things. If several things happened, only the most important might be mentioned in the lead, with the others perhaps appearing later in the story. Or the different things that happened might all be mentioned in the lead—preferably in the order of most to least important—or summarized if they all have something in common.

If *time, day* and *place* appear in the lead, they typically appear after, not before, the *who* and the *what.* If all three are used, they should appear in the order of time-day-place. *Time* comes first in the *time-day-place order*, but is often inexact in the lead. Events are usually described as taking place *Wednesday night* or *Friday morning* or *this afternoon.* Newspapers do not use *yesterday* or *tomorrow. Today* or *tonight* may be used. If important, the exact time of day will appear later in the story (for instance, the moment of an earthquake). For more rules about the *time-day-place* order, see the style section of Chapter 6.

If a hard-news lead doesn't follow this typical order—*who-what* or *what-who*, then *time-day-place* (time being optional)—try to figure out if the lead achieves more the way it is. If it doesn't, it's probably better to use the traditional ordering as the story is introduced. When beginners fail to follow this order, it's usually because they just don't know what they're doing. When professionals switch things around, they usually have a valid reason.

TRIMMING A HARD-NEWS STORY

Because the most important details are presented before the least important ones, trimming a hard-news story to fit a given space is relatively easy. If you cut from the end, you're taking out information the reporter deemed the least important. Sometimes, though, reporters mess up and bury an important detail later in the story, lower down than less important ones. If you, as editor, see this, you should move the more important detail higher in the story, where it belongs.

Features

Features are sometimes called **soft-news stories**. Taking the metaphor too far, some journalists deride features as *fluff pieces*, and some newsrooms even have an unofficial pecking order that places reporters on the government and crime beats at the top and feature writers at the bottom.

Hard-news stories tend to have more sense of **timeliness** than features, despite the fact that hard news is written in past tense and features in present tense. The sense of immediacy in hard news comes from the focus on reporting up-to-date accounts of who did what or what happened to whom. Feature writing, at its best, is more creative, literary, entertaining and emotionally involving than hard-news stories.

The poet Ezra Pound's definition of literature as "news that *stays* news" is an apt description of good feature writing. Good feature writing, in other words, may be more time*less* than time*ly*.

So, features tend to be less timely (such as how-to articles) than hard news. They also are more opinionated (such as columns or reviews) and more focused on personality (such as personality profiles) rather than hard news. And sometimes, a feature will supplement a news story with a behind-the-scenes, colorful account of the news.

Features come in many varieties, but essentially a feature story is a piece of nonfiction writing that uses fiction techniques. It has character and monologue, if not dialog. A feature can have a locale that sets the mood, a colorful description that is sometimes symbolic, a narrative plot with foreshadowing and flashbacks, and sometimes even author's asides.

As an editor of a feature story, you'll often be dealing with more elements than with hard-news stories—photographs, artwork, sidebars and blurbs—and you'll need to make sure these elements all work together. Here are some hints:

- Make sure the various elements agree—especially on spelling of names.
- Make sure your headline doesn't conflict with what the photo portrays or what the photo captions says.
- Use all your big type to get across information to readers just scanning the page—maybe they'll even stop to read the story.

Features are often longer than hard-news stories and typically require more time to edit, even if the headlines aren't expected to be more creative. Still, don't use these facts to sit on a feature too long.

THE FEATURE-STORY LEAD

Feature stories tend to have a beginning, a middle and an end rather than the inverted-pyramid organization of a hard-news stories. The beginning of the article, however, is seldom the chronological beginning of the story behind it. Features often begin *in medias res* (as they say in literature classes)—in the middle of things, at a dramatic moment. The first paragraph is not usually a bottom-line lead, as in a hard-news story, but a more emotionally gripping sample to interest readers in what follows.

A Comparison of Features and News

Hard-news stories are meant primarily to inform. Feature stories are meant to entertain while informing, or even to entertain without informing (as in the case of humor columns and some human-interest stories). As a result, a feature story intentionally aims for the emotions. Human interest alone is enough to justify a feature story, although a **news peg**—a timely, newsworthy event on which to base the story—should be used whenever possible.

Unlike hard-news writers, feature writers tend to be more successful the more personal their literary style. So features tend to have an individual voice—figures of speech and personal observations—that lend them a sense of liveliness, color and personality when compared to the relatively impersonal, give-'em-the-bottom-line approach of hard-news stories. The feature story sometimes conveys a sense of the author's immersion in the lives and events covered, a stark contrast to the objective distance between news reporter and what's being reported.

Reporters and editors need to keep these distinctions in mind when deciding which approach should be taken in the writing or editing of any given story. With some stories, you just want to present the facts straightforwardly. With other stories, you want to throw in some entertainment with the relaying of information.

How do you know which kind of story you're editing? Look for other clues, such as whether the story is in present tense (typical of features) or past tense (typical of hard-news stories), and whether the story has a feature ending or just trails off like a hard-news story.

Remember these common stylistic differences between features and hard-news stories:

- Features are usually written in present tense, hard news in past tense. When it comes to attribution, then, features typically use *says* rather than *said*.
- Features sometimes address the reader directly as *you*.
- Depending on local style, features may refer to people in the stories on second and subsequent references by their first name rather than their last, as is standard for hard-news stories.
- Feature stories may be written in first person if the author is important to the story. But "I" should not be intruded gratuitously—if first-person pronouns can be left out, they should be.

Sometimes, reporters combine the feature and news approaches by starting with a feature-style lead atop a hard-news account. This **mixed approach** is used when a story is primarily informational and about a recent event, so a hard-news approach overall is best, but one brief, dramatic anecdote stands out as too good to pass up in setting the stage. Increasingly, reporters are taking the mixed approach, beginning hard-news stories with feature-style leads that dramatically introduce the story rather than immediately giving the bottom line. These stories can usually be cut from the bottom, but make sure you're not ruining a feature-style ending.

A feature story uses a **soft lead**. Instead of getting to the bottom line of *who-what* and *time-date-place* in the first sentence, a soft lead starts with description, dialog, character, anecdote or personal address to the reader. All except the last provide a sample rather than a summary of what will follow. The personal address is the exception: "You may want to take an umbrella today because the National Weather Service predicts thunderstorms this afternoon."

The purpose of the soft-news lead is to seduce the reader into the story. The bottom line, or summary, or **nut graf**, usually appears a few paragraphs into the story.

Feature leads often use the immediate-ID form of identifying the *who* in the story—that is, using a person's name in the lead—even when the person is not famous. So, when you're editing a story and see an immediate ID in the lead, either the person is well-known to local readers, or this should be the soft lead of a feature. The situation gets more problematic when a reporter uses a soft lead on a hard-news story—as has become more common the past 20 years. (For more information about this mixed approach, see "A Comparison of Features and News" on Page 61.)

The main problem to look for in soft leads is the cliché. Understand that there's a difference between clichés and the hard-news and feature formulas examined here. Formulas represent a genre and permit creative variations. Clichés are particular phrases or approaches that are repeated noncreatively. (A sonata is a genre with a general formula that defines it. But a specific phrase stolen from another musical work and repeated often in various songs is a cliché.)

Feature leads are one of the biggest sources of clichés in journalism. Many cliché leads start with a quotation, a question, one word or a dictionary definition. Others include: "What a difference a day makes," "It's official," "First the good news, then the bad," "Rain couldn't dampen the spirits of . . . ." Because rewriting leads is a major revision, copy editors should draw clichés to the attention of the copy-desk chief or the writer rather than change them on their own.

THE FEATURE ENDING

A feature story should have a definite sense of conclusion. If it doesn't, either it was intended as a mixed-approach story—a hard-news story with a feature lead—or the reporter failed to come up with an ending. Look for something already in the story that would make a good ending. If you don't see anything appropriate, send it back to the reporter.

The two most common types of features endings are:

1. *The snake bites its tail.* The ending ties back to the beginning.
2. *A dramatic quote or statement.* This is used either to summarize the implication of the story in a catchy phrase or image or to point to future implications.

TRIMMING A FEATURE STORY

Unlike an inverted-pyramid story, a feature shouldn't be cut from the bottom. When a feature is too long and you have to make it fit, instead of cutting from the bottom, tighten it from the middle. Take out the weakest points, or extra anecdotes, quotations, facts or details. Then, when the length is close, tighten wordy passages or delete lengthy, uncommon words.

MONITORING THE BODY OF THE FEATURE

Give the reporter more freedom to be personal than you would in a hard-news story. But feature writers shouldn't abuse this freedom by needlessly intruding themselves into a story when they aren't the story. And just as news writers, feature writers should not fall into telling the story through the use of modifiers like *controversial* rather than giving the details so readers can see for themselves that the subject is controversial.

Headlines are expected to be more creative on features than typical hard-news stories, so put more effort into these. Try to make feature heads not just tell the story, but sell it, as well.

Be on the alert for material you could quickly pull out to a sidebar or that would make good graphic possibilities, and pass along the suggestion to the copy-desk chief. Examples include a box with the *time-day-place* of an event, a locator map with directions to a place described in the story, or a list of materials for a do-it-yourself project.

Rules for Both Hard-News and Feature Leads

The lead of a story is its most important element because the lead's quality may well determine whether the reader is hooked or drops the story. Keep the following rules in mind as you are editing.

Keep the Lead Short and Simple.   Don't jam too many facts or figures into it. A lead sentence normally isn't more than about 20 words tops. Don't believe the myth that you need to cram *who, what, when, where, why* and *how* all in the lead.

Most problems arise when reporters try to pack too much into the lead. Either delete unnecessary details, or move minor ones to later paragraphs.

Wordy: The former girlfriend of a man charged with killing a local bartender almost four years ago testified Monday that she has never seen another man who claims he killed the victim and that she was with him that night.

Short and Simple: A man who says he actually committed the murder for which another man is on trial was contradicted in court Monday by his former girlfriend.

Wordy: A Springfield exotic dancer was arrested and charged with indecent exposure last night, officers George Smith and Henry Brown said Monday.

Short and Simple: A Springfield exotic dancer was arrested and charged with indecent exposure last night, police said Monday.

(We don't need the officers' names in the lead.)

Wordy: Former Assistant Secretary of State for Latin American Affairs Lincoln Gordon said today . . . .

Short and Simple: A former U.S. diplomat said today. . . .

(The title is too long, and why should this man receive an immediate-ID lead since few people will have ever heard of him?)

Wordy: A 14-year-old boy fired three shots Friday into a third-floor apartment at 91 Monmouth St. to climax an argument with a 39-year-old mother who had defended her 9-year-old daughter against an attack by the boy, the mother told police.

Short and Simple: A woman told police that a 14-year-old boy fired three shots Friday into her apartment after she had defended her 9-year-old daughter from the boy's attack.

"Short and simple" doesn't mean a lead can't be catchy. The best often are. The editors' eyes brighten when they see leads like these:

They're burying a generation today. (Texas school explosion)

The moon still shines on the moonshine stills in the hills of Pennsylvania.

Fifty thousand Irishmen—by birth, by adoption and by profession—marched up Fifth Avenue today.

Avoid Clichéd Leads.   Cliché leads have been used so often they're not only no longer fresh but also actually irksome. Examples:

Quick action by two alert police officers was credited with saving the life of . . . .

Police and volunteers staged a massive search today for a man who . . . .

Christmas came early for . . . .

Make Sure the Lead Actually Says Something Definite.   It should state a thesis, not merely announce a topic.

Vague Topic: A University of Michigan researcher spoke on campus about cancer Thursday night.

Definite Thesis: A University of Michigan researcher told a campus audience Thursday night that new evidence suggests secondhand smoke may not pose as big of a cancer risk as previously thought.

Don't Start a Lead with a Time, Day, Place, Quotation or Question.   Otherwise, every local story would start with "Today in Springfield . . . ," or with a quotation or question, like a freshman term paper.

Don't Editorialize in a Lead with Value Judgments or Unattributed Paraphrases.

Unattributed Lead: All Delawareans over 45 should be vaccinated now against Asian flu.

(Without attribution, it sounds as though the reporter is editorializing.)

Don't Hype the Story More than It's Actually Worth.   A good lead must be straightforward and capture the flavor of the story. But no matter how well-written, the lead is no good if it misleads the reader into thinking the story is better than it really is.

Don't Bury the Lead or Miss the Real Story.   For example, a wire-service follow-up to a story about a mass killing in a restaurant the previous day began with the condition of the surviving victims. But at the end of the story, the reporter men-

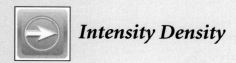

Intensity Density

Intensity density is a term we coined to name a practical, flexible concept that can be applied to both words and visuals, whether in newspapers, magazines and newsletters, books, radio, television, film—even music, video games, advertising and term papers.

The concept is simply this: *Audiences value a media product more if they find more things to like about it in a given space or time.* To give a few examples, you will find a TV situation comedy funnier the more laughs you get in the space of half an hour, and you will find an action movie more involving the more action there is within any 10 minutes, a rock radio station more listenable the more hits played per hour, or a textbook more appealing the less it wastes your time with a lot of fluff between the points worth remembering.

Likewise, TV advertisements and music videos use fast-paced cuts to keep your attention; teachers grade term papers higher that have more original ideas, interesting examples or clever phrasings per page; poetry readers value poems more that have more meaningful lines; and music listeners like songs with interesting **hooks**—whether interesting lyrics (especially in a chorus), a rhythmic groove, a memorable vocal phrasing or an instrumental part.

So it is that magazine, newsletter and newspaper readers find publications more interesting that have more stories, headlines, photos and graphics of interest per page. In other words, make sure that any media product you edit has lots of hooks in a given space or time to grab the audience and make people take notice.

As an editor, this means you need to remember not to waste your readers' time. Get the unnecessary words (the deadwood) out of stories, making them as intensely useful and interesting as possible. Then, use the space saved to get your **story count** up—more quality stories in each copy of your publication. And while you're at it, remember that readers look first at the big type and at photos and graphics. So, try to get more important information into more headlines, second decks, blurbs and captions, and try to get more graphic elements, as well as photos, illustrations, charts, boxes and bullet lists on each page.

Is there an upper limit to intensity density? Yes. You can't have a series of mountains without valleys between, and if a page is too full of graphic elements, it can become too busy and distracting. Likewise, it's possible for an article or book to become so full of ideas, readers have little time to pause and digest them, so the writing becomes too dense, too hard to fathom. This is where the idea of editing as an art comes in again: You have to use your own judgment. Editors tend to err more on the side of being boring rather than exciting, so remembering to pump up the intensity is usually what's most needed.

tioned that the killer, who had died in the attack, had tried calling a local mental-health hot line the morning of the rampage, according to his wife, and had received a recording that because of funding cuts, callers had to make an appointment. Surely, readers would talk more about this fact than the condition of the survivors. The hot line funding cut should have been the lead.

Don't Lead with Old News. Don't put a first-day lead on a second-day story—in other words, lead with the latest, up-to-the-minute news, not yesterday's.

MAKING SURE STORIES ARE ORGANIZED AND FLOW WELL

Here are six steps to making sure stories are well-organized and flow well.

1. Look at the Lead, and Determine Whether This is a Hard-news Story or a Feature. Remember, in a mixed approach, a story may start out with a feature lead but turn into a hard-news story.

If the story has a hard-news lead, check for the typical order of *who, what, time, day* and *place* in the lead. If this order isn't followed, is there a logical reason? *What* or *why* are sometimes better ways to start, and *time, day* or *place* often aren't needed. But it's almost always a bad idea to start a story with *time, day* or *place*.

If you've determined that this is a hard-news story, verify that the story follows the inverted-pyramid structure of most to least important. If anything lower in the story is more important than something higher, move it up. If anything seems irrelevant to the story, delete it.

If you've determined that this is a feature story, check to see whether the lead pulls you into the story. Is it hackneyed or dull or misleading? Did the writer get to the bottom line within a few paragraphs so that you soon knew the "so what"?

If the story has a feature lead, make sure there's a **nut graf**—a paragraph summarizing the bottom line—soon after the lead. If not, readers will have a hard time figuring out the point of the story.

After checking the feature lead, look to the end of the story to see whether there's a definite sense of conclusion, such as a return to the beginning or a dramatic statement or quotation. If so, make sure you don't cut the ending if you need to trim the story for space. If not, then this is either a hard-news story with a feature lead (and you could trim from the end if needed) or the story reads like a feature but needs a better ending.

2. Notice Whether the Lead is an Immediate-ID or Delayed-ID One. If a delayed-ID lead is used, verify that the person is named soon, usually at the start of the second paragraph. If an immediate-ID lead begins the story, verify that the person is well-known to your audience or in the news often, or that this is a feature lead in which immediate ID is appropriate for everyone.

3. Look at Whether the Story Contains Quotes. If the story doesn't have quotes, does it need them? If it is short enough, the story may not need them, but stories 8 inches or more typically do have direct quotes.

If there are quotations in the story, does the writer get to the first quote within the first two to five paragraphs? If not, consider moving up the quote that best summarizes the story or is most dramatic.

Is it always clear who's speaking in a quote? Is a name provided at the beginning of a quote every time the speaker changes? Are all paraphrases attributed so they aren't confused with the reporter making a pronouncement?

Does the story effectively use the **seesaw technique**—when statements and quotations seesaw back and forth, with information presented, are they backed up with a quotation or vice versa? Does the length of the statements and quotations vary so the technique doesn't become too singsong to readers?

4. Look for the Basic Details that Must be Answered in This Kind of Story and in This One in Particular.   In other words, what questions would a reader expect to have answered in this story?

Next, which of these questions is the most important to answer first? Which second and so on? Now, verify the story is organized in the most logical, coherent manner. Does it stick to the subject and explore it completely, or does it ramble off on irrelevant or illogical tangents that should either be cut or made into sidebars?

5. Ask Whether Along the Way Each Step in the Story is Clear.   Are the words and sentences simple to understand? Are all unfamiliar terms explained? Has jargon been avoided wherever possible and defined where unavoidable? If anything is ambiguous, ask the reporter what it means—don't guess. Here are some additional questions to help you seek clarity:

- Is the main point of the story apparent? Does every point and every sentence grow from it and point to it?

- Do sentences vary in length so that the story doesn't sound too choppy?

- Are transitions clear—between sentences and between points in the story?

- Is the full name provided each time a new source in the story is first introduced and an explanation provided of who the person is?

- Are all words used precisely and correctly? (*Admitted, anxious, bureaucrat, claimed* and *refuted* all have specific meanings that may not be intended by the writer but are likely to be inferred by a reader.)

- Have you checked when a story says *today* whether it means the day it was written or the day of publication?

- Are rhetorical techniques such as metaphors, analogies and images used to illustrate the meaning? Are examples given? Does the writer make comparisons? (When a writer makes a statement such as "The room was large," always ask yourself: Compared with what?)

- Does this story need a photo, illustration, chart, summary box, blurb or second deck to make the meaning clearer?

6. Ask Whether the Story Moves Along at a Good Pace. Are points raised given an appropriate depth of treatment before new ones are introduced? Do sentence lengths and structure also vary in an appropriate manner? Is the tone appropriate for this story, and are there any violations of that tone? Does the story hold your interest, or do you get bogged down in irrelevant details?

**MAKING SURE STORIES DON'T LEAVE
UNANSWERED QUESTIONS**

Once in a while, journalists fail to see that the information they present would naturally raise certain questions in a reader's mind. Sometimes, this failure is simply due to carelessness. Other times, it comes from the conflict between trying to be concise (not wasting words) and trying to be complete (making sure everything is said that needs to be said). Although a story should be pared for word economy, it should not be pared for fact economy.

People in the audience for news in any medium want to feel that they're getting at least the gist of the story—the most important details—and as much more of the story as time or space permits. For newspapers, especially, the ability to provide details is the great advantage print has over broadcast media.

Of course, it could be said that an audience doesn't miss what it doesn't know. Those who receive their news primarily in the shortened form of radio or television often feel satisfied that they know what's going on, even though they may be unaware of the greater details provided in newspaper coverage. But whether people are getting their news from newspapers, magazines, radio, television or Web sites, they *are* bothered when something about a story strikes them as incomplete and leaves them with unanswered questions.

If the story says, for example, "Hastings Banda, the leader of Nyasaland, received his education in Ohio," people want to know where in Ohio, at what university and when. Why? No doubt, someone will wonder, "Is that the same Banda I knew at Ohio State in the 1970s?" Here are more cases where the absence of vital information would leave readers confused:

- A man went to court to fight for a seat in the Legislature, but the writer did not tell to which party he belonged.

- A woman was mugged while waiting for a bus at Delaware and Woodlawn avenues, but the writer did not give the time of the incident, which would be of interest to people who ride that bus.

- A drunken chimpanzee supposedly escaped and created havoc around the countryside by trying to break into homes. But the story failed to tell who owned the chimp, what he was doing in the country, how he acquired alcoholic beverages and what finally happened after a game warden arrived.

- A minister was arrested and charged with operating a motor vehicle without a license, failure to carry a car registration card, disorderly conduct and disobeying a police officer. When two of the four charges were dismissed, the story failed to reveal why. (It was standard in that locale to dismiss the license and registration charges when a driver simply forgot to carry the documents.)

A Checklist for Unanswered Questions

- Who will read this story, and what will they want to know about the subject?
- What would have to be in any story on this subject for it to be complete?
- Are there any questions a reader would likely ask about this particular story?

- Are any intriguing angles introduced, then dropped without explanation?
- Are all first references to a person or organization complete?

- A skin diver stayed under water for 31 hours and spent much of his time reading a paperback book. The reporter did not explain what kept the pages from disintegrating. (The paper was a glossy stock.)
- A judge reversed his own conviction of a union leader for breach of the peace. The reversal was described as based on "new evidence," but the writer failed to tell readers what this new evidence was.

In each of these cases, there were basic questions the reporter failed to answer, so the editor should have asked. If any part of a story is confusing, such as the use of technical jargon in a quotation, the editor should supply explanations—after checking with the reporter, if necessary. For example, a story that contains the clause "where family income is below federal poverty levels" should also tell readers what the poverty level is by federal standards.

 MAKING SURE STORIES ARE ACCURATE

Of all the editor's duties, editing for accuracy is one of the most important. A publication that is inaccurate soon loses its credibility and, ultimately, its readers. For years, the importance of accuracy checking was driven home to students at the University of Kansas by the respected copy-editing professor John Bremner, who told them, "If your *mother* says she loves you, check it out."

Good reporting, of course, is the key ingredient in ensuring accuracy. But all who edit the story share that responsibility. City editors ensure accuracy by questioning the reporter about the information and the means by which it was gathered, and copy editors ensure accuracy by checking verifiable facts.

For example, the spelling of names and the accuracy of addresses can be checked in phone books and city directories, as well as through Internet search engines and sources such as Yahoo's People Search. Other facts can be looked up in standard reference volumes (almanac, atlas dictionary, book of quotations or encyclopedia).

Large national magazines have fact checkers who do nothing but verify facts in articles. *The New Yorker's* fact checking is especially famous. But newspapers and broadcast stations, with their much tighter deadlines, seldom have the luxury of being able to check every fact. Instead, they depend more on their reporters to get it right. It's especially important, then, that editors at newspapers and broadcast stations have a heavy dose of suspicion to help them decide when to question a reporter or take the time to look up something that doesn't sound right.

Not everyone, of course, can be as sharp as legendary editor Carr Van Anda, who spotted an error in an Albert Einstein formula. But a well-educated editor with a suspicious nature will detect plenty of mistakes before they appear in print or are broadcast.

Common Kinds of Inaccuracies

Look Out for Inconsistencies Within a Story.   These could include different spellings of a name or statements that contradict something else in the story. Watch for figures that don't add up—such as percentages in a survey that don't add up to 100, figures in a budget story that don't match the total, votes that don't tally with the number cast, or ages that contradict birth and death dates in an obituary. Inconsistencies about age in obituary information from funeral homes are common.

Here are a few examples:

The United Way on Monday awarded $23,000 in supplemental funds to three agencies. . . . The additional funds will go to the Boy Scouts, $11,000; the Girl Scouts, $9,000; and the Salvation Army, $4,000.

Tanglewood Barn Theater ended its regular season with a bang in its production of "Wonderful Town" Wednesday night. . . . [Last paragraph] The show will be repeated at 8:15 p.m. through Sunday.

The largest single cost of the trial was jury expenses, which total $3,807. . . . [Later] Another cost was $20,015 paid to extra guards and bailiffs.

Mrs. John E. Simpson, 86, Columbia, died Sept. 3, 2008, at Boone County Hospital after an illness of several months. Mrs. Simpson was born in Audrain County on Dec. 21, 1922, to the late John and Mary Simpson.

One inconsistency in the last example is that Mrs. Simpson likely did not have the same maiden and married names. Therefore, her parents' surname is probably wrong here. A second inconsistency is that if she was born in December 1922 and died several months before her birthday in 2008, she was not 86 years old but 85.

Look Out for Inconsistencies with Previous Stories or Information You've Heard or Read Elsewhere.   In his State of the Union speech Jan. 25, 1994, President Bill Clinton said 58 million Americans couldn't get health insurance. Two weeks earlier, it was reported the administration had said 39 million. How did 19 million people suddenly lose their health insurance in two weeks? The previous

What to Check for Accuracy and How

- Check spelling of local names in the phone book, city directory or morgue files (electronic, biographical or picture).
- Check spelling of other names in the state manual, morgue picture files, *Who's Who,* almanac or encyclopedia.
- Check local addresses in the phone book (most recent) or city directory (generally less up-to-date). With criminal suspects who move often, you may have to trust the police blotter.
- Check unfamiliar place names in a current atlas.
- Check spellings and whether words are two words, one word or hyphenated, first in *The AP Stylebook,* second in *Webster's New World College Dictionary,* then in *Webster's Third New International Dictionary,* taking the answer from the first one of those you find it in, but checking them in that order. If a compound word is not listed, make it two words as a verb or noun, hyphenated as an adjective.
- Check well-known quotations in *Bartlett's Quotations.* Paul F. Boller Jr. and John George's *They Never Said It* is handy for spotting famous misquotations.
- Check facts and figures against recent stories, morgue files, an almanac, *Facts on File* and an encyclopedia. Jan Harold Brunvand's books are useful for spotting "urban legends" masquerading as news stories.
- Now that newspapers have Internet connections on staff desktops, it's easier to check information on the Web. Even local names and addresses, for example, can often be found through a Yahoo People Search.

year, the figure that appeared regularly in the press was 37 million, and meanwhile, the libertarian-leaning Cato Institute was saying the figure was only about 6 million. Do your audience a favor by checking out such inconsistencies and explaining them. Were different standards being used, resulting in different figures? If so, explain.

Beware of Unwarranted Superlatives.   When reporters write that something is the "first," "only," "biggest," "best" or "a record," good editors question the statement. An excellent example occurred in 1999 after two high school students in Littleton, Colo., opened fire on their classmates.

- *The New York Times* wrote: "It was the largest death toll in an act of terrorism at one of the nation's schools."
- Reuters wrote: "The country's worst school massacre in Littleton, Colo. . . ."
- United Press International wrote: "The worst school massacre in U.S. history."

Unfortunately, all of them were wrong. At Columbine High School in Littleton, 12 students, a teacher and the two gunmen died. On May 18, 1927, 45 people, including 18 elementary students, were killed by a series of dynamite explosions at a school in Bath, Mich. Because it happened so long ago, most reporters knew nothing about it. They should have checked.

Such mistakes are common. Here are a couple more examples:

- A story from Louisville described a conviction as the first under a new law barring interstate shipment of gambling material. Two months earlier, two men had been convicted under the same law.

- A Billy Graham rally was described as having the largest audience for a single meeting. But a Rosary Crusade in San Francisco had been attended by 500,000, a bigger crowd than Graham's.

All superlatives should be checked. If they cannot be verified, at least they can be softened.

Beware of Common False Quotations.   Many common quotations that writers know and repeat turn out to be misstated or misattributed:

- According to the Bible, it's not money that is the root of all evil but "the love of money."

- Ralph Waldo Emerson did not say, "Consistency is the hobgoblin of little minds," but "A foolish consistency is the hobgoblin of little minds."

- François Voltaire did not say, "I may not agree with what you say, but I will defend to the death your right to say it." That was traced back to a woman who wrote an essay that said essentially, "As Voltaire *might* have said, . . ."

- George Santayana did not say, "Those who ignore history are doomed to repeat it." It's often attributed to him, but no one's ever actually been able to find it in his writings.

- William Congreve did not say, "Music hath charms to soothe the savage beast," but rather "Music hath charms to soothe the savage breast."

- In the movie *Casablanca,* Humphrey Bogart did not say, "Play it again, Sam," but rather, "You played it for her and you can play it for me. . . . If she can stand it, I can. Play it!"

- Horace Greeley did not originate "Go west, young man." Greeley merely repeated in one of his editorials the advice actually given by John Babson Lane Soule in 1851.

- Mark Twain didn't write, "Everybody talks about the weather but nobody does anything about it." That credit goes to Charles Dudley Warner, who collaborated with Twain on the book *The Gilded Age.*

- Grantland Rice is often misquoted as saying, "It's not whether you win or lose but how you play the game." Actually, he wrote, "When the One Great Scorer comes to write against your name— / He marks—not that you won or lost but how you played the game."

Beware of Common "Facts" That Aren't.   As with common quotations, many widely known "facts" that writers repeat turn out to be wrong:

- Washington did *not* have wooden teeth—they were ivory.
- The Gettysburg Address was *not* written on the back of an envelope.
- Witches were *not* burned in Salem—they were hanged.
- Lloyd's of London is *not* an insurance company—it's an association of individual underwriters.
- St. Bernard dogs never carried casks of brandy in Switzerland.
- Delilah didn't cut Samson's hair—she had a barber do it, according to Judges 16:19.
- It's the Smithsonian Institution in Washington, not the Smithsonian Institute.

Beware of News That Isn't, Such as Hoaxes and Urban Legends.   Virtually every newspaper, magazine and broadcast station has been victimized at one time or another by a hoax. Such incidents stress the importance of good journalistic technique, particularly the practice of knowing to whom one is talking. **Hoaxes** usually begin when an individual calls or stops by, claiming to be someone he or she is not. Good reporters verify the identity of anyone they do not know. Failing to do so is the surest way to fall victim to a hoax.

The importance of following this rule is clear in the case of a hoax perpetrated on the *Star Tribune,* published in the twin cities of Minneapolis and St. Paul. The *Star Tribune* ran an eight-paragraph story quoting Richard L. Thomas, president of First Chicago Corp., a large bank holding company, as saying his company was interested in purchasing troubled First Bank Systems of Minneapolis for $20 to $22 a share. That day, First Bank stock jumped sharply higher—before First Chicago issued a statement denying that Thomas had talked to the Minneapolis paper. The whole story, it turned out, was a hoax.

"We have absolutely no idea" who the impostor was, said Larry Werner, *Star Tribune* assistant managing editor for business. The problem began when the impostor called a real-estate reporter to talk about an earlier story written by a reporter with a similar name. The real-estate reporter tried to transfer the call, but the caller refused, saying he had already been transferred too often. The real-estate reporter gave his notes to the other reporter, who wrote the story. Neither bothered to call First Chicago to confirm that Thomas had actually made the call. A lesson was learned—the hard way.

Longtime editors know that some hoaxes have a way of reappearing from time to time in various parts of the country. These include the following stories:

- A 16-year-old babysitter was stuck to a freshly painted toilet seat for hours. A doctor administered to her, tripped and knocked himself out. Both were carried off in an ambulance for medical treatment and both sued the family who engaged the sitter.

- A woman driver was flagged by a stalled motorist needing a push. Told she would have to get up to 35 mph to get the stalled car started, she backed off, gunned the motor and rammed his car at 35 mph.

- A sheriff was called to a farm to investigate the theft of 2,025 pigs and discovered that only two sows and 25 pigs were missing. The farmer who reported the loss lisped.

- A farmer armed with a shotgun went to a chicken house to rout a suspected thief. The farmer stumbled and the gun went off, killing all his hens.

- Usually in some obscure hill hamlet in the east of Europe or in Asia, an eagle carried off a 3-year-old child.

- A man called police to report that someone stole the steering wheel and all the pedals from his car. A squad car was sent to the scene, but before police arrived, the man called back and said: "Everything is all right. I was looking in the back seat."

- Someone has found a copy, in near perfect condition, of the Jan. 4, 1800, issue of the Ulster County *Gazette.* The paper is prized not only for its age but also because it contains a statement made to the U.S. Senate by President John Adams following the death of George Washington 21 days earlier. It refers to Washington as "Father of our country." Few copies of the original exist, but there are many reproductions.

- A man received a series of summonses to pay a tax bill. The notices said he owed $0.00 in taxes and $0.00 in penalties. He was warned that his personal belongings would be attached if he didn't pay. He sent the tax office a check for $0.00 and got a receipt for that amount. Sometimes the yarn is applied to the nonpayment of a noncharge from an electric company and a threat to cut off service unless the bill is paid—or to a tuition demand on a student studying at a college on a full scholarship.

- The bricklayer story makes the rounds periodically, usually with a change in locale. The story may have been reworked from a vaudeville gag of earlier days. It is recorded by a comedian with a British accent as a monologue under the title of "Hoffnung at the Oxford Club." Fred Allen used it as a skit on one of his radio shows in the 1930s. In 1945, the story was retold in an anthology of humor edited by H. Allen Smith. Three versions had their setting in Korea, Barbados and Vietnam. In World War II, the bricklayer was a sailor on the USS *Saratoga* requesting a five-day leave extension. Here is the Barbados version, courtesy of UPI:

LONDON (UPI)—The Manchester Guardian today quoted as "an example of stoicism" the following unsigned letter—ostensibly from a bricklayer in the Barbados to his contracting firm:
   "Respected Sir,
   "When I got to the building, I found that the hurricane had knocked some bricks off the top.

So I rigged up a beam with a pulley at the top of the building and hoisted up a couple of barrels full of bricks. When I had fixed up the building, there was a lot of bricks left over.

"I hoisted the barrel back up again and secured the line at the bottom and then went up and filled the barrel with the extra bricks. Then I went to the bottom and cast off the line.

"Unfortunately, the barrel of bricks was heavier than I was, and before I knew what was happening the barrel started down, jerking me off the ground. I decided to hang on, and halfway up I met the barrel coming down and received a severe blow on the shoulder.

"I then continued to the top, banging my head against the beam and getting my fingers jammed in the pulley. When the barrel hit the ground it bursted its bottom, allowing all the bricks to spill out.

"I was now heavier than the barrel and so started down again at high speed. Halfway down, I met the barrel coming up and received severe injuries to my shins. When I hit the ground I landed on the bricks and got several painful cuts from the sharp edges.

"At this point I must have lost my presence of mind because I let go the line. The barrel then came down, giving me another heavy blow on the head and putting me in the hospital.

"I respectfully request sick leave."

Urban legends are really modern folklore—stories that get repeated as factual but that really didn't happen. Two of the more famous examples include the story of the woman who dried her poodle in the microwave oven, and the story of the poisonous exotic snake found in either the imported coat or the basket somebody bought at Kmart or Wal-Mart.

The problem for the news media is that a reporter hears such stories from a friend of a friend who swears it happened to another friend or someone he knew, then the reporter sometimes writes it up even though the story doesn't check out. Why? Because it's too good of a story not to run. A good rule to apply is that if you ever edit a story that sounds too good to be true, it probably is—especially when the story doesn't supply details such as names and direct quotes from the people supposedly involved.

Beware of News Stories or "Facts" and Figures Originating from Potentially Biased Sources.   We're not saying that information from a source with an ax to grind is always deceptive or wrong, just that it bears extra skepticism.

- *Polls funded by politicians or political action groups.* Often, these are **push polls**–consisting of biased questions aimed at influencing the public perception rather than measuring it. Not only are the questions often biased—"Do you oppose fighting terrorists in Iraq or do you support the American troops?"—but also the polls are often conducted of people on mailing lists known to have contributed to a particular side's causes or candidates in the past. The results, then, when either of those things has happened are utterly unscientific and biased.

- *Reports by researchers funded by industries with a vested interest.* In August 2007, *Newsweek* magazine said in a cover story that the oil industry was funding researchers who disputed global warming. That's useful to know. But critics pointed out the article didn't bother to check the funding of the pro-global-warming research: Although anti-global-warming research received $19 *million* in funding, pro-global-warming research had received $50 *billion.*

Further, *Newsweek* editor Robert J. Samuelson himself later called the magazine's coverage "fundamentally misleading" because, as he wrote in *The Washington Post,* although he himself believed the Earth had indeed warmed,

> we simply don't have a solution for this problem. As we debate it, journalists should resist the temptation to portray global warming as a morality tale—as *Newsweek* did—in which anyone who questions its gravity or proposed solutions may be ridiculed as a fool, a crank or an industry stooge. Dissent is, or should be, the lifeblood of a free society.

The lessons would seem to be that journalists should be evenhanded when running stories about how funding may compromise truth, and should not assume that simply challenging the funding of one side's research in itself proves the other side to be right.

• *Information originating on blogs and Web sites lacking gatekeeping checks and balances.* Obviously, there have been times the mainstream media, with their multiple layers of editors, have gotten it wrong, and Web sites or blogs without editorial staff got it right or broke important news first. For example, CBS's airing of documents attacking George W. Bush's military record were later roundly discredited by littlegreenfootballs.com, which showed that the documents were produced using Microsoft Word, not a typewriter of the period. CBS anchorman Dan Rather eventually lost his job over the matter.

Generally speaking, however, because anyone can start a Web site that says anything, it's wiser to be skeptical of information originating from unknown sources or those without a proven track record of accuracy. This is especially true of Web sites and blogs known to have an agenda other than the impartial weighing and reporting of facts

• *Criticism from "media watchdog" groups with political agendas.* Again, we're not saying that criticisms stated by media watchdog groups are always deceptive or wrong. As in a courtroom, the give and take of charges and countercharges can be part of the debate that leads to the truth.

But in September 2007, both conservative talk-radio host Rush Limbaugh and independent but conservative-leaning Fox News commentator Bill O'Reilly challenged reports by the left-leaning Mediamatters.org Web site that Limbaugh and O'Reilly claimed had taken comments of theirs out of context. In both cases, news organizations had printed or broadcast the charges as factual based only on the excerpts and comments made by Media Matters.

O'Reilly and Limbaugh used their platforms as commentators with two of the largest audiences in broadcast to answer the charges by playing tapes of the larger context of their comments, which they said had been misrepresented.

O'Reilly had been portrayed as bigotedly surprised to see black people well-dressed at an event he attended, but he said the larger context showed he was saying that white America assumed black culture was only hip-hop. Limbaugh had been portrayed as calling soldiers who opposed the war in Iraq "phony soldiers," but he said it was in the context of discussing a case of an antiwar activist who had been exposed as lying about having been a soldier in Iraq, not of calling actual soldiers who opposed the war "phony."

Who was right in each case is not so much the question here as the observation that the news media should not have reported only accusations without checking the readily available tapes or transcripts of the shows. Limbaugh said that of all those who reported the story, only Reuters bothered to call to ask his side and to hear a tape of the original comments.

Part of the problem, perhaps, is that journalists assume media watchdog groups have no political leanings of their own. The very names sometimes suggest that. Among those leaning left are Fairness and Accuracy in Reporting, Mediamatters.org and Project Censored. Among those on the right are Accuracy in Media and the Media Research Center. Again, this is not to say that their reports aren't interesting criticism, but the critics themselves need to be viewed critically.

Beware of Imprecise Words or Phrases That Make a Statement Inaccurate or Misleading.   A common source of incorrect writing is the imprecise phrase or word. Legal terms can pose an especially dangerous problem. For example, in some states, *driving while intoxicated* differs from *driving while under the influence of alcohol*. The first is more serious, so if you don't know the local legal difference, using the wrong one could result in a lawsuit for libel.

Here are additional examples:

- The U.S. Supreme Court did *not* ban prayers in school. The court banned the requirement that children pray any particular prayer and the writing by public authorities of a required prayer. The decision had to do with public schools. It did not interfere with required prayers in church-operated schools.

- *Gas* and *gasoline* are not synonymous. Gas is either natural or manufactured. Some explosions are caused by gas, some by gasoline. The story and headline should contain the precise term. Similarly, in stories of food poisoning, the copy should specify whether the story is referring to canned or bottled foodstuffs.

- "A defective 20mm cannon suddenly fired, and the shell killed one airman and injured another." The writer should have used *unexpectedly* rather than *suddenly*, and *bullet*, *slug* or *projectile* rather than *shell*.

- "It is perhaps the most cosmopolitan area in the city, stronghold of the Poles and densely populated with other ethnic groups including Czechs, Bohemians, Slovaks and some Italians," one story reported. But Czechs and Bohemians are one and the same people. The Czech lands include Bohemia and

Moravia. Some Bohemians prefer to be called Czechs. Slovaks are a separate people, although there is a strong language affinity. There is a difference between a *Slovak* and a *Slovenian*, as any editor would soon realize should the two be confused.

Beware of Numbers That Don't Check Out Mathematically.   Numbers add specifics and credibility to a story, and they should make the story more understandable. But, as former British Prime Minister Benjamin Disraeli is often inaccurately quoted as saying, there are "lies, damn lies and statistics."* Sometimes, numbers are inaccurate, confusing or misleading, and the editor needs to correct the situation.

Here's some general advice for editing numbers in a story:

- **Review AP style on numbers.** Basically, spell out zero through nine, then go to Arabic numerals. Know the exceptions, as outlined in *The AP Stylebook.*

- **Don't clutter a lead with numbers.** Nothing is duller than a lead full of numbers.

- **Cite sources for any statistics.** We don't mean footnotes as in a term paper, but name the person or organization that provided them.

- **Double-check all math.** For example, an advocate for the homeless was reported as saying 45 homeless people die in America each second. Do the math. In one minute, that would be 2,700 people; in one hour, 162,000; in one day, 3,888,000; and in one year, that would be 1,419,120,000—far more than the 301 million population of the United States.

- **Round off large numbers.** In the previous example, it would be better to report 1,419,120,000 as *more than 1.4 billion.*

- **Don't assume numbers always explain themselves.** Relate the significance of numbers by putting them in context and in terms people can understand. For example, in a story about an upcoming election over a millage increase in property taxes to fund a new high school, explain how much property taxes would increase on an average-value home in your community.

- **Watch inclusive numbers and numerical comparisons.**
  - Insist on this style: *$5 million to $7 million*, not *$5 to $7 million*, which means five dollars to seven million dollars.
  - Odds should not be written as *3 million to 1* but as *1 in 3 million.*

---

*In his autobiography, Mark Twain attributes the quote "There are three kinds of lies: lies, damned lies, and statistics" to Benjamin Disraeli. No version of this quotation has been found in any of Disraeli's published works or letters. There is a reference to this quotation as being the "words of a Wise Statement" in a speech given by Leonard Courtney in New York in 1895. Perhaps Twain assumed that the "Wise Statesman" was Benjamin Disraeli.

Guidelines for Specific Number-Editing Situations

Percentages
- Appear in stories on budgets, economy, taxes, sports, etc.
- To calculate: Divide the part by the whole, then move the decimal point two places to the right.
- Be aware of how differences in wording affect the accuracy of percentages. For example, all the following statements are true even though the percentage changes:
  1. Five is 50 percent of 10.
  2. Ten is 200 percent of five.
  3. Ten is 100 percent more than five.
  4. Five percent is five percentage points less than 10 percent.
  5. Ten percent is five percentage points more than 5 percent.

Averages Versus Means
- Many uses, such as stories on educational testing.
- To calculate an *average* or an *arithmetic mean:* Add a list of numbers, then divide by the number of numbers you added.
- To find the *median:* List all the numbers from largest to smallest, then find (1) the number in the middle, or (2) if there is an even number of numbers in the list, the average of the two middle numbers.

Per Capita Rates
- Appear in stories on budgets, economy, crime and suicide rates, etc.
- *Per capita* is Latin for "by heads."
- To calculate: Divide the total amount spent by the population it will be spent on.

Interest Rates
- Appear in stories about loans.
- To calculate *simple interest* for a set time, such as one month or one year: Multiply the loan amount (the *principal*) by the rate expressed in decimal form. (To do the calculation, a rate of 5 percent would be expressed as .05.)
- To calculate *compound interest* over a period of time, such as months or years:

1. Express the interest rate in decimal form, but put a 1 in front of it. (A 5 percent interest rate would be written as 1.05.)
2. Multiply this number times itself for each year of the loan past the first. (For a five-year loan, that would be 1.05 to the fourth power, or about 1.22.)
3. Multiply the result times the principal to find the total amount paid by the end of the loan. You can find a calculator online that will do this for you in many places, including www.moneychimp.com/calculator/compound_interest_calculator.htm.

Mortgages
- The *rate* is the interest rate paid on the loan. A *fixed-rate mortgage* stays the same rate during the life of the loan. An *adjustable-rate mortgage* goes up or down during the loan in relation to the *prime interest rate* set by the Federal Reserve Bank.
- *Points* are a percentage of the principal paid up front in order to get a lower interest rate on the loan.

Inflation
- Dollars not adjusted for inflation are called *nominal dollars* or *current dollars.*
- Dollars adjusted for inflation are called *constant dollars* or *real dollars.*
- To convert nominal to constant dollars:
  1. Look up the Consumer Price Index (CPI) for the year you'll use as a base year and the CPI for the year to which you wish to adjust. This is available at ftp://ftp.bls.gov/pub/special.requests/cip/cpiai.txt. Follow the CPI link to the latest press releases.
  2. Divide the base year's CPI by the CPI of the year to which you're adjusting.
  3. Multiply the result in Step 2 by the dollar amount you're adjusting.
- Example: A worker made $20,000 in 1975. What is the equivalent pay in 2008 dollars?
  1. Base year is 1975; CPI in 1975 was 53.8.

Year to which I wish to adjust is 2007 (last full year for which CPI is available); CPI yearly average was 207.342.

2. Divide 207.342 by 53.8 to get 3.85.
3. Multiply 3.85 by $20,000. The equivalent pay in 2003 dollars is $77,000.

Sales Tax

- To calculate the amount that sales tax will add to a purchase, multiply the purchase price of an item by the sales tax rate expressed as a two-place decimal.
- Example: A $500 computer bought in a state with a 6 percent sales tax would carry $500 × .06 = $30 in sales taxes, for a total cost of $530.

Property Tax

- *Assessed value* is what the government appraiser says the property is worth. (The assessed value, though, may be only a percentage of the actual value. In Michigan, it's about half.)
- *Millage rate* is the tax rate per $1,000 value. In 2007, in Washtenaw County, Mich., where Ann Arbor is located, the millage rate was 4.593.

- To calculate property taxes: Divide the assessed value by 1,000—in other words, move the decimal three places to the left. Then multiply the result by the millage rate.
- Example: A home assessed at $250,000 in Washtenaw County (4.5493 millage rate) would require a property tax of $1137.33.

Polls

- Poll results are typically valid within a range of plus or minus 3 percent. This validity is based on the number of people surveyed as compared to the population about which the survey generalizes. Always report this *margin of error,* as well as the number of people surveyed, and realize that surveys with margins of error of larger than 3 percent are not so reliable.
- Make sure the story identifies who conducted or sponsored the survey as well as the exact wording of the questions. These measures will help weed out bias that might invalidate the survey.
- The story should tell when the survey was conducted and how—for example, over the phone, in person or on the Internet.

- *Five times as much as* is not the same thing as *five times more than*. Five times as much as $50 would be $250. But five times more than $50 would be $300—$50 plus five times $50.

Where Editors Create Mistakes

Editors are most likely to create mistakes when editing quotations, rewriting copy, or writing headlines, blurbs and captions.

QUOTATIONS

Don't Turn Paraphrases into Quotations.   Don't insert quotation marks unless you have good reason to suspect the words are a direct quotation. An open quotation mark without a closing one or the use of "I" are obvious clues. Even then, check with the reporter about where the quotation begins and ends rather than guessing.

Don't Doctor Quotes to Make Them Read Better.   If a quotation is weak, consider cutting it, tightly paraphrasing it (remembering to remove the quotation marks) or using partial quotes (quoting key phrases, paraphrasing the rest). Quotation marks are a contract with the reader that these are the exact words someone used, so the safest policy is *don't fix quotes.*

That said, though, probably even the strictest editors have no problem editing out *uh* and *er* and false starts of sentences. Many, if not most, editors would even go a step further and say it's OK to correct minor grammatical errors that needlessly make someone—especially an average person—look foolish. There is, after all, a difference between spoken and written English.

But clearly, it's not a good idea to reshape entire sentences, like a speechwriter would revise text, spicing up a speaker's original words. This is dishonest in a news story, even when it captures the spirit of the speaker's point. Revising quotes also introduces the likelihood that speakers will be misunderstood and their point distorted in the newspaper, thus damaging the news outlet's credibility and opening the possibility of a lawsuit.

REWRITE

Know When Not to Rewrite.   Many copy desks have the explicit policy that they are not rewrite desks. Send major rewrites back to the city editor. Don't rewrite perfectly fine stories the way *you* would have done them. "If it ain't broke, don't fix it."

You may rewrite smaller problems, of course, such as when a passage is unclear. But realize you may have misunderstood it. So, check back with the reporter or the city editor to verify that your revision is accurate. If necessary, call the source.

Be Careful When Writing Headlines, Captions and Blurbs.   Reporters and their sources often complain that the story was correct but the headline, blurb or picture caption was inaccurate. Follow these tips:

- Verify that you have accurately summarized the story in the headline and not distorted it to attract readers or to fit a headline count.
- Make sure blurbs accurately summarize the story. When using a quotation in your blurb, use it word for word, and make sure it will not be misleading or out of context.
- Be certain that facts and spellings of names in headlines, blurbs and captions are consistent with those in the story.

✈ MAKING SURE STORIES ARE OBJECTIVE

Objectivity in journalism typically refers to being factual, being neutral and being fair. In a hard-news story, objectivity also often means being impersonal in style.

Be Factual.   Stick to things that are provable as opposed to opinions, guesses, rumors and predictions. Ask yourself:

- Does the story stick to facts?
- Has the writer avoided all speculation of his or her own, confining any speculation only to quotes or paraphrases from others?
- Has the writer avoided attributions that might imply mind reading, such as saying that someone *believes, doubts, feels, hopes* or *thinks* something rather than sticking to what the source *said?*
- Has the writer avoided predicting that a suspect will be arraigned or convicted? If the person is released without being charged or found guilty, the suspect might have grounds for a libel suit if the story predicted otherwise.

Be Neutral. The writer should not editorialize or intrude his or her own value judgments. Ask yourself:

- Was the writer careful to avoid verbs of attribution that might inadvertently express an opinion, such as *claimed* (implies *disbelief*) or *refuted* (means *successfully answered*)?
- Has the writer avoided saying anything that may disparage or offend someone on the basis of race, sex, religion or ethnic background?
- Did the writer avoid any of the following modifiers or similar words that betray an opinion?

alleged (adj.)	controversial
allegedly	crucial
amazing	definitely
arch-conservative	disturbing
arch-liberal	dramatic
astounding	effectively
awful	evil
bad	exciting
best	fittingly
bizarre	good
certainly	grim
complex	honestly

important	shocking
inevitable	spectacular
insurmountable	still
interesting	stunning
ironically	successfully
luckily	tragic
mysterious	troubling
obviously	ultra-conservative
perfectly	ultra-liberal
poignant	undoubtedly
positively	unique
predictably	unprecedented
quagmire	unquestionably
radical	unusual
respected	very
sadly	worst

Be Fair. Make sure the story represents all sides as evenly as possible.

- Are all sides given? Were enough people interviewed to get the full picture?
- If someone is accused of or criticized for something, does he or she get a chance to reply?
- Is the story legal and ethical?

Be Impersonal in Style in Hard-News Stories. A unique, creative voice is for personal essays and fiction. Ask yourself:

- If this is a hard-news story, has the writer avoided intruding his or her own personality into the story?
- If this is a feature, such as a review or column, does the personality of the writing contribute to the story or merely distract from the subject?

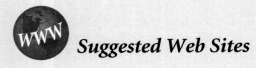

Suggested Web Sites

Great Books Online, with free access to Bartlett's Familiar Quotations, American Heritage Dictionary, Columbia Encyclopedia and much more **www.bartleby.com**

Biography.com **www.biography.com**

FactCheck.org **www.factcheck.org**

Google, for Web searches **www.google.com**

HeadlineSpot.com, for search of magazine, newspaper, radio, TV and wire-service Web sites **www.headlinespot.com**

Information Please **www.infoplease.com**

My Reference Desk **www.refdesk.com**

The Center for Responsive Politics looks at political donations and lobbying **www.opensecrets.org**

Quakwatch.org guide to fraudulent medicine claims **www.quackwatch.org**

Snopes.com for checking out urban legends **www.snopes.com**

TotalNews, for search of news sites **www.totalnews.com**

Suggested Readings

Boller, Paul F. Jr., and John George. *They Never Said It: A Book of Fake Quotes, Misquotes, and Misleading Attributions.* New York: Barnes & Noble, 1989.

Brunvand, Jan Harold. *Too Good to Be True: The Colossal Book of Urban Legends.* New York: Norton, 2001.

Cohn, Victor. *News & Numbers: A Guide to Reporting Statistical Claims and Controversy in Health and Other Fields.* Ames, Iowa: Iowa State University, 1989.

Jackson, Brooks, and Kathleen Hall Jameson. *Un*Spun: Finding Facts in a World of [Disinformation].* New York: Random House, 2007.

Keyes, Ralph. *The Quote Verifier.* New York: St. Martin's Griffin, 2006.

Kirchner, Paul. *Everything You Know Is Wrong.* Los Angeles: General Publishing Group, 1995.

Paulos, John Allen. *A Mathematician Reads the Newspaper.* New York: Anchor, 1996.

CHAPTER 5

MACRO EDITING FOR LEGALITY, ETHICS AND PROPRIETY

Law, ethics and propriety involve principles that help editors decide what not to publish or how to present their stories in a way that poses fewer problems.

American media law is unique in that, theoretically, the First Amendment bans all government limitations on the press. But the Constitution provides for copyright laws the media are not free to violate, and freedom from government censorship doesn't exempt the media from lawsuits by private individuals for libel, invasion of privacy or negligence. Then, too, Congress and the courts have decided that electronic media don't deserve the freedom from regulation the print media have, so broadcast media are licensed, whereas print media are not.

Americans arguably have the freest media in the world, but if the reality were as simple as the First Amendment's commandment that there be "no law . . . abridging the freedom . . . of the press," journalism programs wouldn't need to require entire courses devoted to media law. Also, the law is constantly changing with new statutes and new court cases, and media law varies from state to state. All of this adds to the complications.

Obeying ethical principles is more open to individual choice than obeying legal guidelines. But journalists, in addition to following their own moral compass, need to follow the ethics policies of their employers, which vary from place to place as do state media laws. Beyond their own ethics and those of their employers, journalists should also be familiar with policies that are standard industrywide. This will help them be better informed about which actions are normally acceptable and which aren't.

Propriety could be considered a part of ethics or a part of aesthetics, the field of philosophy that deals with beauty, especially in the arts. When we speak of making decisions about what to publish based on whether it's tasteful or not, we're trying to avoid giving unnecessary offense to our audience. Most American newspapers, for example, do not normally print cuss words beyond the relatively mild *hell* or *damn,* and do not normally print pictures depicting nudity or anything gruesome. But sometimes editors have to decide whether the news value trumps normal taste considerations, as when *The New York Times* decided to print a picture in the 1970s of Vice President Nelson Rockefeller giving a protester the finger.

This chapter will concentrate on bottom-line, practical principles rather than the case approach of the typical media law or media ethics course. These principles should prove useful in spotting problems and avoiding lawsuits. But principles provide rules of thumb, whereas life confronts us with individual circumstances that need to be taken into account—the particular subject matter, the way it's presented and other considerations such as the law of your local jurisdiction.

In short, when you come upon a situation about which you're not sure, seek the help of the editor above you and, if necessary, your company's attorney. Consider this chapter the collective experience of some editors who deal with journalistic decisions. This is not legal advice, which must come from an attorney looking at your individual circumstances.

✦ FREEDOM OF THE PRESS

Before we get to bottom-line, everyday specifics of media law, let's start with the larger context and consider the centerpiece of American media law, the First Amendment, ratified in 1791:

> Congress shall make no law respecting an establishment of religion, or prohibiting the free exercise thereof; or abridging the freedom of speech, or of the press; or the right of the people peaceably to assemble, and to petition the government for a redress of grievances.

Most Americans have no clue what the First Amendment says or means. Time after time over the years, when Americans have been surveyed about it but not told they were being asked about the First Amendment, most haven't recognized it and have opposed it as too radical.

In the early 1990s, students aged 15 to 24 were asked which freedom they would be willing to give up first if America were invaded. Most said freedom of the press, and less than 3 percent thought it important enough to hold on to. Sadly, adults aren't much wiser. Another survey done at roughly the same time found about 59 percent of all Americans thought government should have the ability to censor the media.

It could be argued that our lawmakers, too, haven't understood the First Amendment because we do have laws abridging the freedoms outlined in the First Amendment. In 1966, Supreme Court Justice Hugo Black wrote that in his opinion "no law" means just that: *no* law. He thought even libel and obscenity laws are unconstitutional, but that has never been the general opinion of the court.

Still, we're better off compared to other countries. Many nations today license journalists or exercise some other kinds of **censorship**. Freedom House's 2007 review of 193 countries found that 90 had a free press, 58 a partly free press and 45 a press that is not free. Consider this: When the director of *Police Academy* went to Spain after that movie came out in 1984, he found he was a hero there for having the courage to criticize the police!

Even Canada and the United Kingdom don't have as much press freedom as Americans do. In Canada, for example, judges can order the press not to cover a trial if they deem pretrial publicity could prevent a defendant's fair trial. In the United States, judges instead must resort to measures short of that such as secluding the jury from the news, not depriving the entire public of it. Meanwhile, in the United Kingdom, unlike in the United States, the government may:

- Order the media not to publish something someone alleges, even without proof, is libelous.

- Forbid publication of any information about a case being litigated, even information that has been brought up in open court.

- Prohibit publication of anything the government says involves national security, even though it's often merely something embarrassing to the government.

So, when people say Americans have the freest press in the world, they're not just being chauvinistic.

What Does "Freedom of the Press" Mean?

Freedom of the Press Means No Government Censorship. Alexander Hamilton asked what was meant by **"freedom of the press,"** and James Madison, the author of the Bill of Rights, responded that it meant freedom from despotic control by the federal government. The main idea was to avoid censorship by the government.

What *no censorship* means is *no prior restraint* by government. The government can't tell you what you must or must not publish. The media can severely criticize the government and its officials and have no fear that journalists will be jailed or the door to its publication or broadcast station will be padlocked.

Sometimes students ask, "Could a newspaper print a story about . . . ?" That's not an appropriate question because a newspaper can publish anything. No government censor looks over page proofs before a newspaper is printed, saying what can or can't be included.

And only rarely after something has been published will the newspaper face any government action. Much more likely is the possibility of a civil suit filed by someone named in a story for libel or violation of privacy. In other words, we don't have prior restraint in the United States, but publishers may have to face the consequences after the fact.

Censorship, Pro and Con

Arguments for Censorship

- **We need to protect the young and the ignorant.** The first great philosopher in Western civilization, Plato, around 2,300 years ago, said that in his ideal society the government would censor ideas that might mislead children or even adults. Later, during the Inquisition, the church decided it was better to censor books with ideas not approved by the church than for people to be led astray and lose their souls.

- **We should protect people from words or ideas that might offend them.** Some speech —such as racist hate speech, sexist language or pornographic depictions of women—doesn't help people get to the truth but rather distracts them from it by appealing to prejudice, not reason. This offensive language promotes contempt, not civil discussion. It shocks and intimidates, and it is a threat or a verbal assault.

Both of these ideas add up to this: "We know what's right, and you don't. Further discussion would only be harmful. Force is justified to make sure truth prevails. Anyone who disagrees with us should be silenced."

Arguments Against Censorship

In 1644, John Milton, the English poet who wrote "Paradise Lost," published an essay called "Areopagitica." He argued that licensing of the press, which Great Britain practiced at the time, was censorship, and he demanded that ideas be able to circulate freely. He said freedom of the press was the best way to get at the truth. His essay formed one of the first great defenses of freedom of the press. The first two of the following defenses of a free press derive from him:

- The censored idea might be true, and we'd be depriving ourselves of the truth.
- Even if it's false, being justified in our beliefs and being able to argue effectively for them require exposure to competing ideas.
- The truth is more likely to be discovered if there's a "free marketplace of ideas"—in other words, unconstrained debate, according to English philosopher John Stuart Mill in his classic 1859 book *On Liberty*.
- Freedom of the press makes possible an informed citizenry, which is necessary for wise self-rule. Democracy demands an informed citizenry. As Thomas Jefferson wrote, "Our liberty depends on freedom of the press, and that cannot be limited without being lost."
- Freedom of the press provides a safety valve for the public to let off steam without having to revolt.
- Free expression is a necessary right in order for human beings to realize their potential. To achieve happiness, self-development and individuality, people must be free to gain information on which to base their beliefs and actions, and free to pass on their ideas to others.

Although prior restraint is theoretically prohibited by the First Amendment, on rare occasions courts have allowed it. During the Vietnam War, one lower court temporarily restrained the press from printing the classified "Pentagon Papers" when the government sought an injunction on national security grounds. In addition, the Supreme Court declined to review a judge's prior restraint on Cable News Network's decision to broadcast tapes of former Panamanian dictator Manuel Noriega's conversations with his attorney.

Government licensing of journalists or of presses is considered a form of prior restraint or censorship. For this reason, the print media in the United States are not licensed. But when broadcast media were invented, Congress and the courts decided that those media should not receive the same full freedom as the print media. Radio and television are licensed in the United States and face various regulations, including some regarding content. This situation deserves more debate, especially as the public gravitates toward greater use of electronic and digital media.

As new media are invented, and as print media increasingly go digital, we are likely to lose more of our First Amendment freedoms. That's because people are spending more time with electronic media that are regulated by the government and less with purely print media that the First Amendment more fully protects. For example, both the Congress and former President Bill Clinton signed on to regulate the Internet, although the court later struck down some of their provisions as unconstitutional.

Freedom of the Press Means Freedom to Exercise Editorial Judgment. Because censorship involves the government telling you what you must or must not publish, freedom of the press, then, means those who own the media have the freedom to choose what to publish. The opposite of censorship is the freedom to exercise editorial judgment—to accept or reject any story, advertisement, picture or letter. The media do not have to publish everything handed to them, the way a public utility must provide electricity to everyone in its area who requests it.

For example, the newsletter of the local chapter of the National Association for the Advancement of Colored People does not have to publish an article submitted by the Ku Klux Klan, demanding that it be published for the sake of a diverse viewpoint. Freedom of the press means an editor can reject the KKK's article. If the government required that it be published, that would be censorship.

But broadcast media aren't allowed as full a degree of editorial discretion as print media and have had to face such content regulations as the now-repealed Fairness Doctrine, as well as being required to satisfy the Federal Communications Commission at licensing time that they have operated "in the public interest." Because the airwaves are considered publicly owned, broadcast stations are, to some extent, viewed as limited public utilities.

Freedom of the Press is a Right, Not an Entitlement. *Rights,* in the Bill of Rights, means protections from intervention in your life by the federal government. A right is not an *entitlement*—something the government gives you—as people often use the term today in phrases like *welfare rights* or *right to health care*. The *right* of freedom of the press is not something the government *gives* journalists but instead a *protection against* the government censoring the press.

Freedom of the press also does not entitle you to force someone else to print your ideas or to provide you with a radio microphone or TV time. It's perfectly fine for owners of the media to decide not to publish or broadcast something— that's editorial judgment, not censorship. *Freedom of the press* is the right to exercise editorial judgment.

When a rap artist is turned down by a record company for the violent, sexual content of his music, or a letter to the editor of a magazine is rejected because only the best ones received are printed, that's not censorship but the exercise of freedom of the press—the right to freely make editorial decisions without government mandates.

Freedom of the Press Does Not Mean Responsibilities of the Press. You often hear people say, "With freedom come responsibilities." They go on then to say something like: "I believe in freedom of the press, but if the press doesn't start acting more socially responsibly, the government might have to act."

But freedom of the press is not conditional on the media acting socially responsibly. The First Amendment doesn't say anything about responsibilities. This is the Bill of *Rights*—not the Bill of *Responsibilities.* Besides, who's to define what is "socially responsible"? Does that phrase mean the same to Democrats as to Republicans? Wouldn't government-determined social responsibility lead to censorship of unpopular ideas or those the current party in power doesn't want aired?

Freedom of the Press is Not the Same as the Right to Know. The First Amendment does not guarantee a **right to know**, which actually would be an entitlement, not a right. The phrase *right to know* is used when people think the government should have to give them information. The First Amendment doesn't say the government has to give the press any information—just that the government can't stop the press from printing any information.

The idea of a right to know was first proposed in the 1930s and 1940s. Its main legal apparatus is in state open-meetings and open-records laws passed since the 1950s, as well as in the federal Freedom of Information Act first passed in 1966. But *right to know* is neither a phrase in the First Amendment nor elsewhere in the Bill of Rights, nor a phrase in the Constitution. (By the way, the *right to privacy* is also not in the Bill of Rights or the Constitution. It was first proposed in a law review article in the 1890s.)

Freedom of the Press Doesn't Give Journalists Special Rights. The First Amendment doesn't give journalists any protection from prosecution if they break the law to get a story. If you trespass, misrepresent yourself as a police officer, or pay a bribe, you could go to jail. Nor are journalists protected from a lawsuit just because they quote someone else saying something slanderous. To the law, if you published it, you libeled the person, even though the words weren't your own.

The First Amendment does not grant journalists immunity from testifying at a trial. If you quote an anonymous source who accuses the mayor of being involved in criminal activity, you can be compelled in court to identify who told you that, even if you swore to your source you'd never reveal his or her name. If you refuse to answer, you can go to jail for contempt of court. If you do answer, your source can sue you for breach of contract.

Some states have tried to protect journalists by passing laws extending the same sort of professional-client relationship to them and their sources that lawyers, doctors and priests enjoy. These are called **shield laws**. But when someone's Sixth Amendment right to a fair trial conflicts with such a state statute, the Constitution wins out, and you still have to testify anyway.

Are There Really No Restrictions on American Media? In theory, yes. In reality, no. Despite the absoluteness of the First Amendment's language, the media are restricted in various ways:

- Broadcast media have never been extended all the First Amendment rights of the print media. Electronic media are regulated by Congress, the FCC (broadcast) and, in some instances, by state and local governments (cable and telephones). The airwaves are considered public property, and a broadcaster has to get permission from the government to keep its station on the air. License renewal is at the whim of the FCC. In addition, various rules restrict indecent language, which topics can be discussed on the airwaves, and even mandate that sometimes political ads must be broadcast of which station owners may not approve.

- Commercial speech is not protected by the First Amendment. The government regulates the content of advertisements. The Federal Trade Commission or the Food and Drug Administration can order a company to take corrective measures or pay stiff fines when false or misleading claims are made about products.

Even the print media are not totally free of restrictions. Publication cannot normally be stopped in advance—although that has happened, as in the Pentagon Papers case. And if you work at a high school newspaper, the Supreme Court has ruled that the school can sometimes censor your paper. In addition:

- Publishers can be arrested and go to prison for printing obscenity, although the First Amendment makes no such exception when it says "no law" can be passed abridging freedom of the press.

- A publisher can face criminal charges over copyright infringement—for publishing someone's copyrighted material without getting permission.

- A newspaper or magazine can lose its mailing permit for printing information about a raffle that's technically illegal under state law.

- A publisher or a reporter can face civil suits for libeling someone, invading someone's privacy or treating someone negligently.

Despite restrictions like these, Americans still have the freest press anywhere in the world.

Understanding Our Legal System

Criminal versus Civil Cases

There are two broad categories of law cases: criminal and civil.

Criminal Cases

- *Charges* are filed by prosecutors (not police) against a *defendant*. Arrest *warrants* are obtained from judges. In the federal system, defendants must be *indicted* by a *grand jury* of 21 citizens for the case to go forward.
- Violations of criminal law are called *crimes*. Minor crimes are called *misdemeanors*, and major ones are called *felonies*.
- Penalties range from *probation* (release with supervision) through community service, fines, *incarceration* (imprisonment) on up to death.
- The standard of proof: "beyond a reasonable doubt."
- The judge may take the case away from the jury to order a dismissal but not to overturn a verdict.
- Only the defendant may appeal the decision, not the prosecution.

Civil Cases

- *Complaints* are filed by a *plaintiff* (usually, a private individual, although the government can file a civil action, such as in the antitrust case that was filed against Microsoft) against a defendant. Violations of civil law are called *torts*.
- Penalties usually are payment of *damages*.
- Lawsuits can be filed for virtually anything, but a defendant may countersue, alleging the original complaint to be merely a *nuisance suit*.
- The standard of proof: "preponderance of the evidence."
- Civil cases are usually heard by juries, with the judge making the final decision on damages. A judge may, but rarely does, overrule the verdict of the jury and issue his or her own instead. Or both sides may agree to have the judge decide rather than have a jury trial. If there is no disagreement on facts, only on law, a jury need

not be brought in. Either side may appeal the decision.
- In the United States today, media law is almost exclusively civil law. This was not true historically and is not true in much of the world today.

Sources of Law

Laws are rules of human conduct that carry government-enforced penalties for their violation. Contrast this with *ethics*, which are also rules of human conduct, but which carry no government-enforced penalties, only social or self-imposed ones.

The Common Law

- It developed in England during the 200 years following the Norman Conquest in 1066.
- It was called "common law" because for the first time, the same non-church law applied throughout England.
- Common law was based on community customs existing before that time. Instead of deductively figuring out the law for this particular situation from a general statute, the law is figured out inductively from looking at *precedents* (previous, similar cases). These precedents, however, can be reinterpreted or overruled later.
- The law of libel and invasion of privacy is most often determined by common law and the next area on this list, the law of equity.

Equity Law

- Equity law developed in Britain in the 14th and 15th centuries.
- Like the common law, equity law is judge-made law, and the distinction between the two kinds of law has become blurred. Originally, the difference was that where justice was required but the common law provided no precedents for remedy, judges would have to decide on the basis of what solution seemed fairest to them.

- Equity law decisions are called *judicial decrees*, not judgments, and are made by a judge, not a jury.
- *Injunctions* and *restraining orders*—both issued before someone does something—are matters for equity law because common law decides matters only after something has happened.

Statutory Law

- Statutory law refers to laws passed by legislatures, whether state or federal, as well as city councils—in other words, by bodies of elected officials.
- Statutory laws usually are aimed at larger social issues, whereas common law and equity law are aimed at disputes between individuals.
- All criminal law in the United States is statutory law. Since 1812, common law and equity law have applied only to civil cases.
- Statutory law can anticipate future problems, whereas common law cannot.
- The courts often get involved in "statutory construction"—interpreting the meaning of statutes that have been passed as cases arise involving the matters.

Constitutional Law

- The U.S. Constitution and its (currently 27) amendments together form the highest law of the land. No federal, state or municipal laws may contradict constitutional law. Likewise, the highest state law is the state's constitution and its amendments. Constitutions outline the organization and powers of the various branches of government, as well as detail the restrictions on their powers—the *rights* individuals have against abusive state action.
- All 51 constitutions—the federal and the state ones—guarantee freedom of speech and of the press. The highest media law in the nation is the First Amendment to the U.S. Constitution, which is found in the Bill of Rights.
- A law may be declared unconstitutional because it directly contradicts the Constitution, is overly broad (prohibiting not only the undesired activities but legally protected ones, as well) or is simply too vague (as when a court struck down an Indianapolis ordinance ban-

ning pornography, which the ordinance defined as anything depicting "the subordination of women").

Executive Orders and Other Administrative Rules

- These are orders or rules created by the administrative branch to carry out their executive duties. If such orders or rules exceed the authority of those issuing them, they may be overturned by the appropriate legislature or court.
- Administrative agencies in the federal government have existed only since the 19th century, the first being the Interstate Commerce Commission. These came about as the job of governing became too big.
- The main agency affecting the media is the Federal Communications Commission, created in 1934, with jurisdiction over broadcasting and telecommunications. It has no authority over the print media.

Federal versus State Court Systems

- There are 52 court systems in the United States —one for each state, the District of Columbia and the federal court system.
- Courts are traditionally seen as being either *trial courts* (fact-finding courts where cases are originally heard) or *appellate courts* (law-reviewing courts where appeals are made to previous decisions). Juries exist only in trial courts, not appeals courts. Testimony is taken only in trial courts, not appeals courts. Appeals courts may *remand* a case (send it back to the trial court with instructions to take into account certain things). If new evidence arises after a case was heard by a trial court, an appeals court may order a new trial.

The Federal Court System

- Federal courts hear cases that arise concerning the U.S. Constitution, federal laws and federal treaties; disputes between states, citizens of different states or a citizen of one state and another state itself; ambassadors of other nations; and admiralty or maritime law.
- Media law cases are often heard first on the federal level. For example, if a newspaper, magazine or broadcast network ran a story

possibly invading the privacy of a Michigan resident, the case would be heard in a federal court in Michigan, applying Michigan law.

- Federal judges are political appointments made by the president, so usually from the same party as the one who appointed them. They must then be confirmed by the Senate.
- The appointment of any federal judge is for life. The only way to remove a federal judge involuntarily is by impeachment.

The U.S. Supreme Court

- This is the only federal court prescribed in the U.S. Constitution. Congress could abolish all other federal courts or establish a different federal court system. Likewise, the number of judges on the U.S. Supreme Court is not set by the U.S. Constitution but is at the discretion of Congress. The court has had nine justices since 1869, but originally Congress set the number as six in 1789, and it was as high as 10 from 1863 to 1869. The chief justice is called the *chief justice of the United States*, not chief justice of the Supreme Court.
- Its decisions involving interpretation of the Constitution and federal laws are binding on all federal and state courts. Its power of *judicial review* (to interpret the Constitution) is in fact unconstitutional in that it is not set out in the Constitution itself but was appropriated by the court in the case of Marbury v. Madison in 1803. A rival theory was that the power to declare a law unconstitutional remained with the states under the 10th Amendment.
- It acts occasionally as a trial court (as in the 2003 dispute between Virginia and Maryland over use of water from the Potomac River) but usually as an appeals court.
- Ninety percent of all cases directly appealed to the U.S. Supreme Court are refused, so the usual route is to obtain a *writ of certiorari* (requesting the record of a case for review) after all other means of appeal have failed. Even

then, the Court picks and chooses which cases to hear—for example, only 80 to 90 of the more than 5,000 petitions are reviewed each year. Even if the court hears the case, it is often as much as five years or more after the original trial.

- Court decisions are made by a simple majority, such as 5-4. (If a vote ends in a tie because a justice is absent or excused, the ruling of the highest lower court is affirmed.) Usually, one justice from the majority side of the ruling is asked to write the *court's opinion*. Justices who agree with the decision but not the reasoning or who wish to stress different reasoning for the opinion may choose to write a *concurring opinion*. Those who disagree may write a *dissenting opinion*.

U.S. Court of Appeals

- The old name (until 1948) was the U.S. Circuit Courts of Appeal. The word *Circuit* has been dropped from the official name, even though it persists in the name of the individual courts.
- There are 13 circuits, but only the first 11 are numbered, the other two being for the District of Columbia and the Federal Circuit.
- As the name implies, this is an appeals court only. Typically, a three-judge panel hears a case, although in unusual cases it may be heard by 11. There is no jury. Someone who loses an appeal before a three-judge panel may ask for the case to be heard by all the judges, but such requests are usually denied.
- A Court of Appeals decision on federal matters is binding on all federal and state courts in its region only, although others may look to it as a precedent.

U.S. District Courts

- There are 94 U.S. district courts with 650 judges.
- Justices are called *federal judges* or *U.S. district judges*.

- The first reference is: "U.S. District Court in Detroit." Later references may say "Federal Court in Detroit" but should not say "Detroit Federal Court."
- Most federal cases begin and end in district court.
- About half of all district court cases are heard by a jury.

State Court Systems
- Each state has its own court system.
- Judges are often elected rather than appointed, so they are more politically active and can be removed by voters at elections. About half the states have a system of appointing a judge initially, then making the judge stand for election to retain the appointment.

 LEGAL PROBLEMS

The main legal problems editors must spot and fix involve libel and invasion of privacy. Not quite as common are issues of negligence, obscenity and copyright infringement.

Libel

Part of an editor's job involves looking out for possible libel problems in stories, headlines, photos, graphics, captions and blurbs. If you can edit around the problem, do so, but also alert your supervisor of the problem and what you're doing. If you have doubts or questions, say so, and pass the problem on to your supervisor or the staff attorney.

The editor who lives in constant fear of a damage suit, the copy editor who sniffs libel in every story and tries to make the safe safer, and the broadcast commentator who thinks it's humorous to refer to a politician with whom he disagrees as a "congenital liar" have no place in journalism. The first procrastinates and vacillates, the second makes the story vapid, and the third could land himself or herself and the media outlet in court.

Journalists don't need to be lawyers, but they should know enough about media law to know how to handle common situations and when it's necessary to call an attorney.

Libel is one of the two kinds of **defamation,** meaning a statement that damages someone's reputation or livelihood by bringing that person into hatred, ridicule or contempt in the eyes of a substantial and respectable group. **Slander** is when you say something that defames someone's character. **Libel** is when you publish or, in many states, broadcast something that defames someone's character. (California is one state that defines broadcast defamation as slander.) Making disparaging remarks to someone's face, with no one overhearing it, is neither slander nor libel—the comments may hurt someone's feelings but not damage their reputation.

Examples of defamation include accusing someone of a crime or of immorality; claiming someone is incompetent, dishonest or unethical; saying someone has what the public might consider a loathsome ailment, such as mental illness, venereal disease or AIDS; accusing someone of association with a disreputable cause, such as fascism, communism, terrorism or the Ku Klux Klan; or accusing a woman of being unchaste.

Don't confuse *libel* with *liable*. The second means "likely" and, in legal language, "responsible." And don't think that libel means you must have told a lie about someone. A lie implies something knowingly false was printed. Something unknowingly false may be libelous, too.

In addition, a statement may be untrue but not damage someone's reputation, and that's not libel. For example, it hasn't typically been a problem when newspapers incorrectly report someone died. Or a statement may be true and damage someone's reputation, and that is libel in most states, California being an exception because part of the definition there is that for something to be libel, it must be false.

The misunderstanding that a statement always has to be false to be libelous comes about because essentially you're going to be legally in trouble for libeling someone only when you can't prove what you published or broadcast was true. In other words, something may be legally libelous without being subject to legal action unless it is also false.

That a story damages someone's business or reputation doesn't necessarily mean you shouldn't publish it if it's true and newsworthy. For example, truthfully printing that someone was convicted of a crime may damage his reputation, but no one would argue that it shouldn't be published or that you would be in any danger legally if it were.

SOME COMMON LIBELOUS SITUATIONS

Here are some common situations in which you should be on the lookout for libel:

Make sure accident, crime and court stories contain nothing that convicts a person before trial. All suspects are assumed innocent until they confess or are proven guilty by a jury. If a suspect you convicted in the media is later found not guilty, you could face a libel suit.

Make sure that any damaging statements in opinion pieces concern matters of opinion rather than matters of fact. Opinions are not true or false, but facts are.

Insist that news stories stick to observable, provable facts. Many libel problems could be avoided if editorializing value judgments were edited out of news stories.

Granted that context and proof are important, but when you see words in a story like any of the following, get nervous:

addict	ex-convict	rapist
adulterer	fascist	robber
alcoholic	hypocrit	scoundrel
alleged	incompetent	sexist
bankrupt	influence peddler	sex offender
blackmail	kept woman	sloppy
cheater	Mafia ties	slut
child abuser	mentally ill	stuffed the ballot box
Communist	moron	swindler
corrupt	murderer	thief
crazy	Nazi	traitor
crook	pederast	unchaste
deadbeat	pedophile	unethical
dishonest	peeping Tom	unmarried mother
drunk	racist	unprofessional

Addresses of people who are the subject of damaging stories can be dangerous. Usually, the danger comes from *not* giving the address in the case of a suspect. If someone else in town has the same name, then—unless the age or correct address, or both, are given—the innocent person may sue because people who know the innocent individual thought the story was about him or her.

As for the victim, some papers use the block (for example, "the 2400 block of Main Street") rather than the exact address where the crime was committed. This can help protect the victim's privacy while still informing the public of the general area of the crime.

It's dangerous to make assumptions. For example, if someone has been laid off, that doesn't necessarily mean the person was fired. *Fired* suggests that someone messed up and was kicked out. *Laid off* implies the economy is bad, with no personal blame at all.

Headlines, captions and blurbs can pose special problems. People are more likely to read headlines, captions and blurbs than details in the story, yet the fact that an editor is writing them rather than the reporter means there's more opportunity to get things wrong.

Don't assume that if the details in the story are right, a damaging headline or caption or blurb isn't libelous. As editors, from a legal liability standpoint, it's important to consider the big type as standing alone. But when it comes to the story itself, the courts usually say that statements taken out of context are not libelous—the story must be considered as a whole.

LIBEL LAWSUITS CAN BE COSTLY

Although journalists are no longer imprisoned for libel, as they were in colonial days under British law, carelessness with the facts can cost journalists and their employers staggering amounts of money.

- In 1995, ABC was forced to apologize to the Phillip Morris Co. after alleging the company had intentionally added nicotine to its cigarettes. The suit was settled out of court, but ABC paid an estimated $15 million to $20 million in legal fees.

- In 1997, a Texas jury awarded $222.7 million to a defunct brokerage company following a story in *The Wall Street Journal.* The judge threw out $200 million in punitive damages, but the $22.7 million in actual damages was allowed to stand.

- From 2000 to 2007, about 14 libel cases a year went to trial in the United States, with media companies winning about 54 percent of the time, according to the Media Law Resource Center. Although the winning percentage for media companies is about 18 percentage points higher than 20 years earlier, printing or broadcasting libel can prove costly in dollars and credibility. The average damage award, which does not count legal fees and court costs, is about $3.4 million in libel and invasion of privacy cases.

COMMON QUESTIONS ABOUT LIBEL

How can it be libel when you're just quoting someone else and not saying it yourself?   There's a common assumption that if something originated from an outside source, it's safe. That's wrong because the media are responsible for everything they publish or broadcast from whatever source—their reporters, wire services, syndicates and advertisers.

Don't think quoting a libelous statement by someone else protects journalists because "We're not the ones saying it—we're just reporting it." The newspaper is libeling the person by publishing the remark. This can be a problem not only in news stories but also in letters to the editor in newspapers and magazines, viewer-feedback letters to broadcast stations, information given in press conferences (see Figure 5–1) and audience-feedback forums on Web pages.

When news stories are written about criminal suspects, with accusations in direct quotes, get comments from the person being accused, giving him or her a chance to respond. Like printing a correction, this shows you're at least trying to be fair, although the person could still sue you. In fact, unless the person says "No

Figure 5–1 Television goes live to carry Police Chief Charles Alexander Moose of Montgomery County, Md., addressing a press conference concerning the Beltway Snipe case in 2002.

Photo by Tom Carter/PhotoEdit.

comment" or refuses to speak, any comment can potentially be seen in court as tacit consent for running the story.

Can't I just protect myself with *alleged, allegedly, accused* or *suspected*? Not necessarily. Unfortunately, the *Associated Press Stylebook and Briefing on Media Law* is confusing on the matter.

The *AP Stylebook* acknowledges that *alleged* "must be used with great care" and that it should not be used "as a routine qualifier." It also says you should avoid the appearance of making the allegation. So far, so good, but AP then suggests specifying the source when you use *alleged*, or substituting the words *apparent, ostensible* or *reputed*. Why these three words would be better is not explained.

If you follow AP's suggestion that you also see its rule for the related word *accused*, you are told not to write "accused slayer" because it implies someone is guilty without a trial. Why that differs from "alleged slayer" is not explained, nor why AP's suggested rewording, "accused of the slaying," is any better.

What's the verdict on modifiers like *accused, alleged, allegedly, reputed* and *suspected*? Despite the fact that they are used often, a word like *alleged* before a word like *rapist* in a story may offer little or no legal protection, according to various books and attorneys consulted. But there's not total agreement.

One argument against such words is that they—as well as phrases like *it's alleged that, investigators suspect, police charge* (police don't file charges, prosecutors do), *it's rumored that, sources claim* and *reports say that*—are prejudicial in that they suggest guilt to the reader without offering proof. In other words, they sound as though you're convicting someone.

Another argument against these modifiers is that they are no different from paraphrasing or quoting someone who is saying something slanderous—for example, that someone *allegedly is a thief.* But, as we've seen, by publishing or broadcasting a slander, you become responsible for libel unless you're repeating official charges issued in a warrant or in a courtroom, where you'd have *qualified privilege,* or protection in reporting the allegations in a way that was substantially complete and accurate. Such words, the argument goes, would not legally excuse printing a false, damaging statement if the statement were not privileged or the truth could have been found through reasonable reporting.

One attorney asked rhetorically who was doing the alleging in a phrase like "the alleged murderer." Then he answered: "You are." He added, though, that potentially the word *alleged* could help you with a jury because average people might interpret it to mean what those who misuse it think it means. Another attorney added that she knew of no cases in which a journalist was sued and then lost over the word *alleged* in front of a word like *murderer.* Perhaps victims of the practice—that is, the "alleged" suspects—also are unaware that *alleged* may not be absolute protection.

For the reasons cited, though, it's probably best to avoid *alleged, allegedly* and all similar modifiers. Constructions using *alleged* or *allegedly,* or *rumored* or *reports say,* should be rewritten to be more neutral and objective. Instead, ask: Has a charge been filed? What report says this?

The **"a man" technique** often comes in handy: Change "John Smith allegedly raped the woman at gunpoint . . ." to "A man raped the woman at gunpoint. John Smith was later arrested and charged" (provided he was).

By the way, another mistaken use of *alleged* that's less dangerous but more silly is the misplacement of the word in front of something that is a nonlibelous fact: "Tuesday night, a convenience-store clerk was allegedly hit on the head with a hammer by an unknown assailant."

How can it be libel if I didn't name the person who's claiming damages?   There is a common misunderstanding that if the person libeled isn't named, he or she can't sue. That's not true. If the person is described enough to be identifiable by someone in the know, then that can be the basis of a successful libel suit.

Also, if the harmful statement concerns a group, an individual member of that group can sue. If the group is small enough, such as a jury, a team or a council, each may have a case.

How can it be libel if the person's reputation is already so low it couldn't be damaged more?   A man may be a notorious drunk, but that doesn't make him a thief.

How can it be libel when the story isn't about a person?   Libel may involve a corporation, partnership or trust, or other business, as well as a nonprofit institution—not just individuals.

WHAT PROTECTS YOU FROM LIBEL LAWSUITS?

If your publication's or station's lawyer has read and approved the wording of the story, then, of course, you should feel reassured. But the attorney is usually called only in the trickiest situations when the editors can't solve the problem on their own or are unsure. As an editor, you are the first and main line of defense, so you need to have a good understanding of what to look for and how to fix it.

If you're a rim editor, point out the problem to your supervisor and how you intend to fix it. If your supervisor is uncertain whether there's still a problem, the decision could get kicked up the line of authority and the attorney called if necessary. On some sensitive stories, a good attorney will dictate a legally precise wording that editors should not change. The headline, too, should be carefully phrased.

The best media attorneys understand that your purpose is to get out the news, and they will try to help you do just that in a way that protects you legally. The worst attorneys are the ones who always argue that the safest approach is not to publish or broadcast anything about which you have a legal question. As Benjamin Franklin said, "If all printers were determined not to print anything till they were sure it would offend nobody, there would be very little printed."

Most of the time, the potential problems in a story are obvious enough that experienced editors handle them without calling an attorney. They'll reword the offending passages to convey the information without convicting a suspect or unnecessarily damaging someone's reputation or business.

Experienced editors also are familiar with the legal defenses that justify libel if the story is important enough for the media outlet to run, despite the risk of even an unsuccessful lawsuit.

Libel is legally justified when the story is true and can be proven.   Truth is the best defense against a libel suit, but you have to be able to back it up. It would be a mistake, for example, to rely on the testimony of a doctor to back up a libelous claim if that would violate the doctor-patient privilege of confidentiality.

Legally, the burden of proof is on the plaintiff—the person filing the libel lawsuit—to prove that the statements published by the media are false. But as an editor, make sure reporters can back up any damaging statements in their stories before publishing or broadcasting them.

Courts will settle for *substantial truth* rather than *absolute truth,* meaning that the media must have the story right in at least the most important parts. That's not a license to libel—it's just an acknowledgment that honest mistakes can be made that shouldn't be punished if they don't go to the heart of the complaint.

Libel is legally justified when the story is a fair, substantially accurate and complete account of a judicial, legislative or executive proceeding of local, state or federal government. A quotation you might falsely think is protected is a police officer saying a person is "guilty" or that this arrest "solves a long string of crimes." A suspect is not guilty until convicted, and such remarks are potentially troublesome if printed.

But if the officer makes the remark in court, it is considered *privileged*—that is, not subject to accusations of libel. Also, depending on the jurisdiction, if the officer makes the remark in the line of duty, such as during an official press conference or in a press release, the remark could likewise be privileged. Some states grant a privilege to publish fair and accurate stories based on police reports. But until you know the rulings in your jurisdiction, be hesitant to let such a statement be published or broadcast.

Quoting statements of attorneys, unless made in a courtroom; press releases from government bureaus; and statements by civic organizations are not considered privileged, or exempt from libel-suit claims. Nor are, in many states, quotes from complaints, petitions or affidavits that have been filed.

Libel is legally justified when the story is "fair comment or criticism" (as the courts say)—such as a book, movie, theater, concert or restaurant review—and none of the damaging statements is a matter of fact as opposed to a matter of opinion. Journalists are not protected, even in a review, for misstatements of facts. For example, a restaurant reviewer can safely say the fish tasted bad but could face a problem if he or she insinuates the menu misrepresents frozen fish as fresh, especially if the owner has the receipts to prove the fish was in fact fresh.

Nor could a journalist safely write in a column or editorial, "In my opinion, the mayor is a crook." This statement would not be legally protected. You'd have to have facts to back it up because it's not really a matter of opinion.

Libel is legally justified when the damaging statement is clearly a joke, not to be taken as the truth. A *Saturday Night Live* skit in the early 1990s about Mario Cuomo implying he had organized crime ties is a good example. It was clearly a joke, and Cuomo never sued. "It's only a joke" has traditionally been a libel defense, but after Jerry Falwell's suit against *Hustler* magazine for emotional distress caused by a spoof of him, it appears that even jokes can pose legal problems. Falwell was awarded $200,000 in two courts before the U.S. Supreme Court reversed the ruling in 1986.

Libel is legally justified when the subject of the damaging statement is dead. The maxim is, "You can't libel the dead," meaning someone has to be alive to be libeled.

Traditionally, only the person libeled has cause for action—relatives have no recourse. The offended person must bring suit within the statutory period, ranging from one to six years, depending on the jurisdiction. If the plaintiff dies before—or even during—the trial, the survivors cannot continue the case.

But this is changing. Although the maxim about libel not applying to the dead is still true in most states, many—including California, Texas and New York—are now allowing ongoing suits to continue after the death of the plaintiff. We are also starting to see some lawsuits from trusts or foundations set up by the deceased that nibble away at this protection by claiming that false, damaging statements about their provider are damaging their ongoing legal entity.

Libel is legally justified when the statement, although libelous, is made without actual malice about a public official or public figure, or (in most states) without negligence if the person is a private individual. In a landmark 1964 decision, the U.S. Supreme Court ruled that the constitutional provisions of the First and Fourteenth Amendments could be used as a defense against libel if the defamatory words were used to describe the public acts of public officials and were used without "actual malice." Elected officials, political candidates, judges and police are generally held to be public officials or public figures.

The term *actual malice* is a bit misleading. Plaintiffs do not need to prove that the press had it in for them. The court has interpreted *actual malice* to mean a statement published in "reckless disregard" of the truth. So, if a story comes to you near deadline and you have doubts, you shouldn't "run with it," because that would be reckless disregard of the truth—the actual malice standard for a story about a public official or public figure.

In addition, not taking the usual professional caution, the standard in many states for a story about a private person, could open you up to a charge of negligence. And because the Supreme Court has said plaintiffs can probe journalists' "state of mind" when publishing a story to prove actual malice, you should never make a statement aloud about a story, such as "Sharon really nailed this S.O.B."

To be clear, the actual malice standard for public officials and public figures applies in all the states, but the standard for private individuals is different in various states. At least 20 states and the District of Columbia have decided that to collect damages, a private individual needs only to prove that the libelous statement was false and made negligently. A few have adopted the strict actual malice test for private citizens, but some states require that a private citizen show only that the press was at "fault," a lesser standard even than negligence.

Alaska, Colorado, Indiana and New Jersey require only that a journalist writing about a private citizen meet the same actual malice standard as when writing about public officials and public figures. New York requires that a private citizen prove "grossly irresponsible conduct" by the press to win a libel lawsuit. Generally speaking, though, as an editor, be more worried if the statement is about a private individual than a public official or public figure.

But the question is, how do you know whether someone is a public official or public figure as opposed to a private individual? As things stand today, courts make that determination case by case.

Some people are obviously public officials in that they have prominent governmental decision-making jobs, such as presidents, senators, governors, mayors and City Council members. Career government employees in the civil service, clerks and sanitation workers would probably not be public officials although they work for government. But it's unclear whether some government employees, such as teachers and police officers, are public officials.

As for what makes someone a public figure, the courts have said some people are pervasive public figures in all matters because they are so well-known or influential. A famous actor or musician would fit this category. Others may be public figures only in relation to certain controversial matters in which they have thrust themselves forward—voluntarily or not. Cindy Sheehan, the antiwar protester and mother of a soldier killed in Iraq, might be an example of that.

Libel is sometimes legally justified when the story is fair and includes neutral reporting of both sides of a controversy. This is one of the newest defenses for libel and has not been universally accepted in all jurisdictions—as of 2007, only about 10 states had accepted it. It is accepted in California, for example, but not generally in Texas or New York. Where it does apply, a newspaper might be on more solid ground if it accords someone the right to reply and rebut an attack, and if the response remains pertinent to the charges without upping the ante on the attacker.

Should We Print a Correction?

Although publishing a correction admits the mistake, thus removing the strongest libel defense of truth, it's the ethically proper thing to do if, in fact, the paper was wrong. In many cases, a correction also will avert a lawsuit. In most states, statutes provide for retraction of libel, and the other states typically count corrections as evidence for lessening the damages.

In states with retraction laws, the plaintiff can collect only actual damages—not punitive damages—if the retraction is made on request and within a certain time limit. Sometimes, a newspaper, magazine or broadcast station will offer to run a correction in return for a release from further liability. This saves the time and cost of a trial and may eliminate the possibility of a major judgment against the media outlet.

Here's some advice on handling corrections:

- If you're a copy editor and someone demands a retraction, apology or correction, pass the demand along to your supervisor. It's not your call. The angrier the person and the more potentially troublesome the problem, the more likely the paper's attorney will get involved.

- Before you pass the matter on, don't admit any error or wrongdoing to the person complaining, and don't speak to the complainant's lawyer.

- After investigating a complaint and finding it valid, a media outlet should quickly publish or broadcast a correction, and be sure to avoid republishing or rebroadcasting any libel in the explanation.

Negligence

Negligence means a failure to show enough caution or care in a situation that results in damage or injury to another. As always, the media have no special exemption from laws that everyone has to obey. When the media publish or broadcast something that damages someone, they face possible lawsuits.

Libel itself could be seen as a kind of negligence in that plaintiffs win a libel lawsuit only after being able to show that:

- The published or broadcast material damaged their reputation or business.

- The media did not take the same care that any reasonable journalist would normally under similar circumstances. This applies to private citizens in most states and the District of Columbia suing only for actual damages, not punitive ones.

But in nonlibelous situations, the media can be sued for negligence. In one case, a newspaper printed the name and address of a woman who had successfully fled from an attempted rape. Although the woman's name and address were public record at the police station where she had filed a report, after the paper printed them, the assailant knew her name and where she lived, and he began stalking her. She sued for negligence, and the paper settled out of court. A related example of a situation posing the possibility of a negligence lawsuit would be printing the name or address of a witness to a murder when the suspect is on the loose.

Legal Terms

If you read a story involving legal matters and you don't understand it, this in itself could pose a legal problem for you. The misuse of legal jargon can carry a high risk. Likewise, the following terms could get you in trouble if you think you know what they mean but don't really.

arrested for Contrary to *The AP Stylebook,* don't automatically change *arrested for* to *arrested on a charge of.* Dale Spencer, a copy editor and attorney who taught media law at the University of Missouri for years, used to say that AP was wrong that the phrase *arrested for* connotes guilt.

According to Spencer, *arrested for* is the usual legal wording. In fact, he said, changing the phrase to *arrested on a charge of* could libel a person. That's because *arrested on a charge of* means police picked up the suspect on a warrant, but many people are arrested without a warrant and may never be charged—just questioned and released.

To satisfy both AP and the law, it's safer and more specific to find out whether the suspect was charged. If so, say that instead. If not, say the suspect was arrested in connection with the crime but that as of press time, no charges had been filed.

And while we're discussing charges, never predict in print that someone will be charged. That, too, can pose a libel problem if the person isn't, in fact, charged.

murder Don't call a *homicide* (any slaying or killing) a *murder* until someone has been convicted of that charge. A *murder* is a homicide involving malice and premeditation. A homicide without malice or premeditation is *manslaughter.* It is proper, however, to say someone is "charged with murder" if that is the official charge. That does not mean, though, that you can call the crime a murder. It becomes a murder if the person charged with murder is convicted.

robbery Robbery involves violence or a threat of violence against a person. If someone breaks into a house when no one is there and steals something, it isn't a *robbery* but a *theft*—more specifically, a *burglary.*

Invasion of Privacy

Surveys find that privacy is the right most cherished by Americans, so it's surprising that the right to privacy is named nowhere in the Constitution or Bill of Rights. In fact, as noted earlier, it was invented as recently as 1890 in a law review article and has since been institutionalized in American law by statute and various court rulings, but not by constitutional amendment.

Invasion of privacy can include more than most people realize. To most, it probably means the publishing of embarrassing, private facts or the act of trespassing. Both of these constitute invasion of privacy under U.S. law, but so would depicting someone in a "false light" or using his or her name, voice or image in a commercial context without permission. Notify your supervising editor if you spot any of the following four trouble signs:

A story or picture that reveals private facts about someone, especially embarrassing matters, could pose an invasion-of-privacy problem. This can be a difficult call. The legal questions are: Is the information really newsworthy? Would the information be offensive or objectionable to an average person? (The answer to the first question should be "yes," and the answer to the second question should be "no.")

Be especially concerned if the story or photo discloses information regarding the person's sex life, health or economic affairs. Even with public officials and public figures, it's safer to stick to reporting on their public life. Before revealing personal information, ask yourself, "Does the public really need to know this?"

For example, President Kennedy's sex life was probably no business of the public until his job was affected. His affairs with a woman tied to the Mafia and with an East German spy could have exposed him, and the country, to black-mail.

The main legal defense against an invasion-of-privacy suit is that the information is newsworthy. You might think, "Of course, it's newsworthy, or we wouldn't be publishing or broadcasting it," but the jury will decide, second-guessing your news judgment by playing Monday-morning, armchair editors.

A second defense could be that although the information is embarrassing, it was already public. For example, the information could have come from the public record, or a photograph could have been taken in a public place where many people witnessed the image captured on film.

These two defenses, it should be noted, do not always work. A newspaper in Alabama was ordered to pay damages to a woman pictured with her skirt blown above her waist by an air jet in a carnival funhouse. She was recognizable because her children were with her.

A reporter or photographer who enters someone's private property, without permission, to get a story or pictures could pose a trespassing or intrusion problem. In most states, an exception is typically made after a fire, disaster or crime, when police or fire officials let the press in, although it's sometimes been ruled that only the authorities themselves are privileged at such times against trespass charges, not the press.

Don't think journalists can automatically go anywhere and take pictures without permission. Schools, prisons and mental hospitals, for example, can require written permission. A shopping mall is private property, and mall authorities can ask the press to leave or require approval to take pictures. Even owners of a house or building that has burned down have a right to demand that you not take pictures on the property—and you must obey or be guilty of trespassing.

Pictures of things done in public or viewable from public property (such as a street) are not usually violations of anyone's privacy, although the picture of the woman in the Alabama carnival funhouse with her skirt blown above her waist by a stream of air was taken from public property, and the jury ruled against the newspaper. Also, note that some states have laws against using hidden cameras or privately recording someone's words without permission. (In some states, you must have permission of the other person to record a phone interview. In other states, it's enough that only one of you wants to tape the conversation.) This could potentially be a problem with undercover stories.

A celebrated case in 1997 highlighted the increasing willingness of courts to rule against the news media. ABC, for its *Prime Time Live* show, sent two reporters posing as employees into a Food Lion supermarket in North Carolina. There, they secretly videotaped unsanitary food-handling methods. A federal jury found ABC liable for "fraud, trespass and breach of the duty of loyalty." The jury awarded $5.5 million in punitive damages, but it was later reduced by a federal appeals court to a mere $2.

The best defense against an intrusion lawsuit is that you had permission to be there or to take pictures—usually from the owner but in some situations in certain states, from law enforcement, fire or disaster authorities.

A file photo of someone used to illustrate an unrelated story could bring a "false-light" invasion-of-privacy lawsuit. This is similar in many ways to libel, and this is the only kind of invasion-of-privacy lawsuit against which truth is a valid defense. Using a picture of a woman standing on a street corner to illustrate a story about prostitution is a good example. If the woman in the photograph is a prostitute, you're off the hook. If she's a college student waiting for a bus, you're in trouble.

An advertisement using someone's image, name or voice without permission— considered appropriation—is legal ground for a lawsuit. Woody Allen, Bette Midler, Jackie Kennedy Onassis and Tom Waits have won lawsuits for this. More jurisdictions are even allowing surviving relatives to bring privacy actions against the exploitation of names, images or voices of deceased relatives. The best defense is to make sure permission was first obtained.

Anonymous Sources

Beware if you see an anonymous source quoted in a story, especially if allegations are being made that could result in criminal or civil actions. Readers don't trust anonymous sources—they reduce a paper's credibility. In the District of Columbia and the 35 states with some form of **shield law**—a law protecting journalists from having to reveal the name of their source, similar to protections for attorneys and their clients, doctors and their patients or priests and their penitents—courts have sometimes forced journalists to reveal sources or go to jail. And at least one court case has also decided that if a journalist reneges on a promise of anonymity, the journalist may be liable in a breach-of-contract suit.

Instead of using anonymous sources, a reporter should try to get the source to go on the record. Failing that, the source should be asked to sign an agreement that the journalist will keep the source's name a secret—short of going to jail.

As an editor, check on your paper's or broadcast station's policy on the use of anonymous sources. If the use of an anonymous source violates your employer's policy, then point it out. If not, you might want to protect yourself by not trying to identify the source. If the reporter tells you, then you, too, risk being ordered to reveal the name in court or go to jail.

Obscenity

Chances are, you won't have to worry about **obscenity** while working for a newspaper. But if you're working for a medium with less conservative standards, such as many magazines, you should know that something is considered legally obscene if it:

- Appeals to the "prurient interest" (or would arouse) the average person, applying contemporary community standards to the work as a whole.
- Depicts or describes sexual conduct in a patently offensive way.
- Lacks, as a whole, serious literary, artistic, political or scientific value.

Raffles

That warm story about the neighbors holding a raffle to help raise money for a little girl's surgery could cost your publication. Why? If you run the story, you may lose your mailing permit because all lotteries not run by or licensed by the state are illegal and illegal to promote. The law defines a **lottery** as any contest involving the three elements of prize, consideration (paying to enter) and chance.

Intellectual Property

Intellectual property rights are provided for by the Constitution, and the media are not free to violate them.

Give credit where credit is due. If a wire service sends out a story based on the story of another newspaper, editors should not delete the wire service credit to the originator of the story. Nor should they delete any credit on stories or pictures. They may, if directed, compile stories from various sources into one comprehensive story, adding the sources from which the story was compiled.

When their own paper publishes a story to be copyrighted, editors should ensure that the notice is complete—the notice of copyright, the copyright date and the name of the person or business that holds the copyright.

Quote as little of the copyrighted work as possible. A rule of thumb is to avoid quoting 250-word-plus excerpts (book publishers say 500 words) of books or articles without permission. But this is merely a rule of thumb, not a set number of

Avoiding Trademark Infringement

Here's a list of some of the most commonly misused trademark names and their generic alternatives.

BRAND NAME	GENERIC	BRAND NAME	GENERIC
Aqua-Lung	underwater breathing apparatus	Levi's	jeans
AstroTurf	artificial grass	Little League Baseball	youth baseball
Band-Aid	adhesive bandage	Mace (short for tear-gas spray Chemical Mace)	tear-gas spray
Chap Stick	lip balm		
Coke	cola	Magic Marker	felt-tip marking pen
Crayola	crayons	Novocain	procaine hydrochloride
Crock-Pot	electric earthenware cooker	Oreo	cookie
Day-Glo	fluorescent colors	Palm Pilot	portable digital assistant or organizer
Deepfreeze	freezer		
Dumpster	trash bin	Photostat	photocopy
Fiberglas	fiberglass	Ping-Pong	table tennis
Flair pen	felt-tip or porous-point pen	Popsicle	flavored ice on a stick
Formica	plastic laminate	Post-it	self-stick note
Freon	refrigerant	Q-Tip	cotton swab
Frisbee	flying disk	Realtor	real-estate agent
Fudgsicle	fudge ice-cream bar	Rollerblade	in-line skate
Google	Internet search engine	Rolodex	address-card file
Hi-Liter	highlighting marker	Scotch tape	cellophane tape
iPod	digital music player	Seeing Eye dog	guide dog
Jacuzzi	whirlpool bath	Sheetrock	gypsum wallboard
Jeep	jeep (for military vehicle); otherwise, four-wheel-drive vehicle	Styrofoam	foam plastic
		Tabasco	hot-pepper sauce
		TelePrompTer	TV cuing device
Jell-O	gelatin	TiVo	digital video recorder
Jockey shorts	underwear	Vaseline	petroleum jelly
Kitty Litter	cat-box filler	Velcro	adhesive fastener
Kleenex	tissue	Windbreaker	lightweight jacket
Kool-Aid	soft-drink mix	Windex	glass cleaner
Krazy Glue	super adhesive	Xerox	photocopy
Laundromat	coin-operated laundry	Ziploc	zippered plastic bag

words established by law. Instead, the law specifies that the work cannot be sub-stantially appropriated without permission. That involves looking at what per-centage of the work has been reproduced and what effect that might have on reducing the market value of the original for the copyright holder.

Don't lift photos, art or graphics from other publications, including encyclo-pedias, without permission. Artists who do the graphics for newspapers will often scan a photographic image, such as an airplane from a volume of *Jane's,* convert it to a drawing, add details (for example, of an explosion site) and still credit *Jane's.* Publishers usually appreciate it rather than object when you run a picture of the cover of a book or record album with a review.

Merely linking to other pages from your Web page doesn't seem to pose a legal problem. Some of the Web's more popular sites, such as the Drudge Report (www.drudgereport.com) and WorldNetDaily (www.worldnetdaily.com), pro-vide headlines and descriptions of stories that you click on to be taken to the Web page of origin. A legal problem would arise, however, if the descriptions appro-priated too much of the original story or if the linked pages appeared within a frame, making it appear they were part of the original content of your Web site.

Don't violate trademarks by using them lowercase as generic terms. Companies invest much money into making their brand names known. But if people gener-ically use a brand name, the company can lose the right to its exclusive use, as happened with the former brand names *aspirin* and *nylon.*

So, if you let slip by a mention in a story of a brand-name product in lower-case as though it were a generic term—such as *xerox* for copy, *coke* for soft drink or *styrofoam* for foam plastic—your newspaper is likely to receive a letter from the company explaining you've misused its brand name and threatening a lawsuit if you do it again.

Censorship of School Newspapers

In the 1969 case of Tinker v. Des Moines School District, two students wore black armbands to school to protest the Vietnam War, and in turn, the principals of their schools expelled them. The Supreme Court, however, said students and teachers do not automatically shed their First Amendment rights when they enter the schoolhouse gates, as long as what they are doing doesn't "materially and sub-stantially" interfere with discipline in school.

But courts have long held that students have few Fourth and Fifth Amend-ments rights at school. For example, the lockers are considered school property that may be searched at will with only minimal cause. Students also have few due process rights in disciplinary actions.

So, it's perhaps no surprise that the courts have also said student newspapers do not receive full First Amendment protection from censorship by school authorities. In 1988, for example, in the case of Hazelwood School District v. Kuhlmeier, the Supreme Court said a school board can decide what's appropriate to be printed in a school newspaper, and upheld the decision of the school to delete two pages including an article on pregnancy and divorce.

Justice White wrote for the majority: "Exercising editorial control over the style and content of student speech in school-sponsored expressive activities" is the absolute right of school administrators, as long as their "actions are reasonably related to legitimate pedagogical concerns." Dorothy McPhilips, past president of the Journalism Educators Association, responded, 'What we are teaching the students . . . is that censorship is OK."

In various cases, the courts have said public school authorities may censor student publications that:

- Undermine school discipline.
- Violate rights of students.
- Fail to meet standards of academic propriety.
- Generate health and welfare concerns.
- Are obscene, indecent or vulgar.

An angle the courts have not really addressed is this: The school owns the paper, and in the world outside school, a reporter can't publish what he or she wants if the owner or publisher or editor don't agree. So, why can't the publisher—in this case, the principal—exercise editorial selection? Or, if the school is a public, government-owned one, does that constitute unlawful censorship by definition because a government agent is doing it?

The Hazelwood decision applied to high schools but left open the matter of censorship of college newspapers. Could the same school discipline argument hold with college students, who are, after all, more mature?

Typical reasons administrators use to censor college and university publications include cutting out materials that:

- Portray the institution in an unfavorable light, such as stories and statistics about crime on campus that detract from the blissful image in the recruitment materials. Some colleges have even tried to hide from the public statistics about crime on campus, refusing to release them to the public, although this has been illegal under federal law since 1992.
- Materials that might be confused with official school positions.
- Are not "politically correct" according to the college PC speech code (which by the way, seems to get thrown out by courts whenever challenged, as in the case of Doe v. Michigan in 1989).

- Ads for potentially harmful products like tobacco or alcohol, or about controversial issues, such as denying the Holocaust or opposing reparations to African-Americans for slavery. And administrators can claim that such ads might anger students—student activist groups, almost always on the political left, typically steal entire runs of student newspapers 30 to 40 times each year to try to suppress views with which they disagree.

But for a while, it seemed as though the courts made a distinction between high school and college publications:

- A District Court ruled in 1967 that a student newspaper editor at Troy State College in Alabama could not be punished for failing to print an article the school's administration wanted printed.

- Another District Court ruled in 1983 that the University of Minnesota could not cut funding for the student newspaper when it was not a matter of reducing fees but to punish the newspaper for printing content that some thought was offensive.

- A U.S. Court of Appeals ruled in 2001 that Kentucky State University could not censor the yearbook because it was created as a public forum and was not made by students for a grade.

Then, however, in 2003, in the case of Hosty v. Carter, a U.S. Court of Appeals acting *en banc* (all the judges) overturned the decision of a three-judge panel of the same body and decided that the Hazelwood decision applies to colleges, as well. The Student Press Law Center was joined by other media-rights groups in trying to get the U.S. Supreme Court to overrule the decision, but the court declined to hear it.

Regulation of Electronic Media

The Federal Communications Commission decides the locations where stations will be granted, assigns their frequencies and call letters, classifies them as to what kind of service they must render, regulates the kind of equipment they must use and issues licenses for the station operators (currently renewable every seven years). In addition, the FCC regulates decency of speech and political content.

Why are the rules so different for **electronic media** than for print media? Why is broadcast regulated, whereas print essentially is not? More recently, why has Congress tried to regulate the Internet? Shouldn't the same First Amendment arguments against licensing the press or resorting to other forms of censorship also apply to broadcast and other electronic media? Here are two of the most common reasons given for regulation of broadcast, the original electronic media, along with opposing viewpoints:

Broadcasting is different from print because of the scarcity of the airwaves and the need to allocate frequencies so that stations don't interfere with each other. But it can be argued that broadcast frequencies aren't scarce today and will become less so in the future. First, newspapers are far scarcer now than radio or TV stations. Most cities have one newspaper or fewer but receive many radio and TV stations, not to mention cable stations and Internet sources. And yet, broadcast is regulated, but print is not.

Second, new technologies are changing electronic media. Cable and satellite delivery of radio and TV are giving over-the-air broadcasting serious competition that could eventually drive much of conventional broadcasting out of business. And new compression technologies are making it possible to carry far more station signals in a smaller space, meaning new opportunities are opening up for more stations, even if new spectrum isn't discovered.

What about the idea that someone needs to license and assign frequencies so stations won't interfere with each other's signal? Congress assumed the only way to do this was for the government to own the airwaves and regulate content.

But why not use the same procedure as with land? The government said Western land belonged to whoever claimed it first. The government does not own all land and license it to you. Instead, the government registers deeds and adjudicates disputes. Ayn Rand wrote an excellent article on this, "The Property Status of Airwaves," in *Capitalism: The Unknown Ideal,* and others, such as writers for the Cato Institute, have proposed similar ideas.

The airwaves should belong to the people. Once Congress decided the government would hold ownership of the airwaves on behalf of all the people, the requirement naturally followed that broadcast be operated for the "public interest, convenience and necessity." In other words, licensees had to be "socially responsible," as defined by whoever ran the government. This opens the gate to possible censorship.

QUESTIONABLE USES OF THE POWER TO REGULATE BROADCAST

Whichever side you take on the two reasons most often given to support government regulation of the airwaves, the government has also regulated broadcast for less defensible purposes:

The government has limited eligibility to use the airwaves based on wealth. Historically, the best wavelengths were given to those with the most money and the best equipment. Those without as much money—educational, religious and labor-backed stations—got the worst frequencies and sometimes even had to timeshare them. The result? In 1927, there were 98 educational stations, but by 1937, just three years after the Federal Communications Act was passed, there were only 43.

Unfettering the Electronic Media

Our lawmakers and courts have never fully acknowledged that electronic media should be free for the same reasons as print. Justice Oliver Wendell Holmes said, for example: "The radio as it now operates among us is not free. Nor is it entitled to the protection of the First Amendment. It is not engaged in the task of enlarging human communication." To answer Justice Holmes, here are some reasons electronic media should be as free as the print media and why journalists of all kinds should be concerned:

- Electronic media should be unfettered for the same reasons that we have the First Amendment for print. We need a free marketplace of ideas, an informed public in a democracy, the right of self-expression and the right to consume what messages we want.
- Print journalists argue that the First Amendment is not a special privilege for them but a right of the people. They look like hypocrites then if they reject First Amendment rights for broadcasters.
- Regulation of broadcast creates a climate of opinion favorable to regulating all the media. If broadcasters can be required to give equal time to opposing views, why can't newspapers or magazines or book publishers?
- Media increasingly use electronic technology, which Congress is likely to regulate. The First Amendment doesn't mention radio, television, cable or satellite broadcasting, or the Internet, so Congress has seen fit to regulate them. But even newspapers receive news over phone lines and satellite dishes—technologies Congress has taken it upon itself to regulate. As Ithiel de Sola Pool writes in *On Free Speech in an Electronic Age: Technologies of Freedom:*

  > The industries of print and the industries of telecommunications will no longer be kept apart by a fundamental difference in their technologies. The economic and regulatory problems of the electronic media will thus become the problems of the print media too. . . . The issues that concern telecommunications are now becoming issues for all communications as they all become forms of electronic processing and transmission.

- New technologies mean more voices and the democratization of the media, so why regulate the very technologies that are doing what press critics want? Where's the scarcity now? Where's the high cost? Media critic A. J. Leibling used to say that in America, there's freedom of the press only for those who own one. But many people can own one now with the Web and desktop publishing.

The government has used its licensing power to suppress political opponents. Both Democratic and Republican presidents have used their control over the FCC to harass political opponents. Richard Nixon ordered his people to look into making license renewals tough on *The Washington Post's* broadcast holdings after that paper's Bob Woodward and Carl Bernstein started exposing him in its Watergate stories.

Likewise, President John Kennedy's assistant secretary of commerce, Bill Ruder, admitted: "Our strategy was to use the Fairness Doctrine to challenge and harass right-wing broadcasters and hope that the challenges would be so costly to them that they would be inhibited and decide it was too expensive to continue."

SPECIAL RULES FOR BROADCAST

The famous Fairness Doctrine of 1949 is no longer legally mandated, although it's often confused with the still enforced Section 315 of the FCC Act of 1934. So we begin with the Fairness Doctrine to help sort out which content is still regulated and which is not.

The Fairness Doctrine was an FCC rule, not a statute. It applied not to candidates, as does Section 315, but to controversial issues of public interest. Each broadcaster was required to give reasonable opportunity for the presentation of conflicting viewpoints on controversial issues of public importance.

There were various later additions to the Fairness Doctrine provisions.

The FCC ruled in 1963 that if a paid ad gave one side of an issue, the media had to give the other side free time if it couldn't afford to pay for an opposing ad. An example: In Missouri during the 1970s, right-to-work supporters bought TV and radio ads presenting their side of the issue on a state referendum. The unions spent all their money on newspaper ads, then demanded free Fairness Doctrine time from TV and radio stations on the grounds they had no money.

The FCC granted free time to antismoking messages under the Fairness Doctrine. A Court of Appeals went one step further, saying the cigarette ruling could not be limited to cigarettes. Friends of the Earth then argued that gasoline ads were only one side of the issue, and antipollution messages should be aired free. But the FCC refused, insisting that cigarettes were unique—a legal product, nonetheless controversial, with one-sided advertisements.

As of 1967, the Fairness Doctrine came to include an entitlement to reply to an editorial and an entitlement to reply to a personal attack. The Personal Attack Rule of 1967 said that when an attack was made on the honesty, character, or integrity of a person or group during public discussion, that person or group must be given the opportunity to respond.

The Political Editorializing Rule of 1967 said that when a licensee editorialized for or against a particular candidate—or even for or against an issue identified with a particular candidate, even if the candidate's name wasn't mentioned—the broadcaster had to notify rivals and afford them time to respond. For years, the broadcaster wasn't protected if someone given Fairness Doctrine time libeled someone else, but that was eventually changed.

With the Fairness Doctrine, the FCC was saying, in essence, that the public's entitlement to be informed took precedence over the right of the station to exercise editorial judgment. The government could override editorial discretion in the electronic media to force them to carry opposing views.

But in 2000, the U.S. Court of Appeals for the District of Columbia ordered the FCC to repeal the Personal Attack and Political Editorializing rules immediately. The court said that the rules "interfere with editorial judgment of professional journalists and entangle the government in day-to-day operations of the media."

The FCC established the Fairness Doctrine in 1949, it said, to try to make sure there was a greater diversity of opinions presented in broadcasting. The FCC's power to require stations to air opposing views was upheld by the Supreme Court in 1969.

But the Fairness Doctrine didn't kick in until one side of a controversy was already aired, so stations would sometimes try to get around it by not airing controversy, especially after the U.S. Supreme Court ruled in 1976 that the licensee could determine what was a controversial issue of public importance. Broadcasting became more bland and less controversial for fear of having to provide free time to special-interest groups or face license challenges. Whatever the intention, the result was actually self-censorship and less presentation of public issues.

After the FCC repealed the Fairness Doctrine in August 1987 (Congress tried to reinstate it by law, but it was vetoed by President Ronald Reagan), controversy returned to radio in the form of more news-talk formats. For example, in 1980, there were 110 all-news stations in the United States; in 1992, 530—up 381.8 percent. In 1980, there were 244 stations with talk-radio formats; in 1992, 349—up 43 percent. In 1990, there were no news-talk stations in America; in 1992, there were 530. In 1980, there were *no* public affairs format stations in America; in 1992, there were 50. And in 1989, there were only 11 noncommercial all-news stations in America, but by 1993, there were 184.

Although the Fairness Doctrine is gone, the FCC still regulates broadcast content in these ways:

All candidates in a primary or general election must be given an "equal opportunity"—not "equal time," as many people mistakenly think—to buy commercial time and be charged the lowest rate. Section 315 of the Communications Act of 1934 says that all candidates must have available to them an "equal opportunity" to air their views if one candidate for the same office has already done so on any given station. After Ronald Reagan announced his candidacy for president, stations had to give equal opportunity to other candidates every time a Reagan movie ran. And you can't get around Section 315 by putting supporters on the air rather than the candidate, according to the Zapple rule.

News coverage is exempt from Section 315's equal opportunity provision under a 1959 amendment that says each candidate does not have to be equally covered because one may be making more news than another.

By the way, broadcasters cannot censor a political advertisement, but neither can they be held responsible in case of a legal action over the political ad.

Broadcast stations generally don't have to accept ads they don't want to run. The Supreme Court ruled in the 1973 case of CBS Inc. v. Democratic National Committee that the "public interest" standard of the Communication Act does not require broadcasters to accept editorial advertising. Chief Justice Burger wrote: "For better or worse, editing is what editors are for, and editing is selection and choice of material. That editors—newspaper or broadcast—can and do abuse this power is beyond doubt, but that is not reason to deny the discretion Congress provided." One might wonder then why broadcast is regulated at all.

The FCC regulates indecency. The FCC traditionally outlawed "the seven dirty words" (*shit, piss, fuck, cunt, cocksucker, motherfucker* and *tits*) made famous by George Carlin's comedy routine. In a 1978 case challenging the broadcast of that comedy bit over the radio, the court ruled it was not obscene but could be deemed unfit for broadcast by reason of indecency.

The FCC now defines *indecency* as "language or material that depicts or describes, in terms patently offensive as measured by contemporary community standards for the broadcast medium, sexual or excretory activities or organs." Congress passed a 24-hour ban of indecent broadcasts in 1988, but this was ruled unconstitutional in 1991. After a series of new partial bans by the FCC, eventually, in 1995, a panel of judges decided the FCC could ban indecency except between 10 p.m. and 6 a.m.

The Prime Time Access Rule of 1970 mandates non-network programming from 7:30 p.m. to 8 p.m. EST six days a week. This rule was pushed by Westinghouse, a company that sold alternative programming to the networks, although it later bought CBS. The result of the rule was not more local programming but more syndicated programming, such as game shows and tabloid-television shows.

Every seven years at license-renewal time, each station owner must show that the station has operated in the public interest and be able to withstand any challengers from the community who might want to claim it has not. In 1943, the U.S. Supreme Court ruled in NBC v. U.S. that the Federal Communications Commission is not restricted merely to supervising traffic on the broadcast airwaves. The FCC must also make sure stations serve "public interest, convenience or necessity." This phrase was taken from a South Dakota public utilities regulation, and indeed the broadcast media are treated in some ways more like public utilities to be regulated rather than part of a system of free press left unlicensed and uncensored.

SATELLITE BROADCAST LAW

The FCC was going to exempt direct-broadcast satellite networks from ownership and political access requirements that other broadcasters must follow, but broadcasters sued. In National Association of Broadcasters v. FCC (1984), the court said satellite broadcasters must meet the same standards as over-the-air broadcast.

INTERNET LAW

Media law is constantly changing, and one of the latest major areas of development comes from the government's attempts to figure out what to do about the Internet. This is where things stand so far:

It's safer to assume that laws applying to both print and broadcast—such as libel, privacy and intellectual property—also apply to the Internet. For example, the Digital Millenium Copyright Act of 1998 says that copyright law applies to material posted online, including e-mails and discussion forums. So, get permission before reprinting online material, including photos or graphics linked to another site but stripped out of the original context. But a brief description of an article with a link to the whole article on another site does not violate copyright unless the article was stripped out of context by being imported into a frame or page that makes it appear to be your own content.

It's unlikely the government will eventually permit greater freedom to the Internet than to print if it's technologically feasible to limit it. But to what extent Internet law will remain relatively free, like print, rather than more restrictive, like broadcast, remains open. Given the government's reluctance to apply full First Amendment protection to previous electronic media, it's probably more likely that the Internet will see greater regulation in the future.

Attempts so far to censor offensive content on the Internet have largely failed. The Supreme Court ruled that parts of the Communications Decency Act passed in 1996 are unconstitutional by reason of being overly broad. Likewise, a federal appeals court in 2001 struck down a federal judge's ban on the anti-abortion Web site The Nuremburg Files from publishing wanted posters of doctors who performed abortions.

Ironically, the more an Internet medium tries to edit or moderate its content for legal problems, the less legal protection it currently seems to have. This has been shown in a case against CompuServe and two against America Online in which courts have let the Internet services off the hook because they were seen as common carriers, like phone companies, rather than as publishers exercising editorial judgment.

ETHICAL ISSUES

The joke is that journalism ethics is an oxymoron, a contradiction in terms—that in journalism, ethics don't matter—all that matters is getting the story.

Believe it or not, most journalists don't think that way. People who go into journalism mainly care greatly about their fellow human beings. So, for most journalists, deciding whether to publish information shouldn't end with asking whether it's news and whether publishing it might pose legal problems. Sometimes, newsworthy, legally safe information won't get published because of ethical objections. **Ethics** involves doing what's right even when it's legal to do what's wrong.

First, let's look at some matters you might have thought were legal problems but which in America are really mainly ethical ones.

Confessions

It's legal to print that someone has confessed to a crime. But most news outlets will tell you generally to avoid printing that someone confessed, even when police tell you this. Why? Confessions can be recanted or thrown out of court if they were derived under duress or before someone's Miranda rights were read to them. Printing a confession before it's been admitted into court can bias a jury, denying someone a fair trial if it's later thrown out by the judge.

Printing Names and Addresses

It's legal to print the names of juvenile defendants and the names or addresses of victims of sexual crimes. The Supreme Court has said newspapers have the right to print the names of rape victims and details about the crime. And although the law may prevent authorities from releasing the names of juvenile offenders, it can't prevent a newspaper from publishing those it knows. Not printing such names, then, is an ethical rather than a legal consideration for the press.

But addresses can be another matter. Printing the address of a victim of an attempted rape may constitute negligence if the assailant is still on the loose. (He might use that information to find the victim again.) But the newspaper might be legally safer printing the address of a person charged in a crime because if someone else in the area has the same name, that person could sue, claiming readers might mistakenly think he or she was the suspect.

Ethical Flashing Lights

You may think of yourself as an ethical person and that a discussion of ethics is something you can skip over. But many times, as an editor you will find yourself facing a possible ethics problem and not even know it.

The No. 1 reason journalism students give for going into the field is that they want to change the world. But consider this: If you sign a petition, wear a candidate's button or have a bumper sticker on your car that supports a cause, you are probably violating your employer's ethics policy. News outlets often ban such displays of political viewpoints even by journalists not covering politics. (But publishers may belong to groups like Rotary Club and be friends with the powerful people the paper covers.)

Here's another example of being in a possible ethics violation without knowing it. Accepting anything from a source can be a conflict of interest. For example, if you're a travel writer and accept a free trip to Cancún, you could find yourself out of work. It could also be considered unethical to let a City Council member buy you a cup of coffee and a piece of pie while you conduct an interview.

Even though you think you can't be bought, and that no strings are attached to the trip or the snack, your objectivity is compromised by the acceptance of favors, and your credibility, too. (But most papers wouldn't insist sports writers buy their own tickets to sporting events, and many would allow reviewers to receive free books or CDs.)

To help you determine whether you may be facing an ethical problem, here are the kinds of ethical questions you might face as a journalist, along with a number of examples of each and even some typical answers. Think of this as a list of warning signs that what you are about to publish deserves a second look—not that publishing such information would necessarily be ethically wrong in all cases.

Should you publish information that is not objectively true or that may be deceptive?

- *Misinforming or failing to inform in a story if the deception might serve a public good.* What if the government asks you to print or not print certain information, perhaps to ease or prevent public fears or to deny a terrorist publicity? What if promoters of a good cause ask you not to report adverse reaction to a social program of theirs aimed at a desirable goal? What if African-American leaders, for example, requested you not run negative stories about affirmative-action failures or backlash to quota proposals? (Most papers would refuse.)

- *Leaving out information that might be relevant to a story if people involved ask you to.* What if the family of a person who died of AIDS or suicide asks you not to include that information in the obituary? What if the victim of a non-sexual assault asks you to leave his name out of the story because he's embarrassed he was beat up? (Most papers would refuse.)

- *Stretching the facts or stressing only the most sensational angle to have a more interesting story.* (Most journalists would say this is wrong but nonetheless sometimes do it.)

- *Quoting out of context.* (Journalists, as opposed to propagandists, would say this is wrong, but not everyone will likely agree on what the real context is.)

- *Selecting material to fit a preconceived story idea.* (Many journalists haven't thought about this one and do it more often than they would if they did think about it.)

- *Creating a pseudo event, staging a photograph or writing a letter, ostensibly from a reader, to reveal certain information or to begin an advice column.* (This was more common in the past than now.)

- *Taking a side, other than in an editorial, a news analysis or, to a lesser extent, a sports story or a feature.* (Most journalists try to be objective, but they're not always successful at keeping out their biases.)

- *Blurring distinctions between ads and copy.* (Good publications avoid this.)
- *Not covering an important story or burying it inside as a small story.* (No one will tell you this is a good idea, but people disagree about the relative news value of stories.)

Should you obtain information in nonopen, nonlegal or questionable ways?

- *Use of anonymous sources.* (This can pose both legal and ethical problems but is commonly done.)
- *Use of off-the-record statements.* (This can pose not only an ethics problem, but a legal one, as well, if a source sues you for breach of contract. But what would you do if someone told you, off the record, information that would be an important scoop? Some reporters might break their promise, for good or bad.)
- *Use of stolen or otherwise illegally obtained information.* If someone told you he'd broken into an office and found documents proving who killed Jimmy Hoffa, what would you say? (This may or may not be illegal, as the Pentagon Papers case proved. That is, it's normally illegal, but the Supreme Court OK'd it in that case because of its importance. Is it ethical, though? Do the ends justify the means?)
- *Use of information obtained in trade for favorable treatment.* (Probably no one would tell you this is ethical, but it is sometimes done if the information is important enough and the favorable treatment is small enough.)
- *Sting operations, undercover investigations, eavesdropping, clandestine recording or photography, nonidentification of the reporter as such.* Is it ever OK to research a story without telling your sources you're a journalist and that what they say may be printed? Is it ethical to impersonate someone else to get a story? Is it ethical to go undercover as a patient to get a story about abortion counseling or conditions in a state mental hospital? (These can make some of a news outlet's most important investigative stories, and sometimes there may be no better way to get them. But there is much debate about the ethics of such techniques. Awards have been denied to newspapers for such stories because of their questionable nature.)
- *The appearance of conflict of interest, even if it doesn't influence what is published*—such as holding stock investments in a company you or your paper covers; freelancing as a media consultant, PR adviser or speech writer; or taking honorariums to speak to corporations or lobbying groups your paper might cover. (Most papers would not allow this.)
- *Accepting special privileges or gifts not accorded the general public.* What freebies, if any, are acceptable while working as a journalist? Lunch bought by a source? Records or books that come in the mail for review? Tickets to concerts, games or speeches? Special press seating at a game? Special preview

showings not open to the public of movies or plays? Trips on chartered planes to cover sporting events? Transportation and accommodations for a travel story? (The policies on this are mixed. A common principle seems to be such freebies are acceptable only if they are not worth more than a certain small dollar amount.)

- *Plagiarism*—such as incorporating information from stories by your competition into your own without acknowledging the source. What about lifting whole paragraphs of background information from morgue stories written by a different reporter? (Plagiarism is a legal, as well as an ethical, problem. Journalists often get facts from other stories, even without crediting them, but they usually won't take direct quotes. Lifted quotes should be kept to a minimum, and credit should be given to the original source unless it was another writer at the same publication.)

- *Involvement in politics or causes.* To what extent can you be a journalist (as opposed to a commentator) and be involved in politics? Should a journalist run for political office? What if it's for the school board? How about putting a political bumper sticker on your car or wearing a campaign button? What about becoming involved in the Rotary Club, the PTA or a neighborhood crime-watch group? Should a publisher have any more latitude than a reporter? Should a journalist publicly take sides on political or social issues such as abortion, the death penalty, affirmative action or a balanced federal budget? Would it make any difference if this were not an issue the reporter covers? Why do you suppose many newspapers take stands on issues like these on their editorial page? (Policies vary and are often inconsistent.)

Should you publish information that is harmful to individuals in stories?

- *Information that violates someone's privacy.* Is it ever ethical to invade someone's privacy to get the news? Is it ethical to go through someone's trash for information? To stake out a politician's house to see whether he or she is cheating on a spouse? To publicize crimes or sins of people related to someone famous? (Of course, this poses severe legal consequences as well as ethical questions.)

- *Information that may conflict with someone's right to a fair trial.* (Although legal to print it, a media outlet should also consider the fairness of its coverage. After all, what if the suspect is not guilty and the coverage railroads him or her?)

- *Names and addresses.* What about victims of crimes other than sexual assaults? Are the common practices of routinely printing the ages and addresses of people in stories an invasion of privacy and possibly a threat to their safety? What about printing addresses in obituary notices? Burglars often use the obituaries in a newspaper as a shopping list. They know the survivors will be out of their houses attending the funeral, so they hit the best houses during the services. Should newspapers stop printing the addresses of the survivors of the deceased, or doesn't it matter because the burglars could just look them up in the phone book? (Names and addresses are usually published except for victims of sex crimes and juvenile offenders. Addresses aren't usually published for the deceased or survivors of the deceased in obituaries.)

- *Names of juvenile offenders.* (Most news outlets typically withhold these but may release them in the case of a particularly serious and famous crime.)

- *Expunged criminal records, information about previous convictions (especially misdemeanor crimes such as minor drug arrests), or information about mental-health problems.* (These are legally publishable if obtained, although all of them pose an ethics issue. Many papers typically won't publish them—and in the case of someone's medical records, publishing could potentially spark an invasion-of-privacy lawsuit.)

- *Confessions.* (News outlets often won't publish or broadcast a confession until it is accepted as evidence in court, but if the case is important enough, one outlet is likely to release it, and the others will then typically follow suit once the information is out there.)

Should you publish information that is potentially harmful to society?

- *How to commit a crime.* You learn that a con game is being played in your area to cheat elderly people out of their savings. Should you run a story explaining the con so readers can avoid it, or might that teach others how to run the con themselves? (Most outlets would run it.)

- *Information that could hamper a criminal investigation.* (Most outlets probably won't publish such information if specifically asked not to. In big stories, the press does sometimes get in the way of police investigators as it pursues scoops.)

- *Information the government says must be kept secret for national security reasons.* You learn the president of the United States plans to invade a certain foreign country. Should you scoop your competition and announce this? (Most media outlets would not.)

- *Publicity crimes—when the press is held hostage.* This occurs when someone takes hostages until publicity is granted for a cause. (*The New York Times* decided to print the Unabomber's manifesto, and doing so eventually helped authorities capture him. But taking such action should spark a spirited debate in the newsroom before the decision is made.)

- *Ads of harmful products, such as tobacco and alcohol.* (Some publications exercise more restrictions than others on which dollars they will or will not accept for advertising.)

Should you accept restraints on the press?

- *From the government.* Should editorial pages champion a free press, then inconsistently promote the causes of social responsibility of the press, restraining sex and violence on TV, mandating more children's educational or quality programming, and banning or restraining certain kinds of advertisements? (Journalists often have mixed premises that prevent them from seeing how all of these positions place limits on the freedom of the press they cherish.)

- *From the owners or managers.* If your publisher asks you to slant a story a certain way because it involves a friend, should you abide by that wish? (Of course, the owner gets to make the rules, but you have to decide whether your job is more important than your ethics. Because it's sometimes hard to have the luxury of your ethics when you have no money in your savings account, it's a good idea to put 10 percent of each paycheck into a "go to hell" fund that would permit you to tell your boss, "Go to hell," rather than do something you consider wrong.)

- *From yourself.* Self-restraint over a story because the reporter is shy or wants to be a "nice guy" to sources can restrain the press from getting to the truth. Likewise, when the press sees itself as a town booster, editors may not want to print negative news. After all, the press has to keep up good relations with residents in order to survive economically. (You need to maintain independence to be objective, which may sometimes mean you have to stand up for yourself as a journalist more than you might as a private individual.)

- *From sources.* If someone gives a reporter good information, then afterward asks the paper not to print it, should you abide by this request? Should a reporter read a story back to a source to make sure it's accurate? If so, should you let the source reword a quotation to improve it? Or because he or she has now decided it would be better to say it in a less-pointed way? If a source says you've missed the point and taken an angle that suggests the wrong tone, what should you do? (Some papers see double-checking quotes with sources as responsible, but most see it as giving the source too much control over the story. The key is making clear that this is just an accuracy check, not a license for the source to rewrite the story as he or she would like.)

Finding Ethical Answers

Once you've identified a potential problem, where do you go for help in deciding whether it would be ethical?

- Abide by your own religious and philosophical convictions about right and wrong.

- Consider the written or unwritten policy of your newspaper, magazine or station on such matters. If there's not a written policy, consult with your editor.

Deciding Ethics Issues

General Questions

- Does this involve something that's ever right?
- Does the situation make this ethical even though it may generally be wrong?
- What is our intent in running this? Is our intent honorable?
- What will be the consequences for everyone involved? Will this accomplish more harm than good for most of the people?
- Is there a way to lessen the harms? Could we be more moderate in our approach?

Audience and Community

- Is this material appropriate for our audience?
- Should we decide whether the public should see this or have this information, or should we let people make up their own minds about its appropriateness?
- Is this something our audience needs to know, even though it may not want to?
- Would this information help our audience in any way, such as better understanding the world?
- Would this information hurt our audience by offending or prejudicing it? Does the information glamorize something destructive?
- Does this information point out a problem that needs to be solved?
- Would this information help prevent a similar situation from occurring again?

Sources and Those Concerned

- Are we treating this person as we treat everyone else in the same situation?
- Is this fair to all concerned?
- Is this public information?
- Would getting this information out violate anyone's trust?

- Does this information violate anyone's privacy?
- Would this information stigmatize innocent people?
- Are we exploiting anyone by running this?
- Does the public's need to know this information count for more than the harm we might be causing an individual?
- Is there some way to publish this that would minimize the harm?

The Material Itself

- Is this newsworthy?
- Is this true?
- Is this well-done?
- Is this biased?
- Does it sensationalize?
- Is this information relevant to the larger news story?
- Is this legal?

Ourselves

- How would we feel if someone published this about us?
- Are we being consistent in our policies?
- Will publishing or broadcasting this information damage our credibility?
- Will *not* publishing or broadcasting this information look like we are hiding something or protecting somebody?
- Will this have repercussions on fellow journalists or the public's right to know?
- What does your conscience say? Will we later feel proud or ashamed of ourselves for running this?
- Can we afford the backlash in terms of lost subscribers, lost revenue, lost credibility and expensive lawsuits?

- Consult the written policies of other media outlets or professional organizations. The Society of Professional Journalists publishes a code of journalistic ethics, as do a number of newspapers and other news organizations. We've included SPJ's code of ethics on the following pages, and others are available in various books and on professional Web sites.

SPJ Code of Ethics

The most widely accepted code of ethics for journalists is the one published by the Society of Professional Journalists. It is reprinted here with permission.

Preamble

Members of the Society of Professional Journalists believe that public enlightenment is the forerunner of justice and the foundation of democracy. The duty of the journalist is to further those ends by seeking truth and providing a fair and comprehensive account of events and issues. Conscientious journalists from all media and specialties strive to serve the public with thoroughness and honesty. Professional integrity is the cornerstone of a journalist's credibility. Members of the Society share a dedication to ethical behavior and adopt this code to declare the Society's principles and standards of practice.

Seek Truth and Report It

Journalists should be honest, fair and courageous in gathering, reporting and interpreting information.

Journalists should:

- Test the accuracy of information from all sources and exercise care to avoid inadvertent error. Deliberate distortion is never permissible.
- Diligently seek out subjects of news stories to give them the opportunity to respond to allegations of wrongdoing.
- Identify sources whenever feasible. The public is entitled to as much information as possible on sources' reliability.
- Always question sources' motives before promising anonymity. Clarify conditions attached to any promise made in exchange for information. Keep promises.
- Make certain that headlines, news teases and promotional material, photos, video, audio, graphics, sound bites and quotations do not misrepresent. They should not oversimplify or highlight incidents out of context.
- Never distort the content of news photos or video. Image enhancement for technical clarity is always permissible. Label montages and photo illustrations.
- Avoid misleading re-enactments or staged news events. If re-enactment is necessary to tell a story, label it.

- Avoid undercover or other surreptitious methods of gathering information except when traditional open methods will not yield information vital to the public. Use of such methods should be explained as part of the story.
- Never plagiarize.
- Tell the story of the diversity and magnitude of the human experience boldly, even when it is unpopular to do so.
- Examine their own cultural values and avoid imposing those values on others.
- Avoid stereotyping by race, gender, age, religion, ethnicity, geography, sexual orientation, disability, physical appearance or social status.
- Support the open exchange of views, even views they find repugnant.
- Give voice to the voiceless; official and unofficial sources of information can be equally valid.
- Distinguish between advocacy and news reporting. Analysis and commentary should be labeled and not misrepresent fact or context.
- Distinguish news from advertising and shun hybrids that blur the lines between the two.
- Recognize a special obligation to ensure that the public's business is conducted in the open and that government records are open to inspection.

Minimize Harm

Ethical journalists treat sources, subjects and colleagues as human beings deserving of respect.

Journalists should:

- Show compassion for those who may be affected adversely by news coverage. Use special sensitivity when dealing with children and inexperienced sources or subjects.
- Be sensitive when seeking or using interviews or photographs of those affected by tragedy or grief.
- Recognize that gathering and reporting information may cause harm or discomfort. Pursuit of the news is not a license for arrogance.
- Recognize that private people have a greater right to control information about themselves than do public officials and others who seek power, influence or attention. Only an overriding public need can justify intrusion into anyone's privacy.
- Show good taste. Avoid pandering to lurid curiosity.
- Be cautious about identifying juvenile suspects or victims of sex crimes.
- Be judicious about naming criminal suspects before the formal filing of charges.
- Balance a criminal suspect's fair trial rights with the public's right to be informed.

Act Independently

Journalists should be free of obligation to any interest other than the public's right to know.

Journalists should:

- Avoid conflicts of interest, real or perceived.
- Remain free of associations and activities that may compromise integrity or damage credibility.
- Refuse gifts, favors, fees, free travel and special treatment, and shun secondary employment, political involvement, public office and service in community organizations if they compromise journalistic integrity.
- Disclose unavoidable conflicts.
- Be vigilant and courageous about holding those with power accountable.
- Deny favored treatment to advertisers and special interests and resist their pressure to influence news coverage.
- Be wary of sources offering information for favors or money; avoid bidding for news.

Be Accountable

Journalists are accountable to their readers, listeners, viewers and each other.

Journalists should:

- Clarify and explain news coverage and invite dialogue with the public over journalistic conduct.
- Encourage the public to voice grievances against the news media.
- Admit mistakes and correct them promptly.
- Expose unethical practices of journalists and the news media.
- Abide by the same high standards to which they hold others.

Sigma Delta Chi's first Code of Ethics was borrowed from the American Society of Newspaper Editors in 1926. In 1973, Sigma Delta Chi wrote its own code, which was revised in 1984 and 1987. The present version of the Society of Professional Journalists' Code of Ethics was adopted in September 1996.

PROPRIETY

When we speak of **propriety** in journalism, we mean selecting and presenting material that is *appropriate* for a specific audience. Media outlets with fairly selective, niche audiences—such as most magazines, newsletters and Web sites—may be liberal in the language and illustrations they use. Those with more general audiences—such as newspapers, broadcast outlets and some large Web sites—are typically more conservative in their standards.

The key question to ask here is: Would this give unnecessary offense to our audience? Publish the material only if your audience would be receptive and if the material is newsworthy. Here are some examples:

- *Nudity.* Usually, nude photographs are not published in a newspaper. But such photos might be if the nudity occurred in public or involved a legitimate news story, or if the nudity is covered enough in the photo to become less objectionable.

- *Obscene gestures, obscenity and profanity.* These, also, usually are not published in a newspaper without offsetting circumstances. An obscene gesture by a public official, candidate or religious leader might be published. Swear words might be published, provided they are mild, such as *damn* or *hell.* Offensive language might be published if part of a powerful quote, such as a man convicted of murdering his girlfriend telling a reporter, "I'm glad I killed the bitch," or a man at a Martin Luther King Jr. rally saying, "I'm here to say thanks that my son won't have to grow up in a world where people call him 'nigger.'"

- *Gore, tragedy and grief.* Newspapers usually reject these photos, despite the public's opinion that newspapers run them to increase sales. Actually, when such photos are run, people call to cancel their subscription in protest. Even television newscasters, for whom the slogan "if it bleeds, it leads" is well-known, face public outcry over broadcasting gruesome images or ones that intrude into private grief and suffering.

Sometimes, though, the news event captured is important enough or the message strong enough or the aesthetic quality great enough that the image is published anyway. But be prepared: Even photos that have won a Pulitzer Prize or other journalism awards have received large public outcries when originally published or broadcast. Examples include Eddie Adams' Pulitzer Prize–winning shot of the execution of a Viet Cong prisoner, a photo of children falling to their death from a fire escape, and a family sobbing over the body of a drowned toddler.

Being Sensitive

Included in propriety, and strongly related to both taste and objectivity, is the idea that journalists must show **sensitivity** to stereotyping or unfairly labeling people because of their **race,** ethnic or religious background, age, sex, sexual preference or handicap. For most journalists, bias along these lines is unconscious and unintentional, which makes it harder for an editor to spot. Journalists should strive to remove bias from their writing—not to push a politically correct agenda but because bias of any kind flies in the face of objective journalism.

We suggest these guidelines:

Avoid any obviously offensive language. EXAMPLES: words like *bitch* (a woman), *queer, gook, wop, Holy Roller, geezer* and *gimp*.

Avoid merely gratuitous references to the categories of race, ethnicity, religion, age, sex, sexual preference and handicaps. EXAMPLES: Why say, "Police are looking for a suspect who is a black male in his early 20s"? Such a description fits so many men as to be useless. Why comment on a woman's looks, dress or marital status when they have nothing to do with the story and when these would not be mentioned in a similar article about a man?

Some questions are less easy to answer: Are courtesy titles such as *Miss* and *Mrs.* sexist because they identify a woman by her marital status while the courtesy title *Mr.* does not? Is the practice many newspapers follow of routinely printing someone's age an ageist policy? Is it an invasion of privacy?

Avoid passages that may be prejudicial in effect even when not intended as such. One reason Americans so often talk at cross-purposes about subjects like racism and sexism is that people in power—whites or men, for example—usually define such terms by whether the offending user "meant anything by it," while people out of power—minorities or women—usually define them by the results, regardless of the speaker's intention, or lack thereof.

People could probably communicate better with each other if they learned to appreciate each other's perspective. And the fact is, both the *intent* and the *effect* of a statement deserve to be examined. After all, the severity of punishment for a crime is determined in part by trying to judge the intent of a perpetrator—a lighter sentence for unintended manslaughter than for a coldly plotted murder. Likewise, effect matters, too. We've all been a victim at one time or another of someone's ill-chosen words that stung deeply regardless of the innocent intent of the person speaking.

Beware of story premises meant as positive but that betray a paternalistic attitude. EXAMPLES: "He has such a good sense of humor, you forget he's handicapped." "She's a woman—and she's a doctor." "Tiger Woods is articulate" (as if you wouldn't expect that from a man who's an athlete or a minority, or both).

Words and phrases offensive in origin but perhaps not recognized as such by a speaker may be offensive to the people involved, even if no offense was intended by the user. EXAMPLES: *nigger toes* (Brazil nuts); *to Jew someone down* (to drive a hard bargain), *basket case* (originally meant a paraplegic), *gyp* (from *gypsy*). Is there a difference between words like *gyp*, of which gypsies—although they prefer *Romany*—have made an issue, and *basket case*, which has not generally been made an issue by the disabled?

On a related note, the use of Native American names for teams may be offensive to the people involved, even when racism is no longer intended—if it ever was. This was the case with Eastern Michigan University's old team name, the Hurons, which was offensive to one of the two major groups of Hurons. Complicating this issue was not only supporters' loyalties to the traditional team name but also the view of some—including one of the Huron tribal groups—that the name was an honor rather than a disgrace.

But it shouldn't be too difficult to see that Native American culture is demeaned by the spectacle of drunken sports fans in headdress and war paint—like old-time Hollywood's portrayal of "Indians"—beating tom-toms, swinging hatchets and shouting slogans such as "Scalp 'em, Chiefs!" Would similar stereotypes be tolerated today of African Americans? Journalists can't change the names of the teams, but they should refuse to use cliché phrases like "the Braves are on the warpath."

Edit out assumptions that people who share a skin color, ethnic background, sex, disability, religion, or sexual orientation are all alike, whether in negative or positive characteristics. EXAMPLES: "Women are bad drivers and are more emotional than men." "Vietnam veterans are powder kegs ready to explode." "African Americans are poor." "Jews are smart and make great doctors." "Asians are model minorities, good at math and successful in life." "Elderly people are infirm, forgetful, stubborn, conservative, frumpy and stooped."

Edit out assumptions that certain jobs are male or female jobs. EXAMPLES: Calling a man a *male nurse* or *male secretary* assumes that nursing and secretarial work are female occupations. Calling a woman a *lady lawyer* or *woman doctor* assumes that law and medicine are male occupations.

A reporter began her story this way: "Mothers aren't the only ones who can tell us how to eat properly. A computer can, too." And so can a father. This reporter reinforced the stereotype that it is the mother's role to look out for the needs of children. The editor could have changed the lead to: "Parents aren't the only ones . . . ."

Don't describe a woman's appearance, clothing, marital status, motherhood or grandmotherhood in situations where you would not say similar things about a man. EXAMPLES: "The first lady entered wearing a red dress and large gold earrings and received an ovation. Then the president arrived a minute later to thunderous applause." "The pretty mother of three was hospitalized following the accident." "Local Grandmother Wins Bowling Tourney."

Edit out assumptions that you can tell by physical characteristics alone, such as someone's sexual orientation, religion, ethnicity or even race. EXAMPLES: A story about a bomb threat to a northern Wisconsin high school included this: "According to the complaint filed at the Minocqua Police Department, [the secretary] reported that the threat came from a male Indian's voice." Just how does a male Indian sound? Besides, couldn't someone be faking a dialect to mislead authorities? Sometimes, such descriptions tell us more about the prejudices of the sources than about the person described, as when someone is described as "looking Jewish" or "sounding gay." Someone who looks white may be a light-skinned African American, and someone who looks African American may actually be from India, Pakistan or Haiti.

Make an effort to include women and minorities in stories that have nothing to do with their being women or minorities. EXAMPLES: Interview women and minorities for business stories, for stories about community events and for lifestyle features. But don't turn these into "He's black, but he owns a yacht" stories.

Generally speaking, use designations preferred by the group being covered.

- *African-American* has gained wide support, but *black* is still OK. *Negro* is passé, *colored people* is offensive, but *people of color* is acceptable for nonwhites as a group.

- *Disabled* versus *handicapped* versus *special people* versus *otherly abled* versus *physically challenged:* Generally, use *disabled,* but follow local preference. Editors tend to resist terms like *special people,* which seem to imply you're special only if you're disabled.

- *Gay* is acceptable in place of *homosexual* (for a male), but either is OK.

- Native Americans prefer their tribal name or *Native American* as a generic term. Avoid *Indian. American Indian* is gaining in acceptance.

- *Fundamentalist* versus *Pentecostal* versus *charismatic* versus *Holy Roller: Fundamentalist* is the broadest term. Only *Holy Roller* is offensive.

EXCEPTIONS: Be reluctant to accept loaded terms as standard designations—such as *sanitary engineer* in place of *garbage collector.* At some point, however, euphemisms and loaded terms may become so standard that they lose their emotional charge. When they seem preferred, widespread and neutral, it's time to adopt them—as has happened with *senior citizen* and, to some extent, with *pro-life* and *pro-choice.*

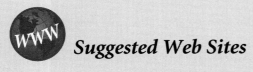

Suggested Web Sites

American Society of Newspaper Editors, ethics codes
www.asne.org/ideas/codes/codes.htm
First Amendment Center **www.firstamendmentcenter.org**
Indiana University Bloomington School of Journalism, ethics cases
www.journalism.indiana.edu/Ethics/
Media Law Resource Center **www.ldrc.com/index2.html**
The Poynter Institute, media ethics bibliography
www.poynter.org/content/content_view.asp?id=1208
Reporters Committee for Freedom of the Press "The First Amendment Handbook"
www.rcfp.org/handbook/viewpage.cgi
Society of Professional Journalists, ethics page **www.spj.org/ethics.asp**
Student Media Law Center **www.splc.org**
United States Copyright Office of the Library of Congress **www.copyright.gov**
University of Iowa Library, index to World Wide Web media law sites
http://bailiwick.lib.uiowa.edu/journalism/mediaLaw/index.html

Suggested Readings

Brooks, Brian S., James L. Pinson and Jean Gaddy Wilson. *Working With Words: A Handbook for Media Writers and Editors.* 6th edition. Boston: Bedford/St. Martin's, 2006.

Carter, T. Barton, et al. *Mass Communications Law in a Nutshell.* 6th edition. St. Paul, Minn.: West, 2006.

Miller, Casey, and Kate Swift. *The Handbook of Nonsexist Writing.* 2nd edition. New York: iUniverse, 2001.

Patterson, Philip, and Lee Wilkins. *Media Ethics: Issues and Cases.* 6th edition. New York: McGraw-Hill, 2007.

Pember, Don R., and Clay Calvert. *Mass Media Law 2007–2008.* 15th edition. New York: McGraw-Hill. 2006.

CHAPTER 6

MICRO EDITING FOR PRECISION IN LANGUAGE

At first glance, micro editing may not seem as important or as fun as macro editing. Instead of dealing with the big, important problems of a story, micro editing focuses on checking for correct grammar and usage, making the mechanics conform to local and wire-service stylebooks, fixing spelling errors and typos, and tightening the wording.

Although many reporters might consider micro editing to be an obsession with picky, little details, if the details aren't correct, they distract from what *is* important—the information the writer is trying to get across. The writer and editor, then, should both try to make sure the mechanics are correct so that instead of becoming a distraction, the mechanics are invisible to the reader.

This is the hardest of the copy-editing skills to learn for most people because it involves mastering so many rules. Micro editing requires technical knowledge as well as skill and art. To be a master of micro editing, you must become a master of the language. Studying it makes you a better editor or reporter.

GRAMMAR

Problems with the mechanics, such as grammar and usage, destroy the credibility of a publication among well-educated readers, listeners or viewers. Grammatical errors can ruin otherwise clear writing or distort the meaning of a **sentence**.

Just as a carpenter must learn to use a saw, hammer and nails, so, too, must journalists learn to use words. And although journalists should learn basic grammatical terms, just as that carpenter needs to learn the names of tools, the focus here is mainly on practical tips for using grammar.

These tips are the minimum a good journalist should know, and after you master these, pick up some more detailed grammar guides (such as Margaret Shertzer's *The Elements of Grammar,* written for a general audience, or *Working*

With Words by Brian S. Brooks, James L. Pinson and Jean Gaddy Wilson, written specifically for journalists) and some usage guides (such as the classic *Modern American Usage* by Wilson Follett and *The New Fowler's Modern English Usage* edited by R. W. Burchfield).

Sentence Problems

Avoid fragments.   To be a sentence, a group of related words must have a subject and verb, and express a complete thought. If it doesn't, it's a **fragment** and should be rewritten as a complete sentence.

> *Wrong:* The War on Poverty. An idealistic attempt to help people but largely a failure at reducing overall poverty rates.
>
> *Right:* The War on Poverty was an idealistic attempt to help people but largely a failure at reducing overall poverty rates.

Avoid fused sentences.   When two sentences have been jammed together with no punctuation between them and without capitalizing the first word of the second sentence, it is called a **fused sentence**. To fix it, choose one of the following:

- End the first sentence with a period, and capitalize the first word of the second.

- Put a semicolon after the first sentence, and leave the first word of the second sentence lowercase.

- Put a comma and conjunction *(but, and)* after the first sentence, and leave the first word of the second sentence lowercase.

- In some cases, put a dash after the first sentence and leave the second one lowercase. (This is used for a dramatic pause.) In other cases, put a colon after the first sentence and capitalize the first word of the second sentence. (This is used when the first sentence clearly points to the second.)

> *Wrong:* The Cleveland Rockers needed to do something they hadn't done all season they needed to beat the Detroit Shock.
>
> *Right:* The Cleveland Rockers needed to do something they hadn't done all season. They needed to beat the Detroit Shock.
>
> *Right:* The Cleveland Rockers needed to do something they hadn't done all season: They needed to beat the Detroit Shock.

Avoid comma-splice sentences.   A **comma splice** is like a fused sentence, only a comma has been used to separate the two independent clauses. A comma by itself is not enough to separate two full sentences. The remedies are the same as for a fused sentence.

> *Wrong:* The Cleveland Rockers needed to do something they hadn't done all season, they needed to beat the Detroit Shock.

Avoid run-on sentences.   A **run-on sentence** is not just any long sentence, but one that rambles on forever, not knowing when to quit. As a result, too many ideas get jumbled together in an unclear way. The fix is to separate the various ideas into separate sentences. Some books refer to fused sentences and comma splices as *run-ons*.

> *Too Long:* Strict, new federal guidelines meant to improve homeland security by restricting access to explosives are also being applied now to fireworks displays, making it more diffi-cult to hold Fourth of July celebrations in communities across the country, according to local officials and pyrotechnics-industry spokespeople who say their business was already heavily regulated and safe.

> *Better:* Strict, new federal guidelines meant to improve homeland security by restricting access to explosives are also being applied now to fireworks displays. This is making it more difficult to hold Fourth of July celebrations in communities across the country, according to local officials. And pyrotechnics-industry spokespeople say their business was already heav-ily regulated and safe.

Be on the lookout for reader stoppers.   Readers get stuck on passages that are fuzzy in meaning, often because the word order makes the sentence unclear. If you're not sure what a sentence means, ask the reporter to clarify it.

> An insufficient water supply problem for firefighting at Fitch Senior School will be discussed next Thursday.

(Try this: "The problem of insufficient water supply for firefighting at Fitch . . .")

> White segregationists waving Confederate flags and black integrationists marched past each other Tuesday.

(Or did white segregationists waving flags march past black integrationists Tuesday?)

> Joseph H. Hughes Jr. of Los Angeles wrote to many of his late son's, Coast Guard Ensign Joseph H. Hughes III, friends.

(Translation: "wrote to many friends of his late son, . . .")

> As explained by one engineer to Reed, one of the reasons for the high cost of repairing the streets is that the space between the concrete and the ground presents problems of pump-ing liquid concrete between.

(We can only hope that Reed understands.)

> Gangs of white rowdies roamed the area last night, attacking cars bearing blacks with base-ball bats, bricks and stones.

(Who had the bats?)

> Three counties, Meigs, Pike and Vinton, get more than 85 percent from the state. Morgan gets 90.3 percent.

(How many counties?)

> Many of the 800 executives and clerical people will be transferred, and some probably will be eliminated.

(That's rough on people.)

Victims in the other cars were not hurt.
(Then why were they victims?)

Monday will be the first day of a new way of delivering an expanded hot-meal program to senior citizens in Genesse County.
(Would the "program" or the "meals" be delivered?)

The delegation. . . was welcomed by 20,000 mostly black supporters.
(What color was the other part of each supporter?)

Many of the players hovered around 5 feet 2.
(They must have looked funny up in the air like that.)

Parents protesting the closing of Briensburg School on Monday tried to . . .
(A misplaced time element leads to awkward construction. Did they protest on Monday only? Was the school closed on Monday? Or did they "try to" on Monday?)

Avoid suggesting false connections by combining unrelated ideas in a sentence.

A guard at the Allied Kid Co., he died at 7:10 a.m., about five minutes after one of the youths implicated in the attack was taken into custody.
(This implies that guards die at 7:10 a.m.)

Worn on a chain with swivel and button, this model retails at $39.95.
(How much does it cost if I just carry it loose in my pocket?)

"Because breath is so vital to life," Burmeister explained, "the field of inhalation therapy and the development of breathing equipment have become increasingly important in medical science today."
(It may be true that these things are increasingly important, but not because breath is vital to life. Breath was just as important to life 3,000 years ago as it is today.)

Stored in an air-conditioned room in lower Manhattan, the tapes contain information on the reading habits of 1 million Americans.
(The nature of the information on these tapes is not in any way related to the place of their storage or the condition of the air there. An easy way to edit this sentence is to start with the subject: "The tapes, stored in an air-conditioned room in lower Manhattan, contain information . . .")

Planned by Jones, Blake and Droza, Detroit architects, the new school has 18 classrooms in addition to such standard facilities as cafeteria and library.
(This implies it's natural to expect a school planned by that particular firm to have 18 classrooms and the other features.)

Completed three years ago, the plant is 301 feet by 339 feet and is a one-story structure containing . . .

(A plant of exactly that size could have been completed 50 years ago or yesterday.)

Unmarried, Jones is survived by his mother, Mrs. . . .

Born in Iowa, he worked on two newspapers in Illinois before coming to St. Louis.
(This particular error crops up often in obituaries.)

Avoid mixed metaphors.

Legislative Hall was swarming with lobbyists as the second session of the 121st General Assembly got under way Monday.

With lawmakers treading water while awaiting Gov. Elbert N. Carvel's state and budget messages, due Wednesday, lobbyists had a field day.

(In two paragraphs, the story pictured Legislative Hall as a beehive, a swimming pool and an athletic field.)

Breaking domestic ties with gold would make the nation's gold stock a real barometer of international fever for gold.

(Do you shove that barometer under your tongue or what? Try *thermometer.*)

They hope to unravel a sticky turn of events that was further complicated recently.

(Did you ever try to unravel glue, molasses, maple syrup or other similar strings or yarns?)

Nouns and Pronouns

PRONOUN-ANTECEDENT AGREEMENT

Every pronoun should clearly refer to a previous noun.   The previous **noun** a **pronoun** refers to is called its **antecedent.** A pronoun without a clear antecedent makes for a **vague pronoun reference,** which needs to be fixed—perhaps by restating the noun.

Vague: When Beth and Dana were young, she was always the one who was more adventurous.
(Which one?)

Clear: When Beth and Dana were young, Beth was always the one who was more adventurous.

Vague: The Smiths have two children. Both are 54.
(The Smiths or their children?)

Clear: The Smiths, both 54, have two children.

A pronoun and its antecedent should be the same number. If the antecedent is singular, the pronoun should be singular, also. If the antecedent is plural, the pronoun should be plural, too.

Wrong: The committee will make their decision next week.

Right: The committee will make its decision next week.
("Committee" is singular.)

PRONOUN CASE

Learn, understand, and remember the difference among subjective pronouns, objective pronouns and possessive pronouns.

- These pronouns are used as the **subject of a clause**: *I, you* (singular), *he, she, it, one, we, you* (plural), *they.* They are also used when the pronoun serves as a **predicate nominative**—a noun or pronoun following a **linking verb,** which is a verb that equates the subject with something else.

    Marilyn and I are close friends.
    ("I" is part of the compound subject.)

    It is I.
    ("I" is a predicate nominative here following the linking verb "is": "It" equals "I.")

- These pronouns are used as any **object** of a phrase or clause: *me, you* (singular), *him, her, it, one, us, you* (plural), *them.* They are also used as the **subject of an infinitive**—a noun or pronoun in front of a verb in its *to* form, such as *to go.*

    The lawyer questioned her.
    ("Her" is the direct object.)

    Many of us coal miners have black lung disease.
    ("Us" is the object of a preposition.)

    The Tigers wanted him to be traded.
    ("Him" is the subject of the infinitive.)

- These pronouns are **possessive:** *my, mine, your, yours, his, her, hers, its, one's, our, ours, your, yours, their, theirs, whose.* Possessive pronouns are also used as an adjective (a type of modifier) in front of a **gerund** (a noun formed from a verb ending in ing).

    My husband will mow the grass. (possessive)

    Joe likes mine better. (possessive)

    Her dropping the course was ridiculous, the professor said. (adjective before a gerund)

THAT VERSUS WHO, THAT VERSUS WHICH, WHO VERSUS WHOM

Learn, understand, and remember the different uses of relative pronouns. A **relative pronoun** is used to connect a subordinate clause to the main clause of a sentence. These words are relative pronouns, and they are often confused with each other: *that, who, whoever, whose, whom, whomever, which.*

When you find a relative pronoun in a sentence, first determine whether the sentence needs a word from the *that* family or the *who* family. If you determine the word should be from the *that* family, then choose between *that* and *which.* If you determine instead that the word should be from the *who* family, choose between *who* and *whom.* Here are these three steps outlined in more detail:

- To choose between the *that* and *who* families, ask whether the word refers to a person or to an animal with a pet name. If it refers to either of these, then you need a word from the *who* family. If it refers instead to a thing or an animal without a pet name, then you need a word from the *that* family.

  The book that she read . . .
  (The book is not a person, nor an animal with a pet name.)

  Spot, the dog who loved him . . .
  (Spot is an animal with a pet name.)

- If you need a word from the *that* family, choose between *that* and *which.* Ask yourself whether the word introduces something **parenthetical**—something not essential to the meaning of the sentence, like something you might put in parentheses. If it does, you need the word *which,* and you need to put a comma in front of *which* and another at the end of the parenthetical item unless that item ends the sentence. If the word doesn't introduce something parenthetical, you need the word *that* with no comma in front of it or after the clause it introduces.

  The deer that got away was a 10-pointer.
  ("That got away" is not parenthetical—it points to the exact deer we're talking about.)

  The deer, which was a 10-pointer, got away.
  ("Which was a 10-pointer" is parenthetical in this sentence. The main thought is that the deer got away—and by the way, it was a 10-pointer.)

- If you need a word from the *who* family, choose between *who* and *whom*—or *whoever* and *whomever,* for that matter. To do that, use this trick:

  1. Start reading the sentence only after the choice between *who* and *whom.*

  2. Finish the sentence using either *he* or *him,* wherever either would fit. If neither works, it's probably because there is a *to* before or after the choice. Move the *to* or cut it out, then try again.

  3. If *he* works, the answer is *who* or *whoever.* If *him* works, the answer is *whom* or *whomever.*

  Hand the fliers back to who brought them.
  (*He* brought them, so the word is *who.*)

  To whom should he hand them?
  (Should he hand them to *him*? Yes, so the word is *whom.*)

  After his decision to cancel the trip, he sent a letter to all of the officials whom he had invited to attend.
  (He had invited *them,* so the word is *whom.*)

POSSESSIVES AND PLURALS

One of the most common mistakes in written English involves putting an apostrophe where it doesn't belong. Many people just don't know how to write plurals and possessives.

The only time an apostrophe is used to make a simple, nonpossessive plural is when it's the plural of a single letter like A's. Here are some examples of common kinds of mistakes people make:

Wrong: Carbon arrow's are his favorite for archery practice.
Right: Carbon arrows are his favorite for archery practice.

Wrong: the decade of the 90's
Right: the decade of the '90s
("The '90s" isn't possessive here, so there's no apostrophe before the *s*. There is an apostrophe before the 9 because it takes the place, as in a contraction, of the missing "19" in 1990s.)

To make the plural of a noun ending in almost anything but *s*, add *s*. Exceptions: If the noun ends in *s* already, make the plural by adding *es*. If a common noun ends in *y*, make the plural by changing the *y* to *i* and adding *es*. If a proper noun ends in *y*, just add *s* without changing the *y* to *i*.

toys
(didn't end in *s*, so *s* was added)

gases
(ended in *s*, so *es* was added)

jellies
(common noun ended in *y*, so the *y* was changed to *i* before adding *es*)

the O'Reillys
(proper noun ended in *y*, so just add *s*)

To make the possessive of a noun not ending in *s*, add *'s*. To make the possessive of a noun ending in *s*, add just an apostrophe if the noun is a name, is plural or if the next word starts with an *s*. Otherwise, add *'s*.

Bill's car
(didn't end in *s*, so *'s* was added)

Jesus' home
(singular possessive name, already ended in *s*, so just an apostrophe was added)

the troops' weapons
(plural possessive, already ended in *s*, so just an apostrophe was added)

"*Sorry, but I'm going to have to issue you a summons for reckless grammar and driving without an apostrophe.*"

the hostess' seat
(singular possessive but next word starts with s, so just an apostrophe added)

the bus's windows
("Bus" ends in *s,* but it's not a name, is singular rather than plural, and the next word doesn't start with an *s.* So an apostrophe *s* is added.)

Here are a few examples of plurals and possessives using people's surnames:

	SINGULAR	PLURAL
Regular	Smith	Smiths
Possessive	Smith's	Smiths'
Regular	Jones	Joneses
Possessive	Jones'	Joneses'
Regular	Kelly	Kellys
Possessive	Kelly's	Kellys'

The only possessive pronouns that end in *'s* are those ending in *one* or *body*.

theirs   yours

anyone's   everybody's

Verbs

Verbs express action or a state of being.

PARALLEL CONSTRUCTION

Keep verbs and other items in a series in a parallel, or similar, form.

Wrong: We love to hunt, fishing and snowboards.

Right: We love hunting, fishing and snowboarding.

Wrong: First, read the instructions, then you should practice on your own.

Right: First, read the instructions, then practice on your own.

TENSES

Don't confuse the word *of* with the word *have* or its contraction *'ve*.

Wrong: could of, might of, must of, shall of, should of, will of, would of

Right: could have or could've, might have or might've, must have or must've, shall have or shall've, should have or should've, will have or will've, would have or would've

Know the correct principal parts of the commonly misused irregular verbs. The **principal parts of a verb** are the present tense, the past tense and the past participle. These are the basis for forming the six basic verb tenses in English. For most English verbs, you merely add *ed* to the end of the present tense to make both the past tense and past participle. (If the present tense ends in a consonant and the last syllable is stressed, double the consonant before adding *ed*.)

For example, take the verb *correct*. If we use the *you* form to illustrate, the present tense would be *you correct* and the past tense would be *you corrected*. The past participle form would also be *corrected: you have corrected*. From these three principal parts, all six of the following verb tenses can be formed:

Past Perfect: you had corrected

Past: you corrected

Present Perfect: you have corrected

Present: you correct

Future Perfect: you will have corrected

Future: you will correct

Although the three principal parts of all English verbs will let us form the verb tenses this way, some verbs in English are **irregular verbs**—they don't form the past or past participle with *ed.* Look over "Principal Parts of Common Irregular Verbs" on Page 147, and memorize any principal parts that you know you use incorrectly in conversation.

Use the correct verb tense to best describe the time when something took place. Here are some tips:

- Stick to one basic verb tense in a story as much as possible. Don't make a tense change for no apparent reason. For example, don't switch back and forth between *said* and *says* in the same story. Hard-news stories are usually written in past tense. Features are generally written in present tense. Of course, if a story requires writing at some point about something that happened earlier or later than something else, then it's appropriate to switch the verb tense.

- You know the order *past, present, future.* That's half of the six tenses right there. Next, remember that there's a tense that describes something further in the past than each one. In other words, older than the *past* is the *past perfect.* Between the past and the *present* is the *present perfect.* And between the present and the *future,* there's the *future perfect.*

  If that seems confusing—as in how can something be further in the past than the past?—think of it this way: If you're writing about something that happened in the past and you want to mention something that happened even earlier, use the past perfect. Follow a similar rule for the other perfect tenses:

  Past: The City Council approved the antismoking ordinance in August.

  Even Earlier: The City Council had considered the matter for three months when it approved the antismoking ordinance in August.

  Present: The City Council considers proposals at each meeting.

  Earlier: The City Council has considered proposals at each meeting.

  Future: The City Council will hold a retreat in the fall.

  But Before Then: The City Council will have held a retreat in the fall before it will start (or starts) its new term.

- Many editors insist that when you paraphrase after the attribution *said,* you must change the tense of the original remark. A statement that was originally in present tense will then be paraphrased in past tense (*correct* becomes *corrected*), past tense becomes past perfect (*corrected* becomes *had corrected*), and *will* in the future tense or future perfect becomes *would* (*will correct* becomes *would correct, will have corrected* becomes *would have corrected*).

  Original in Present Tense: "I'm pleased."

  Paraphrased in Past Tense: She said she was pleased.

Original in Past Tense: "I corrected the proofs."
Paraphrased in Past-Perfect Tense: She said she had corrected the proofs.

PASSIVE VOICE

Use verbs in the active voice rather than the passive voice. In the **active voice,** the subject does something:

The president fired the secretary of state.

But in the **passive voice,** the subject is not the one acting; rather, the subject is being passively acted upon:

The secretary of state was fired by the president.

The passive voice is wordier and less direct. Sometimes, it's even less clear, as when the actual doer is left out entirely:

The secretary of state was fired.

For these reasons, it's generally better to avoid passive voice.

Use passive voice only when you want to stress the receiver of the action rather than the doer. This is especially applicable in a crime or accident story:

The victim was assaulted and robbed as she left the convenience store.

CONDITIONAL AND SUBJUNCTIVE MOODS

Learn to use the conditional mood. Use *could, might, should* or *would* instead of *can, may, shall* or *will* when something is not now true but could, might or would be true under a certain condition. This is called the **conditional mood.**

Wrong: The bill will cut taxes.
Right: The bill would cut taxes.
(It would if passed into law.)

Learn to use the subjunctive mood. With verbs that convey a demand, desire, doubt, hope, prayer or wish, use the **subjunctive mood** form of a verb to express a condition contrary to fact.

Wrong: I wish I was rich.
Right: I wish I were rich.
(But I'm not.)

Wrong: If she was here, something would be done.
Right: If she were here, something would be done.
(But she's not here.)

Principal Parts of Common Irregular Verbs

In this list, the *present tense* is shown first, then the *past tense* and finally the *past participle*.

awake, awoke, awakened
bear, bore, borne
bid (offer), bid, bid
bid (command), bade, bidden
break, broke, broken
bring, brought, brought
broadcast, broadcast, broadcast
burst, burst, burst
cling, clung, clung
come, came, come
dive, dived, dived
do, did, done
drink, drank, drunk
drive, drove, driven
drown, drowned, drowned
eat, ate, eaten
fall, fell, fallen
flow, flowed, flowed
fly (to soar), flew, flown
fly (hit a baseball high), flied, flied
forbid, forbade, forbidden
forsake, forsook, forsaken
get, got, got or gotten
go, went, gone
hang (suspend), hung, hung
hang (execute), hanged, hanged
have, had, had
hide, hid, hidden
kneel, knelt or kneeled, knelt or kneeled
lay (set down), laid, laid

lead, led, led
lie (recline), lay, lain
pay, paid, paid
plead, pleaded, pleaded
prove, proved, proved (proven is only an
   adjective)
raise, raised, raised
ring, rang, rung
rise, rose, risen
see, saw, seen
set (place or put down; also, hens, cement
   and the sun set), set, set
shake, shook, shaken
shine, shone, shone
show, showed, showed or shown
shrink, shrank, shrunk
sit (seat oneself), sat, sat
slay, slew, slain
spring, sprang, sprung
steal, stole, stolen
strive, strove, striven
swear, swore, sworn
swim, swam, swum
swing, swung, swung
tear, tore, torn
tread, trod, trodden or trod
wake, woke, waked
weave, wove, woven
wring, wrung, wrung

Wrong: If dissent is treason, then we've lost our freedom.
Right: If dissent be treason, then we've lost our freedom.
(The writer is suggesting dissent is not treason.)

Wrong: They demand that he leaves.
Right: They demand that he leave.
(A demand requires the subjunctive.)

Note that the past tense of the subjunctive for the verb *to be* is always *were,* but the present tense of the subjunctive for *to be* is always *be.* For all other verbs, the subjunctive is used only in present tense and is always the infinitive minus the *to.* That means for most verbs, the only different subjunctive form is the third-person singular, which typically just drops the *s.*

SUBJECT-VERB AGREEMENT

A singular subject needs a singular verb. A plural subject needs a plural verb.

Wrong: The monotony of the concrete walls painted in dull green and blue are broken only . . .
Right: The monotony of the concrete walls painted in dull green and blue is broken only . . .
(Monotony . . . is . . .)

Wrong: A two-thirds vote of both houses of Congress and ratification by three-quarters of the states is necessary.
Right: A two-thirds vote of both houses of Congress and ratification by three-quarters of the states are necessary.
(A vote . . . and ratification . . . are necessary.)

The verb must agree in number with the subject. Ignore any other noun or pronoun. It's common for a sentence to have a plural object of a preposition between the subject and verb or a plural predicate nominative after a linking verb. But remember, the verb agrees with the subject—not anything else.

Wrong: The majority of the senators favor the measure.
Right: The majority of the senators favors the measure.
("Majority" is the subject and is singular, so the verb must be singular. "Senators" is the object of the preposition, so the verb does not have to agree with it.)

Wrong: An American Bar Association team, in addition to a citizens' panel, have recommended this.
Right: An American Bar Association team, in addition to a citizens' panel, has recommended this.
("Team" is the subject, so the verb must be "has." Parenthetical material should be ignored in choosing whether a verb should be singular or plural.)

Wrong: The panel are Ann, Steve and Craig.
Right: The panel is Ann, Steve and Craig.
(Make the verb agree with the subject, "panel," which is singular. The predicate nominative is "Ann, Steve and Craig.")

A conjunction in the subject influences the number of the verb. A conjunction is a word that connects other words, phrases, clauses or sentences.

- If the subject contains the word *and* connecting two or more items, the verb should be plural, unless the *and* is part of the name of a single item.

  Fran and Carol are here.
  The potatoes and gravy tastes great!
  ("Potatoes and gravy" is considered one dish.)

- If the subject contains the word *or*, the verb should be singular unless one of the items it connects is plural. In that case, the verb agrees in number with the nearest of the items.

  A degree in journalism or English is necessary for the job.
  One or two guides are available.

- If the subject contains the words *along with, as well as, in addition to, including, such as, together with* or any other parenthetical words or phrases set off by commas or dashes, the number of the subject is not affected.

  Joseph, as well as Melissa, is a Republican.

Learn the confusing singular words that are subject–verb stumbling blocks.

- **Collective nouns** like *committee, council, jury* and *team* normally take a singular verb. The exception is when the focus is on the committee members (plural) rather than the committee as a unit (singular). Use the plural form of the verb when the members that make up the collective noun are *not* acting in agreement.

  Wrong: The committee have decided on an agenda.
  Right: The committee has decided on an agenda.
  (The singular verb "has" is used because "the committee" is acting as a single unit.)

  Wrong: The committee disagrees with each other.
  Right: The committee disagree with each other.
  (The plural verb "disagree" is used because "the committee" is *not* acting as a single unit.)

- These **uncountable nouns** (nouns with no separate singular and plural forms) are singular even though they end in *s: apparatus, athletics, civics, economics, kudos, linguistics, measles, mumps, news, shambles, summons, whereabouts.*

- These **indefinite pronouns** are normally singular, even though some of them may sound plural: *another, anybody, anyone, anything, each one, everybody, everyone, everything, little, much, nobody, no one, nothing, other, somebody, someone, something.*

- The word *none* normally means *no one* or *not one*, so it usually takes a singular verb.

Wrong: None were going.
Right: None was going.
(No one was going, or not one was going.)

Occasionally, *none* means *no two* and will take a plural verb.

Wrong: None on the committee agrees.
Right: None on the committee agree.
(No two on the committee agree.)

- *Either* and *neither* are singular by themselves, but in the expressions *either . . . or* and *neither . . . nor,* the verb should agree in number with the closer noun or pronoun.

Wrong: Neither were right.
Right: Neither was right.
(By itself, "neither" is singular.)

Wrong: There are two things that either the Sloanes or Hollenbach have.
Right: There are two things that either the Sloanes or Hollenbach has.
("Hollenbach" is closer to the verb "has" and is singular, so the verb should be singular, as well.)

- The words *majority, number* and *total* are singular when preceded by the word *the.* But they become plural if preceded by the word *a.*

The majority of voters is in favor.
A majority of voters are in favor.

- Fractions and percentages are singular when referring to the amount of one thing but plural when referring to a number of things. A helpful guide is that what the fraction or percentage refers to is often stated immediately after, as the object of a preposition, so make the verb agree with the object of that preposition.

Half of the work is done.
("Work," the object of the preposition "of," is singular, so "is" is singular.)

Half of the students were there.
("Students," the object of the preposition "of," is plural, so the verb "were" is plural.)

Learn these confusing plural words that are subject–verb stumbling blocks.

- These uncountable nouns are plural: *assets, barracks, earnings, goods, odds, pants, pliers, proceeds, remains, riches, scissors, shears, tactics, thanks, tongs, wages.*
- These indefinite pronouns are plural: *both, couple, few, many, others, several.*

Use your own judgment with these confusing words, which can be either singular or plural.

- These uncountable nouns are sometimes singular, sometimes plural: *ethics, headquarters, mechanics, politics, savings, series, species, statistics.*
- These indefinite pronouns are sometimes singular, sometimes plural: *all, any, more, most, plenty, some, such.*

Modifiers

Modifiers are words that describe other words; adjectives, adverbs, and interjections are modifiers.

ADJECTIVES VERSUS ADVERBS

Don't use an adjective in a sentence when an adverb is required. Many people mistakenly use an adjective in place of an adverb when they're describing the manner in which something is done.

- **Adjectives** modify a noun, pronoun or gerund.
- **Adverbs** modify a verb, adjective or another adverb.

Look at what's being modified, then pick the appropriate kind of modifier.

Wrong: The car ran smooth.
Right: The car ran smoothly.
(The modifier tells *how* the car "ran." It modifies the verb, not the car itself, so an adverb is needed.)

Once you can tell whether the adverb or the adjective form is required, how do you tell the two apart?

- Most adverbs end in *ly*. Exceptions include *well, very, quite, rather.*
- A few other words that are *not* adverbs end in *ly*: *friendly, lonely, manly, surly* (adjectives); *family* (noun).

FORMS AND PLACEMENT OF MODIFIERS

Use the proper form of a modifier.

- The **positive form** for a simple modifier with no comparison.

Adjectives: tall; controversial
Adverb: quickly

- The **comparative form** when two things are compared.

  Adjectives: taller; less controversial, more controversial
  Adverbs: less quickly, more quickly

- The **superlative form** when three or more things are compared.

  Adjectives: tallest; least controversial, most controversial
  Adverbs: least quickly, most quickly

Notice that shorter adjectives form the comparative by adding *er* to the end of the positive and form the superlative by adding *est* to the end of the positive. Longer adjectives, as well as adverbs, tend to form the comparative by adding *less* or *more* in front of the positive and form the superlative by adding *least* or *most* in front of the positive.

Some words, however, have irregular comparative and superlative forms:

good, better, best
well, better, best
little, less, least
much, more, most

Place modifiers next to what they describe. If you don't follow this rule, you'll end up with the error called a **misplaced modifier.** The most common misplaced modifier is the **dangling participle.**

Wrong: If convicted of the assault-and-battery charge, the judge will impose the sentence.
("If convicted . . ." applies to the defendant, not the judge, so this is a misplaced modifier.)

Right: The judge will impose the sentence if the defendant is convicted of the assault-and-battery charge.

Wrong: Besides being cut on the left cheek and bloodied in the nose, Zeck's wallet was stolen with $825.
(Zeck was "cut and bloodied . . . ," not his wallet, so this is a misplaced modifier.)

Right: Zeck's left cheek was cut, his nose was bloodied, and his wallet with $825 was stolen.

Wrong: Trying to arrest the man, the suspect fled from police.
("Trying to arrest the man" is a misplaced modifying phrase because it's next to "the suspect," but the suspect was not trying to make the arrest.)

Right: The suspect fled from police as they tried to arrest him.

The last example above is also an example of a dangling participle because "trying to arrest the man" is a modifying phrase built on the *ing* form of a verb—

a **participle**, in other words—but it dangles because it's not next to what it modifies.

COORDINATE VERSUS COMPOUND MODIFIERS

Coordinate modifiers are equal adjectives that take a comma between them. The test is whether you could reverse them and put *and* between them. Exceptions: Don't use a comma if one or both of them refers to age, color, ethnicity, material, nationality, number or race.

> the tall, skinny boy
> ("Tall" and "skinny" can be reversed with *and* between them, so use a comma.)

> the red brick building
> (Red is a color and brick a material, so don't use a comma.)

Compound modifiers are an adverb (or another word acting as an adverb) modifying an adjective, with the two together modifying a noun or pronoun. Punctuate with a hyphen between the adverb and adjective. Exceptions: Don't use a comma after the word *very* or after an *ly* adverb.

> pressure-cooker situation
> ("Pressure" modifies "cooker," and together they modify "situation." So use a hyphen.)

> heavily guarded entrance
> ("Heavily" is an *ly* adverb, so don't use a hyphen.)

> family-oriented event
> ("Family" is a noun, not an *ly* adverb. It modifies "oriented," and together they modify "event," so use a hyphen.)

Interjections

An **interjection** is a word that expresses emotion and often takes an exclamation mark—one only!—either immediately after or at the end of the sentence it introduces.

> Ouch! That hurts.
> Ouch! That hurts!
> Ouch, that hurts!

When the interjection represents only a mild emotion, an exclamation mark is not used.

> Gee, I don't know.

Connecting Words

PREPOSITIONS

A **preposition** is a connecting word that shows a relationship between its object and some other word in the sentence. Most prepositions show a spatial relationship, so if you think of a bird and some trees, you can think of a number of prepositions: The bird can fly *to* the trees, *from* the trees, *under* the trees, *over* the trees, *through* the trees and *around* the trees. All of the words before *the trees* are prepositions. In addition to spatial relationships, some prepositions show time relationships, such as *before* and *after,* and some show agency, such as *by* and *for.*

Don't end a clause or sentence with a preposition.

> *Wrong:* National security is something he said he cares deeply about.
> *Right:* National security is something about which he said he cares deeply.

The object of the preposition should be in objective case if it's a pronoun. This doesn't change with a plural object of the preposition.

> *Wrong:* Give it to I.
> *Wrong:* Give it to myself.
> *Right:* Give it to me.
> ("Me" is the object of the preposition "to.")

> *Wrong:* Give it to Sheila and I.
> *Wrong:* Give it to Sheila and myself.
> *Right:* Give it to Sheila and me.
> ("Sheila and me" is the plural object of the preposition "to.")

In a headline, a prepositional phrase should not be split over two lines.

> *Wrong:* Floods recede in
>   rural Missouri
> *Right:* Floods recede
>   in rural Missouri

But don't split apart on different lines a verb from a preposition that's part of the verb.

> *Wrong:* Husband: Let's work
>   out our marriage problems
> *Right:* Husband: Let's work out
>   our marriage problems

A preposition is part of the verb when it changes the meaning of the verb, as in the example just cited. *Work out* means something different from merely *work.*

Separate proper nouns. Instead of letting them run together, separate proper nouns with a preposition, or otherwise move them apart in the sentence.

Wrong: He married Filipa Franks June 10, 1999.

Right: He married Filipa Franks on June 10, 1999.

Right: He was married June 10, 1999, to Filipa Franks.

Repeat a preposition in a parallel construction if it will avoid confusion.

Wrong: The prime minister said she would push for lower interest rates and tax cuts. (Does she want the "tax cuts" lower, as well?)

Right: The prime minister said she would push for lower interest rates and for tax cuts.

CONJUNCTIONS AND CONJUNCTIVE ADVERBS

Understanding conjunctions and conjunctive adverbs will help you make clearer transitions between ideas and help you correctly punctuate sentences.

It's OK to start a sentence with a conjunction like *and* or *but*. It's a common myth that you can't start a sentence with *and* or *but*, but there's no such grammar rule. You may start a sentence with any kind of conjunction, but it seems particularly odd to think you can't start one with a coordinating conjunction, like *and* or *but*, because by definition a **coordinating conjunction** is one that begins an *independent clause*—one that can stand alone as a complete sentence.

The comma goes in front of a coordinating conjunction, not behind it.

Wrong: The FBI arrived at the scene and, agents began gathering evidence.

Right: The FBI arrived at the scene, and agents began gathering evidence.

Put a comma between a dependent clause and an independent clause only when the dependent clause comes first.

Wrong: They went home early, because the power went out.

Right: They went home early because the power went out.

Wrong: Because the power went out they went home early.

Right: Because the power went out, they went home early.

If you're unsure whether a **clause** is independent or dependent, ask yourself whether it could stand alone as a complete sentence. The word that begins the clause can also help you decide. These are common coordinating conjunctions that begin an **independent clause** (*one that could stand alone as a complete sentence*):

and	but
for	nor
or	yet

A **subordinating conjunction,** like any of the following, tells you what follows is a **dependent clause** *(one that could not stand alone as a complete sentence):*

although	as
because	if
since	until
whether	while

Learn how to use conjunctive adverbs. A **conjunctive adverb** (an adverb joining two clauses) in the middle of a sentence needs a semicolon in front of it and a comma behind it. Better still, in journalism, make the conjunctive adverb the first word of a second sentence with a comma behind it.

Wrong: The Jackson City Council approved the plan, meanwhile the county had second thoughts.

Right: The Jackson City Council approved the plan; meanwhile, the county had second thoughts.

Best for Journalism: The Jackson City Council approved the plan. Meanwhile, the county had second thoughts.

Some of the most common conjunctive adverbs include:

also	instead
as a result	in the first place
at the same time	likewise
besides	more important
consequently	moreover
first, second, third, etc.	nevertheless
for example	on the contrary
for this reason	otherwise
furthermore	so
however	still
in addition	then
indeed	therefore

Note that the same word may be used as either a regular adverb or a conjunctive adverb.

He said that shouldn't have stopped him; however, it did.

("However" is used as a conjunctive adverb, with a semicolon before it and a comma after it.)

He didn't, however, agree.

("However" is used as a regular adverb, requiring only commas around it to set it off as parenthetical.)

Know which words always go together as correlative conjunctions. Some coordinating conjunctions are always used in pairs. There are called **correlative conjunctions.**

as . . . as	neither . . . nor
not so . . . as	not only . . . but also
either . . . or	if . . . then

USAGE

Correct **usage** is mainly a matter of vocabulary. But we're not talking about mastering big words that people seldom use in conversation. We're talking mainly about recognizing everyday words we use—and sometimes misuse—in conversations and knowing how to use them correctly.

Vocabulary contributes to clearer communication. When some people think *prioritize,* for example, they think about making something a priority rather than its actual meaning, to rank items. No wonder instructions are likely to be misunderstood. Other times, though, correct usage and grammar seem to act more like signals to your audience that you're educated because you've mastered the King's English rather than succumbing to colloquialisms and slang. Before you put that down as superficial, realize that correct usage helps establish the credibility of a publication or station.

The problem is that language is always changing, and today's usage or grammar error may become tomorrow's preferred way. The reverse is also true, and today's preferred usage may come to sound stilted to your audience. But until a change becomes widely recognized—not only by the general public but also by writers, editors, teachers, stylebooks and usage manuals—it's usually safer to revise the wording to reflect current standards.

The two main usage problems are *confused words* and *misused idioms.*

Confused Words

Good reporters are meticulous in presenting the facts for a story. Others are not so precise in their choice of words. By habit, they write *comprise* when they mean *compose, affect* when they want *effect, credible* for *creditable.* They use *include,* then list all the elements.

Each time a word is misused, it loses some of its value as a precision tool. AP reported that "U.S. officials connived with ITT." There was no *connivance,* which means closing one's eyes to wrongdoing. The precise word would have been *conspired,* if, indeed, that is the charge.

Note these examples that got by the copy desk:

He has been an "intricate part of the general community."
(The writer meant *integral,* meaning essential.)

The two officers are charged with dispersing corporate funds.
(The word is *disburse*—to pay out, to expend. *Disperse* means to scatter in various directions, to distribute widely.)

A story indicating that a man might not be qualified for his job says: "Miller refutes all that," and then he says why he is capable.
(*Denies* would have been much better because *refutes* means he proved the charges wrong.)

A football pass pattern was referred to as a "flair out."
(*Flair* means a natural talent or aptitude. The word is *flare* or expansion outward in shape or configuration.)

Mrs. Reece, a spritely woman . . .
(She may be a *sprite*—an elf or pixie—but what the writer probably meant was *sprightly*—full of life.)

His testimony about the night preceding the crime was collaborated, in part, by his mother.
(*corroborated,* perhaps?)

The MSD could be the biggest benefactor in Kentucky under a . . . reimbursement program.
(It should be *beneficiary,* one who receives. The *benefactor* is the giver.)

Other terms often misused:

- A lot—two words; better yet, change to *much* or *many.*
- Adopted, passed—Resolutions are *adopted* or *approved;* bills are *passed.* In legislative jargon, *passed* also can mean *passed by for the day* or *for that meeting.*
- Affect, effect—For a noun meaning result, use *effect.* As a verb, *affect* means influence, and *effect* means cause.
- Aggravate, annoy, irritate—The first means *to make worse.* The second and third mean *to incite, provoke or bother, but the third also means to make the skin itch.*
- Although, though, while—*Although* is used at the start of a clause, *though* is used in the middle. *While* may be used to show contrast, also, but should only be used when it means "at the same time."
- Amateur, novice—An *amateur* is a nonprofessional. A *novice* is a beginner.

- Among, between—*Among* is used for three or more. *Between* is used for two.
- Amount, number—*Amount* indicates the general quantity. *Number* indicates an enumerable quantity.
- Amused, bemused, confused—No one confuses *amused* and *confused,* but many people think *bemused* means slightly amused. Instead, it means confused. It's better to avoid the confusion by not using *bemused.*
- Avenge, revenge—Use *avenge* for another, *revenge* for self.
- Bale, bail, bond—A farmer's hay is *baled;* water is *bailed* out of a boat; a prisoner is released *on bail.* (*Bond* is cash or property given as a security for an appearance or for some performance.)
- Because of, due to, since—These can mean basically the same thing, but *due to* must always follow a *to be* verb, and *since* is best used when the stress is on something happening after something else rather than in the sense of cause.
- Biannual, biennial—The first means *twice a year.* The second means *every two years.* The copy editor could help the reader by substituting "every six months" for *biannual* and "every other year" for *biennial.*
- Bills, laws, legislation—A *bill* is proposed legislation. If it's passed, it becomes a law. Legislation is the law enacted by a legislative body. Do not write or say, as is often heard, "The president will send legislation to Congress." He may propose legislation, but it only becomes legislation if Congress passes it.
- Canvas, canvass—The first is a cloth. The second means *to solicit.*
- Celebrant, celebrator—A *celebrant* presides over a religious rite. A *celebrator* celebrates.
- Center around—Something can be centered *in,* centered *at* or centered *on,* but it cannot be centered *around.* If you want to use *around,* try "revolves around."
- Collision—Two objects can *collide* only when both are in motion and going— usually but not always—in opposite directions. It is not a *collision* when one car is standing still. If a car *collided* with a power pole, it must have been in the bed of a moving truck.
- Compared to, compared with—Use the first to stress similarities. Use the second to stress differences.
- Complement, compliment—The first means to complete something by adding what's missing. The second refers to a flattering statement.
- Compose, comprise, constitute—The whole *is composed of* the parts; the whole *comprises* the parts; the parts *constitute* the whole.
- Concert, recital—Two or more performers give a *concert.* One performer gives a *recital.*

- Continuous, continual—If it rains steadily every day for a week, it rains *continuously.* If it rains only part of every day for a week, it rains *continually* or *intermittently.*
- Dais, podium, lectern—A speaker stands on a *dais* or *podium* but behind a *lectern.*
- Damage, destroy—The first refers to partial destruction. The second refers to complete destruction. It is wrong, then, to say something was "partially destroyed" and redundant to say it was "completely destroyed."
- Ecology, environment—*Ecology* can mean the interrelationship of organisms and their environment but more properly it refers to the science that studies that. *Environment* means surroundings.
- Enormity, enormousness—The first means evil. The second means hugeness. A common error is to speak of the *enormity* of a task or issue that is not particularly evil, as in "The *enormity* of her new responsibilities overwhelmed her."
- Etc.—The abbreviation for the Latin *et cetera* is *etc.,* not *ect.*
- Farther, further—*Farther* is used for literal distance. *Further* is used to mean deeper.
- Fewer, less—*Fewer* is used with plural nouns. *Less* is used for singular nouns. *Less* is also used with plural amounts of money or weight. A trick is to remember that *fewer* is used for things about which you could ask, "How many?" while *less* is used for things about which you could ask, "How much?"
- Flaunt, flout—The first means *to wave or flutter showily.* The second means *to mock or treat with contempt.* "The students *flouted* the authority of the school board."
- Flier, flyer—*The AP Stylebook* prefers the first for either aviators or handbills, reserving the second only for proper names, as in the names of some buses, trains, bicycles or wagons.
- Flounder, founder—Horses *flounder*—struggle, thrash about—in the mud. Ships *founder* or sink. Of course, horses can *founder* when they become disabled from overeating.
- Gender, sex—Originally, *gender* referred to whether a noun or pronoun was feminine, masculine or neuter. In recent decades, it has more commonly been used to refer to sex-based roles in society—a sociological distinction. The word *sex,* not *gender,* is the better word to refer to biological differences.
- Grant, subsidy—A *grant* is money given to public companies. A *subsidy* is help for a private enterprise.

- Grisly, gristly, grizzly —"Karmel begins her work in a valley of shadows that deepens and darkens as she heaps one grizzly happening upon the next." One *grizzly* heaped upon the next produces only two angry or aroused bears. The word the writer wants is *grisly, meaning gruesome. Tough meat can be described as gristly for having lots of gristle.*

- Half-mast, half-staff— The first term refers to a flag lowered on a ship or at a naval base. The second refers to any other flag that's lowered.

- Hardy, hearty—A story of four visiting police officers from Africa said they expressed appreciation for their *hardy* welcome. If that's what they said, they meant *hearty. Hardy means bold or rugged, and hearty means jovial or nourishing.*

- Healthful, healthy—The first refers to something that promotes good health. The second refers to a person, plant or animal that has good health. A common mistake is to speak of "eating *healthy*" when what is meant is a person eats a *healthful* diet.

- Hopefully—This is incorrect for *it is hoped* or *I hope.* It really means *in a hopeful manner.*

- If, whether—*If* is used for conditions (if A, then B). *Whether* is used for choices ("I don't know whether I'll go"). Notice *whether* does not require *or not* following it. Many people use *if* when *whether* is needed. To get the distinction right, see whether you could put *whether* in the sentence. If yes, *whether* is the right word. If no, then leave it as *if.*

- Impassable, impossible—The first is *that which cannot be passed.* The second is *that which can't suffer or be made to show signs of emotion.*

- Imply, infer—The speaker does the *implying,* and the listener does the *inferring.*

- Its, it's—*Its* is possessive. *It's* means *it is* or *it has.*

- Lay, lie—The first means to set or put something down. Its principal parts are *lay, laid, (have) laid,* and *(is) laying.* The second means to rest or recline. Its principal parts are *lie, lay, (have) lain,* and *(is) lying.* A common mistake is to use the first verb in place of the second.

- Mantel, mantle—The first is a shelf. The second is a cloak.

- Mean, median—*Mean* is the average. If the high is 80 and the low is 50, the mean is 65. *Median* means that half are above a certain point and half are below.

- More than, over—*The AP Stylebook* used to insist that *over* should be used only in a spatial sense, and *more than* should be used for anything else, as in

"The proposal costs *more than* (not *over*) $3 million." AP no longer insists on this, but many editors still prefer it.

- Oral, verbal—All language is *verbal*—of words. But only *oral* language is spoken.

- People, persons—A *person* is a human being. *People* is the plural.

- Prejudice, prejudiced—The first means bigotry. The second means bigoted. Many speakers and writers make the error of leaving off the *d* in the second.

- Pretense, pretext—Both refer to putting on a false front, but the first refers to the false show itself. The second refers to a false motive behind it. Someone's flattery may be a *pretense* that she likes someone when she doesn't. But if someone acts under a false *pretext*, he gives a reason other than the real one.

- Principal, principle—The first means main and by extension the supervisor of a school, who in England, was the main teacher. "The principal is your pal," is a mnemonic many have used to remember this spelling. The second means a rule or law.

- Raise, rise—The first means to lift something up. Its principal parts are *raise, raised, (have) raised,* and *(is) raising.* The second means to get up. Its principal parts are *rise, rose, (have) risen,* and *(is) rising.*

- Set, sit—To *set* means to put or lay something down. Its principal parts are *set, set, (have) set,* and *(is) setting.* To *sit* means to put one's bottom down, as in a chair. Its principal parts are *sit, sat, (have) sat,* and *(is) sitting.*

- Sewage, sewerage—*Sewage* is human waste, sometimes called *municipal* or *sanitary waste. Sewerage* is the system to carry away sewage, which goes to *sewerage* (not *sewage*) *plants. Industrial waste* is the waste from factories. Some cities have *storm sewers* to carry away rainwater and have *sanitary sewers* for sewage.

- Stationary, stationery—The first means not moving. The second means writing paper.

- Supposed to—Note the *d.*

- Sustenance, subsistence—"The two survived despite little besides melted snow for *subsistence.*" No wonder they almost starved. The word is *sustenance. Sustenance* is food. *Subsistence* is survival or means of support.

- Their, there, they're—*Their* is possessive. *There* is used in the phrase "there are" or as the direction ("over there"). *They're* means they are.

- To, too, two—*To* is the preposition ("to the trees"). *Too* is an adverb meaning also or excessive ("That's too much, too"). *Two* is the number.

- Used to—Note the *d*.
- Your, you're—*Your* is possessive. *You're* means *you are.*

Misused Idioms

Careless use of the **idiom** (the grammatical structure peculiar to our language) occurs often in the news. Usually, the fault lies in the prepositions or conjunctions. In the following examples, the bracketed word is the preferred usage.

Three times as many Americans were killed than [*as*] in any similar period.
It remains uncertain as to when the deadline for the first payment will be.
(Omit *as to.*)

The economist accused him with [*of*] failing to make a decision.
(You charge somebody with blundering, but you accuse him *of* it.)

He said the guns are against the law except under [*in*] certain specified situations.
(But *under* conditions or circumstances.)

Dressen is no different than [*from*] other experts.
(*Different* may only be followed by *than* when introducing a clause: "The patient is no different than he was yesterday.")

Five men were pelted by [*with*] stones.
The reason for the new name is because the college's mission has been changed.
(". . . is *that* the college's mission has been changed.")

He said he would not call on [*for*] assistance from police except as a last resort.
(*Call on* the police, but *call* the police *for* assistance.)

At other times, the fault lies in entire phrases that must be used verbatim to be idiomatic:

These men and women could care less about Bush's legislative magic.
(The correct phrase is "couldn't care less.")

Gerunds, but not present participles acting as adjectives, require the possessive:

It was the first instance of a city [*city's*] losing its funds.
He said he didn't know anything about Hollenbach [*Hollenbach's*] interceding in his behalf.

An example of a present participle used in a similar context is:

I do not like the man standing on the corner.
(The possessive is not required because *standing on the corner* is used to identify *man.*)

↗ STYLE

By far, the main stylebook American journalists need to study and learn is the one published by the Associated Press, *The Associated Press Stylebook and Briefing on Media Law.* United Press International has a similar one, and many large newspapers have their own. Some newspapers—such as *The New York Times, Los Angeles Times* and *The Washington Post*—have published their stylebooks and distribute them nationwide to bookstores.

If you're familiar with *The AP Stylebook,* you'll find when you look in any of the others that the rules usually differ from AP's in relatively few major ways. If you know AP **style,** it's easy to learn a local style. Just look for two things: where the local stylebook disagrees with AP and any entries that supplement AP. Often, the main differences are not disagreements but rather the addition of entries such as place names that have a strictly local value. A number of newspapers, in fact, save money by publishing only a pamphlet of local additions and exceptions to use alongside *The AP Stylebook.*

To learn AP style, begin with the following list of rules any journalist should know. This will cover the most common rules—about 80 to 90 percent of those you regularly use—and the grouping here will make learning far easier than the alphabetical listing in *The AP Stylebook.*

When you have these rules mastered, read through *The AP Stylebook* at least once to get a feel for what's there. Sure, it's like reading a dictionary, but how will you know what to look up if you don't have a passing familiarity with what's in it and where? Read a few entries a day until you get through it all.

Journalists with a special interest in sports or business should also study carefully the chapters on the topics following the main section of the stylebook. In fact, it's a good idea to note typical style issues that arise commonly in all the different types of stories you edit. We'll look at some of those in Chapter 7.

Abbreviations and Symbols

- Days of the week are never abbreviated.
- Months are abbreviated only when followed by a date during the month: Feb. 2 or Feb. 2, 2008, but not February 2008. The months with five letters or less are not abbreviated: *March, April, May, June, July.*
- States are abbreviated only when following the name of a city. The abbreviations used are not the two-letter postal abbreviations (*MI* for Michigan), but rather the older, more easily recognized abbreviations (*Mich.* for Michigan). The following eight states are never abbreviated: *Alaska, Hawaii, Maine, Utah, Texas, Ohio, Iowa* and *Idaho.*

- See "Addresses" on Page 171 for which names of thoroughfares are abbreviated and when.
- Most initials of three letters or more do not take periods. Exceptions: *c.o.d., U.S.S.R.*
- Use a dollar sign ($) with any actual dollar amount, but always write out the word *cents* rather than using the cents symbol.
- Always write out *percent* rather than using the symbol, except in a headline if the space is tight.
- An ampersand (&) is always written as *and* unless it's part of a company's actual name.

Capitalization

- Common nouns are lowercase: *dog, apple.*
- Proper nouns are uppercase: *Fido, Sears.*
- Names of months and days of the week are capitalized, but seasons are not: *Wednesday, January, spring.*
- Actual names of races are capitalized, but colors are not: *Caucasian, white.*
- Capitalize names of departments in government, but for departments anywhere else, capitalize only the parts that would be proper nouns by themselves: *State Department, Department of Defense, Fire Department, English department, history department, returns department.*
- For names of varieties of plants and animals or of particular foods, capitalize only the proper noun: *German shepherd, MacIntosh apple* (the fruit—the computer has a lowercase *i*), *red delicious apple, Boston cream pie.*
- Political party names are capitalized, but not the names of philosophies unless based on a proper noun: *Democratic Party, socialist philosophy, Marxism.*
- Capitalize regions, but lowercase mere directions: *the South, Southern accent, driving south.* Exception: Do not capitalize a region in front of a proper noun, unless that forms the actual name or a place well-known around the country: *southeast Michigan, southern United States, South Carolina, Southern California.*
- Many product names that people think are generic terms (common nouns) are actually trade names (proper nouns) and should be capitalized: *Band-Aid, Dumpster, Frisbee, Jell-O, Kitty Litter, Kleenex, Scotch tape, Styrofoam, Vaseline, Velcro, Windbreaker, Xerox.* For more examples, see "Avoiding Trademark Infringement" on Page 110.
- Oddly, AP lowercases pronouns for God or Jesus, but capitalizes *Mass* and *Communion.* It capitalizes *pope* only in front of the pope's name.

Numbers

- Generally speaking, the numbers zero through nine are written out, and the numbers 10 and above are written as numerals.
- Exceptions to the general rule about numbers: Use numerals, even if less than 10, with addresses, ages, clothes sizes, dates, dimensions, money, percentages, recipe amounts, speeds, temperatures, times, weights and years. Most numbers in sports references are numerals, as well as the expressions No. 1, No. 2, etc.
- Despite the two previous rules, the only numeral that isn't written out at the beginning of a sentence is a year: *2007 was a bad year financially for many people.*
- Always write out the words *million, billion* and *trillion: 1 million, 13 billion.*
- Fractions are written out if less than one but written as numerals if greater: *one-third,* $1\frac{1}{3}$.
- Add the suffixes *nd, rd, st* and *th* to numerals for designations of courts, military terms and political divisions (such as precincts, districts and wards). Also, use them for amendments or street names in which the number has two or more digits: *First Amendment, 10th Amendment.*

Punctuation

COMMAS

- Use between independent clauses joined by a conjunction.
- Use after a dependent clause followed by an independent one but not vice versa.
- Use to introduce a quote of one sentence.
- Use instead of parentheses around parenthetical items.
- Use between coordinate modifiers—when you can reverse them and put *and* between them. Example: *The tall, thin man. . . .* Exceptions: See "Coordinate versus Compound Modifiers" on Page 153.
- Use after an introductory word, phrase or clause.
  Introductory word: Suddenly, it started raining.
  Introductory phrase: In the fall, it turned chilly.
  Introductory clause: Because he voted for the war, he came under attack.
- Differences between English usage and journalism usage:
  1. Don't put a comma before the word *and* in a series unless it would be confusing not to do so.

2. Don't put a comma before *Jr.* or *Sr.* for names of people, or before *Inc.* or *Ltd.* in names of businesses

3. Put a comma both before and after a state, after a city or a year, and after a date.

SEMICOLONS

- Use a semicolon (;) to join independent clauses—those that could stand alone as complete sentences—when there is no conjunction between the two. A semicolon should never be used to join a dependent clause to an independent one. But journalists don't often use semicolons to join independent clauses. They typically would either make the clauses separate sentences or join them with a comma and a conjunction.

- Use a comma between items in a series when at least one of the items contains a comma. (Include a semicolon before the *and.*)

- Do not capitalize after a semicolon.

COLONS

- A colon (:) is used to introduce a list or to join two closely related independent clauses when the first is meant to introduce and point to the second.

- A colon is also used instead of a comma to introduce a quote of two sentences or more.

- Capitalize after a colon only if what follows is a complete sentence.

DASHES

- Don't overuse them.

- Use a dash instead of a comma for a dramatic pause in a sentence.

- Use dashes in place of commas around parenthetical items already containing commas.

- You may use dashes as bullets to set off items in a list.

HYPHENS

Put a hyphen between compound modifiers—that is, when you have two modifiers in a row, the first modifies the second and the two of them together modify something else.

the well-liked teacher

The exceptions are that you should not hyphenate after the words *very* or *most,* or after an adverb ending in *ly.*

Quotations

ATTRIBUTION

It's important that the reader always be clear who's saying what. Beginning writers often confuse the reader when they paraphrase what a speaker said without saying the speaker said it. Every paraphrase needs to be attributed, but every quote does not.

> *Wrong:* Privacy is our most cherished right.
>
> (Without attribution this paraphrase sounds as though the writer is editorializing.)
>
> *Right:* Gonzalez said that privacy is our most cherished right.
>
> *Acceptable But Unnecessary Attribution:* Horner said he approved of the plan. "I'm all in favor of it," he said.
>
> (The "he said" after the quotation is unnecessary because the previous sentence told us he said it.)
>
> *More Concise:* Horner said he approved of the plan. "I'm all in favor of it."

A second way that failure to attribute can confuse a reader is when there's more than one speaker. Whenever more than one person is quoted in a story, attribution is required—and it should be placed in front of the quotation—whenever the speaker being quoted changes. This is important so the reader doesn't think it's the same person speaking. When there's only one speaker, it's not necessary to put an attribution with every sentence quoted as long as it's clear the same person is speaking.

> "This type of evaluation isn't based on a score," he said. "It is based on ideas and areas that should be addressed."
>
> (Notice it's clear the same person is saying the second sentence even without another *he said,* which would only seem redundant.)

The first time a quotation is used, the speaker's qualifications are also usually cited, as well as the person's full name. On second reference, the person's last name only is cited. If the person has a title that was used on first reference—such as *the Rev., Dr.* or *Gov.*—that title is dropped on all following references. Sometimes the title (written out and without capital letters) can be used in place of the name on some of the secondary references: *The governor said . . . .*

In a detailed recounting of what someone said, rather than repeat *says* or *said* so often, introduce a longer account with a sentence like, "He gave the following account to police."

> A Memphis man was arrested early Monday morning after a high-speed chase through South Memphis that resulted in serious injury to a pedestrian.

Police arrested Jerome Caldwell, 22, of 303 S. Third St., and prosecutors charged him with resisting arrest, aggravated assault and burglary.

Police gave this account of the events:

Officers Jill Southerland and Carlos Rodriguez responded to a silent alarm at Southside Hardware, 2028 E. Miller St., about 4:30 a.m. They entered the building and surprised a burglar, who fled through a rear door.

The man jumped into a car and led the officers on a three-mile chase through South Memphis, which ended when another squad car was summoned to help block the intersection at Hernando and Main streets. The car came to a stop there but not until it had struck Antonio D'Amato, 29, who was crossing Main Street when the car and police arrived.

Starting the description of the sequence of events with "Police gave this account of the events" made it unnecessary to attribute each sentence with "police said." Here are some additional tips regarding attributions.

- Reporters should stick to one tense in attributions—either *said* or *says* throughout but not both. Don't mix the two because then you'll have unnecessary shifts in verb tense from past to present. Instead, use *said* for hard-news stories, and use *says* for feature stories. Journalists usually avoid *stated* or *states* for attribution.

- The order should usually be *source said,* not *said source.* The *source-said* order is more conversational because usually the subject precedes the verb in English. You may want to use the *said-source* order, however, if the *source* and the *said* are separated by a long description, such as a title.

- Journalists prefer *said* and *says* to other attributions because of their brevity and neutrality. For example, *stated* is longer. *Claimed* and *according to* can imply doubt. (Some editors prefer *according to* when a document is being quoted. *According to* is also correct when you mean "in accordance with rules" and then should refer to the content not the speaker.) *Admitted* implies guilt. *Conceded* implies someone agreed reluctantly. *Refuted* means successfully answered. *Added* means the statement was an afterthought. And nobody ever *beamed, grinned, laughed, smiled* or *winced* in words.

- Avoid attributions that imply mind reading. Mind reading occurs when a reporter says, for example, that someone *believes, doubts, feels, hopes* or *thinks* something. How does the reporter know? Only if he or she is a mind reader or the person said it.

- Here are a few special problems with *said* and *says:*

  1. If *said* or *says* is followed by a time element, follow the time element with the word *that.*

  2. If a person is paraphrased as saying two clauses in one sentence, don't separate the clauses with a comma.

3. If a person is paraphrased after the word *said,* the clause following it must be in an earlier tense to maintain the proper sequence of tenses.

He said he was going. ("Was," not is.)

HOW TO CAPITALIZE AND PUNCTUATE QUOTATIONS

- Capitalize the first word of a quotation only when it is a complete sentence that is directly quoted.
- When the attribution precedes the paraphrased or quoted statement:
    1. Quotations of more than one sentence are introduced with a colon.
    2. Quotations of one sentence are introduced with a comma.
    3. Partial quotes are not introduced with commas or colons.
- When the attribution follows the paraphrased or quoted statement:
    1. Put a comma before the attribution and after the paraphrase or quote when it's a full sentence or less long.
    2. If the quotation is more than a sentence long, move the attribution either after the first sentence or before both of them, punctuating according to the above rules.
- What punctuation marks go before the final quote mark? A comma or a period will always go inside the quote. An exclamation mark or a question mark will go inside or outside, depending on whether it's part of the actual quote. *The AP Stylebook* says the latter is true for colons and semicolons, as well. But in practice, they always seem to go outside the quote.
- Don't go from a partial quotation to a complete one within the same paragraph. Don't write:

Jones said he was "happy to be alive. I can't believe it happened."

Instead, put a quotation mark after the period following "alive," then begin a new paragraph with a quotation mark in front of "I."

- How to handle quotations of more than one paragraph:
    1. Don't put quotation marks at the end of the paragraph if the quote in that paragraph is a full sentence and the quotation continues in the next paragraph.
    2. If the quotation in the paragraph is a partial one that continues into the next paragraph, it *does* have quotation marks at the end.
- The use of quote marks means the reporter is using the exact words the speaker or writer used. Reporters shouldn't rewrite another person's words

and leave them in quotations. They should quote them exactly, paraphrase them (no quotations but attribution still used) or use partial quotes (paraphrase of some words with quotation marks around direct quotes).

- Journalists don't usually use an ellipsis (. . .) to indicate words being left out of a quotation as a student would in a term paper. That doesn't mean journalists rewrite the quote and deceptively leave it in quotation marks. Rather, journalists will instead use paraphrases (putting the quotation in the reporter's own words but taking off the quotation marks) or partial quotes (quotations of a few words or phrases only while paraphrasing the rest).

Miscellaneous

TIME-DAY-PLACE

- Journalists write about events in time-day-place order because it is usually the most efficient way. For example, don't say an event will take place "at City Hall on Friday at 3 p.m." Instead write that it will take place "3 p.m. Friday at City Hall" (saving two words).
- Do not include both a day and a date. Use only the day for events within a week forward or backward. Use only the date for events beyond a week forward or backward.
- Do not write *yesterday* or *tomorrow,* but you may write *today* or *tonight, this morning, this afternoon* or *this evening* if you mean the day of publication. Be careful, however, not to write *today* to refer to something you're writing today but that won't be printed until the next day.
- If you write a month without a date, don't abbreviate the month. If you write a month with a date, abbreviate it unless it's one of those with five letters or fewer (March, April, May, June, July): *August; Aug. 9; Aug. 9, 2007; August 2007* (year but no date, so not abbreviated).

ADDRESSES

- Words like *street, avenue, boulevard, drive* and *lane* are always written out when a specific address is not given. If an address is given, then the words *street, avenue* and *boulevard* are the only three such words abbreviated (*St., Ave., Blvd.*): *Ninth Street; 1039 Ninth St.; 1826 Circle Lane.*
- If the street name has a direction in it, abbreviate the direction only with a specific street address: *West Hickory Avenue, 103 W. Hickory Ave.; Southeast Avalon Drive, 2608 S.E. Avalon Drive.*

- When an address follows a person's name, either separate them with the word *of* and no commas, or use commas around the address without the word *of*: *Hank Jones of 678 S. Elm was arrested.; Hank Jones, 678 S. Elm, was arrested.*
- When an address follows a person's name and age, separate them with both a comma after the age and the word *of* in front the address. Do not put a comma after the address in this instance because the comma is there to separate the age, not the address: *Hank Jones, 36, of 678 S. Elm was arrested.*

TITLES

- A person's official title is always capitalized if it appears in front of the name, lowercase afterward or without the name: *President George W. Bush; George W. Bush, president of the United States; the president.*
- Mere job descriptions (such as *astronaut, announcer, teacher*) are not capitalized either before or after a name. (If you are not sure whether a title is a formal, official title or merely a job description, put the title after the name and lowercase it.) AP now always lowercases the titles *coach* and *professor.*
- Use the abbreviations *Dr., Gov., Lt. Gov., Rep., Sen.* and *the Rev.* (note that the word *the* is part of the title) only in front of a name and on first reference. In later references, just use the person's last name. The titles *president* and *professor* are never abbreviated.
- Courtesy titles *(Mr., Mrs., Miss, Ms.)* are usually not used. Instead, a person is referred to on first reference by first and last name, then on subsequent references by last name only. Exceptions include direct quotations or when a woman requests it. Newspapers also commonly use courtesy titles for the deceased in obituaries, and a few do in editorials.
- In stories where it's necessary to distinguish between two people with the same last name, AP suggests using the first and last name in all references or a courtesy title for a woman if her preference is known. In the latter case, however, many editors would find it sexist to include the courtesy title for a woman but not a man. Some newspapers will use only first names on second reference in cases where two people have the same surname, but they'd typically do this only in features.

DATELINES

A **dateline** is the designation before the start of a story of the city from which the story was filed. It appears only in front of a nonlocal story. The name of the city in a dateline is written in capital letters, the name of the state or country in upper and lowercase: GRAND RAPIDS, Mich.

Some cities (such as Washington) are so well-known that they are not followed by a state or country. A list of cities in the United States and abroad that stand alone can be found in *The AP Stylebook* under the *dateline* entry. In addition, your editor may designate other cities within your state or readership area as dateline cities that stand alone in your publication.

Notice, especially, that *Washington* and *New York* always refer to the cities by those names, not the states, unless otherwise indicated. In other words, you would not normally write *Washington, D.C.,* or *New York City* but simply *Washington* or *New York.*

- If a city is a *dateline city*—that is, one that stands alone without a state or country in a dateline—it would also stand alone within the body of a story.
- The dateline is typically followed by parentheses in which is written the name of the wire service providing the story, then by a dash. The story would then follow, beginning on the same line:

WASHINGTON (AP)–The Senate voted 52–48 on Thursday . . .

Spelling

Here are some questions you might ask when checking spelling:

1. Have you checked for typos?
2. Have you looked up all compound words to see whether they should be written as one word, two words or hyphenated?

Journalists have a specific and unique way of determining the way a word is spelled. This can result in some words being spelled differently from how you may be accustomed. For example: *adviser, doughnut, hot line.* Follow these steps:

1. Look it up in *The AP Stylebook.* If the word is in there, spell it that way.
2. If the word is not in AP—and only then—look it up in *Webster's New World Dictionary.* Don't look in a different dictionary. Don't look in the small paperback version of this one. If the word wasn't in AP and it *is* in here, spell it that way.
3. If the word isn't in either AP or *Webster's New World*—and only if it wasn't in either—look it up in the latest *Webster's Third International* (unabridged). If the word wasn't in the previous two but it is in here, this is the way to spell it.
4. If the word isn't in any of the three, consider a different word. If the word isn't in any of the three, and it is a compound about which you wonder whether it should be one word, two words or hyphenated, then make it two words as a noun or verb, or hyphenate it as a compound adjective in front of a noun.

Spelling Words to Know

Some often misspelled words you should commit to memory:

acceptable	boyfriend	exhilarating
accessory	burqa	existence
accommodate	buses (vehicles)	February
accumulate	busses (kisses)	firefighter
acknowledgment	Canada geese	fluorescent
acoustics	caress	forward*
adherence	Caribbean	fourth
admissible	cave-in	fraudulent
advertise	cemetery	fulfill
adviser*	chaperon	goodbye*
aficionado	chauffeur	grammar
afterward*	collectible	greyhound
aggressor	consensus	guerrilla
already	consistent	harass
all right	consul	hemorrhage
alleged	council	heroes
allotted, allotment	counsel	hitchhiker
appall	deductible	homicide
Arctic	demagogue	hypocrisy
assistant	descendant	ifs and buts
attendance	diarrhea	impostor
ax*	dietitian	inadmissible
backward*	disastrous	incredible
bankruptcy	dissension	indestructible
battalion	divisive	indispensable
beginning	do's and don'ts	innocuous
bellwether	doughnut	innuendo
benefited	drowned	inoculate
berserk	drunkenness	irreligious
blond (adj., noun for male)	embarrass	irresistible
	emphysema	irreverent
blonde (adj., noun for female)	employee*	jeopardy
	espresso	judgment*

*Preferred spelling. Words in parentheses also indicate common newspaper usage.

kidnapped*
kindergarten
knowledgeable
lambaste
largess
leisure
liaison
license
likable
liquefy
marijuana
marriage
marshal
massacre
medieval
memento
misspell
naïve
nerve-racking
nickel
ninth
nuisance
occasion
occurred
OK'd
opposum
overrule
paid
papier-mâché
parallel
paraphernalia
pastime
pavilion
peacable

penicillin
percent*
percentage
permissible
personnel
Philippines
picnicking
playwright
pneumonia
poinsettia
politicking
pompon
potoatoes
preceding
preferred
privilege
procedure
prodigy
prostate
publicly
quandary
questionnaire
queue
rarefy
reconnaissance
relevant
restaurateur
rhythm
rock 'n' roll (rock-and-roll)
sacrilegious
seize
separate
siege
sizable

skiing
skillful
strait-laced
strong-arm
subpoena
summonses
supersede
surprise
tariff
theater*
thoroughly
till
tomatoes
tornadoes
toward*
traveled*
tumultuous
twelfth
ukulele
vacuum
veterinarian
vice versa
vilify
villain
volcanoes
voyageur
Wednesday
weird
whiskey* (whisky for Scotch)
wield
wondrous
X-ray (noun, verb and adj.)
yield

Measures of Readability

Broadcast news is written to be spoken, so sentences are short and to the point. Newspaper and magazine writing is more literary, so the print media constantly run the risk of making stories too difficult to read. Difficult reading results in lost or confused readers. As a result, newspapers and magazines periodically test their stories for readability. Researchers have devised formulas that measure the ease with which an item can be read. Or, more accurately, they try to gauge some of the factors that make reading difficult.

Most readability formulas are based on concepts familiar to newspaper editors. Short sentences generally are easier to read than long ones, and short words are more comprehensible than long ones. Two of the better-known formulas developed by readability experts use sentence and word lengths as key ingredients.

The **Flesch formula,** devised by Rudolph Flesch, uses 100-word samples to measure average sentence length and number of syllables. The formula multiplies the average number of words in the sentence by 1.015 and the total syllable count by 0.846. The two factors are added, then subtracted from 206.835 to arrive at a readability score.

A formula devised by Robert Gunning determines the **fog index.** It adds the average sentence length in words and the number of words of three syllables or more (omitting capitalized words; combinations of short, easy words like *butterfly;* and verb forms made into three syllables by adding *-ed, -es* or *-ing*). The sum is multiplied by 0.4 to get the fog index.

Suppose the sample contains an average of 16 words to the sentence and a total of 150 syllables. By the Flesch formula, the sample would have a readability score of 64, which Flesch rates as standard or fitting the style of *Reader's Digest.* In the same sample, assuming hard words make up 10 percent of the text, the fog index of the Gunning scale would be 10, or at the reading level of high school sophomores and fitting *Time* magazine's style.

Neither Flesch nor Gunning tests content or word familiarity. All they suggest is that if passages from a story or the whole story average more than 20 words to the sentence and the number of hard words in a sample of 100 words exceeds 10 percent, a majority of readers will find the passages difficult to understand.

The formula designers would not recommend that editors pare all long sentences to 20 words or fewer and all long words to monosyllables. Long sentences, if they are graceful and meaningful, should be kept intact. Mixed with shorter sentences, they give variety to style and provide the pacing necessary in good writing. A long word may still be a plain word.

An editorial executive of *The New York Times* preferred to measure density of ideas in sentences

☀ TIGHTENING

A few words may say a lot, and a lot of words may say little.

The average newspaper reader reads the paper for only 22 to 24 minutes a day. The average broadcast story lasts 30 seconds or less. So, don't waste your audience's time with unnecessary words. Get to the point as quickly as possible, conveying as much news as you can within the time the reader, viewer or listener spends with you.

Cut any words that wouldn't change the meaning of the sentence if they were gone. In the following sentences, the underlined words can be deleted:

She shopped <u>very</u> late each afternoon at the store at <u>the corner</u> of 10th and Elm streets.

rather than sentence length itself and came up with a pattern of "one idea, one sentence." A special issue of the newsroom publication *Winners & Sinners* was devoted to this pattern and reports of reading tests on two versions of the same articles. One test was done on the comprehensibility of the articles as written originally, another on the articles when rewritten to lower the density of ideas in the sentence. The "one-idea, one-sentence" dictum is not taken literally even at the *Times,* but the editors insist, "Generally, it speeds reading if there is only one idea to a sentence."

The number of unfamiliar words in passages also has been found to affect readability. Edgar Dale and Jeanne S. Chall at The Ohio State University prepared a list of 3,000 words known to 80 percent of fourth-graders. The word-load factor in the **Dale-Chall formula** consists of a count of words outside the list. Only 4 percent of the words on the Dale-Chall list have three or more syllables.

Editing stories to reduce the number of words outside the word-familiarity list would be time-consuming and impractical. The lists would have to be revised periodically to take out words that no longer are familiar and to add new words that have become part of everyday language—even to fourth-graders.

Most readability formulas use a few fundamental elements but neglect context or story structure. Thus, a passage in gibberish could rate as highly readable on the Flesch, Gunning and Dale-Chall scales. This was demonstrated by Wilson L. Taylor at the University of Illinois Institute of Communications Research.

Taylor developed the **cloze procedure** (from "close" or "closure" in Gestalt psychology) to test context. In this procedure he omitted certain words—usually every fifth word—and asked respondents to fill in the missing words. He then graded passages on the number of correct words respondents could fill in.

Of passages from eight writers, the Taylor method ranked samples of Gertrude Stein's semi-intelligible prose as the second most difficult. The most difficult was a passage from James Joyce. Both the Dale-Chall and the Flesch scales rated the Stein passage as the easiest to read and the Joyce passage in a tie for fourth with a passage from Erskine Caldwell.

To test for human interest, Flesch measures personal words and sentences. Sentences that mention people and have them saying and doing things increase readability. The cloze procedure suggests that unfamiliar words may be used and understood if they are placed in a context in which the reader can guess their meaning.

For years, editors were quick to point out that in the fast-paced world of newspapers, magazines, radio and television, there is no time to worry about the academic exercise of measuring readability. Now that news stories are written on computers, that no longer is a valid argument. Many word processors have utilities for measuring the readability of an article. Some even have the capability built in. If editors truly want to connect with readers, they will make regular use of these tools.

From one week to the next, Esther went from <u>being the</u> goat to hero.

Enrique shot from the top of the box, and <u>in an instant,</u> the ball ripped into the upper-right corner of the net.

The mayor read from a <u>prepared</u> statement.

She was on the operating table from 8 p.m. Monday <u>night</u> until 5 a.m. Tuesday <u>morning.</u>
(*Night* and *morning* are redundant because *p.m.* and *a.m.* mean the same thing.)

He said the USDA is <u>currently</u> spending. . .

Justice said Double Spring had been <u>in the process of</u> phasing out its operation. . .

Hayley has some 30 <u>different</u> (fish) tanks in his home.

Retired Adm. Jackson R. Tate slipped away to a secret retreat Tuesday for his <u>first</u> meeting with the daughter he has never met.

Omit extraneous facts. News presents the pertinent facts. Every story should answer all the questions the reader or viewer expects answered. If a big story returns after having been out of the news, it should contain a short background or reminder. Readers don't carry clips to check background.

But Robert J. Casey, an author and former reporter for the defunct *Chicago Daily News,* once observed, "Too many facts can louse up a good story." If a fact isn't vital in telling the news, it should be omitted. Stray bits have a way of bringing trouble. A buried reference to a 30-year-old hanging "from an apple tree on Joe Smith's farm" brought a libel suit. Joe Smith was still living and the hanging wasn't on his farm. The reference added nothing to the story but taught the editor a lesson. The following could be reduced to a paragraph or two—it is not worth five column inches of type:

> Robert F. Kelley today was named chairman of this year's Democratic Jefferson–Jackson Day dinner.
>
> The appointment was announced jointly by Democratic State Chairman John M. C— and National Committeeman William S. P—.
>
> Kelley, administrative assistant for 12 years to ex-Sen. J. Allen F— Jr. in Washington, said he will name a dinner committee, site, date and speaker in a "few days."
>
> The Jefferson–Jackson Day dinner, traditionally held in late April or early May, is the largest meeting of its kind held by the Democrats each year.
>
> Kelley said he already is trying to line up a "nationally known" speaker for the occasion.
>
> Kelley, now associated with the legal department of the D— Co., has been a member of the dinner committee for several years. This is his first assignment as chairman of the affair.
>
> Kelley was a vice chairman of last year's Community Fund drive and has a wide background in party and civic affairs.
>
> He is a past president of the Delaware State Society and the Administrative Assistants and Secretaries Club in the nation's capital.

Substitute fewer words for more if they mean the same thing.

Wordy: prior to
Concise: before

Wordy: applying its stamp of approval
Concise: approving

Wordy: work in the field
Concise: field work

Wordy: The field is 50 feet in length.
Concise: The field is 50 feet long.

Wordy: The vase was blue in color.
Concise: The vase was blue.

Wordy: He is said to be resentful.
Concise: He is said to resent.

Wordy: wrote a formal letter of resignation
Concise: resigned

Wordy Phrases to Avoid

Most experienced editors can add to this list. The preferred form is in parentheses.

a bolt of lightning (lightning)
a great number of times (often)
a large number of (many)
a period of several weeks (several weeks)
a small number of (few)
a sufficient number of (enough)
absolute guarantee (guarantee)
accidentally stumbled (stumbled)
advance planning (planning)
advance reservations (reservations)
all of a sudden (suddenly)
as a general rule (usually)
assessed a fine (fined)
at a later date (later)
at the conclusion of (after)
at the corner of 16th and Elm (at 16th and Elm)
at the hour of noon (at noon)
at the present time (now)
at 12 midnight (at midnight)
at 12 noon (at noon)
bald-headed (bald)
called attention to the fact (reminded)
climb up (climb)
commute back and forth (commute)
completely decapitated (decapitated)
completely destroyed (destroyed)
completely surrounded (surrounded)
consensus of opinion (consensus)
cost the sum of $5 (cost $5)
despite the fact that (although)
disclosed for the first time (disclosed)
draw to a close (end)
due to the fact that (because)
during the winter months (in the winter)
end result (result)
entered a bid of (bid)
exact replica (replica)
exchanged wedding vows (married)
few in number (few)

filled to capacity (filled)
first priority (priority)
first prototype (prototype)
for a period of 10 days (for 10 days)
foreign imports (imports)
free gift (gift)
free pass (pass)
general public (public)
grand total (total)
heat up (heat)
hostile antagonist (antagonist)
in addition to (and, besides, also)
in back of (behind)
in case of (if, concerning)
in order to balance (to balance)
in the absence of (without)
in the event that (if)
in the immediate vicinity of (near)
in the near future (soon)
in the not too distant future (eventually)
incumbent governor (governor)
introduced a new (introduced)
is going to (will)
is in the process of making application (is applying)
is of the opinion that (believes)
Jewish rabbi (rabbi)
kept an eye on (watched)
large-sized man (large man)
lift up (lift)
made good his escape (escaped)
major portion of (most of)
married his wife (married)
merged together (merged)
midway between (between)
new bride (bride)
new construction (construction)
new innovation (innovation)
new record (record)

(continues)

Wordy Phrases to Avoid (Continued)

off of (off)
old adage (adage)
old cliché (cliché)
on account of (because)
on two different occasions (twice)
once in a great while (seldom, rarely)
partially damaged (damaged)
partially destroyed (damaged)
past history (history)
period of time (period)
placed its seal of approval on (approved)
possibly might (might)
postponed until later (postponed)
prior to (before)
promoted to the rank of (promoted to)
qualified expert (expert)
receded back (receded)
recur again (recur)
reduce down (reduce)
refer back (refer)
remand back (remand)
revise downward (lower)
rise up (rise)

rose to the defense of (defended)
self-confessed (confessed)
short space of time (short time)
since the time when (since)
sprung a surprise (surprised)
started off with (started with)
strangled to death (strangled)
summer season (summer)
sworn affidavits (affidavits)
tendered his resignation (resigned)
there is no doubt that (doubtless)
total operating costs (operating costs)
true facts (facts)
underground subway (subway)
united in holy matrimony (married)
upward adjustment (increase)
voiced objections (objected)
went up in flames (burned)
whether or not (whether)
widow of the late (widow)
with the exception of (except)
young juveniles (juveniles)

Use words that are more common. Usually, they're also the shorter ones. But sometimes, it's better to use a longer word, or two or three smaller words, rather than one less-common one.

LESS COMMON	MORE COMMON
aggregate	total
attempt	try
component	part
conceptualize	think of
contusion	bruise
currently	now
discover	find
enable	let, allow to
enormous	big

Clichés to Avoid

The Associated Press ran almost 400,000 words of its copy through a computer to determine which of the tired words and phrases were used most often. The result: *hailed, backlash, in the wake of, informed, violence flared, kickoff, death and destruction, riot-torn, tinder dry, racially troubled, voters marched to the polls, jam-packed, grinding crash, confrontation, oil-rich nation, no immediate comment, cautious (or guarded) optimism, limped into port.*

Editors can add to this list of tired expressions:

acid test
area girl
average (reader, voter, etc.)

banquet (never a dinner)
belt tightening
bitter (dispute)
blistering (accusation)
bloody riot
bombshell (announcement, etc.)
boost
briefing
brutal (murder, slaying)

cardinal sin
caught the eye of
controversial issue
coveted trophy
crack (troops, etc.)
cutback

daring (holdup, etc.)
deficit-ridden
devastating (flood, fire)
devout (Catholic, etc.)
do your own thing
dumped

experts
eye (to see)
eyeball to eyeball

fiery holocaust
fire broke out, swept
fire of undetermined origin
foot the bill
freak accident

gap (generation, credibility, etc.)
-gate (added to name to indicate a scandal)

hammer out
hard-core, hard-nosed
hike (for *raise*)
historical document
hobbled by injury
hosted
hurled

identity crisis
in terms of
initial (for *first*)
-ize (finalize, formalize)

junket

keeled over

led to safety
luxurious (apartment, love nest, etc.)

made off with
miraculous (cure, escape, etc.)
momentous occasion

name of the game

opt for
overwhelming majority

passing motorist
plush (hotel, apartment, etc.)
police were summoned

pressure (as a verb)
probe

race card
relocate (for *move*)
reportedly, reputedly

seasoned (observers, etc.)
senseless murder
shot in the arm
staged a riot (or protest)
standing ovation
stems from
stinging rebuke
sweeping changes
swing into high gear

task force
tense (or uneasy) calm
terminate (for *end*)
thorough (or all-out) investigation
timely hit
top-level meeting
tragic accident
turn thumbs down

uneasy truce
unveiled
upcoming

vast expanse
verbalize
violence erupted
violent explosion

whirlwind (tour, junket)

young boys

LESS COMMON	MORE COMMON
frequently	often
implement	start, do
numerous	many
obtain	get
remainder	rest
subsequently	later
transport	carry
utilize	use

Cut clichés, or insist on a more original restatement. A good writer uses a fresh and appropriate figure of speech to enhance the story. The editor should distinguish between the fresh and the stale. This isn't always easy because some words and phrases are used repeatedly in the news report. See "Clichés to Avoid" on Page 181.

Don't cut descriptions from feature stories if they help set the scene or add color.

> On stage, she is surrounded by musicians in greet suits and cowboy boots. Stuck there in the middle, Tammy looks like one smooth pearl in a bucket of green peas.
>
> (Such descriptive language might be cut from a hard-news story but should be left in a feature to help set the scene and tone.)

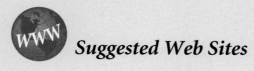

Suggested Web Sites

Grammar Girl Web site and podcast
http://grammar.quickanddirtytips.com/default.aspx
Grammar Now! **www. grammarnow.com**
Linguist List **www. linguistlist.org**
The Online English Grammar **www.edufind.com/english/grammar/**

Suggested Readings

Bremner, John B. *Words on Words: A Dictionary for Writers and Others Who Care About Words.* New York: Columbia University Press, 1980.

Brooks, Brian S., James L. Pinson and Jean Gaddy Wilson. *Working With Words: A Handbook for Media Writers and Editors.* 6th edition. Boston: Bedford/St. Martin's, 2006.

Burchfield, R. W., Ed. *The New Fowler's Modern English Usage.* 3rd edition. New York: Oxford University Press, 2000.

Follett, Wilson. *Modern American Usage: A Guide.* Revised by Erik Wensberg. New York: Hill & Wang, 1998.

Ross-Larson, Bruce. *Edit Yourself: A Manual for Everyone Who Works With Words.* New York: Barnes & Noble, 2003.

Shertzer, Margaret, *The Elements of Grammar: The Essential Guide to Refining and Improving Grammar.* New York: Barnes & Noble, 2001.

Walsh, Bill. *Lapsing Into a Comma: A Curmudgeon's Guide to the Many Things That Can Go Wrong in Print—And How to Avoid Them.* Chicago: Contemporary Books, 2000.

HOLISTIC EDITING
Integrating the Macro and the Micro

In Chapters 4 through 6, we discussed macro versus micro approaches to editing. Earlier, in Chapter 3, we discussed the Three R's approach to editing and mentioned also the Seven C's Plus One formulation. All of these represent different ways to think about the editing process and to keep the basics in mind. You can use any or all of them that seem useful to you.

In this chapter, we introduce one more approach: **holistic editing.** You may find this a particularly practical technique in helping you edit stories speedily yet thoroughly. The idea is simple. The news each day is full of the same kinds of stories—accidents, crimes, meetings, sports, weather, etc. After you've edited enough of each kind, you gradually learn what needs to be in each kind of story, even the typical order in which they're presented, as well as the most common problems big and small.

So, when experienced editors read stories, they can edit more quickly because they know what to look for in stories of that type. As a beginning editor, you can use this chapter as a checklist of the problems a seasoned editor looks for in various kinds of stories. Simply identify the type of story you're editing, then turn here for advice.

Of course, while editing any kind of story, be on the lookout not only for what's typical in stories of that type but also for other kinds of problems, large and small, that might appear. For example, all fields of journalism stress short paragraphs; short sentences; short, common words; use of a common stylebook, usually AP; and some standard of objectivity, although that can mean different things in hard-news versus features.

Speaking of that, all hard-news stories share certain common structures that differ somewhat from features. Likewise, all the writing for a specific medium like newspapers has certain features in common compared to another medium such as television. So, incorporate knowledge of these various formulas into your editing as well as the story-genre approach described in this chapter.

How you do that is up to you. You might, for example, read a story several times with a different focus each time—macro, micro, then headline writing. Or you might first read a story to get an overall sense of whether it's a hard-news story or a feature, and which kind of story it is.

Remember, a story might be more than one kind at a time. You might edit, for example, a story from a police press release about the arrest of a man wanted for a crime reported previously in the paper. For that, you might want to review the advice for press-release stories, follows and crime stories (all discussed in this chapter).

It should also be pointed out that journalists tend to use two approaches in classifying stories: Sometimes they classify them by content, such as a crime story, and sometimes by approach, such as a first-person story. The classifications presented in this chapter incorporate both methods of classification, so here's another reason an individual story might fall into more than one type.

This holistic approach, then, involves recognition at one time of all the various patterns a particular story fits and how it might differ from what's typical. The variances you spot will usually be errors to correct, but it's important to be on the lookout for creative variations that introduce intelligent, fresh approaches. Don't try to fit every story into a straitjacket of preconceptions. Being able to recognize the difference between a mistake and useful innovation takes experience and an open, alert mind—demonstrating that good editing requires lots of knowledge, but it's also ultimately an art, not a science.

ACCIDENT AND DISASTER STORIES

Car crashes, boating accidents, drownings, fires, tornadoes, floods—all fall under the category of accident and disaster stories.

Accident-story leads are often in passive voice, with the victim having been killed or having been injured or the property having been damaged, rather than active voice, with someone doing these things to the person or property.

Why, then, are we usually told to avoid passive voice? In a disaster story, we may not know who did this, and even if we do know, we don't want to write the story in such a way that someone is convicted in print before being found guilty at a trial. Conclusion: The *who* is probably the victim or the damaged or destroyed property.

The *what* is that someone died or was injured, or that property was destroyed or damaged. If more than one of these happened, deaths are more important than injuries, injuries are more important than destroyed property and destroyed property is more important than damaged property—unless the injuries were slight and the destruction or damage widespread or costly.

If the lead is a delayed-ID, then the name typically starts the second paragraph. The first full-sentence quote often appears in the second paragraph, as well, or sometimes in the third paragraph. The first quote in the story should be the most dramatic or the best summary of the significance, drama or tragedy of the accident.

From there on, the story's details will be presented from most-to-least important, while seesawing back and forth between the reporter's presentation of details and quotes from those involved.

Accident stories should answer these questions:

- *Who was involved?* What are the names, ages (especially children) and addresses? Are there any relatives or friends who might be able to add details or character information to that gathered from authorities, participants and witnesses?

- *What happened?* What was the nature of the accident? What was the extent of injuries (condition of victims) and damages (monetary or other description)? These should be answered by the investigating officer; participants, if possible; and witnesses.

- *When did it happen?*

- *Where did it happen?*

- *How and why did it happen, as the officer on the scene, participants and witnesses understand it?*

Warning: Be sure the description of what happened doesn't assume or imply anyone's guilt. There has not yet been a trial, so don't convict anyone beforehand in print. Best bet: Tell what charges were filed or tickets given. For example, rather than saying, "While driving drunk, Jones crossed the median and hit an oncoming car," report that he received a ticket for driving while intoxicated and striking a vehicle in the other lane.

In *train and plane crash stories*, you should include the train or flight number, the place of departure, the destination and the times of departure and expected arrival. Airplanes may collide on the ground or in the air (not *midair*). Let investigators *search* the wreckage, not *comb* or *sift* it.

Most *earthquake stories* describe the *magnitude* of the tremor. One measurement is the Richter scale, which shows relative magnitude. It starts with magnitude 1 and progresses in units, with each unit 10 times stronger than the previous one. Thus, magnitude 3 is 10 times stronger than magnitude 2, which in turn is 10 times stronger than magnitude 1. On this scale, the strongest earthquakes recorded were a 9.5 in Chile in 1960 and a 9.2 in Alaska in 1964. *Intensity* generally refers to the duration or to the damage caused by the shock.

In *fire stories*, the truth is that in nine of 10 cases when people are "led to safety," they're not. Except for an occasional child or infirm adult, they simply have the common sense to leave the building without waiting for a firefighter to "lead them to safety." Eliminate terms such as *three-alarm fire* and *second-degree burns* unless they are explained.

In *fire and flood stories*, the residents of the area are rarely "taken from their homes or asked to leave." Instead, they "vacate their homes," or they're "told to evacuate," or they "are evacuated."

ACCIDENT STORY USAGE

- Damage, damages—"The full tragedy of Hurricane Betsy unfolded today as the death toll rose past 50, and damages soared into many millions." *Damage* was the correct word here. You collect *damages* in court.

- Damaged, destroyed—*Damaged* refers to partial destruction, *destroyed* to complete. "An estimated $40,000 worth of damage was done Jan. 29." *Damage* isn't worth anything. Quite the contrary.

ACCIDENT STORY CLICHÉS TO AVOID

fiery holocaust
flames (licked, leaped, swept)
raging brush fire
rampaging rivers
searing heat
tinder-dry forest
(traffic, triple) fatals (police station jargon)
tragedy, tragic
weary (firefighters, rescue workers)

ACCIDENT STORY TIGHTENING

The preferred form is shown in parentheses:

autopsy to determine the cause of death (autopsy)
blazing inferno, flaming inferno (inferno)
came to a stop (stopped)
completely destroyed, partially destroyed (destroyed, damaged)
vehicle (car, truck)

ADVANCE PIECES

Advance pieces announce an upcoming event but go beyond a simple calendar-style listing by interviewing the principal people involved and doing a personality profile or history behind an event or organization.

These stories often, but not always, originate from a press release. When a press release arrives at a newspaper, editors judge whether it will be covered at all by asking themselves whether it gives some genuine news that readers would want to know or whether it is just a request for a free ad disguised as a press release.

A press release should never be printed as a publicity puff but rather rewritten and expanded into a news feature. Make sure all self-serving, self-promoting, nonobjective language gets removed and that the focus is on what the readers might find interesting, not merely what the sponsor wants to say.

Advances are often written as personality profiles of a key person involved or as a historical piece about the person or group. In such a case, the news-peg event may be teased in the story, but often it's best to take the time-day-place and cost details out and put them into a box.

Don't save calendar items just for post mortems. If you're ever called on to open the mail and sort through the press releases for likely stories, don't simply set aside an announcement of an interesting event for a story *after* the event occurs. By letting your readers know of an event they might want to attend rather than simply documenting it afterward, you serve your readers better. Also, the one event can now be the subject of two stories, one before and one after, giving the paper more news and making the sponsor happier, as well.

ANALYSIS PIECES

Analysis articles explain and interpret news events, offering the perspective of an expert in the field or at least of a reporter or commentator who has closely followed the events.

Alert the copy-desk chief if you are ever mistakenly given an analysis piece to brief. A **brief**—a small two- or three-inch story—appears in a **digest**, which is a collection of small stories under a heading like "News in Brief." The slot person tends to assign digest items on the basis of the wire-service budget rather than after reading the whole story, so it happens fairly often that you'll be mistakenly given an analysis piece that the slot thought was a news story that could be cut.

Don't remove the byline from an analysis piece unless it has a byline logo with it, like those you see with regular contributing commentators. When paginating or proofing a news page with an analysis piece on it—as opposed to an editorial or opinion page—make sure the story has an *Analysis* or similar logo with it.

The headline on an analysis piece should reflect the opinion taken in the story, so it does not have to be objective.

BOATING AND SHIPPING STORIES

If your media outlet is near the water, you may have to edit stories with nautical terms.

Make sure all nautical terms are used properly. Commercial ships are measured by volume, the measurement of all enclosed space on the ship expressed in units of 100 cubic feet to the ton. Fuller description gives passenger capacity, length and age. The size of vessels is expressed in *tonnage,* the weight in long tons of a ship and all its contents (called *displacement*). A *long ton* is 2,240 pounds.

All this is confusing to most readers, so editors should translate into terms recognized by readers, who can visualize length, age and firing power more readily than tonnage: "The 615-foot Bradley, longer than two football fields, . . ."

A *knot* is a measure of speed, not distance (nautical miles an hour). A *nautical mile* is about $1\frac{1}{7}$ land miles. The term *knots per hour* is redundant.

Port is left when facing the front, *starboard* is right, *forward* is as it sounds and *aft* is back. The *stern* is at the back of the ship,.

BOATING AND SHIPPING STORY USAGE

- Boat, ship, etc.—A story referred to a 27-foot ship. Nothing as small as 27 feet is a ship. *Ship* refers to big seagoing vessels such as tankers, freighters and ocean liners. Sailors insist that if it can be hoisted onto another craft, it is a boat, and if it is too large for that, it is a ship. Specific terms such as *cabin cruiser, sloop, schooner, barge* and *dredge* are appropriate.

  "A rescue fleet ranging from primitive bayou pirogues to helicopters prowled the night." A *pirogue* is a canoe or a dugout, so why not simply use the more common term?

- Gangplank—"The youths got to the pier just before the gangplank was lowered." When a ship sails, the gangplank is raised.

- Half-mast, half-staff—A flag can be flown at *half-mast* only on a ship or at a naval base. On land, it's at *half-staff.*

- Helm, tiller, wheel—"Capt. Albert S. Kelly, 75, the pilot who manned the Delta Queen's tiller on Monday . . ." What he manned was the *helm* or *wheel.* Few vessels except sailboats are guided with a *tiller.*

- Under way, underway—For anything non-nautical, *under way* is two words, not one. Even in nautical uses, it is only one word as an adjective in front of what it modifies: "the underway fleet."

🖋 BUSINESS STORIES

Business news is increasingly consumer news. Back in the penny press era, it was discovered that business news could be made interesting to a wider audience by including more "news you can use." After all, news has the most impact when it has the power to affect people personally—in the pocketbook, in the way they live or in their emotions. But business features don't have to end with how-to articles. **Focus pieces**, **analysis pieces** and **personality profiles** play a big role on business pages, as well.

Some common recurring types of business stories include *personal finance stories* (on topics like jobs, credit, college, cars, mortgages, leases, investment, insurance) and *local business features,* which look at new businesses, earnings of big local employers, big shake-ups in management, heroes (personality profiles) and villains (investigations).

Stories about growth indicators look at recurring measurements such as:

- Gross Domestic Product—The quarterly total output of goods and services; newer than the Gross National Product, which included citizens abroad
- Consumer Price Index—A monthly basket of about 400 items
- Unemployment rate—Reported monthly
- Housing starts—Responds quickly to interest rates; reported monthly
- Index of Industrial Production—Monthly index of factories and cars, mines, electricity and gas.

Business news, like any other kind, is most interesting when focused on people rather than things. If a business story seems dull, check whether it's focused on a person acting or reacting, or merely on an abstract business topic. If the latter, let your desk chief know your concern and ask whether it might be sent back for refocusing on a person involved with the issue.

Pay attention to numbers in a business story. Sometimes, business stories get bogged down with lots of figures that are not clearly explained. Insist that figures be explained so readers can more easily relate to them and understand their significance. Also, don't let too many numbers be crammed into a lead. Pick the number that is most important to the reader, then move the others down. People are interested in how the news affects them, not in the figures per se. (See Chapter 4 of this book.)

All who edit business stories should have at least an elementary knowledge of business terms. If you can't distinguish between a *balance sheet* and a *profit-and-loss statement,* between *earnings* and *gross operating income,* and between a *net profit* and *net cash income,* you have some homework to do. It may be helpful to take classes in economics and accounting to learn economic concepts and be able to analyze a budget. At minimum, you should learn how to calculate percentages, read Henry Hazlitt's classic little book, *Economics in One Easy Lesson,* and know a little about the federal agencies that regulate business.

BUSINESS STORY USAGE

- Ampersand—Use an ampersand (&) in a company's name if that is how the company writes it—otherwise, write *and. Company, incorporated* and *limited* are abbreviated at the end of a name, not in the middle. But if a name ends with both *company* and *incorporated*, both are abbreviated.

- Dividends—Dividends reports should use the designation given by the company—*regular, special, extra, increases, interim, quarterly*—or say what was paid previously if there is no specified designation. The story should say whether there is a special or extra dividend paid with the regular dividend and include the amount of previously added payments. When the usual dividend is not paid or reduced, some companies issue an explanatory statement, the gist of which should be included in the story.

- Dow Jones average—The Dow Jones average is one of several indexes used to gauge the stock market. It bases its index on 30 stocks. Changes in it are changes in the index number, not a percentage change.

- *Firm*—*Firm* should not be used interchangeably with *company*. A *firm* is a partnership or unincorporated group. By the way, include the location of the home office.

- Lloyd's of London—Contrary to what most people think, Lloyd's does not itself sell insurance. You cannot have a policy from it. Instead, it's a group of insurance companies, one of which may sell you insurance.

- Savings and loans—These should not be called *banks.* They may be referred to as *companies, institutions* or *associations.*

- Technique, technology—A *technique*, idea or method is not a *technology*, but for some reason, groups that put on seminars like to speak of their "groundbreaking technology" when all they're doing is teaching their ideas.

BUSINESS STORY CLICHÉS TO AVOID

biggest, best, first, groundbreaking, revolutionary (these terms are too often used without checking that they are accurate)
new and improved
product (instead of the kind of item or its name)

BUSINESS STORY TIGHTENING

The preferred form is shown in parentheses:

depreciate in value (depreciate)
merchandise (goods)
merchandize (sell)

CALENDAR ITEMS

See "Press-Release Stories" on Page 212.

✦ CELEBRITY NEWS

One of the main characteristics that makes something newsworthy is the prominence of the person involved. Prominence has to do with how famous, powerful or rich someone is.

Celebrities are newsworthy. Sure, Britney Spears' losing custody of her children or Paris Hilton's latest driving violation may not be the most important things going on in the world on a given day, but they will certainly be talked about by your audience. The trick is not to become too tabloid-ish, though, because too much coverage of such news causes readers to associate you with the **tabloids** and can damage your credibility.

A number of legal points discussed in Chapter 5 should be kept in mind when editing stories about celebrities:

Celebrities have less protection than an average person when it comes to suing the media for libel. Celebrities must prove that the article was published or broadcast with "actual malice," meaning "reckless disregard of the truth," not just that it was wrong and negligent. This doesn't mean, however, journalists should intentionally lower their standards when reporting on celebrities.

The public fascination celebrities engender doesn't mean they don't deserve private lives. The main defense the media have against an invasion of privacy lawsuit is newsworthiness, but celebrity status doesn't mean the media should seek and reveal all embarrassing private information about prominent people for public titillation. Nor does it entitle the press to stalk or trespass to get stories.

Celebrities have a right to endorse or not endorse products and causes of their own choosing without advertisers appropriating their name, voice or image without permission. Appropriation of these for commercial purposes can result in an invasion of privacy lawsuit.

CELEBRITY NEWS USAGE

- Debut, host, premiere—*The AP Stylebook* says none of these words should be used as a noun. The movie *will debut* or *have its premiere*. The star *will be host* of the event.

CELEBRITY NEWS CLICHÉS

controversial
lovely and talented
whirlwind (courtship, romance)

CHRONOLOGICAL STORIES

Stories presented in chronological order—earliest to most recent—were common during the colonial press period but are seldom used today because they can be boring to modern readers. Readers today tend to prefer that reporters start most stories with the latest news, not the earliest, and get to the point sooner. There are exceptions, however:

Use the chronological approach when the subject of an interview relates a complicated series of events. There's nothing wrong with allowing the subject to tell the story with a minimum of interference from the writer as long as it's interesting.

Use the chronological approach when reporting a detailed event. For example, an account of a gunman's siege may lend itself to this treatment. So might the reconstruction of a pilot's frantic final moments before an airplane crash or a step-by-step account of how the Legislature altered a bill to appease lobbyists.

Start with a lead summarizing the story, then transition to the chronological account, concluding, perhaps, with a dramatic ending or continuing in inverted-pyramid style.

COLOR PIECES

The purpose of a **color piece** is to make the readers feel as though "they are there"—to give them a word picture of the sights, sounds, smells, and even touch and taste, if possible, of an event or locale. Color pieces are often assigned as side-bars or follows to hard-news stories.

Use a nut graf near the top of the story to give readers a main point on which to focus.

Don't overuse modifiers. Although a color piece involves more description than is typical in news stories, that's not a license to overuse modifiers. What constitutes overuse is a matter of experience and taste, but modifiers are usually unnecessary when a more specific noun or verb is available, or when the reader may have a sense that details are coming fast and thick with no apparent theme or reason.

COLUMNS

Sports, entertainment, humor, editorial, food, garden, home improvement, religion, antiques and advice are some of the main kinds of columns.

It's especially important to remember when editing them to know when to put your fingers on the keys and when to take them off. Columns are generally the most personal of feature stories, and nothing will infuriate a reporter so much as a copy editor needlessly rewriting a column.

Columns often contain elements of a review, so it's important for legal purposes to beware of false statements about matters of fact as opposed to mere negative opinion.

Columns are one of the places where the news media most often pass on famous misquotations or misinformation. This is because columns are more personal and involve more writing off the top of the head rather than reporting. See Chapter 4.

🚀 COURT STORIES

Editors must have some knowledge of legal terms and the legal process if they are to make the story and headline technically correct yet meaningful to the public. See Chapter 5.

The most important point to remember: Make sure the reporting does not incriminate anyone not yet convicted in court. Journalists are legally protected in reporting libelous statements made in court proceedings provided the coverage is fair and accurate. Similar statements made outside the courtroom, though, do not receive the same protection.

The Fifth Amendment guarantees the right against self-incrimination. The report should not suggest that the use of this protection is a cover-up for guilt. Phrases such as "hiding behind the Fifth" should be eliminated.

To say "the grand jury failed to indict Jones" implies it shirked its duty.

Consider the ethics of reporting names and addresses of victims. Names of women, men or children in rape cases or attempted rape cases generally should not be used. Nor should the story give any clue to their addresses in a way by which they can be identified, especially if the perpetrator has not been apprehended. But in other cases, some feminists have argued that rape victims' names should not be withheld because rape victims have no reason to feel shame.

Avoid legalese. For example, "In a petition for a writ of mandamus, the new bank's incorporators asked the court to . . ." should be changed to "The new bank's incorporators asked the court to . . ."

Referring on second reference to the *appellee* or the *appellant* is confusing. The best way is to repeat the names.

Lawyers are fond of word doubling: *last will and testament, null and void, on or about, written instrument, and/or.* "The maximum sentence is a $20,000 fine and/or 15 years' imprisonment." The maximum would be the fine and 15 years.

Make sure the headline accurately reflects the story. An accurate story with an inaccurate headline can still pose a legal problem, especially because many readers will read only the headline and not the story.

In some civil suits, the main news peg is the enormous sum sought by the plaintiff. The headline should be accurate, of course, but whether the same angle should be included in the headline is questionable. In some damage claims, the relief sought is far greater than the plaintiff expects to collect. The judgment actually awarded is the news and the headline.

COURT STORY USAGE

- Arraignment, preliminary hearing—An *arraignment* is a formal proceeding at which a defendant steps forward to give the court a plea of guilty or not guilty. It should not be used interchangeably with *preliminary hearing*, which is held in a magistrate's court and is a device to show probable cause that a crime has been committed and that there is a likely suspect.

- Bail, parole, probation—*Bail* is the security given for the release of a prisoner. The reporter reveals ignorance when writing, "The woman is now in jail under $5,000 bail." She can't be in jail under bail. She can be free on bail, or she can be held in lieu of bail. *Parole* is a conditional release of a prisoner with an indeterminate or unexpired sentence. *Probation* allows a person convicted of some offense to go free, under suspension of sentence during good behavior and generally under the supervision of a probation officer.

- Charge—"The psychologist charged last night that black high school students generally do not think of the university as a friendly place." The statement is more an observation than a charge.

- Decisions, judgments, opinions, rulings, verdicts—A *verdict* is the finding of a jury. A judge renders *decisions, judgments, rulings* and *opinions*, but seldom verdicts, unless the right to a jury trial is waived. Although verdicts are returned by juries in both criminal and civil actions, a guilty verdict is found only in criminal actions. Attorneys general or similar officials give *opinions*, not *rulings*.

- Divorce—Divorces are *granted* or *obtained* not *awarded* like a medal.

- Fines, sentences—Fines and sentences are not *given*—they are not gifts. Rather, the defendant was fined or sentenced.

- Insanity—Someone is found "not guilty by reason of insanity," not "innocent by reason of insanity."

- Judge, jurist, justice—Members of the Supreme Court are *justices*, not *judges* or *supreme judges*. The title of the U.S. Supreme Court's chief justice is "Chief Justice of the United States." A *jurist* is an expert in the law, not any judge or jury member.

- Mistrial—Judges *declare*, but do not *order*, mistrials.

- Pleas—Someone can plea *guilty, not guilty* or *nolo contender* (not admitting guilt but not contesting the charge). There is no such thing as a plea of innocence. And the past tense is *pleaded*, not *pled*.

- Sentences—A jail sentence does not mean, necessarily, that a person has been jailed. The individual may be free on bail, free pending an appeal or on probation during a suspended imposition of sentence. Prison sentences may be consecutive or concurrent. If a man is sentenced to two *consecutive* three-year terms, he faces six years of imprisonment. If his sentences are *concurrent*, he faces three years. But, why use these terms? The total sentence is what counts with the readers and the prisoner. Note also that if a person has been sentenced to five years but the sentence is *suspended*, he or she is given a suspended five-year sentence, not a five-year suspended sentence.

- Statements—Statements are either *written* or *oral*, not verbal (which just means in words).

COURT STORY TIGHTENING

The preferred form is shown in parenthesis:

apprehended (arrested)
court litigation (lawsuit)
file a lawsuit against (sue, file suit against)
statutory grounds for divorce (grounds for divorce)
taken into custody (arrested)

LEGAL TERMS REQUIRING EXPLANATION

Knowing these terms will help make you a more knowledgeable journalist when it comes to court stories, or at least help you enjoy more an episode of *Boston Legal*.

- Accessories before the fact—Those charged with helping another who committed the felony

- Acquitted—Found not guilty

- Arraigned—Brought to court to answer to a criminal charge

- Bequest—Gift

- Civil action—Pertaining to private rights of individuals and to legal proceedings against other individuals, businesses or government entities

- Continuance—Adjournment of the case

- Corpus delicti—The evidence necessary to establish that a crime has been committed; not restricted to the body of a murder victim—it can apply as well to the charred remains of a burned house

- Debenture—Obligation

- Demurrer—A pleading admitting the facts in a complaint or answer but contending they are legally insufficient.

- Domicile—Home

- Extradition—Surrender of the prisoner to officials of another state
- Extortion—Oppressive or illegal obtaining of money or other things of value
- Felony—A crime graver in nature than a misdemeanor, usually punishable by imprisonment or death; misdemeanors, however, can carry sentences of up to one year
- In camera—In the judge's chambers
- Indicted—Accused or charged by a grand jury
- An information—An accusation or a charge filed by a prosecutor
- Liquidate—Settle a debt
- Litigant—Participant in a lawsuit
- Paralegal—Legal assistant
- Plaintiff—Person filing the lawsuit
- Plat—Map
- Released on personal recognizance—Released on word of honor to do a particular act, such as not to leave the district and to show up in court on a certain date
- Remanded—Sent the case back to a lower court for review
- Res judicata—Matter already decided
- Stay order—Stop the action or suspend the legal proceeding
- Venire—Those summoned to serve as jurors
- Writ—A judge's or a court's order
- Writ of habeas corpus—An order to bring the prisoner to court so the court may determine whether the prisoner has been denied rights
- Writ of mandamus—A court order telling a public official to do something

CRIME STORIES

As with accident and court stories, the worst thing you can do in a crime story is to imply someone is guilty who has not been convicted. Even if a police officer tells you someone is "guilty as sin" or that "this arrest solves 32 burglaries," such statements would convict the suspect in print. Here's an example of a lead that convicts:

> Two Marines are being held without bond after terrorizing a family, stealing a car and trading shots with officers.

As written, that lead convicts the men who had not yet stood trial. The writer, instead, should have reported what charges were filed against the Marines.

Listing the wrong name in a crime story is a route to libel action. Thorough verification of first, middle and last names, of addresses and of relationships is a necessity in editing the crime story.

Avoid *alleged* and *allegedly* as modifiers of the suspect or his or her possible deeds ("the *alleged* rapist," "the suspect *allegedly* raped"). Instead, use a construction such as, "The victim said a man climbed through her bathroom window and raped her. Police later arrested William Jones."

Don't identify someone as a *suspected criminal*. Also, don't say someone is a "reputed organized crime figure" unless you're quoting privileged reports, such as transcripts from hearings before Congress. The term *would-be rapist* makes someone guilty of attempted rape.

Crime stories usually have a delayed-ID lead because most victims aren't well-known.   The stories also often are written in passive voice because usually the perpetrator is unknown and a descriptive phrase about him or her would be less important than a descriptive phrase about the victim. Examples:

> An Ypsilanti woman was held at gunpoint for four hours Monday by her ex-husband before police were able to talk the man into releasing her. (passive voice)

> An Ann Arbor youth was severely beaten by a group of teenagers after a rock concert Monday night and robbed of $17. (passive voice)

> A man in a ski mask abducted a Southfield woman from a shopping-mall parking lot Monday and forced her to drive to a secluded location where he raped her. (active voice)

Other advice for editing crime stories:

- Avoid printing confessions until they have been admitted into court as evidence.
- Avoid printing names or addresses of juvenile offenders or victims as well as victims of rape, sexual assault or sexual abuse.
- Generally, avoid gruesome photos of victims.
- Avoid saying a victim was *unharmed* if he or she was involved in a psychologically harrowing situation such as a kidnapping or an attempted rape.
- Avoid unconscious sexism and racism, which often pop up in descriptions of victims or suspects.

CRIME STORY USAGE

- Attempted (holdup, robbery)—There's no such thing as an *attempted holdup*. A holdup is a robbery even if the bad guy got nothing from the victim.
- Burglary, larceny, robbery, theft—A *robber* steals by force. A *thief* steals without resorting to force. *Theft* suggests stealth. A *burglar* makes an unauthorized entry into a building. If a person is caught in the act, pulls a gun on the homeowner and makes off with the family silverware, that person is a robber. *Theft* and *larceny* both mean taking what belongs to another. *Larceny* is the more specific term and can be proved only when the thief has the stolen property. Pickpockets and shoplifters are thieves. By the way, money is not

robbed. A bank is *robbed*; the money is *stolen.* "A man in uniform swindled $1,759 from a woman." No, the person is swindled, not the money.

- Drugs, narcotics—All narcotics are drugs, but many drugs are not narcotics.
- Homicide, murder—Avoid calling a homicide a *murder* until someone has been convicted. But you may call the trial a *murder trial,* if the defendant has been charged with murder.
- Lawman—The word *lawman* can mean too many things: a village constable, a sheriff's deputy or the sheriff, a prosecutor, a bailiff, a judge, an FBI agent or a revenue agent. It is also sexist. A more precise word is almost always more suitable in a newspaper.
- Looting—It is incorrect to write:

  Two men were fined and given suspended sentences Friday in Municipal Court for stealing newsracks and looting money from them.

  Thieves broke into 26 automobiles parked near the plant and looted some small items.

  Money or other property is not looted. That from which it is taken is looted.

- Sheriff's deputies—Not *deputy sheriffs.*

CRIME STORY CLICHÉS TO AVOID

daring daylight robbery	thorough investigation
hail of bullets	tragic crime
senseless murder	

CRIME STORY TIGHTENING

The preferred form is shown in parenthesis:

armed gunman (gunman)	self-confessed (confessed)
badly decomposed body (body)	was in possession of (had)
fatal killing (killing)	

➤ EDUCATION STORIES

Examples of education stories are the local Board of Education's meeting; personality profiles of teachers, students or administrators; issues facing education, such as cheating, plagiarism, taxes to support education; and so on.

EDUCATION STORY TIGHTENING

The preferred form is shown in parentheses:

educator, educationist (teacher)	language on paper (write)
facilitator (teacher, leader)	resource center (library)

ENTERTAINMENT STORIES

Entertainment stories can be reviews of movies, plays, books, music, art shows or restaurants; personality profiles of celebrities; advance stories on entertainment events, such as movie or theater openings, tonight's TV shows or the release of a new album by a popular performer; focus pieces on issues, controversies and trends in the arts; entertainment columns; and so on.

For editing advice, see the entries for the specific kind of story it is, such as a review, advance piece, focus piece or column.

ENTERTAINMENT STORY CLICHÉS TO AVOID

feel-good movie
in a world where . . . , one (man, woman) . . .

 ## FIRST-PERSON STORIES

First-person accounts—where the reporter speaks as *I*—should be used sparingly because the focus should normally be on the news, not on the reporter. But first-person stories are perfectly acceptable when the reporter is an eyewitness to an event. A personal column is often written in first person, as is a story based on a day the journalist spent riding along with an ambulance driver or a police officer (participatory journalism).

 ## FOCUS PIECES

The focus piece is used primarily for writing an analysis of an issue, but it's adaptable to other kinds of features, as well. The writer E. B. White once advised: "Don't write about Man. Write about a man." That's basically what the focus piece does. It's also sometimes called *The Wall Street Journal* approach.

A story about a particular person dealing with a particular problem serves as a frame around a discussion in the middle of the broader issue. After starting with this person, the article has a nut graf in which readers find out why they're reading this—the larger controversy, issue or problem of which this person's experience is an example. The nut graf is actually a transition to the discussion and analysis that makes up the bulk of the story, then the ending is a return to the person with whom the story started.

The story can be particularly effective if the writer uses the person in the beginning and end of the story, and as a thread running through the discussion and analysis part, as well. This isn't mandatory, but when the writer does it, the article can gain narrative cohesion.

Make sure there is a nut graf in a focus piece, and make sure it comes right after the feature lead. If the nut graf is missing or too far down in the story, readers get confused and put off.

A common variation of the focus piece is the *multiple-interview story*. The story starts with a single person, moves to a nut graf, then quotes from various sources to develop points in the body. The ending may return to the person in the lead, or it may end, instead, with a strong quote from one of the other sources.

In any story with more than one source, make sure that it's always clear which person is being quoted and that all second references to names (last name only) are preceded by a first reference with full name and title.

⤴ FOLLOWS

A **follow** is an update to a previous story. The original story may have broken off your cycle and has already been reported by your competition, whether newspaper or broadcast media. We'd call that a **second-cycle story**. Or the original story may have run on a previous day in your own newspaper. Then, we'd call it a **second-day story**. Of course these days, with fewer than 20 cities having more than one paper, the idea of a second cycle seems almost obsolete.

The story may be a **developing story** that runs consecutively over several days as new events unfold, such as the war in Iraq, political campaigns or trials.

The story may be an **update** on a story that happened weeks, months or years earlier. This is the "Where are they now?" story that often looks at how someone or something has changed since being in the news. For example: What kind of military threat does militant Islam still pose after U.S. actions in Afghanistan and Iraq?

A follow may contain:

* Information not available earlier.
* Information obtained through reporter enterprise.
* Fresh details, such as color or background.
* Analysis about the news of the first story.
* Reaction from those affected by the original story.
* Local reactions to a state, national or international story.

Make sure a follow has a second-day lead—one stressing new information that advances the story. The cardinal sin of follow stories is putting a **first-day lead** on a second-day story—that is, beginning with the old news rather than the new. This mistake is made for one of two reasons: Either the reporter has not kept up with the news and doesn't know the old information has already been reported, or the reporter makes the mistake of thinking that the old news is more important because it's more general than the newer news. But what's important is what's new.

Somewhere in the story, there should be a tie-back paragraph leading to a brief explanation of previous developments for readers who missed the original news or need to be reminded. Often, the **tie-back paragraph** will follow the lead, then the story will return to its main focus on new information, ending with more details recapping the original story.

Follow-Up Features

When a big news event breaks, a feature story will often be assigned to provide color and human interest as a sidebar to the main story, or to provide a new angle that can keep a story in the public eye and move it along in the absence of fresh developments. Sometimes, reporters who provide color pieces neglect making the point clear. *Make sure there's a nut graf near the top that lets readers know what's going on and ties this piece to the news peg.*

As with any follow, the news that should be stressed is what's new, not merely a repeat of what's already been made public. A color or human-interest piece may not have any new developments to report, but what's new are the details or the inside angle reported here first. So, for example, a feature follow to a plane crash providing a firsthand account by an observer or passenger should begin with what's new to this story—calling attention to the inside scoop—not simply repeating that a plane crashed the day before.

Commemorative features appear at the first anniversary of an event and perhaps every fifth anniversary thereafter, reminding people of important events on this date in history. Reporters typically interview survivors who experienced the event firsthand and try to capture its color and significance for people today.

FOOD FEATURES

Often, these stories are written as a personality profile of a cook or a feature story about a particular kind of food—ice cream, barbecue or Chinese food, for example—to which some relevant recipes are added at the end.

Unless your local paper's style is to uppercase all the main words in the recipe title as though it were a book title, remember that the wire-service rule for names of foods is that only words that would be proper names by themselves are capitalized:

Wrong: Boston Cream Pie
Right: Boston cream pie

Recipes use numerals and fractions exclusively—don't follow the usual rules for writing them out.

Recipe writers tend to forget the rule about putting a comma before an independent clause. A sentence like "Mix thoroughly and bake for 30 minutes" should take a comma before the "and." After all, we have two independent clauses with *you* as the understood subject of each. How do we know this isn't a compound predicate? You are supposed to bake for 30 minutes, but you don't mix for 30 minutes, as well.

HISTORY PIECES

Local-history stories can be immensely popular features. If your paper doesn't run them often, suggest them to the lifestyles editor. The basic structure is often like that of the personality profile or sometimes that of a chronological narrative topped with a teaser to interest readers in the story that follows. The more the piece is written like a short story, though, the more questions you should ask about the details (such as the weather) and the quotes (especially dialog) to make sure these parts are not simply made up for the sake of the story.

HOW-TO ARTICLES OR SERVICE JOURNALISM

Not all **service-journalism** pieces are in the how-to format. Others, for example, include calendar listings, lists of the 10-best type, and focus or multiple-interview pieces on lifestyle issues. But the how-to is the most common service-journalism piece, and the two terms are sometimes used synonymously. Food, home improvement, interior design, gardening and photography are some subjects often written about in the how-to format.

The reporter should not pretend to be an expert if he or she isn't. How-to features take either the **writer-as-expert approach** or the **outside-expert approach.** Unless the feature writer is an expert on the subject, the latter approach should be taken, with an interview of at least one expert to quote in the piece. A common mistake of beginning feature writers is to try to write a how-to piece like a term paper—consulting published sources and then writing as though an expert.

Make sure the directions are clear and easy to follow. If they're not, get clarification from the reporter before assuming you know what was intended. Generally speaking, the big question is whether the reader could do this based on these instructions alone.

Suggestions that will make the how-to work better for the readers are to include a list of materials needed for a project, safety-precaution notes and a sidebar about how to troubleshoot. Also, be on the lookout for technical jargon that can be rewritten in more common language.

HUMAN-INTEREST STORIES

The term **human-interest story** is often used as a synonym for *feature*, but here it refers more specifically to a story focusing on an unusual or emotionally involving event. Such stories often appear on Page One, despite the lack of a news peg, because they are interesting, humorous or odd and are likely to cause people to talk about them.

Beware of human-interest stories lacking specific source names that could verify the story. Folklorist Jan Harold Brunvand has documented a number of urban legends that have been reported as news by the media. Beware, too, of common hoax stories, such as those in Chapter 4.

LABOR DISPUTES

Stories of labor controversies should give the reasons for the dispute, the length of time the strike has been in progress and the claims by both the union and the company.

Editors should be on guard against loaded terms. There is a tendency in labor stories to refer to management proposals as *offers* and to labor proposals as *demands.* The correct word should be used for the correct connotation.

Strikebreaker and *scab,* which are loaded terms, have no place in the news if used to describe men or women who individually accept positions vacated by strikers. The expression "honored the picket line" often appears in the news, even though a more accurate expression is "refused (or declined) to cross a picket line."

On estimates of wages or production lost, the story should have authoritative sources, not street-corner guesses. An individual does not speak for the majority unless authorized to do so. Statements by workers or minor officials should be downplayed until they have been documented.

Make sure you understand any math involved in the various claims or proposals. If a worker gets a 10-cent-an-hour increase effective immediately, an additional 10 cents a year hence and another 10 cents the third year, that worker does not receive a 30-cent-an-hour increase. The increase at the time of settlement is still 10 cents an hour.

LABOR STORY USAGE

- Arbitrator, concilator, fact finder, mediator—A *fact finder* listens to both sides' positions and tries to determine what the facts are when they are disputed. A *conciliator* or *mediator* in a labor dispute recommends terms of a settlement. The decision of an *arbitrator* usually is binding.
- Closed shop, union shop—In a *closed shop,* the employer may hire only those who are members of the union. In a *union shop,* the employer may select employees, but the workers are required to join the union within a specified time after starting work.
- Labor leader, union leader—*Union leader* is usually preferred to *labor leader.*

- On strike, struck—It also is common to read, "The company has been on strike for the last 25 days." No. The employees are *on strike*. The company has been *struck*.

⭐ MEDICAL NEWS

Translate technical terms into plain English. See the Medical Story Tightening list below.

Avoid trade names of drugs. Use the generic term unless the story is about a particular manufacturer's drug.

MEDICAL STORY USAGE

- Anesthesiologist—A doctor who administers anesthesia is an *anesthesiologist,* not an *anesthetist.*
- Babies—Babies are *born,* not *delivered.* Mothers deliver. Use *Caesarian section,* not *C section.* Remember that weights of babies are always written as numerals even if in single digits, and ages of babies are always written as numerals, even if single digits or days or weeks or months rather than years.
- Condition—Don't write that someone is in *serious condition* if the person wasn't even taken to the hospital. Avoid *guarded condition* or *resting comfortably.*
- Heart condition—To write someone has a *heart condition* or a temperature means nothing. Everyone has both. It's only news when either is abnormal.
- Illnesses—The illness, not the patient, is *diagnosed.*
- Injuries—An injury is *sustained* only if it is capable of causing death. If it wasn't sustained, it was *suffered*—injuries are not *received.*
- Jaundice—Jaundice is a symptom, not a disease.
- Opthalmologist, optometrist—An *ophthalmologist* is a doctor who diagnoses eye disease. An *optometrist* tests for and prescribes glasses;.
- Slings—A person wears a sling *on* his or her arm. That person doesn't wear his or her arm *in* a sling.
- Temperature—It means nothing to say someone *has a temperature* because everyone does. What's important is if it's abnormal.

MEDICAL STORY TIGHTENING

The preferred form is shown in parentheses:

abrasion (scrape)	hemorrhaging (bleeding)
contusion (bruise)	laceration (cut)
fracture (break, crack)	physician (doctor)

MEETING STORIES

When only one main thing is decided at a meeting, use a **single-element-what lead**. To focus on the one most important thing decided of several that were discussed, use the **most-important-element-what lead**.

> The City Council voted 5-1 Monday to approve unit-plan zoning for a 60-acre tract north of Interstate 70 on U.S. 63 North.

If a group decides at a meeting on several things that all have something in common, use a **summary-what lead** that summarizes them by focusing on what they have in common.

> The City Council took advantage Monday of a light agenda to approve a variety of zoning matters.

Occasionally, more than one thing is decided at a meeting, and each is important enough to mention in the lead. This is a **multiple-element-what lead**. It tells with parallel verbs two or more actions that were decided. Even though all the elements mentioned are important enough to be in the lead, you should still try to make sure that they're listed in the order of most-to-least important.

> The City Council on Monday rejected a bid by beverage-container-ordinance opponents to put a repeal measure on the ballot for spring election and restored $1.2 million in funding to the Columbia Arts Council.

If the group reached a decision about something, the story usually stresses the action taken, the vote, the reasons for it and against it, and the expected consequences of the action.

If the group discussed an issue but failed to reach a decision, the story usually stresses the most significant issue raised, any consensus reached and reasons given on different sides of the arguments. Or the reporter may take a feature approach that stresses, for example, one person's colorfully expressed views. The body of the story might include the following:

- Background of the issue
- Arguments for and against it
- Name and identification of those on each side
- Time and location of the meeting
- Additional matters discussed
- Makeup of the audience, the number attending, audience reaction
- Agenda for the next meeting

Government News

City Council and *County Commission* are capitalized with or without the city or county; *council* and *commission,* however, are lowercase. In most states, the *Legislature,* without the state's name, is capitalized, but AP says *legislature* should be lowercase in states like Missouri that have a body with a different formal name like General Assembly.

AP says: "Amendments, ordinances, resolutions and rules are adopted or approved. Bills are passed. Laws are enacted."

OBITUARIES

The **formula obit** is the most common type of obituary. It starts as a notice from the funeral home, often the result of filling out a form provided by the newspaper. The obituary is then written following a typical order that is varied primarily for the timing of the services and the individual circumstances of the person's life.

Each newspaper has its own obituary formula that will vary somewhat. Usually, you'll just have to figure out the formula from comparing previously run obits.

The standard **formula obit** usually leads with the person's name and date of death. A variation is to lead with the services if they are timelier than the date of death. The **feature obit**, though, usually leads with some distinguishing characteristic or achievement of the deceased.

Both the standard and feature obit should be distinguished from the paid funeral notice. Although it may look like an obituary, it's paid for and run as an ad. Because it's an ad, the family or friends can say pretty much what they want and not be edited the way the other two types would be.

Copy editors should check obits to make sure they conform to the local standard obit formula and local policy matters. Here are some typical policies concerning matters in obits. Of course, your newspaper's policy will likely vary in some ways, but this will give you an idea of the sort of issues involved.

Addresses Burglars often burglarize the homes of relatives of the deceased when the address is printed in an obituary. That's because they can safely guess the relatives will be out of the house at the time of the funeral. As a result, many newspapers will not print street addresses of the deceased or of survivors. All individual's addresses, in town or out, are reported in obits simply by town.

Some addresses, however, are helpful in an obit: the place where visitation and services will be held (often the funeral home but many times a place of worship), as well as the cemetery. Notice, by the way, the spelling of *cemetery*—there are no *a*'s in it. Another common misspelling in obits is *cremation* (not *creamation,* as though the person were going to be made into a dairy product). Addresses for visitation, services and burial let interested people know where to go to pay their respects.

Cause of Death   All deaths are *sudden,* even ones preceded by long suffering; *unexpected* is the word you want. People die of injuries *suffered* or *sustained,* not *received.* People do not die of an apparent heart attack—it's not visible.

Also, people die *of* not *from* a disease; of *heart illness,* not *heart failure;* after a *long illness,* not an *extended illness;* and *following* or *after* an operation, not *as a result of* it unless malpractice has been proved.

Sometimes, relatives do not want the newspaper to list the cause of death if it is suicide or AIDS or some other cause embarrassing to them. They may withhold it; they may tell you but ask you not to print it; they may actually ask you to lie about it. Not all newspapers will want to investigate every unlisted cause of death. But no newspaper should ever knowingly lie. As for withholding known information, the trend is not to withhold newsworthy information and instead to tell the truth—however embarrassing it may be to the family and no matter how much they protest.

Courtesy Titles   Use courtesy titles—for the deceased only—on second and subsequent references: *Mrs. Jones, Miss Jones, Ms. Jones* (ask family for woman's preference), *Dr. Jones, Mr. Jones.*

Dates   Because obits are clipped and saved for years, some newspapers use the date rather than the day for describing the time of death, visitation, services and burial. For dates of birth, wedding and death, use month-date-year order. For dates of visitation, services and burial, use time-month-date order.

Always check that the birth date subtracted from the death date agrees with the age listed. Remember, too, you cannot simply subtract the years and stop—you have to make sure the person's birthday has occurred this year, otherwise subtract one more. Example: A person born Aug. 3, 1928, who died May 18, 2007, was 78, not 79.

Flowers   If the family requests that flowers not be sent, ask whether they prefer donations be sent to a favorite charity. If yes, get the name and address, and print that in the obituary—in addition to or in place of sentences like "The family requests no flowers," according to local policy. Some newspapers never used to print phrases like *in lieu of flowers* out of deference to the florist industry, but such a policy is now commonly rejected.

Negative Information   Sometimes, in the description of a person's life, journalists have to decide whether to include unsavory things about the deceased. Should a minor crime committed a quarter century ago be included in the obituary? Probably not. But good editors should not hesitate to include negative information if they deem it important.

Semantics   Never write euphemisms such as someone *passed away, succumbed, met her Maker* or *is resting in the arms of Jesus.* The deceased is referred to as *Mr. Jones,* not *the dearly departed.*

Do not write that a spouse *preceded him in death*. Instead, write, "She died in 2006" or "She died earlier." Do not make matters worse by writing "She died before him," which sounds as though she died before his very eyes.

Survivors A man is survived by his *wife,* not his *widow*. A woman is survived by her *husband,* not her *widower*.

Do not write that survivors are *of the home*. This means they live at the same address as the deceased. Instead, give the town for the address as for everyone else.

When listing groupings of survivors (usually only the spouse, parents, siblings, children, grandchildren and great-grandchildren), use a comma after the name of the grouping, commas within the items and a semicolon between them: "Survivors include two brothers, John Hill of Ann Arbor and Ben Hill of Ypsilanti; three sisters, Macy Weinhurst of Buffalo, N.Y., Sarah Peters of Port Huron and Jane Sommers of Detroit; and five grandchildren." Note the semicolon before the final *and* in the series.

OBITUARY USAGE

- Body—Not *corpse* or *remains*
- Burial—Not *internment*
- Casket—Not *coffin*
- Mortician—Not *undertaker*
- Services—Not *obsequies or funeral services*. It is permissible to say a minister either *conducts* or *officiates* at services. If the deceased is Catholic, a funeral Mass is *offered,* not *held*.

Feature Obituaries

Feature obits are written as feature stories about the deceased rather than in the typical formula-obit fashion.

Obituaries have always been one of the most often read parts of a newspaper, but the obit beat traditionally has been palmed off on cub reporters. Perhaps that's because obituaries were usually among the most formulaic of newspaper writing, and seasoned reporters were called to the task only when the deceased was prominent enough to warrant a feature obit, which often ran on one of the news pages rather than with the regular obits.

Now, however, journalists are at last beginning to recognize the importance of obits, and awards for outstanding reporting are sometimes going to obituary writers who take the time to featurize obits of interesting people, even if they aren't well-known. If obit reporters have enough time before deadline, they should consider making a few calls to the deceased's friends and family and writing a feature obit.

The feature obit is usually organized around a theme—a distinguishing characteristic or achievement of the deceased that serves as a summing up of that person's life. Here's an example of a lead from a feature obit that demonstrates this:

Ben Jeffers had a city in his basement.

Mr. Jeffers himself built all the houses, factories, schools, churches, even the farm buildings in the surrounding countryside. He also built the roads and laid the train track connecting them all. It was a 27-year project for the model railroader, who died May 25, 2007.

"Ben loved playing with his trains and building a little world around them," said Fran Jeffers, his wife. "He told me once that one of his first memories of life was traveling with his father on a train to Chicago."

One of the biggest problems with feature obits is that writers sometimes try to build the feature around a trite theme rather than finding something unique or more interesting. Here are three examples:

Stephanie Benson dreamed of one day dancing on Broadway. But the 21-year-old Eastern Michigan University theater major will never get her chance. She was killed in a car wreck Aug. 18, 2007.

Pat Albrecht could always make her friends laugh. There was the time. . . .

His family and friends remember Hank Petrovik as a man who never had an unkind word for anyone.

Although the structure of a feature obit is different from that of the typical formula obit, it obeys the same style rules.

PERSONALITY PROFILES

A personality profile is used when the focus is on a person rather than an event or thing.

Although personality profiles are generally about a living person the reporter has interviewed, the feature obit, in which the reporter interviews friends and family of the deceased and perhaps researches the paper trail, is also a kind of personality profile.

The personality profile is also often used as a top for cooking stories—cook-of-the-week features, for example.

Although ostensibly about a thing, odd-hobby and odd-occupation stories usually end up as variations on the personality profile because they are best written by focusing on a person engaged in the activity.

One note of warning: With rare exceptions, we are past the days when the point of a story can acceptably be about a person engaged in a hobby or occupation that's odd only because of a person's race or sex.

Remember that personality profiles are selective and themed—they shouldn't just be a collection of assorted facts about someone. Although the following advice is aimed mainly at feature writers, it can also help copy editors know what typically will work best. Rene J. Cappon, feature editor with the Associated Press, offers this thought on personality profiles in his book, *The Word:* "Don't cram a profile with routine biographical detail; keep that for the obit. Look for the characteristics, habits, traits, working methods and experiences that make your subject different."

Cappon suggests that in profiles of newsworthy people, it's a good idea for the writer "to concentrate on qualities that got them there" and especially steer clear of reporting the clichés that celebrities spout in answer to routine questions they hear all the time. (There's an amusing scene in the movie *Bull Durham* in which an experienced baseball player teaches a rookie a number of clichés to use when answering questions from the press.)

Beginning writers often overquote in personality profiles. You'll know this is the case if the writer is a **cub reporter** (an intern or a new hire) and you see many long quotations that remind you of a student trying to fill space in a term paper. Alert the copy-desk chief if this is the case, and get permission to whittle down the quotes, paraphrase and use partial quotes. Get permission first, as this could cause not only a personnel dispute but also could throw off the layout if the story length is changed much.

POLITICAL STORIES

Political stories include profiles of candidates, analyses of issues, stories about polls on issues or candidates, columns, stories about speeches and meetings and votes.

Perhaps the single biggest problem with political stories is making sure there's no bias in them. Opinion pieces are a different matter, of course, because readers expect those to take a side. A good rule of thumb is whatever your own political beliefs, make a special effort to make sure the other side is represented fairly.

Remember to cover the issues, not just the horse race. A study in 2007 found that horse-race stories—those concentrating on who's leading in the polls or has gathered more money—outnumber issue stories in the media by 7-1. Readers need to see more stories explaining the issues better.

POLITICAL STORY CLICHÉS TO AVOID

arch conservative, arch liberal—(The use of *arch* is more of a value judgment than the more simply informative *conservative* or *liberal*.)
closed-door hearing, closed-door meeting)—(drop the *door*)
dark horse

PRESS-RELEASE STORIES

Don't let any press release be published without a reporter checking it out and rewriting it. Why? Press releases are often written by people with no journalistic training. The result is that press releases typically come in written more like ads than news—full of self-serving propagandistic language. Often, there's no sense of what in the release is the real news that would interest your audience—sometimes, important information such as the time of an event is even left out. To top it off, the releases are almost never in AP style and may even contain misspellings, poor grammar and awkward, vague or wordy writing.

People send press releases to newspapers to get free publicity. You're not obligated to give it to them. Read the release, and determine whether it's really news. Ask yourself: Does it contain information your readers would want to know or should know? If not, raise the matter with the copy-desk chief.

Be on the lookout for any nonobjective language the reporter might have missed. Cut everything that is self-serving rather than informative—anything that editorializes or sounds opinionated or like an advertisement.

Improve the wording, if necessary, to make it clearer and simpler while leaving in all the real information. Look for anything that's unclear or missing or could mean more than one thing. Were any of your questions unanswered? If so, then you need to ask the reporter to find the answers or get on the phone to the source yourself, depending on your paper's policy.

Consider whether the press release could be made more effective by restructuring it. Does this have the best lead for your audience? Does it stress something that affects people? If not, does it stress something that would interest your readers? At the very least, people should be stressed rather than things.

Be especially careful editing for AP and local style, as well as spelling. Press releases seldom come written in AP style, and you usually find capitalized words like *association, board, center, club* and *institute* on second reference, such as "The Center will begin a weekly newsletter next month." Lowercase such words when standing alone on second reference.

Calendar Items

Usually, these items run in the community calendar part of the newspaper—smaller than briefs, with a time and date rather than a headline. They can also be a good source of feature stories.

Many press releases are mailed at the last minute and don't arrive in time to get the information into the calendar before the event. Conversely, if the press release has a later **release date**—a time before which the people who sent it don't want it run—honor the release date, and don't run the story earlier than that time.

Remember the time-day-place formula (and don't use both day and date). Time examples: 7 a.m. to 5 p.m.; 3 to 5 p.m.

Know the newspaper's policy about whether profit-making events are given free publicity. For example, some newspapers may put a listing in the calendar for a band playing at a bar or for the movies playing this week at the theaters. Others demand these be promoted only through paid ads.

Look out for profit-making enterprises trying to appear as nonprofit to avoid taking out an ad—for example, a mutual-funds investment company promoting a "free lecture on how to achieve financial independence," when the lecture is really just a vehicle for selling shares in a mutual fund.

Here are some other tips to keep in mind when writing or editing calendar items:

- The plural of *person* is *people,* not *persons.*
- Don't write "For additional information, *contact* Jan Smith at 555-1212." Instead, write: "For more information, *call* Jan Smith at 555-1212" (or ". . . stop by the Columbia Art League at . . . .").
- Rather than say "No admission," say "The event is free."
- Change "The event is free and open to the public" to "The event is free." If it weren't open to the public, why would we be running this calendar item?
- Change "A free-will offering will be taken" to "An offering will be taken" or "Donations will be collected."

Personnel: Appointments, Promotions, Training, Retirement

Find out your paper's policy on this category of item. Newspapers usually run these items as briefs, often without headlines, on the business page or in the feature section, often on Sunday, under some standing heading like "Academics," "Local Celebrities" or "About Town." Seldom are these worth a larger story—only if they're something particularly unusual.

The way the company writes its name is not necessarily written in AP style. For example, AP abbreviates *Company* at the end of a name and before *Inc.* or *Ltd.* Also, AP puts no comma between *Co.* and *Inc.* or *Ltd.* But AP does honor the company's use of an ampersand (&) in its name.

Remove self-serving plugs for the employer, as well as quotations by or about the employee, leaving just the news of who got promoted to what at which company.

Does this item let burglars know someone will be out of town during a certain time to attend a training program or take a long retirement trip? If so, reword the item so travel times are not also burglar tips.

Personal: Weddings, Engagements, Anniversaries, Reunions

Look at previous examples from your newspaper for the format. For example, for names in the headlines or captions, does your newspaper print the woman's name first or the man's name first? Are courtesy titles used? Find out, too, whether your paper limits anniversaries to significant numbers like 25th, 50th, etc.

Avoid pretentious words and phrases. Examples include *holy matrimony, bonds of matrimony* and *exchanged nuptial vows.*

Avoid descriptive, judgmental adjectives. *Attractive, beautiful, charming, lovely* and *pretty* are judgmental adjectives. Also, the trend is not to print descriptions of wedding gowns in wedding announcements.

Avoid non sequiturs such as "Given in marriage by her parents, the bride wore . . . ."

Couple is a collective noun, so it's singular when referring to the pair as a unit, but plural when referring to individuals acting separately.

Cause-Promoting Releases

Is it a "good" cause? Is it a "legitimate" cause?. Newspapers will generally run announcements about a wide variety of causes on various political and religious spectrums, weeding out only those of a commercial, fringe or hate-group nature.

Often, these are noncontroversial press releases promoting something like a community blood drive, a fund-raiser for United Way or an American Cancer Society smoke-free day. These are usually worth at least a brief, often even an 8- to 10-inch story.

Image-Building Releases

These items can be from an individual or an organization but generally come from politicians—either those in office trying to keep their name before the public or candidates seeking office.

Ask yourself whether this is only self-serving or also public-serving. In other words, is this just an attempt at free advertising, or does it contain some legitimate news? Sift out the self-serving quotes and self-congratulations, leaving in only the real news, if any.

Consider whether the other candidate or other side in a controversy should be called for comment.

QUESTION-AND-ANSWER INTERVIEWS

The **Q-and-A interview** should be used in place of a more conventional personality feature only when the words of the person interviewed are so important or unique that readers would rather read the person's words quoted in full than a more selective, arranged and descriptive account.

RELIGION STORIES

Make sure the terminology is correct for the particular religion. *Sect* and *cult* have a derogatory connotation. Generally, they mean a church group espousing Christianity without the traditional liturgical forms. *Religion* is an all-inclusive word for Judaism, Islam, Christianity and others. Not all denominations use *Church* in the organization's title. It is the First Baptist Church but the American Baptist Convention. It is the Church of Jesus Christ of Latter-Day Saints (but *Mormon Church* is acceptable). Its units are *missions, stakes* and *wards.* It is the *Episcopal* Church, not the *Episcopalian* Church. Its members are Episcopalians, but the adjective is *Episcopal:* Episcopal clergymen.

Mass may be *celebrated, said* or *sung.* The rosary is *recited* or *said.* The editor can avoid confusion by making the statement read something like this: "The Mass (or rosary) will be at 7 p.m." The Benediction of the Blessed Sacrament is neither *held* nor *given;* services close with it.

The order of the Ten Commandments varies depending on the version of the Bible used. Confusion can be spared if the commandment number is omitted.

The usual style in identifying ministers is *the Rev.,* followed by the individual's full name on first reference and only the surname on second reference. If the minister has a doctorate, the style is *the Rev. Dr.* The title *Reverend* should not be used alone, nor should plural forms be used, such as "the Revs. John Jones and Richard Smith." Churches of Christ do not use the term *reverend* in reference to ministers. They are called *brothers.*

Rabbis take *Rabbi* for a title. Priests who are rectors, heads of religious houses or presidents of institutions and provinces of religious orders take the *Very Rev.* and are addressed as *Father.* Priests who have doctorates in divinity or philosophy are identified as *the Rev. Dr.* and are addressed either as *Dr.* or *Father.*

The words *Catholic* and *parochial* are not synonymous. There are parochial schools that are not Catholic. The writer should not assume that a person is a Roman Catholic simply because he is a priest or a bishop. Other religions also have priests and bishops. Use *nun* when appropriate for women in religious orders. The title *sister* is confusing except with the person's name (Sister Mary Edward).

Jews and *Judaism* are general terms. *Israelis* are nationals of the state of Israel, and *Jews* are those who profess Judaism.

Jewish congregations should be identified in news stories as *Orthodox, Conservative* or *Reform.* To help readers, the editor should insert "branch of Judaism" or whatever other phrase might be necessary to convey the proper meaning. The terminology of the congregation concerned should be followed in naming the place of worship as a *temple* or a *synagogue.* Most Orthodox congregations use *synagogue.* Reform groups use *temple,* and Conservative congregations use one word or the other, but *synagogue* is preferred. The generic term is *Jewish house of worship.* It is never *church,* which applies to Christian bodies. *Jewish rabbi* is redundant—just use *rabbi.*

Islam is the name of the world's second-largest religion. Its followers are called *Muslims.* The adjective is *Islamic.* The correct spelling is now *Qur'an,* not *Koran.* The two main branches of Islam are *Sunni* (the largest) and *Shiite* (the second largest). *Wahhabi* Muslims are a fundamentalist subgroup within the Sunni branch. Titles for Muslim clergy vary from group to group but include *sheik, ayatollah, hojatoleslam, mullah* and *imam.*

Hinduism is the world's third-largest religion after Christianity and Islam. Hinduism has no formal clergy, but it does have *monks.*

Buddhism is the world's fourth-largest religion and is divided into three main kinds: *Theravada* or *Hinayana, Mahayana,* and *Vajrayana* or *Mantrayana. Zen* is a subcategory of Buddhism developed in Japan. Buddhist clergy may be called *priests,* and Buddhism also has *monks.*

REVIEWS

Movies, books, music, drama, art and restaurant reviews are the main kinds of reviews.

Negative reviews are protected from libel judgments provided they state opinions about things that are matters of opinion and facts about things that are matters of fact. Reviewers create legal problems if they make false statements about matters of fact—as opposed to matters of opinion—that can harm a person's reputation or business.

As opinionated pieces, allow reviews more latitude when it comes to standards of objectivity. That is, reviews are more opinion than fact, aren't neutral, aren't impersonal in style and don't have to be fair in the sense of giving both sides. But they should be fair in the sense of being honest and open-minded rather than prejudiced beforehand.

SCIENCE AND HEALTH STORIES

Science and health stories may be written as hard-news stories, but they are often turned into features by focusing on a researcher or someone dealing with a science or health problem, by following a wire story with reactions from local experts or people involved, by analyzing a new development and explaining what it means, or in some cases by taking a how-to approach.

SEASONAL FEATURES

Some features are assigned every year like calendar work. July seems to be the time, for example, when food editors assign stories about homemade ice cream, and sometime during the summer, there will likely be a spread on barbecuing and another on picnics.

In October, look for a feature on Halloween safety and another on the latest fashions in costumes.

In November, look for a food page on Thanksgiving-dinner ideas, and the day after Thanksgiving, look for a story about the biggest shopping day of the year.

In December, look for a story on what the items in "The Twelve Days of Christmas" would cost at today's prices and another on the latest toy fads.

You get the idea. As you might guess, many feature editors keep a **futures file** of seasonal story ideas. You might prepare yourself for advancement by beginning your own futures file as you find repeatable ideas in various newspapers or even on TV, radio and Internet reports.

Seasonal stories may be assigned each year, but that doesn't mean they have to be trite. Whenever possible, insist on new angles in seasonal stories. Every Yuletide, for example, there are countless stories beginning "Christmas came early" for a certain family. Don't let writers get away with such stale approaches. If you get such a feature to edit, take it to the copy-desk chief and suggest that it be sent back for a new lead.

SPEECH STORIES

Speech stories are based on the answer to the question: *Who* said *what* to *whom, when* and *where?* Some speech stories also describe *how* it was said, *why* it was said and *to what reaction.*

An important point to note about both speech and meeting stories is that the reporter should not try to include everything that was said. If the better story were the one closest to having everything, then we might as well fire the reporters and just run uncut transcripts of speeches.

Instead, a reporter's job is to select what is most important. The reporter shouldn't bother with unimportant points. Usually, speech stories cover no more than the three or four most important points. Also, the reporter shouldn't overquote but use only the quotations that best make the points—not every one that was relevant.

The speech-story lead usually follows the order of who said what, although if what was said is more important than who said it, this order may be reversed.

> Researchers at the University of Michigan are charging that the U.S. Food and Drug Administration is dragging its heels on approval of a new treatment for AIDS.

> The U.S. Food and Drug Administration is dragging its heels on approval of a new treatment for AIDS, researchers at the University of Michigan are charging.

Time, day and place may follow in the lead but often appear in later paragraphs instead, especially if they would make the lead unwieldy.

The *what* in a speech story is the most important point made in the speech—a thesis statement, not a mere statement of a topic. A *topic* can be like a vague title that hints at the subject but doesn't say exactly what the speaker said or what position was taken. A *thesis,* however, takes a specific stand.

To say, for example, that someone "spoke about cancer" is to state a topic, not a thesis. A thesis might be that someone "said new studies have found that secondary smoke is not nearly so big a cancer threat as earlier studies had indicated."

A hint for making sure a speech-story lead states a thesis rather than a topic is to make sure it avoids the following attributions: *commented on, discussed, spoke about* or *spoke on, talked on* or *talked about.* It's grammatically impossible to use these with a thesis statement. On the other hand, if the lead uses *said* (for a hardnews story) or *says* (for a feature), it's almost impossible *not* to follow the attribution with a proper thesis.

After the lead paragraph summarizes the most important news of the speech as the reporter sees it (which is not necessarily what the speaker thought was the main point or spent the most time on), the speech story typically uses a quote in the next paragraph or two to back up the thesis.

The first full-sentence quote of a speech story should typically come anywhere from the second paragraph to about the third or fourth. Much later than that, and the reader probably wonders where the quotes are or stops reading. A full-sentence quote earlier, in the first paragraph, doesn't usually summarize the story as well as a statement of the thesis and looks like a beginner's work.

Here's an example from the Associated Press that doesn't use *said* in the first paragraph but nonetheless states a thesis. Notice, also, how it begins with an immediate-ID *who,* gives a thesis *what* statement and backs it up in the next paragraph with the first full-sentence quote:

> WASHINGTON—House Speaker Newt Gingrich today rejected talk of an immediate deal with President Clinton to avoid a possible impeachment inquiry despite polls showing most Americans don't want the president removed from office.

> "For anybody to talk about doing anything before we finish the investigative process simply puts the cart before the horse," Gingrich, R-Ga., told reporters following a meeting between GOP and Democratic House leaders.

Note that the second paragraph, in addition to containing a quote amplifying the thesis from the lead and the name of the speaker (if this was a delayed-ID lead), often includes the name of the organization sponsoring the speech and sometimes when and where it was given.

In case you're wondering about the variations on the who-what-time-day-place in this example, the following explanations are in order:

- "WASHINGTON" at the beginning is called a *dateline.* Whenever a story takes place out of town for the newspaper covering it, the name of the city appears at the start in all capital letters. The dateline is not considered part of the lead.
- The use of the day element "today" before the *what* ("rejected talk of an immediate deal . . .") is a common variation when the reporter has an adverb that should be placed grammatically next to the verb "rejected."

After the lead, the story should proceed using the seesaw technique. The story seesaws back and forth between paraphrasing key points and direct quotations that are one, two or three sentences long.

The order of the story typically follows an inverted-pyramid style. The most newsworthy point in the lead is followed by supporting points and points of lesser importance as the story proceeds.

The body of the story might also include some facts about the speech if they weren't already given in the lead: the purpose, time and place of the speech. It might describe the nature and size of the audience, including any prominent people in attendance, and describe the audience's reaction—such as a standing ovation or the number of hecklers.

The story might include background information about the speaker and material gathered from a question-and-answer period or from an interview with the speaker.

Occasionally, in the case of misstatements of fact made by the speaker—as opposed to a mere difference of opinion—the reporter might include corrections.

Don't say, "The president said in prepared remarks . . ." because presidential speeches—indeed most speeches—are typically prepared.

Review the guidelines in Chapter 6 about selecting quotations.

SPORTS STORIES

Sports stories are often player interviews and profiles, advances on upcoming games and tournaments, analysis and commentary about games, focus stories on issues in sports and personal columns on anything sports or recreation related.

Sports journalists too often assume their audience is as knowledgeable as they themselves are and don't define technical terms. Sometimes, writers even assume readers will understand what sport they're talking about from the technical terms used. Likewise, sports journalists sometimes assume that just by mentioning the name of a manager or player, their audience will know the sport and team.

But even if these assumptions were correct, why limit sports coverage to those in the know? If sports journalists would take a little time to mention the sport, mention the teams and define technical terms, perhaps more casual readers would find the stories useful, as well. And they should put statistics in perspective so that their relevance is clear to the readers. Comparisons are always a useful way to promote understanding.

Look out for flamboyant overuse of modifiers and sports-writing clichés—use genuine color instead, such as great quotes. Examples of clichés:

coveted trophy
crunch time
drought
field of battle
field of dreams
good speed
hammered
He'd [she'd] like to have had that one back
hoopsters
in your face
last-ditch effort
paydirt
the pride is back
roared back
roared from behind
rocky road
sea of mud
seconds ticked off the clock
a shooting contest
slammed
standing-room-only crowd
sweet revenge
turned the tables
unblemished record
What a difference a season makes.

Also, make sure reporters press beyond the clichés athletes use when they're talking:

I just try to take it one day at a time, and with the help of my teammates and the good lord, I'll get through this slump.

Insist on better, fresher quotations.

Editors should insist, too, that reporters resist the temptation to use synonyms extravagantly. For example, use the verbs *wins, beats* and *defeats, not annihilates, atomizes, batters, belts, bests, blanks, blasts, boots home, clips, clobbers, cops, crushes, downs, drops, dumps, edges, ekes out, gallops over, gangs up on, gouges, gets past, H-bombs, halts, humiliates, impales, laces, lashes, lassoes, licks, murders, outslugs, outscraps, orbits, overcomes, paces, pastes, pins, racks up, rallies, rolls over, romps over, routs, scores, sets back, shades, shaves, sinks, slows, snares, spanks, squeaks by, squeezes by, stampedes, stomps, stops, subdues, surges, sweeps, tops, topples, triggers, trips, trounces, tumbles, turns back, vanquishes, wallops, whips, whomps* or *wrecks.*

Reporters should let the ball be *hit,* not always *banged, bashed, belted, blooped, bombed, boomed, bumped, chopped, clunked, clouted, conked, cracked, dribbled, drilled, dropped, driven, hacked, knifed, lashed, lined, plastered, plunked, poked, pooped, pumped, punched, pummeled, pushed, rapped, ripped, rocked, slapped, sliced, slugged, smashed, spilled, spanked, stubbed, swatted, tagged, tapped, tipped, topped, trickled, whipped, whistled, whomped* or *whooped.*

Reporters should let a ball be *thrown* and only occasionally *tossed, twirled, fired* and *hurled.* They should let a ball be *kicked or punted* and never *toed* or *booted.*

Reporters should resist the shopworn puns: Birds (Eagles, Orioles, Cardinals) soar or claw; Lions (Tigers, Bears, Cubs) roar, claw or lick; Mustangs (Colts, Broncos) buck, gallop, throw or kick.

Editors must insist on neutrality in most sports copy. Slanting the story in favor of the home team is not acceptable. Sportswriters, like feature writers, are allowed more leeway as far as objectivity, but this shouldn't be abused. Sports editors tend to tolerate much more opinion in their writers' stories than elsewhere in the paper. Although often thought of as necessary for a lively sports page, the same argument could be made for other categories of news, as well. The reality is that greater tolerance of both clichés and opinion is granted sportswriters, and cutting a bit of extra slack is required, but you should still fight excessive and gratuitous clichés and opinionating on sports pages as elsewhere.

Local people love to see their kids' names in print in high school sports stories. Remember, too, that these players are just kids.

The AP Stylebook has a special section on sports style. Most helpful hint: Almost every number is a numeral.

✒ TRAVEL PIECES

Travel stories tell about interesting places to visit and often suggest tours, routes, accommodations and restaurants.

If the story is about a nearby locale and no sidebar or graphics are included, suggest to the copy-desk chief that a map be made or a directions-box be included, as well as, perhaps, a list of accommodations or tours, with prices, pulled from the story.

Don't let travel stories fall into the trap of long, boring descriptions. Remember, most readers find lengthy descriptive passages a turnoff because mere description focuses on things being rather than on people acting.

Because travel pieces contain more description than most other features, editors are more likely to find adjectives and adverbs overused in them. Remember Mark Twain's advice that modifiers should be used only sparingly.

Be on the lookout for travel-piece clichés such as a particular locale that is "a quaint blend of old and new." This description applies to almost everywhere. Likewise, rather than simply labeling a place "historic" or "scenic," describe what makes it historic or scenic, *showing* the readers rather than *telling* them.

If you're working as an assignment editor, be aware that it's usually considered unethical to accept free travel arrangements.

WAR STORIES

Find out what the policy is at your newspaper, magazine or station about whether war reports must be neutral and whether it's permissible to wear flag-style clothing or accessories, such as a flag lapel pin.

Military titles use numerals when a number is involved: 1st Sgt. Bill Taylor. Also, it's redundant to say someone was promoted to the rank of major. She was simply *promoted*.

WAR STORY CLICHÉS TO AVOID

massive attack
pitched battle
powder keg (used as a metaphor)

WEATHER STORIES

An editor said, "Ever since the National Weather Service started giving hurricanes human names, reporters can't resist the temptation to be cute." He then cited, as an example, the lead, "Hilda—never a lady and now no longer a hurricane—spent the weekend in Louisiana, leaving behind death, destruction and misery." That, the editor said, is giddy treatment for a disaster causing 35 deaths and millions of dollars in property damage. The potential for passages in poor taste is not lessened by the fact that men's names are used for hurricanes, too.

Another editor noted that a story referred to "the turbulent eye of the giant storm." Later in the story, the reporter wrote correctly that the eye of the hurricane is the dead-calm center. Good, colorful writing is to be encouraged, but a simply written story with no gimmicks is better than writing that goes awry.

Blizzards are hard to define because wind and temperatures may vary. The safe way is to avoid calling a snowstorm a *blizzard* unless the National Weather Service describes it as such. Generally, a blizzard occurs when there are winds of 35 mph or more that whip falling snow or snow already on the ground and when temperatures are 20 degrees above zero Fahrenheit or lower.

A *severe blizzard* has winds that are 45 mph or more, temperatures 10 degrees above zero or lower and great density of snow either falling or whipped from the ground.

The National Weather Service insists that ice storms are not sleet. *Sleet* is frozen raindrops. The service uses the terms *ice storm, freezing rain* and *freezing drizzle* to warn the public when a coating of ice is expected on the ground. The following tips will help editors use the correct terms:

- Temperatures can become *higher* or *lower,* not *cooler* or *warmer.*
- A *cyclone* or *tornado* is a storm or system of winds rotating about a moving center of low atmospheric pressure. It is often accompanied by heavy rain and winds.
- A *hurricane* has winds above 74 mph.
- A *typhoon* is a violent cyclonic storm or hurricane occurring in the China Sea and adjacent regions, chiefly from July to October.
- The word *chinook* should not be used unless so designated by the National Weather Service.

Here is a handy table for referring to wind conditions:

light	up to 7 mph
gentle	8 to 12 mph
moderate	13 to 18 mph
fresh	19 to 24 mph
strong	25 to 38 mph
gale	39 to 54 mph
whole gale	55 to 75 mph

Temperatures are measured by various scales. Zero degrees Celsius is freezing, and 100 degrees Celsius is boiling. *Celsius* is preferred over the older term *centigrade.* On the Fahrenheit scale, 32 degrees is freezing, and 212 degrees (at sea level) is boiling. On the Kelvin scale, 273 degrees is freezing, and 373 degrees is boiling. To convert degrees Celsius to Fahrenheit, multiply the Celsius measurement by nine-fifths and add 32. To convert degrees Fahrenheit to Celsius, subtract 32 from the Fahrenheit measurement and multiply by five-ninths. Thus, 10 degrees Celsius is 50 degrees Fahrenheit. To convert degrees Kelvin to Celsius degrees, subtract 273 from the Kelvin reading. (Kelvin is used for scientific purposes, not for weather reporting.)

WEATHER STORY CLICHÉS TO AVOID

Old Man Winter Wednesday stretched his icy fingers and dumped a blanket of snow on the state.

adverse weather conditions

biting (bitter) cold

current temperature

fog rolled (crept or crawled) in fog-shrouded city

golf-ball–sized hail

hail-splattered

hurricane howled

mercury dropped (dipped, zoomed, plummeted)

rain failed to dampen

storm-tossed

winds aloft

How would reporters ever write about the weather without Old Man Winter, Jack Frost, Icy Fingers and Old Sol? Why do rain and snow never *fall?* They are always *dumped.*

At least two people were killed in Thursday's snowstorm, marked at times by blizzard-like gales of wind.

By National Weather Service standards, this is an exaggeration and a contradiction. By any standard, it is a redundancy. A blizzard is one thing. Gales are something else. Gales of wind? What else, unless maybe it was gales of laughter from discerning readers.

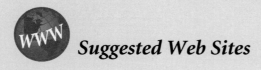# Suggested Web Sites

Bureau of Labor Statistics **www.bls.gov**
My Reference Desk **www.refdesk.com**
National Weather Service **www.nws.no22.gov**

Suggested Readings

Blundell, William E. *The Art and Craft of Feature Writing.* New York: Plume, 1988.
Cappon, Rene J. *The Word: An Associated Press Guide to Good News Writing.* New York: Associated Press, 1982.
Hazlitt, Henry. *Economics in One Lesson.* New York: Three Rivers Press, 1988.
Missouri Group. *News Reporting and Writing.* 9th edition. New York: Bedford/St. Martin's, 2007.
Schwartz, Jerry. *Associated Press Reporting Handbook.* New York: McGraw-Hill, 2002.

CHAPTER 8

WRITING HEADLINES, TITLES, CAPTIONS AND BLURBS

GETTING PEOPLE TO READ

An axiom of the media industry is that to get people to read newspapers and magazines, listen to radio, watch television and surf the Internet, you first must get their attention. Radio accomplishes this with sound, while television provides a compelling combination of sound and pictures. The print media and the Internet, on the other hand, rely primarily on still photographs and large type to accomplish the same end.

In this chapter, we review the importance of what print journalists call *display type—headlines, titles and blurbs—*and the words, called *captions* or *cutlines,* that accompany still photographs. For the print or Web journalist, these are critical means of drawing an audience.

SOME THOUGHTS ON HEADLINES

Newspapers have developed **headline** writing into an art form. The copy editor who writes compelling *heads,* as they are called, is a valuable member of the staff. While the copy editor's first task is to correct and refine copy, as outlined in earlier chapters, a second task is to write a headline that:

- Attracts the reader's attention.
- Summarizes the story.
- Helps the reader index the contents of the page.
- Depicts the mood of the story.
- Helps set the tone of the newspaper.
- Provides adequate typographic relief.

Although all these functions are important, none is more important than attracting the reader's attention.

The Laws of Newspaper Readership

We get a much clearer view of the job of a newspaper journalist when we grasp this simple truth: *The average reader does not read the average newspaper story.* That's a depressing thought at first—one most newspaper editors don't want to hear and don't want to believe. But, unfortunately, it's true.

The fact is that the average reader reads the newspaper only about 24 minutes a day, according to recent studies. That's more than the 15 minutes Walter Lippmann estimated readers spent with papers each day early in the 20th century.

But, of course, that 24 minutes is not all spent reading news—not by a long shot. From that time, we should subtract the minutes spent looking at the classifieds and other advertising, as well as the TV listings, the horoscope, the comics and the bridge column.

We should also subtract the time spent reading columns such as Dear Abby and the 60-Minute Gourmet. Some also would suggest subtracting the time spent reading sports scores and obituaries, but to many these are the most important news in the paper.

How much time is left to read the news? Not much. But think about it. Do you read the whole paper word for word? Few people, even journalists, do so. Why should we expect the average reader to spend more time with a newspaper than we do? What almost all newspaper readers do, journalists included, is look at the pictures and graphics and big type—the headlines, captions and blurbs—and use them as both a quick news summary and an index to what we may want to read in depth.

Now here's the good news: If we accept this as a fact of newspaper life rather than just get depressed about it, we're in better shape to make better papers.

Another axiom of the newspaper industry is this: *The people most likely to read a newspaper story in its entirety are those most likely to find fault with it.*

Let's start with a word of encouragement for reporters—those most likely to find this news disturbing. After all, we've just told you that the prize-winning stories you labored to craft and are so proud of probably aren't read by many of your paper's subscribers.

If you write a story about a new kidney machine at the local hospital, it doesn't matter whether Hemingway himself couldn't have done a better job. The people most likely to read it, aside from your editor and maybe your family and friends, probably work at the hospital or have kidney problems. Those are the same people who likely know more about the subject than you do and who are most likely to find fault with your story.

That's encouraging? It can be. If you're in the doldrums about complaints over stories, let that motivate you to be more accurate. Also consider who's complaining before you let frustration burn you out.

Editors and publishers who pay more and more attention to studies showing low credibility ratings for newspapers should keep that reality in mind—not just as an excuse but also as a part of the problem that now can be more easily tackled because we've identified it as such.

Assume the Reader Won't Read the Story

Let's turn our attention to page designers and headline writers for whom the implications are particularly strong for our initial observation—that the average reader doesn't read the average newspaper story.

If the average reader is mainly reading just the big type, then a big part of a reader's impression of the newspaper's usefulness—and how interesting it is—is determined at the newspaper copy desk, where the headline is written.

That big type is likely to be all a reader will read of a story. As a result, it should be so clear that the reader will feel, and be, informed by reading it alone.

Thus, we offer the single-most powerful bit of advice for improving headlines: *When you write a headline, assume the reader won't read the story.*

The problem with many heads is that the copy editor has forgotten that he or she had the benefit of having read the story before encountering the headline. The reader does not. Too many headlines by beginners read like vague titles on term papers. That won't do.

The test is this: After you've written a headline, forget you know what the story is about long enough to read the headline and ask yourself whether you have a clear idea of the news from reading just the headline. If the answer is that you don't, then the headline should be rewritten or the page designer should redesign the story's space to include a longer headline, a second deck, a blurb or some other display-type device.

Here's a tip for page designers: You can design pages that will better inform your readers if you recall the advice that newspaper readers are big-type readers. Every bit of big type on a page is another chance to give them additional news they might not otherwise read.

For example, why use an **underline** (a one-line caption) with a photo when a full **cutline** (a multiple-line caption) would allow the copy editor to pull some additional information from the story and highlight it?

This is especially helpful when the photo is a portrait of someone prominent in the story and the only information the photographer gives you is the person's name. Allow room to put in a cutline with an interesting quotation that otherwise might remain unread in the body of the story.

The Evolution of Headlines

Styles of headlines, like fashions, change constantly, even though their functions remain the same. Because style is an important factor in determining what can and cannot be included in a headline, it may be useful to review the historical development of headline styles.

Newspapers' first news display lines were short and slender, usually a single **crossline** giving little more than a topical label: **LATEST FROM EUROPE.** By adding more lines or by varying the length of the lines, designers created the **hanging indention,** the **inverted pyramid** and the **pyramid:**

        XXXXXXXXXXXX
          XXXXXXXXX
          XXXXXXXXX

        XXXXXXXXXXXX
          XXXXXXXXX
            XXXXXX

            XXXXXX
          XXXXXXXX
        XXXXXXXXXX

Later, by centering the second line and making the third flush with the right-hand margin, they developed the **stepline.** It became one of the most popular styles of headlines and is still in use at a few newspapers:

> **Heavy Rain**
> **Shuts Down**
> **All Beaches**

The next move was to combine these elements—a stepline, an inverted pyramid, a crossline, then another inverted pyramid. The units under their introductory head became known as **banks** or **decks.** An article in *The Quill* cited one found in a western newspaper describing a reporter's interview with Gen. Phil Sheridan in 1883:

FRISKY PHIL

GAZETTE REPORTER HOLDS
INTERESTING INTERVIEW
WITH HERO OF WINCHESTER

THE GREAT WARRIOR RECEIVES THE
NEWSPAPERMAN WITH OPEN ARMS;
HE IS MORE OR LESS BROKEN UP ON
THE CRAFT ANYWAY

HE TRAVELS IN A SPECIAL
MILITARY COACH AND LIVES
ON THE FAT OF THE LAND

SHERIDAN IS MANY MILES AWAY,
BUT THE CHAMPAGNE WE DRANK
WITH HIM LINGERS WITH US STILL

WE FEEL A LITTLE PUFFED
UP OVER OUR SUCCESS
ATTENDING OUR RECEPTION BY
LITTLE PHIL, BUT MAN IS
MORTAL

MAY HE WHO WATCHES OVER THE
SPARROWS OF THE FIELD NEVER
REMOVE HIS FIELD GLASSES FROM
THE DIMINUTIVE FORM AND GREAT
SOUL OF PHIL SHERIDAN

Throughout most of America's history, newspaper headlines have tended to depict the mood of the times as well as the tone of the paper. **JERKED TO JESUS,** shouted the *Chicago Times* on Nov. 27, 1875, in headlining the account of a hanging. Another classic:

> **AWFUL EVENT**
> **President Lincoln**
> **Shot by an Assassin**
>
> The Deed Done at Ford's
> Theatre Last Night
>
> **The Act of a Desperate Rebel**
>
> The President Still Alive at
> Last Accounts
>
> No Hopes Entertained of His
> Recovery
>
> *Attempted Assassination of*
> *Secretary Seward*
>
> **Details of the Dreadful Tragedy**
> *The New York Times*

(continues)

Big type and clamoring messages still weren't enough for some newspapers in the late 1800s. According to Gene Fowler, an executive told the owners of the *Denver Post,* "You've got to make this paper look different. Get some bigger headline type. Put red ink on Page One. You've got to turn Denver's eyes to the *Post* every day, and away from the other papers." So the *Post* ran its headlines in red to catch readers' attention. The message had to be gripping. According to Fowler's version, Harry Tammen, co-owner of the *Post,* was so incensed over a lifeless banner that he grabbed a piece of copy paper and composed one of his own: **Jealous Gun-Gal Plugs Her Lover Low.** When the copy desk protested the headline wouldn't fit, Tammen snapped, "Then use any old type you can find. Tear up somebody's ad if necessary." Still, the desk wasn't satisfied. "It isn't good grammar," the desk chief argued. But Tammen wouldn't budge. "That's the trouble with this paper," he is quoted as saying. "Too damned much grammar. Let's can the grammar and get out a live sheet."

The battle for circulation was hot. So were the headlines. Many were also colorful:

Demon of the belfry sent through the trap

Dons planned to skedaddle in the night

Does it hurt to be born?

**Conductors robbing little girls
of their half-fare tickets**

Do you believe in God?

During and after the Spanish-American War, some newspapers used as many as 16 decks, or headline units, to describe the story. Often, the head was longer than the story.

With improved presses and a greater variety of type available, designers were able to expand the headline. Eventually, the main Page One head stretched across the page and became known as the **banner, streamer** or **ribbon**. On some papers it was called, simply, the *line.* This headline sometimes called for the largest type available in the shop. When metal type wasn't adequate for the occasion, printers fashioned letters from wood (called *furniture*). A 12-liner meant that the line was 12 picas, or 144 points (two inches).

During this period, the names of headline forms were derived from their use or position on the page. A story placed above the nameplate and banner headline is called a **skyline**, and the accompanying headline is known as a *skyline head.* Sometimes, the skyline head stands alone but carries a notation about where the story can be found.

A headline may have several parts—the main headline and auxiliary headlines known as *decks, dropouts* or *banks.* These are not to be confused with *subheads* or lines of type (usually in boldface) sometimes placed between paragraphs in the story.

A **kicker** headline is a short line of display type, usually no larger than half the point size of the main headline and placed over the main part of the headline. On some papers the kicker is termed the *eyebrow* or *tagline.*

A **stet head** is a standing headline such as **Today in history.** A **reverse plate** headline reverses the color values so that the letters are in white on a black background. A **reverse kicker,** in which one line in larger type is above the deck, is called a **hammer** or **barker.**

As the tone of the newspaper was moderated at the turn of the 20th century, so were the headlines. Banner headlines still shout the news, occasionally in red ink, but gloom-and-doom headlines have virtually disappeared. Understating is more likely to be found in headlines today than overstating. Extra editions have been out of fashion for a long time. And no longer do circulation managers hurry into the city room to demand a banner headline that will increase the newspaper's street sales.

Between World Wars I and II, the cult of simplification, known as *streamlining,* brought changes in the newspaper headline. Designers put more air, or white space, into the head by having each line flush left, with a zigzagged, or ragged, right margin:

```
XXXXXXX
XXXXXXX
XXXXXX

XXXXX
XXXXXXX
XXXXXXXX

XXXXXXXX
XXXXXXX
XXXXXXXX
```

Urged by this spirit of simplification, they abolished the decorative **gingerbread**, such as fancy boxes, and reduced the number of banks or eliminated them altogether except for the deck reading out from a major head—called a *readout* or *dropout*. They argued that the flush-left head was easier to read than the traditional head and that it was easier to write because the count was less demanding.

Another part of the streamlining process was the introduction of modern **sans serif** typefaces to challenge the traditional typefaces such as Century, Caslon, Goudy and Garamond. Advocates of the new design contended that sans serif faces such as Helvetica and Univers were less ornate, gave more display in the smaller sizes, contained more thin letters (thus extending the count) and allowed a greater mixture of faces because of their relative uniformity.

Headlines in all-capital letters gradually gave way to capital and lowercase letters, which are easier to read. In modern headline design, only the first word of the headline and proper names are capitalized. This form of headline capitalization is known as **downstyle**.

The wider columns in contemporary newspaper design give headline writers a better chance to make meaningful statements because of a better count in one-column heads. The trend away from vertical makeup and toward horizontal makeup provides more multicolumn headlines on the page. Such **spread heads** can be written effectively in one line.

Traditionally, the headline has headed the column and hence its name. But the headline need not necessarily go at the top of the news column.

Increased emphasis on news display in recent years has prompted designers to discard established rules in favor of headline styles that complement the story. More and more, they are borrowing design concepts from magazines. Thus, newspapers now contain flush-right headlines, hammer heads are proliferating, and decks, or dropouts, are returning. Through it all, the flush-left headline remains dominant.

And, of course, when you place any story on the page, ask yourself how complicated the story is and whether the headline specs you're considering will allow enough space to summarize it adequately.

Although the size of type is important to attract attention, and the number of words the designer allows is critical to communication, the most important part of the headline-writing process is crafting a head that says as much as possible.

Good headlines attract the reader's attention to stories that otherwise may be ignored. The day's best story may have little or no impact if the headline fails to sell it or attract the reader's attention. Headlines sell stories in many ways, but often they do so by focusing on how the reader's life will be affected. For example, if the City Council has approved a city budget of $30 million for the coming year, one approach is to headline the story:

Council approves $30 million budget

Another approach, which does a better job of selling the story, might be this:

City tax rate to remain unchanged

The second approach answers the question the reader is most likely to ask about the council's action: How will it affect me?

Some headlines attract attention because of the magnitude of the event they address:

Earthquake in Algeria kills 20,000

Others attract attention because the headline is clever or unusual:

Hunger pangs
Thief finds sandwich goodies,
wine provide appetizing loot

Each story requires a different approach, and the headline writer who is able to find the correct one to attract the reader's attention is a valued member of the newspaper's staff.

Most headlines that appear over news stories are designed to inform, not entertain, so the headline that simply summarizes the story as concisely and accurately as possible is the bread and butter of the headline writer:

U.S., China to sign major grain deal

Such headlines seldom win prizes for originality or prompt readers to write letters of praise. But a newspaper full of headlines that get right to the point is a newspaper that is easy to read. The reader knows what the story is about and can make an intelligent decision about whether to read more. The headlines summarize the news, much as five-minute radio newscasts do.

If the headlines on a page do a good job of summarizing the stories, the editors have created for their readers a form of index to the page. This also helps readers determine what to read and what to bypass. In one sense, good headlines help readers determine what *not* to read. While that may seem counterproductive to the newspaper's objectives, it is realistic to recognize that readers will partake of only a small percentage of the newspaper's offerings. Newspapers help by providing a choice of fare, much as supermarket managers offer their customers various brands of green beans. That may not be an appealing comparison to those who view newspapers as entities above that sort of thing, but it *is* realistic. To ignore that reality is a mistake.

The headline also sets the mood for the story. The straightforward news headline indicates that the story it accompanies is a serious one. Similarly, a headline above a how-to-do-it story should reflect the story's content:

It's easy to save by regularly changing your car's oil

Setting the mood is even more important when writing headlines for humorous stories. One newspaper hurt readership of a bright story during the streaking craze by using a straight headline:

Judge lectures streaker

The story was a humorous account of the court appearance of a group of college students who had run across a softball diamond in the nude. In the second edition, the headline writer did a much better job:

Streaker gets the pitch
It's a whole nude ball game

The mood was set for the reader to enjoy the story.

Headlines probably reveal as much about the tone, or character, of a newspaper as anything it contains. If the top story on the front page is headlined **Cops seek lover in ax murder** and the second story carries the headline **Britney flips over new beau**, there can be little doubt about the nature of the publication. Serious tones, as well as sensational ones, can be set with headlines.

Finally, headlines provide typographic relief (see Figure 8–1). They separate stories on the page and relieve the tedium that would exist with masses of text-sized type.

The Reader's Favorite Newspaper

All the jokes about *USA Today*'s short-article, fast-food journalism aside, that newspaper could teach even *The New York Times* a thing or two about being informative. That's because *USA Today,* the nation's largest-circulation newspaper, is probably most in tune with how people actually read a newspaper, not how journalists think they should.

TICKS
The best defense? A good, strong dose of prevention.

Mayor orders investigation of park police

5 Days of Testimony End
Jury Gets Zimmer Case

Police Expand Task Force
Missing Persons Bureau Placed Under Redding's Command

Figure 8–1 Headlines come in all sizes and typefaces. Sizes are measured in points, a printer's unit of measurement equal to $1/72$ of an inch. Because there are 72 points in an inch, 24-point type would be about one-third inch in height. Typefaces are given distinctive names, such as Bodoni and Helvetica.

In an ideal world, everyone would have the time to read in-depth articles about everything. But that's not the world in which readers live. Readers skim the headlines because they don't have time to read more than the articles of particular interest to them.

When we as journalists say *The New York Times* is the standard for journalistic excellence—as in many ways it is—we are not looking at how readers actually read. A typical *Times* inside page may have only one or two stories on it because they're so long and in-depth. But what does the average reader read? The big type. How much information, then, did the reader really get from that page?

Compare a *Times* inside page with a typical inside page in *USA Today,* loaded with photos and graphics and numerous small stories. More stories means more items can be covered in the same amount of space with a larger array of big type. The average reader probably spends more time reading the average page of *USA Today* than the average page of *The New York Times.* That reader will, in turn, be more informed on a greater number of topics.

We're not suggesting that *The New York Times* change what it does. For one thing, the average *Times* reader is probably an atypical newspaper reader—one who buys *The Times* for the greater depth it offers compared with the alternatives.

But most of us can better serve our readers—actually better inform them and keep them more interested—if we put together newspapers in a way that takes into account how most people actually read.

Shorter Stories—And More of Them

If we take the ideas outlined above and apply them to our local paper, it clearly would make sense for us to run shorter stories and more of them. We're not ruling out occasional lengthy, in-depth pieces. Readers should get these, too, but they should probably be limited to one per open page. It's unrealistic to think readers will read much more than that.

Despite that, it sometimes seems that reporters think every planning and zoning committee meeting is worth 15 to 20 inches of space or more. When papers run all these lengthy stories, some stories are held until they are less timely or are squeezed out of the newspaper altogether. Reporters' efforts are wasted, and the readers are more poorly informed.

THE HEADLINE-WRITING PROCESS

Readers read the headline first, then the story. Copy editors work in reverse; they first read the story, then write the headline. This often leads to confusing heads because copy editors mistakenly assume that if readers will only read the story they will understand what the headline is trying to convey. Except in rare cases

Headline Writing is Fun

It's fun to write headlines because headline writing is a creative activity. Copy editors have the satisfaction of knowing that their headlines will be read. They would like to think that the head is intriguing enough to invite the reader to read the story. When they write a head that capsules the story, they get a smile from the executive in the slot and, sometimes, some praise.

Somerset Maugham said you cannot write well unless you write much. Similarly, you can't write good heads until you have written many. After copy editors have been on the desk for a while, they begin to think in headline phrases. When they read a story, they automatically reconstruct the headline the way they would have written it. A good headline inspires them to write good ones, too.

Sometimes they dash off a head in less time than it took them to edit the copy. Then they get stuck on a small story. They might write a dozen versions, read and reread the story and then try again. As a last resort, they may ask the desk chief for an angle. The longer they are on the desk, the more adept they become at shifting gears for headline ideas. They try not to admit that any head is impossible to write. If a synonym eludes them, they search the dictionary or a thesaurus until they find the right one.

If they have a flair for rhyme, they apply it to a brightener: **Nudes in a pool play it cool as onlookers drool.**

Every story is a challenge. After the writer has refined the story, it almost becomes the copy editor's story. The enthusiasm of copy editors is reflected in a newspaper's headlines. Good copy editors seek to put all the drama, the pathos or the humor of the story into the headline. The clever ones, or the "heady heads," as one columnist calls them, may show up later in office critiques or in trade journals:

Council makes short work of long agenda
Hen's whopper now a whooper
Stop the clock; daylight time is getting off
Lake carriers clear decks for battle with railroads
'Dolly' says 'Golly' after helloful year
Tickets cricket, legislators told
Quints have a happy, happy, happy, happy, happy birthday
(First birthday party for quintuplets)

deliberately designed to tease the reader, the headline must be instantly clear. In most cases, the reader will not read a story simply to find out what the headline means.

Headline writing, then, involves two critical steps:

- Selecting which details to use.
- Phrasing them properly within the space available.

The copy editor exercises editorial judgment in completing the first step in the process. Most use the **keyword method** in which the copy editor asks: Which words must be included in the headline to convey to the reader the meaning of the story? In its simplest form, this involves answering the question: Who does what?

Thus, most good headlines, like all good sentences, have a subject and predicate, and usually a direct object:

Tornado strikes Jonesboro

That done, the copy editor tries to make the headline fit. Synonyms may be necessary to shorten the phrase, and more concise verbs may help:

Twister rips Jonesboro

That, in simplified form, is the essence of headline writing. But it is seldom that easy. All newspapers have rules to define the limits of what is acceptable, and consideration must be given to such factors as the width of the column and the width of the characters in the typeface to be used. In the sections that follow, the complexity of headline writing will become apparent. Through it all, however, it may be useful to keep in mind the two critical steps previously outlined.

Understanding Headline Orders

Traditionally, the instructions for headlines are written as three numbers separated by hyphens. Here are four examples: 1-24-3, 3-36-2, 4-48-1, 6-60-1.

The first number in a headline order is the number of columns the headline will cover; the second is the point size of the headline (its height in points measured from the bottom of a descender like *g* to the top of an ascender like *h*); and the third is the number of lines in the headline. So, a 1-24-3 headline is one column wide, 24-point type, three lines long.

A note on print measurements: In publishing and printing, we don't measure in inches or centimeters but in picas and points. There are 12 points in a pica and 6 picas (or 72 points) in an inch.

Traditionally, graphic elements and column widths are measured in picas and points, but the height of type is measured just in points. So, we'd say a headline is 36 points (half an inch tall) but a photograph is 38.6 picas wide and 24.6 picas deep.

By the way, 38.6 (read as 38 point 6) means $38\frac{1}{2}$ picas. Why? The point is not a decimal point but a dividing mark between picas and points. The photograph referred to is 38 picas and 6 points wide—or, since there are 12 points in one pica, $38\frac{1}{2}$ picas. In many layout programs, 38 picas 6 points would be written 38p6. (In so-called new math terms, we are in base 12, not base 10.)

It will save you time writing headlines if you first visualize their size so you'll have an idea about how much to write and where to break lines. It's easy to "see" the number of columns and lines, but visualizing the point size may be hard at first. Just remember that 72 points equals an inch, so 54 points would be three-fourths of an inch, 48 would be two-thirds of an inch, 36 half an inch, 24 one-third of an inch and 18 one-fourth of an inch. Other point sizes can be visualized like this: 60 would be between three-fourths and an inch tall, 30 would be between one-third and one-half inch tall.

Headline Terminology

Copy editors have various terms for different kinds of headlines so that editors doing the design can tell copy editors editing the stories and writing the headlines exactly what they want. Here are the terms you should know:

Main head. If there's only one headline over a story, it's usually just called the *headline.* But if there is more than one, the headline that makes the main point is the **main head.** The main head may typically have between one and three or four lines.

Second deck. If the story has more than one headline, the **second deck** adds additional details or a different angle beyond what's said in the main headline. A second deck may be one to four lines long. Don't confuse a second deck with merely a second line of the main head. Here are some differences:

- The second deck will be a sentence of its own and not simply a continuation of a sentence in the main head.
- The second deck will be in a lighter typeface than the main head and at some papers will be italic.
- The second deck will be either half the point size of the main head or the next larger standard point size above half. (The standard head sizes are 14, 18, 24, 30, 36, 42, 48, 54, 60, 72, 90 and 96.) So, a second deck under a 48-point head would be either 24 or 30 points. Example:

This is a main head
This is a second deck beneath the main one

Hammer. A *hammer* is a label head, typically one to three words long, above a main head. It's used mainly with features. When a story has a hammer, the hammer is in bold type, and for once the main head is in lighter, smaller type. When you have a hammer, the main head is either half the point size of the hammer or is the next larger standard point size above half. The hammer itself should not be longer than half the width of the main head. Example:

Hammer
Here's the main head beneath the hammer

Kicker. Like a hammer, a *kicker* is a label head (but of up to about five words) above a main head. But with a kicker, the main head is the bold one while the kicker is half the point size (or the next standard size above half) of the main head and in lighter type. At some papers, a kicker is italic or underlined, or some combination of lighter, italic and underlines. Kickers are much less common today than hammers because people tend to read type from biggest to smallest, so a kicker tends to be read after the main head—not what the designer wants—and leads people's eyes away from the story. Example:

This is a kicker up here
Here's the main head

Headline Mechanics

There are a few headline conventions with which all headline writers must be familiar. Here, by category, are a few must-know items about the mechanics of crafting a newspaper headline:

PUNCTUATION

- Most editors write downstyle headlines in which only the first word of the headline and other proper names are capitalized.
- Don't put a period at the end of a sentence.
- If you have two sentences within one headline, separate them with a semi-colon (and do not capitalize the first word of the second sentence). A semi-colon should not be used in a headline unless both what precedes and follows are complete sentences with subjects and predicates.
- Use single rather than double quotation marks.
- A comma is used in place of the word *and.*
- Attribution is best shown with the word *says*, but it is often shown with a colon instead. If a colon is used, capitalize the first word that follows if it begins an independent clause. A third way to show attribution, a way that is the least desirable, is with a dash at the end of the thought, followed by the name of the person who said it. But beware of confusing headlines like this one:

Cause for AIDS found – scientists

GRAMMAR

- Except for hammers, kickers, catchlines (one or two words in headline type accompanying a photograph) and a few magazine-style titles, headlines should be complete sentences but with the articles and adjectives missing.
- Write in present tense about events that have happened since the last day's newspaper.

- Past tense, usually used for events in a more distant past, is rarely used. Example:

  Pearl Harbor was `no picnic,' witness recalls

- Future is shown by changing will to *to*. Example:

  City Council to discuss sewer bonds

- Write in active voice.
- Eliminate articles (*a, an, the*) and *to be* verbs.

LINE BREAKS

- Multiple-line headlines should break at logical places—at pauses between natural breath units.
- If you have a literary background, think of multiple-line headlines as little poems, and put the line breaks only where they would come in a poem.
- Don't split modifiers from the word they modify.
- Don't split a prepositional phrase over two lines.
- Don't split the parts of an infinitive over two lines.
- Some leeway is permitted in one-column heads—but only as a last resort. Typically, this involves modifiers (prepositional phrases would still not usually be split).

ABBREVIATIONS

- Never abbreviate days of the week.
- Never abbreviate months unless followed by a date.
- Most newspapers allow abbreviations for states without a city name preceding.
- Never abbreviate months or states that AP does not.
- Typically, it is permissible to abbreviate these cities: Kansas City as K.C., Los Angeles as L.A. and New York as N.Y.
- Never abbreviate a person's name (Wm. F. Buckley, J. Jones).
- Do not eliminate *the* in front of *Rev.*
- Most newspapers will let you use a numeral for a number less than 10.
- You may use a percent sign (%) for the word *percent.*
- As in text, you may abbreviate any headline reference for *U.S., U.N. CIA* or a university commonly known to readers (*M.U., USC*, etc.).
- Some, but probably not most, newspapers will let you abbreviate *county* as *Co.* or department as *Dept.* if the rest of the name is present.

HOW TO WRITE THE HEADLINE

Some editors leave the wire service's suggested headline on top of the story to help them get started. If you do this, don't rely too heavily on it or your headline will sound too much like those of other papers. But it does make a good starting point, a check that you've understood the story and a fallback if you're stuck.

Start by writing your ideal head for the story—what you'd like to say if space were no object. Then try to fit it into the space you have. Cut the head to its essentials if it's too long. If it's too short, add more information. To improve the fit, you can also simply pick synonyms that say the same thing in a shorter or longer space (see Figure 8–2).

Some editors find it useful to jot down key words from the story that need to be in the headline. Then they build the head around these key words.

Headlines That Tell

Here are some tips on writing informative headlines:

- Remember that the headline and other big type may be all the reader will read, so get in the key words and be as specific as possible in presenting the news.

- After you've written a headline, forget for a moment what you've read in the story. Would you have a clear understanding of the news just from reading

Figure 8–2 A copy editor tries to craft a headline for a news story.
Photo by Philip Holman.

the big type (headlines, blurbs and captions)? If not, rewrite the head. Example:

No: **Jury hears how man was slain**

Yes: **Victim slain with his own gun**

- Make sure the headline is accurate—don't exaggerate or mislead. Reread the story to make sure.

- Try to match the tone of the story in the headline. A light story demands a light head. A tragic story should not have a head that is a pun.

- Don't editorialize. Attribute all controversial statements. Make sure the headline over a news story is neutral and fair.

- Get information from the top, but don't repeat the lead or give away a punch line or ending. If the best headline information really is down further, consider moving that information up.

- Be conversational and clear. Make the language vivid, and appeal to the reader. Don't write a headline in the negative (using *not*)—it's harder to grasp quickly. Don't try to get more than one idea in a deck, or things can get confusing.

- Don't overabbreviate. Use only abbreviations everyone knows: *CIA, FBI, UFO.* Examples of unacceptable abbreviations: *DOS* for Department of State, *FD* for Fire Department.

- Don't use obscure names or terms in the headline.

- Don't use common last names (Jones or Smith) in a headline. Use a name only if the person is well-known and easily identifiable. The exception, of course, is an obituary.

- Pay special attention to verbs. Write in active, not passive, voice. Try to get a verb in the top line, but don't start with a verb, or the headline may sound like a command. Likewise, avoid label heads (those without verbs) except in hammers, kickers and catchlines. If a label head is appropriate, beware of nouns that can also be read as verbs because they can introduce double meanings:

Dead cats protest

- Avoid "headlinese" whenever possible: *blasts, rips* (ridicules); *nixes* (rejects); *solons* (lawmakers, Legislature). Reserve, when possible, the old standby headline terms for deadline.

- Don't pad a line to make it fit. Say something.

- Question heads seldom work. Avoid them unless the point of the story is to raise a question to which it doesn't present the answer.

- Don't repeat words in the big type—within a headline, or between heads or captions or blurbs.

- If your paper still uses **upstyle** or **all-cap heads** (few do anymore), be especially aware of how some names may be misread:

Right: **Chargers may lose Butts for rest of year**

Wrong: **CHARGERS MAY LOSE BUTTS FOR REST OF YEAR**

Headlines That Smell

To the advice above, let's add more tips based on examples of actual headline bloopers by professionals. Such examples are collected monthly in the back of *Columbia Journalism Review* and *American Journalism Review*. Almost every August, the *National Lampoon* also collects examples in its True Facts issue. You might also like to look at Jay Leno's collections of headlines, the royalties from which he donates to pediatric AIDS programs and research.

BEWARE OF TYPOS

Poll says that 53% believe media offen make mistakes
Re-electing Lincoln: The Battle for the 1964 Presidency
Defective show officially starts new TV season
Schools to call for pubic input
Nicaragua sets goal to wipe out literacy
13% of U.S. adults unable read or write English
Are young Americans be getting stupider?
Tribal council to hold June meeting in June
Man booked for wreckless driving
56-year-old man shoots shoots daughter twice
Despite our best efforts, black employment is still rising

AVOID VAGUE HEADLINES THAT SAY NOTHING

City Council to meet
Strike continues in fifth day
School Board Agrees to Discuss Education
New Bar Exam to Include Test of Legal Skills
Religion Plays Major Part in the Message of Easter
Cold Wave Linked to Temperatures
Researchers call murder a threat to public health
Some students walk, others ride to school
Don't leave kids alone with molester
Carcinogens cause cancer, book says
8 American men left

BEWARE OF DOUBLE ENTENDRES

After dogs died in heat, should owners have gotten off?
Marijuana issue sent to a joint committee
City Council takes up masturbation
Breaking wind could cut costs

Muggers beat man with empty wallet
Why do we tolerate demeaning gays, women?
Bad coupling cause of fire
Plan to deny welfare to applicants still alive
Textron Inc. Makes Offer to Screw Co. Stockholders
Spot Searches Dog Bus Drivers
Narcolepsy may be more prevalent in women than thought
Tahoe-area man sentenced to 28 years in Calif.
Many who moved to Florida leave after death
High-crime areas said to be safer
Beating Witness Provides Names
Unpaid subway fare led police to murder suspect
Culver police: Shooting victims unhelpful
Police begin campaign to run down jaywalkers
Man executed after long speech
Man admits killing widow to avoid facing death penalty
More Judicial Fertilizer Use Advised
Condom Week starts with a cautious bang
Jerk Injures Neck, Wins Award
Doctors offer sniper reward
Blind workers eye better wages
Navy Jet Preparing for Air Show Crashes
Woman off to jail for sex with boys
Stiff opposition expected to casketless funeral plan
Dolls sent to flood homeless
Do-it-yourself pregnancy kit to go on sale
Dr. Tackett Gives Talk on Moon
Mad cow speaker at Arts Center
Aging Expert Joins University Faculty
No dad's better than abusive one
Dad wants 3 charged for sex with daughter
Prostitutes appeal to pope
Wives kill most spouses in Chicago
Professor of Greek thought dead at 59
Murder suspect gets appointed attorney
Bill to help poor facing early death
Dole and Bush dead even in Kansas polls
Clinton makes domestic violence appeal to men
OJ blamed for Disney salmonella outbreak
Teacher strikes idle kids
USA to seek new location
Woman dies after 81 years of marriage
Singer John Denver dies in experimental plane crash
Clinic gives poor free legal help
Giant women's health study short of volunteers
Senate presses vets' suits
Lebanon chief limits access to private parts
Potential witness to murder drunk
S. Florida illegal aliens cut in half by new law

ISU revokes doctorate in plagiarism
A Promising Medical Specialty Emerges to Help Torture Victims
Jude delays ruling on paddling principal
New drugs may contain AIDS, but not all can afford them
A record walker admits she skipped 1,000 miles
Army Focuses On Second Base In Sex Probe
Jessica Hahn pooped after giving testimony

BEWARE OF MISPLACED MODIFIERS

Scotland Yard arrests three men carrying explosives and seven others
40,000 at Mass for Polish priest reported killed
Threatened by gun, employees testify
Bomb found on Gaza road to be used by Arafat

WRITE ACCURATE HEADLINES

The key to ensuring accuracy is close and careful reading of the story. Erroneous headlines result when the copy editor doesn't understand the story, infers something that is not in the story, fails to portray the full dimension of the story or fails to shift gears before moving from one story to the next. Some examples:

Minister buried in horse-drawn hearse
(The hearse and horse participated in the funeral procession, but they were not buried with him.)

Cowboys nip Jayhawks 68-66 on buzzer shot
(The lead said that Kansas [the Jayhawks] beat Oklahoma State [the Cowboys] by two points in a Big XII conference basketball game.)

Paducah's bonding law said hazy
(The details were hazy; the subject of the story was hazy about the details.)

3 in family face charges of fraud
(They were arrested in a fraud investigation, but the charges were perjury.)

Black child's adopted mother fights on
(The child didn't select the mother; it was the other way around. Make it "adoptive.")

Do-nothing Congress irks U.S. energy chief
(The spokesman criticized Democrats, not Congress as a whole, and the "do-nothing" charge was limited to oil imports.)

Four held in robbery of piggy bank
(The bank was the loot; the robbery was at a girls' home.)

White House hints at ceiling on oil spending
(The subject of the story was oil imports.)

DON'T REHASH OLD NEWS

Some stories, like announcements, offer little or no news to invite fresh headlines. Yet, even if the second-day story offers nothing new, the headline cannot be a repetition of the first-day story lead.

Suppose on Monday the story says that Coach Mason will speak at the high school awards dinner. If Mason is prominent, his name can be in the head: **Mason to speak at awards dinner**. On Thursday comes a follow-up story, again saying that Coach Mason will be the awards dinner speaker. If the headline writer repeats the Monday headline, readers will wonder if they are reading today's paper. The desk editor will wonder why copy editors won't keep up with the news. The problem is to find a new element, even a minor one, like this: **Tickets available for awards dinner.** So the dinner comes off on Friday, as scheduled. If the Saturday headline says **Mason speaks at awards dinner,** readers learn nothing new. The action is what he said: **Mason denounces 'cry-baby' athletes**. Or if the story lacks newsworthy quotes, another facet of the affair goes into the head: **30 ATHLETES GET AWARDS.**

WATCH FOR LIBEL

Because of the strong impression a headline may make on a reader, courts have ruled that a headline may be actionable even though the story under the head is free of libel. Here are a few examples:

> **Shuberts gouge $1,000 from Klein brothers**
> **'You were right,' father tells cop who shot his son**
> **McLane bares Old Hickory fraud charges**
> **Doctor kills child**
> **A missing hotel maid being pursued by an irate parent**
> **John R. Brinkley—quack**

A wrong name in a headline over a crime story is one way to involve the paper in a libel action.

The headline writer, no less than the reporter, must understand that under the U.S. justice system a person is presumed innocent of any crime charged until proved guilty by a jury. Heads that proclaim **Kidnapper caught, Blackmailer exposed, Robber arrested** or **Spy caught** have the effect of convicting the suspects (even the innocent) before they have been tried.

If unnamed masked gunmen hold up a liquor store owner and escape with $1,000 in cash, the head may refer to them as "robbers" or "gunmen." Later, if two men are arrested in connection with the robbery as suspects or are actually charged with the crime, the head cannot refer to them as "robbers" but must use a qualifier: **Police question robbery suspects.** For the story on the arrest, the headline should say **Two arrested in robbery**, not **Two arrested for robbery**. The first is a shortened form of *in connection with;* the second makes them guilty. Even *in* may cause trouble.

Three women arrested in prostitution should be changed to **Three women charged with prostitution**.

The lesson should be elementary to anyone in the publishing business, but even carefully edited papers and Web sites are sometimes guilty of publishing heads that jump to conclusions. This was illustrated in the stories concerning the assassination of President John F. Kennedy. Lee Harvey Oswald was branded the assassin even though, technically, he was merely arrested on a charge of murder. In a statement of apology, the managing editor of *The New York Times* said his paper should not have labeled Oswald an assassin.

In their worst days, newspapers encouraged headline words that defiled: **Fanged fiend, Sex maniac, Mad-dog killer**. Even today, some newspapers permit both reporter and copy editor to use a label that will forever brand the victim. When a 17-year-old boy was convicted of rape and sentenced to 25 to 40 years in the state penitentiary, one newspaper immediately branded him "Denver's daylight rapist." Another paper glorified him as "The phantom rapist." Suppose an appeal reverses the conviction? What erases the stigma put on the youth by the newspaper?

The copy editor who put quotation marks around **Honest count** in an election story learned to his sorrow that he had committed libel for his paper. The implication of the quotes is that the newspaper doesn't believe what is being said.

DON'T OVERSTATE

Akin to the inaccurate headline is one that goes beyond the story, fails to give the qualifications contained in the story or confuses facts with speculations. Examples:

> **West Louisville students at UL to get more aid**
> (The lead said they may get it.)
>
> **Pakistan, U.S. discuss lifting of embargo on lethal weapons**
> (The story said, correctly, that the embargo may be eased. And aren't all weapons lethal?)
>
> **Arabs vote to support PLO claim to West Bank**
> (The story said that Arab foreign ministers voted to recommend such action to their heads of state. The head implies final action.)
>
> **Schools get 60% of local property tax**
> (This reflects fairly what the lead said but fails to reveal an explanation, later in the story, that the schools get a proportion of the contributions of various levels of government—federal, state and local. Although the local property tax contributes 60 percent, the amount is far less than 60 percent of the total local property tax.)

DON'T COMMAND THE READER

Headlines that begin with verbs can be read as commands to the reader and should be avoided. A New York City newspaper splashed a 144-point headline over the story of the shooting of Medgar Evers, a civil rights advocate. The head: **Slay NAACP leader!** Another head may have given the impression that a murder was being planned: **Slaying of girl in home considered**. In reality, police were trying to determine whether the murder took place in the girl's house or in a nearby field.

Here are some examples of heads that command:

Save eight from fire	**Buy another school site**
Arrest 50 pickets in rubber strike	**Find 2 bodies, nab suspect**
Assassinate U.S. envoy	

AVOID EDITORIALIZING

The reporter has ample space to attribute, qualify and provide full description. The copy editor, however, has a limited amount of space in the headline to convey the meaning of the story. As a result, there is a tendency to eliminate necessary attribution or qualification and to use loaded terms such as *thugs, cops, pinkos, yippies* and *deadbeats* to describe the participants. The result is an editorialized headline.

Every word in a headline should be justified by a specific statement within the story. Was the sergeant who led a Marine platoon into a creek, drowning six recruits, drunk? Most headlines said he was, but the story carried the qualification "under the influence of alcohol to an unknown degree."

Even though the headline reports in essence what the story says, one loaded term will distort the story. If Syria, for reasons it can justify, turns down a compromise plan offered by the U.S. concerning the Golan Heights problem, the head creates a negative attitude among readers when it proclaims **Syria spurns U.S. compromise.**

It is often difficult to put qualification in heads because of count limitations. But if the lack of qualifications distorts the head, trouble arises. A story explained that a company expected to bid on a project to build a fair exhibit was bowing out of the project because the exhibit's design was not structurally sound. The headline, without qualification, went too far and brought a sharp protest from the construction company's president:

Builder quits, calls state World's Fair exhibit 'unsound'

AVOID SENSATIONALIZING

Another temptation of the headline writer is to spot a minor, sensational element in the story and use it in the head. A story had to do with the policy of banks in honoring outdated checks. It quoted a bank president as saying, "The bank will take the checks." In intervening paragraphs, several persons were quoted as having had no trouble cashing their checks. Then in the 11th paragraph was the statement: "A Claymont teacher, who refused to give her name, said she had tried to cash her check last night, and it had been refused." She was the only person mentioned in the story as having had any difficulty. Yet the headline writer grabbed this element and produced a head that did not reflect the story:

> **State paychecks dated 1990**
> Can't cash it,
> teacher says

DON'T MISS THE POINT

The process of headline writing begins as soon as a copy editor starts reading the story. If the lead can't suggest a headline, chances are the lead is weak. If a stronger element appears later in the story, it should be moved closer to the lead.

Although the headline ideally emerges from the lead, and generally occupies the top line (with succeeding lines offering qualifications or other dimensions of the story), it often has to go beyond the lead to portray the full dimensions of the story. When that occurs, the qualifying paragraphs should be moved to a higher position in the story. Example: **U.S. company to design spying system for Israel**. The lead was qualified. Not until the 15th paragraph was the truth of the head supported. That paragraph should have been moved far up in the story.

The head usually avoids the exact words of the lead. Once is enough for most readers. Lead: "Despite record prices, Americans today are burning more gasoline than ever before, and that casts some doubt on the administration's policy of using higher prices to deter use." Headline: **Despite record gasoline prices, Americans are burning more fuel**. A paraphrase would avoid the repetition: **Drivers won't let record gas prices stop them from burning up fuel**. Since the story tended to be interpretive, the head could reflect the mood: **Hang the high price of gasoline, just fill 'er up and let 'er roar**. Most copy editors try to avoid duplicating the lead, but if doing so provides the clearest possible head, it is a mistake to obfuscate.

DON'T GIVE AWAY THE PUNCH LINE

Some stories are constructed so that the punch line comes at the end, rather than at the beginning. Obviously, if the point of the story is revealed in the headline, the story loses its effectiveness. The following story calls for a head that keeps the reader in suspense until the end:

> One Saturday afternoon not long ago, a night watchman named Stan Mikalowsky was window-shopping with his 5-year-old daughter, Wanda, and as they passed a toy shop the child pointed excitedly to a doll nearly as big as she was.
>
> The price tag was only $1 less than the watchman's weekly pay check, and his first impulse was to walk away, but when the youngster refused to budge he shrugged and led her into the store.
>
> When Stan got home and unwrapped the doll, his wife was furious.
>
> "We owe the butcher for three weeks, and we're $10 short on the room rent," she said. "So you got to blow a week's pay for a toy."
>
> "What's the difference?" said the night watchman. "Doll or no doll, we're always behind. For once let the kid have something she wants."

One word led to many others, and finally Stan put on his hat and stomped out of the house.

Mrs. Mikalowsky fed the child and put her to bed with the doll next to her and then, worried about Stan, decided to go looking for him at the corner bar and make up with him. To keep his supper warm, she left the gas stove on, and in her haste threw her apron over the back of the chair in such a way that one of the strings landed close to a burner.

Fifteen minutes later when the Mikalowskys came rushing out of the bar, their frame house was in flames and firefighters had to restrain the father from rushing in to save his daughter.

"You wouldn't be any use in there," a police officer told him. "Don't worry, they'll get her out." Firefighter Joe Miller, himself a father, climbed a ladder to the bedroom window, and the crowd hushed as he disappeared into the smoke. A few minutes later, coughing and blinking, he climbed down, a blanket-wrapped bundle in his arms.

The local newspaper headlined its story with the line that should have been saved for the finish:

Fireman rescues life-size doll
as child dies in flames

Headlines That Sell

A good headline tells the story; a great headline tells it and sells it. Remember, though, that headlines that sell must also tell. Selling is something you do in addition to telling, not in place of it. Here are some techniques to make a headline sell a story by explaining it in a way that is striking:

ALLITERATION

Alliteration is the repetition of sounds. It's often overused but can still be effective. Alliteration should sound natural or at least make sense.

Crowds cry encore to street-corner Caruso
(about a man who dresses in a tux and sings opera arias on the street for tips)

RHYMES

Rhymes can sometimes work.

Dollars for scholars
(hammer over scholarship story)

The urge to converge
(hammer on a story about business mergers)

BALANCE AND CONTRAST

Examples of this technique are:

They bring new life to old towns
(about remodelers of historic buildings)

Hot pursuit of the common cold

GRAPHIC DEVICES

Graphic devices occasionally work but can be cheesy, too.

> **Photocopying made easy Photocopying made easy**
>
> **Missing l tt rs in sign puzzl curators at mus um**
>
> **$port$ and money**
>
> **It's a boy, it's a boy, it's a girl, it's a girl: Quadruplets born to local couple**

PUNS

This is one of the most-often used headline tricks. In fact, it's used so much, most editors, if not readers, get tired of it. Not only that, it's often misused. Still, puns can be effective when they are appropriate to the mood and content of the story. Don't try to brighten a serious story with an inappropriate one.

> *No:* **Mother of all deadbeat dads gets six months in prison**
>
> *No:* **MacMassacre! 23 killed in Big Mac attack**
> (about a mass murder at a McDonald's)
>
> *Yes:* **Clockmaker puts heart into tickers**
>
> *Yes:* **Business picking up for pooper-scooper firm**
>
> *Yes:* **Last brew-ha-ha: 'Cheers' ends 11-year-run**

PUT A TWIST ON THE FAMILIAR

This technique is similar to the pun but specifically involves taking a well-known saying, title or cliché, and playing off it. (We're indebted to educator and magazine expert Don Ranly for many of these examples.)

> **Forgive us our press passes**
> (story about criticism of the press)
>
> **'Tis a Pity' it's a bore**
> (review of production of play *Tis a Pity She's a Whore*)
>
> **Where there's smoke, there's ire**
> (about no-smoking controversy)
>
> **Take this job and love it**
>
> **There's no business like shoe business**
> (feature about a shoe-repair shop)
>
> **Canada's game**
> (headline in *Toledo Blade* when the Toronto Blue Jays won the World Series)
>
> **English bathrooms out of the closet** (about British decorating their bathrooms)

LEARN FROM MAGAZINES, TABLOIDS AND USA TODAY

Although these sometimes sensationalize, you can learn from some of them.

- Headlines with personal pronouns such as *you* or *we:*

  We're eating out more
  (survey story, *USA Today* style)

- Advice headlines:

  How to sell your old baseball cards for a fortune
  Five ways to flatten your thighs

- Analysis headlines:

  Why the U.S. is losing the drug war

- Striking or superlative statements:

  The iron woman of softball
  (hammer)

  Threat of terrorism has Rambo quaking
  (Sylvester Stallone cancels trip to Europe after terrorism threat)

AVOID "HEADLINESE"

Avoid the words that get overused in headlines and that make them sound alike. Examples of "headlinese" to avoid include: *blasts, cops, eyes, gives nod* (approves), *grill* (question), *hike, OK's, probe, raps, row* (clash), *set, slated.* These are all overused.

SPEAK THE LANGUAGE OF THE STORY

Think of words associated with the subject of the story, and use them in the headline to bring the reader into the spirit of the topic:

  What a long, strange trip it's been: Summit marks LSD's 50th year
  After the pomp, tough circumstances
  (about poor job prospects for grads)

LET THE STORY SPEAK FOR ITSELF

Sometimes you don't want to be cute—the story is odd or interesting enough by itself. Stories about dinosaurs, space aliens, diets and medical breakthroughs fit this category. You just need to get the keyword in the headline and people will read it.

  Are 33 orgasms a day normal at age 75?
  (Dr. Ruth column)
  Man acquitted in mayonnaise slaying case

What to Do If You're Stuck

Every headline writer has a mental block at one time or another. Here are some tips for when that happens:

- If you can't get a line to fit, look for synonyms for each individual word in that line that might be longer or shorter as needed. If that doesn't work, only then should you try rewriting the whole headline with a different approach.

- Look at the suggested head from the wire service, if it's still atop the story. Maybe that will help you come up with a different idea.

- Ask another editor for help. If neither of you can think of something, ask your superior. If none of you can come up with something, ask that the size or number of lines be changed or that a blurb or second deck be added.

- If you're having trouble capturing a feature story's focus, the story itself may need more focus. But if it's too late to send it back, consider turning a quote from the story into the head. This is an especially helpful technique for a personality profile. But don't get in the habit of doing this all the time.

- This last idea is sneaky and should be used only as a last resort: If you're having trouble not repeating a great lead in the headline, consider stealing the great lead for the head, then rewriting the actual lead. But don't even think of doing this with a local story—only a wire one where the reporter won't be around to chew you out.

TITLE HEADS IN MAGAZINES

Newspapers have headlines, and magazines have **titles.** Sometimes they are similar, and sometimes they are not. Carl Riblet Jr., an expert on title and headline writing, suggested that beginners start by listing the titles of all the books they have read. This is to demonstrate that readers can recall titles even if they have forgotten the contents. It also demonstrates the effectiveness of an apt title.

A good title helps sell the story, as illustrated by these originals and the revisions given them by alert publishers:

Old: **Old-Time Legends Together With Sketches, Experimental and Idea**
New: **The Scarlet Letter**

Old: **Pencil Sketches of English Society**
New: **Vanity Fair**

Old: **The Life and Adventures of a Small-town Doctor**
New: **Main Street**

Old: **Alice's Adventures Underground**
New: **Alice in Wonderland**

Old: **Tales of a Country Veterinarian**
New: **All Things Wise and Wonderful**

Typically, a newspaper uses illustrations to focus the readers' attention on a page. It relies on the headline to lure readers into the story. But in a magazine, the

The Magazine Title

Most of the headline-writing techniques discussed in this chapter are those that have evolved at newspapers. But newspapers increasingly are adopting techniques pioneered at magazines. These include a title, as opposed to a headline, with a conversational deck, a secondary headline written more like a sentence than a headline. *Sports Illustrated*, whose editors are masters of writing titles with conversational decks, yields some excellent examples:

What Parity?
With 11 Super Bowl losses in a row,
the AFC has a way to go to beat NFC powers
Dallas and San Francisco

Run for the Roses
After Michigan stunned previously unbeaten
Ohio State, joy bloomed at Northwestern

Love Story
The death of 28-year-old Sergei Grinkov was the
final chapter in one of sport's great romances

Rolling Rocks
The Rockies' remarkable streak *will* come to an end
(we think); their talent base, though, is built to last

Newspapers sometimes call this convention a *hammer head*, but its marriage with a **conversational deck** rather than a secondary headline was popularized in magazines. The idea is to catch the reader's eye with a bold title, then follow with an explanation that gives more detail.

whole page—title, pictures, placement—is designed to stop the readers in their tracks. They may get part of the story from a big dramatic picture before they ever see the title. This combination of elements must make readers say to themselves, "I wonder what this is all about."

The magazine editor is not confined to a few standardized typefaces for headings. Instead, the editor may select a face that will help depict the mood of the story. Nor is the editor required to put the heading over the story. It may be placed in the middle, at the bottom or on one side of the page.

The heading may occupy the whole page or only part of a page. It may be accented in a reverse plate or in some other manner. It may be overprinted on the illustration. More often, it will be below the illustration rather than above it. Almost invariably it is short, not more than one line. Often, it is a mere tag or teaser. A **subtitle**, then, gives the details:

Oil from the Heart Tree
An exotic plant from Old China produces
a cash crop for the South

I Can HEAR Again!
This was the moment of joy, the rediscovering
of sound: whispers... rustle of a sheep...
ticking of a clock

The Pleasure of Milking a Cow
Coming to grips with the task at hand
can be a rewarding experience,
especially on cold mornings

In magazines, only a few of the rigid rules that apply to newspaper headlines remain in force. Rules of grammar and style are observed, but almost anything else goes. Magazine title writing is free-form in both style and content.

BLURBS AND CAPTIONS

Most readers don't completely read many stories in the newspaper. Instead, they look at the photos, graphics and big type. They use the headlines, captions and blurbs as an index to the news, deciding which stories to read. It's important, then, that editors try to sneak across as much information as possible in the big type. Readers should feel—and be—informed merely by perusing the paper in their normal way.

So, tell the story as completely as possible in the main head, then use any additional devices available to you—second decks, blurbs or captions—to add as much other important news as possible.

- View second decks, blurbs and captions as opportunities to get across more information to people who won't be reading the story, as well as hooks to people who might be tempted to read more.
- Put the main idea in the biggest type, the next most important idea in the next biggest type, etc. Usually, this means the following order: *main head, second deck, blurb, caption.*
- Don't repeat information from one graphic element to another. That's just wasting the opportunity to get across more information.
- Make sure none of the information contradicts information in the other elements or in the story. Especially, make sure the spelling of names is consistent.
- Write in full sentences. Don't cut articles or *to be* verbs from blurbs or captions.
- You don't have to worry about where the lines break with blurbs or captions.
- Learn local style on matters like whether your paper uses single or double quote marks in blurbs and captions.

Blurbs

Blurbs go by different names at different papers—**pullouts, pull quotes**, etc.—but the key thing to remember is that whatever they're called, they are information in big type that either provides a summary or a sample of the story.

External blurbs are always summary blurbs. They generally come between the headline and the lead of the story, in which case they're sometimes called *read-out blurbs,* although they have many other names, as well. **Read-out blurbs** are similar in function to second decks, but they permit more flexibility and generally greater space to say more.

Sometimes, generally on feature stories, an external blurb may be above the headline, in which case it's called a **read-in blurb** because it reads into the headline.

Internal blurbs are always sample blurbs. They are placed somewhere within the story itself, usually with rules above and below them. Most often, they're used for pull quotes, the most interesting quote or quotes from the story. Sometimes, especially when none of the quotes are that colorful but the page designer has planned for the space, an internal blurb may simply be interesting information from the story rather than a quote.

Captions

Writing photo **captions** is an art. Here are some tips to remember:

- Don't waste the opportunity to get across more information. Fill up the space as much as possible and don't say obvious things like "Janet Hemmings looks on as . . ."
- Feel free to add information from the story to the cutline if you have extra space. It's also fine for the cutlines to have information not in the story.
- If there are multiple captions, put the main cutline information under the dominant photo, the one people will look at first.
- Write in present tense. It's helpful to avoid days or dates in cutlines. This will avoid awkward mixes of present tense with past days.
- When more than one person is pictured, a caption usually names them *from left*.

There are several kinds of captions:

Nameline. A **nameline** is a one-line caption under a **mugshot** and consists only of the person's name. A nameline under a full-column mugshot will have the person's first and last name. A nameline under a thumbnail (half-column mug) will have only the person's last name.

Nameline-Underline. Some papers will put a one-line description under a nameline. That's called a nameline-underline. Example:

Hillary Clinton
Mum on Giuliani's divorce

Underline. An underline is a one-line caption. Except for when it's part of a nameline-underline, the underline should be a full sentence and have a period or question mark at the end. An underline should never be less than half the space width that was allowed for it, and ideally, it should fill the line.

Cutline. A *cutline* is a multiline caption and is used to provide more information than a mere underline would allow. A cutline in one or two columns may be any number of lines long. In three columns or more, a cutline is usually divided into two or more wraps (such as two wide columns of type under a three-column photo), and each column should have an even number of lines so the wraps are equally long.

Catchline. A catchline is a label head (like a hammer) over the cutline of a **standalone photo** (a photo with no story other than the information in the cutline). It's typically one to three words.

HEADLINES AND TITLES FOR THE INTERNET

Almost all of the basic conventions of headline and title writing apply equally to the Internet. Typically, news sites follow the conventions of newspaper headline writing, and other sites employ a mixture of headline and title writing. But Web site editors increasingly realize that there are some significant differences between writing heads for print and Internet sites.

Suzanne Levinson, director of site operations for MiamiHerald.com and ElNuevoHerald.com, argues that for several reasons Web headlines must be different from those that appear in the newspaper or magazine:

- There is often no context for the head. In other words, on the Web there often is no photo, caption, subhead or section label (national, international, sports, etc.) to help the reader figure out what the story is about. And even if some of those exist, search engines allow readers to drill straight to the story, sometimes without the surrounding context.

- Print headlines often are too long or too short for the Web. As a result, they don't automatically work on the Internet.

- Print headlines are often written awkwardly to fit space available in the print edition, which might not correspond to the space available online.

- Clever heads for which print editors are known often don't work on the Web. Internet scanners want information and don't want to be teased.

- Keywords often are missing in print heads, a fatal flaw in online heads. In print, for example, keywords that must be included in a Web headline often are missing. A story about a football game may have a head without Miami or Dolphins.

That last point is an important one. Many users are driven to an Internet story by search engines. If the user enters keywords that aren't contained in the headline, there's no assurance the user will find the story. Even when entire texts are indexed, without the requisite keywords the story will rank lower in the list of search results.

Levinson argues that readers tend to search for topic and location. Example:

Schools in Miami

If those words aren't in the headline, there's a strong possibility the user will never find it. Why is this important? Web sites must attract as many readers as possible to become financially viable. Web editors, then, must write headlines that index the news even better than printed publications. Levinson cites examples of headlines from the *Miami Herald* that were rewritten for the Web:

Print: **Ripe for growth**

Online: **Wine superstore sign of industry's growth**

Print: **Divorce was out of the question, husband says**

Online: **Divorce was never an option, Terry Schiavo's husband says in new book**

Levinson suggests that editing text for the Web is different, too. As an example, she notes that *here*, when used in the *Miami Herald*, clearly refers to Miami. But with readers coming directly to a story on MiamiHerald.com from a search engine such as Google or Yahoo!, the reader may not even be aware that he or she is reading an article from Miami. Similarly, *today* may work well in a printed publication for the date of publication; it doesn't work at all on the Web, where the day of week or date is essential.

Teresa Schmedding, news editor of the *Daily Herald* in suburban Chicago, agrees with Levinson that the Web demands a different approach. Like Levinson, she warns against cute headlines that tease rather than inform. Says Schmedding, "Studies show that readers do not like headlines that force them to click on something by teasing, but they do like those that help them evaluate whether they want to read."

Like Levinson and Schmedding, executives nationwide are rethinking how they edit their Web sites. Increasingly, they realize that while the fundamentals of editing and headline writing for print remain, the Web is a different medium that requires new approaches.

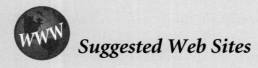

Suggested Web Sites

American Copy Editors Society **www.copydesk.org**
Folio (the magazine of the magazine industry) **www.foliomag.com/**
The Poynter Institute **www.poynter.org/**

Suggested Readings

Brooks, Brian S., George Kennedy, Daryl Moen and Don Ranly. *Telling the Story: The Convergence of Print, Broadcast and Online Media.* 3rd edition. New York: Bedford/St. Martin's, 2007.

Brooks, Brian S., James L. Pinson and Jean Gaddy Wilson. *Working With Words: A Handbook for Media Writers and Editors.* 6th edition. New York: Bedford/St. Martin's, 2006.

CHAPTER 9

USING PHOTOS, GRAPHICS AND TYPE

Only one news medium—radio—attempts to reach large audiences without strong graphic appeal. We live in a world in which visual stimulation is important in attracting and holding the attention of television viewers, newspaper and magazine readers, and Web surfers. Indeed, in today's world it's almost unthinkable to ignore the power of design and the impact of video, photos and graphics.

Unfortunately, too many journalists are so focused on written or spoken content that they fail to appreciate the power of visuals. Writes Monica L. Moses, deputy managing editor for visuals at the *Star Tribune* in Minneapolis: "Making traditional journalists more visually literate is difficult because of a deep and unspoken wariness of visuals and visual journalists. While visual work is the most visible in the newspaper, visual journalists are the least visible in the industry."

Moses adds that many writers and editors think what they provide is content while visual journalists deal in form or presentation. She notes that visuals are content, too, and an important part of content at that. Research from The Poynter Institute tells us:

- About 90 percent of readers enter pages through large photos, artwork or display type (such as headlines and promos).
- Running a visual element with text makes it three times more likely that at least some of the text will be read.
- Headlines are more likely to be read when a photo is nearby.
- The bigger the photo, the more likely readers are to read the caption.

While these findings relate most directly to newspapers and magazines, it's equally undeniable that visuals make television what it is and that visuals are extremely important in driving traffic through Web sites. ESPN's Web site (www .espn.com) has become one of the most popular in the country, thanks to strong content, good design and ample use of digital video and graphics.

As a result, in today's world the wordsmith on the magazine editing staff and the newspaper city hall reporter need to be just as attuned to the power of visuals as the television videographer and the magazine designer. Although one journalist may spend all or part of her day working entirely with visuals, and another may spend all of his day working with words, both must recognize and respect the power of visual communication. Moses notes:

- Photographs and information graphics markedly increase both comprehension of text and interest in stories.
- Graphics, photographs and headlines get far more attention from readers than text does.

The same is true in television and on the Web. When television stories are merely read by anchors, and Web stories are told only with text, news consumers show little interest. Add video, photos, graphics and display type, and the equation changes.

Television, of course, lives and dies with video and graphics. The television **videographer** oversees all aspects of the video image, including lighting and the operation of the camera. The videographer in many ways is television's ultimate editor because of the incredible power of sound and video in that medium. But whatever the medium—except, of course, radio—the power of visuals is strong and undeniable. In this chapter, we address the fundamentals of using photos, graphics and type, devices available in all of the media capable of visual communication.

EDITING FOR GRAPHIC APPEAL

Editors can do much to help increase graphic appeal. Here are some tips that apply equally well to newspapers, magazines and Web sites:

- **Be on the lookout for sidebars.** If a story seems too long and moves in several directions, consider breaking it into a main story and separate sidebars. Remember, the average person reads the paper only about 24 minutes a day—perusing the photos and reading mainly the headlines and other big type except on a few stories of interest. Breaking sidebars out of longer stories means the material looks shorter and more inviting. In addition, you spoon-feed the readers some extra information in the sidebar's headline.

  Boring: A 30-inch story describes the events of an upcoming town-history festival, relates some of the history to be commemorated and profiles the organizer of the event.

  Better: The three parts of the story should be made separate stories, packaged with appealing photos or artwork. The events should probably be listed in an accompanying box. Don't automatically make the history the centerpiece; the profile may be the better choice. People usually prefer to read about people rather than things or events.

  Boring: A 75-inch investigative piece examines who lives in public housing, the history of public housing in the area, the complaints people in public housing have about life in the projects, the complaints neighbors have about having public housing nearby and responses from officials in charge.

Better: Organize this into separate stories that can run over several days as a series. Or run the stories as a package, probably on a Sunday, on a special page devoted to the issue. Promo it on the front page, or even consider starting the main story, probably a summary, on the front page and then jumping it to the special page. Another alternative: It could run in the Sunday magazine if you have a locally produced one. The less earth-shattering the revelations, the more likely this alternative would be considered.

- **People will be more attracted to stories with photos or graphics, so keep the visual possibilities of each story in mind when designing a page.** Even if you're a newspaper copy editor, it may be helpful to your supervisor if you mention that a particular story has great quotes that could be used for blurbs or a list that could make a good chart. Is the story so complicated that the headline could use an extra deck? Adding that may result in better communication. Encourage reporters to think about visual possibilities for their stories. Remind them that stories almost always receive better play if accompanied by photos or graphics. Visual possibilities should be considered early in the writing and editing process, not as an afterthought.

- **Bullets permit you to list a lot of items in a minimum amount of space and with added contrast.** Bullets are solid circles, dashes, check marks or black boxes used to set off items in a list. *USA Today* makes extensive use of bullets to keep its stories short.

- **If a story is long, subheads could help break it into shorter, logical parts.** Use subheadings instead of transitional paragraphs between the parts. Magazines and Web sites use them frequently; newspapers use them less frequently, except in the longest of stories.

- **Make sure the photographer knows the mood and theme of the story and takes pictures of the main people being interviewed.** Too often, newspapers will have a sad piece with a smiling photograph or a feature with a photograph of one person and a story about someone else.

- **Drawings, often called line art,** are sometimes preferable to photos for series logos and for situations where a camera could be intrusive. They also can explain complicated processes or things by stripping away the exterior and showing the inner workings of the object.

- **Double-check charts for accuracy of figures.**

USING PHOTOS

At good newspapers, the days are gone when a city editor would say to a reporter, "That's a good story; now get me a photo to go with it." Today, good newspapers treat graphical elements—photos, charts and illustrations—as the editorial equivalent of stories. Accordingly, they are assigned with the same care, and often at the same time, as news and feature articles.

That development came about late in the last century as newspapers faced increasing competition for readers' attention. Editors found that newspapers needed to be more attractive if they were to hold or increase readership. The result was an era in which newspaper design became almost as important to many editors as content. In general, the size and quality of newspaper photographs increased, and charts, graphs and maps proliferated. All of these elements were increasingly likely to be printed in color.

None of that should be surprising. We live in a visual society in which color and design play important roles. Visual appeal is used to market everything from television to cereal boxes, and newspapers are not exempt. This has necessitated a change in the way almost all newspapers look. The gray, vertical columns of the past have given way to modular design, color, more and larger pictures, and charts, graphs and maps, which editors call *information graphics.* To make these changes, newsrooms have been forced to change their internal structures, too.

Today, photo editors are key members of the newsroom management team, usually equal in rank to news, city or metropolitan editors. Design desks have been added in many newsrooms to relieve the copy desk of the chore of designing as well as editing. Many metros have gone so far as to appoint assistant managing editors for graphics. And graphic departments, which produce charts, graphs and maps, have sprung from nowhere, even at relatively small dailies.

Not surprisingly, technological advance has helped. Few newsrooms today are without personal computers with design and charting software. These machines allow editors and artists to create graphics that would have taken days to execute through traditional methods.

Now, the art of photography itself has changed as digital cameras make silver-based photography obsolete. Both local and wire service photos are being processed with computers and digital-imaging software (see Figure 9–1). Once again, the newspaper industry is embracing technology to help it remain competitive. Those who work digitally agree that the computer has allowed for greater creativity while saving time and money.

No fancy technology, however, can make a bad picture good or help an editor determine whether a graphic accomplishes what it purports to do. This chapter is designed not to make photographers or graphic artists of editors but to give editors an appreciation of the role of photos and graphics in the appeal of newspapers, magazines and Web sites. **Visual literacy** is critical to the competent editor.

Rewriting can turn a poorly written news story into an acceptable one. Little can be done to change the subject matter of clichéd photos—tree plantings, ribbon cuttings, proclamation signings and the passing of checks, certificates or awards from one person to another. Some newspapers, magazines and Web sites use photographs of these situations simply because of the tradition that "chicken-dinner" stuff must be photographed. It is a tradition that should be scrapped, and most good publications have already done so.

Figure 9–1 Photos are now edited on computer workstations at most newspapers.
Photo by Philip Holman.

A photo editor is almost as essential to a newspaper as a city editor. Some executive—preferably one with a background in photography—should be responsible for assigning photographers to news and feature events. Someone in authority should insist that all photos, including those from news agencies, be edited and that captions be intelligently written.

If it is a good picture, it should get a good play, just as a top story gets a big headline. If pictures are a vital part of the story, editors should be willing to cut back on words, if necessary, to provide space for photographs. Some events can be told better in words than in pictures. Conversely, other events are essentially graphic, and editors need little or no text to get the message across.

Photographer–Editor Relationships

An encouraging development in recent years has been the trend toward making photographers full partners in the editorial process. Historically, photographers were second-class citizens in the newspaper and magazine hierarchy. They did not enjoy the prestige of the reporter or the copy editor, and with rare exception their opinions were not solicited or were ignored.

Many insightful editors now realize that photographers possess an intangible quality known as visual literacy, a trait sometimes lacking in even the best of word-smiths. Photographers should have a voice in how their pictures are displayed, and editors who have given them that voice invariably have been pleased with the results. The number of publications using pictures well is increasing each year, although leading photo editors agree that there is ample room for improvement. For every newspaper, magazine and Web site using pictures well, it is easy to find two still using the line-'em-up-and-shoot-'em approach.

A key to improvement in the quality of pictures is allowing the photographer to become involved in the story from the outset. If possible, the photographer should accompany the reporter as information for the story is gathered. If that is impossible, allowing the photographer to read the story—or to take time to talk with the reporter about the thrust of it—will help ensure a photograph that complements the story. Publications throughout the country each day are filled with pictures that fail to convey a message because the reporter, photographer and editor failed to communicate with each other.

An important part of this communications process involves writing the photo order, the document given to the photographer when an assignment is made. A photographer for the *Columbia Missourian* once received an order for a picture of an elementary school principal. The order instructed the photographer to meet the principal in his office at 3:15 p.m. and to take a picture of him at his desk. It mentioned that the principal would be unavailable until that time. The story focused on how the principal went out of his way to help frightened first-graders find the right bus during the first few weeks of school. Because the reporter failed to mention that when he wrote the photo order, the photographer followed his instructions exactly. He arrived at 3:15 and took the picture. Only after returning to the office did he learn the thrust of the story and discover that the principal was unavailable 15 minutes earlier because he had been helping students find their buses. The best photo opportunity had been missed.

Editing Decisions

Most photographs, like most news stories, can be improved with editing. The photo editor, like the copy editor, must make decisions that affect the quality of the finished product. The photo editor must determine:

- Which photo or photos complement the written story or tell a story of their own.
- Whether cropping enhances the image.
- What size a photo must be to communicate effectively.
- Whether retouching is necessary.

SELECTION

Photo selection is critical because valuable space is wasted if the picture does nothing more than depict a scene that could be described more efficiently with words. The adage that a picture is worth a thousand words is not necessarily true. If the picture adds nothing to the reader's understanding of a story, it should be rejected. Conversely, some pictures capture the emotion or flavor of a situation more vividly than words. In other situations, words and photographs provide perfect complements.

A talented photo editor, experienced in visual communication, can provide the guidance necessary for successful use of pictures. Smaller newspapers, magazines or Web sites without the luxury of full-time photo editors can turn to their photographers for advice, but often the news editor or copy editor must make such decisions. When that is necessary, an appreciation for the importance of visual communication is essential for good results. At Web sites, there are often no photographers or photo editors, which means those who produce the site must possess visual literacy.

Internal procedures reflect the media outlet's picture-selection philosophy. Some allow the photographer to make the decision; the pictures he or she submits to the desk are the only ones considered for publication. This procedure may ensure selection of the picture with the best technical quality, but that picture may not best complement the story. A photo editor, working closely with the photographer, the reporter, the city editor and the copy editor, should have a better understanding of the story and be able to make the best selection. Contact prints, miniature proofs of the photographer's negatives, allow the photographer, reporter and editors to review all frames available so the best selection can be made. In digital photography, the same results can be had by reviewing photos on a computer monitor.

CROPPING

A photograph is a composition. The composition should help the reader immediately grasp the picture's message. If the picture is too cluttered, the reader's eyes scan the picture looking for a place to rest. But if the picture contains a strong focal point, the reader at least has a place to start. A prime job of a photo editor, therefore, is to help the photographer take out some unnecessary details to strengthen the overall view.

Certain elements within the picture could be stronger than the full picture. Some photo editors try to find these interest points and patterns by moving the digital photo around in an art box with a mouse or by moving two L-shaped pieces of cardboard over the picture. This helps to guide the editor in cropping. The editor looks for a focal point, or chief spot of interest. If other points of interest are present, the photo editor tries to retain them. The editor searches for patterns that can be strengthened by cropping. The pattern helps give the picture harmonious and balanced composition. Among these patterns are various letter shapes—L, U, S, Z, T, O—and geometric patterns such as a star, a circle, a cross or a combination of these.

Because most news and feature photos contain people, the editor strives to help the photographer depict them as dramatically as possible. The editor must decide how many people to include in the picture, how much of each person to include and what background is essential.

Historically, publications have opted for the tightest possible cropping to conserve valuable space. Severe cropping, however, may damage a photo to the point that not printing it would have been preferable. Those who win awards for photo editing appreciate the fact that background is essential to some photographs. As a result, they tend to crop tightly less often than editors with more traditional approaches to picture editing. In Figure 9–2, tight cropping allows the reader to see interesting detail. But in Figure 9–3, tight cropping eliminates the environment and damages the meaning of the picture. Those who can distinguish between these approaches are valuable members of newspaper and magazine staffs. They possess visual literacy.

Through all this, the photo editor attempts to reserve the rule of thirds. Imagine a photo divided into thirds both horizontally and vertically. The four points where these lines intersect are considered the best focal points, or centers of interest, for the photo.

SIZING

The value of the picture, not the amount of space available, should determine the reproduction size of a photograph. Too often, editors try to reduce a photograph to fit a space and destroy the impact of the photo in the process. Common sense should dictate that a picture of 15 individuals will be ineffective if it appears as a two-column photo. More likely, such a photo will require three or even four columns of space.

Talented photo editors know that the greatest danger is making pictures too small. If the choice is between a two-column picture and a three-column picture, the wise photo editor opts for the larger size. Photos can be too large, but more often they are damaged by making them too small. Another alternative may be available. Modern production techniques make it easy for the editor to publish a half-column photo with text wrapping around it to fill the space.

Sizing of any photograph is an important decision, but sizing of pictures in multiphotograph packages is particularly important. In such packages, one photograph should be dominant. The use of multiple pictures allows the editor flexibility that may not exist in single-picture situations. If a picture editor selects a photo of a harried liquor store clerk who has just been robbed and a photo of the outside of the store where the robbery occurred, the editor has three choices:

- Devote equal space to the two pictures. This is the least desirable choice because neither picture would be dominant and, consequently, neither would have eye-catching impact.

- Make the outside shot dominant and the close-up of the clerk secondary. This would work, but the dominant photo, which serves merely as a locater, would

A

B

Figure 9–2 Foot-print on the lunar soil. An example of how cropping (B) can bring out an interesting detail in a photograph (A). The close-up view was photographed with a lunar surface camera during the Apollo 11 lunar surface extravehicular activity.

Photographs courtesy of the National Aeronautics and Space Administration.

A   B

Figure 9–3 Tight cropping can occasionally destroy the impact of a picture. (A) Tight cropping takes the farmer out of his environment by making it difficult or impossible for the reader to determine that the setting is a barn (B).

Columbia Missourian photo by Manny Crisostomo.

have little impact. The impact of human emotion, evident in the clerk's face, would be diminished.

- Make the facial expression dominant with good sizing and make the outside shot as small as $1\frac{1}{2}$ columns. The outside shot, standing alone, would look ridiculous if used in that size, but used in conjunction with another, larger photo, it would work well.

Dramatic size contrast is an effective device in multipicture packages (Figure 9–4). An editor trained in visual communication understands the usefulness of reversing normal sizing patterns for added impact.

RETOUCHING

Some photographs can be improved by **retouching,** the process of toning down or eliminating distractions within the frame. Minor imperfections in photos can be retouched with computer programs such as Adobe PhotoShop. Care must be exercised, however, to ensure that retouching does not change the meaning and content of the photo. Changing a photo to alter its meaning is as unethical as changing a direct quotation to alter a speaker's meaning.

An unscrupulous editor can move one of the Great Pyramids in relation to the Sphinx to improve a picture's composition or place the head of one person on the body of another. Both these things have happened in recent years as magazines, newspapers and Web sites have grappled with the ethics of altering photographs.

Most good editors have taken the solid ethical position that nothing more than changing the brightness, contrast or sharpness of a picture should be tolerated. Anything more than that leads to deception, which is sure to destroy a publication's integrity.

Pictures as Copy

When the picture has been processed, someone—reporter or photographer—supplies the information for the *caption,* also known as the *cutline.* The picture and caption information then go to the appropriate department, where the editor decides whether to use the photo and, if so, how to display it.

Before submitting a picture to the production department, the editor supplies information to get the correct picture in the correct place with the correct caption. A picture, like a story, generally carries an identifying slug. To ensure that the photograph will match the caption and the story, the editor uses a *slugline.*

A slip of paper clipped on the picture or taped to the back normally contains information such as:

- The slug or picture identification.
- The size.
- Special handling instructions.
- The department, edition and page.
- The date the photo is to appear.
- The date and time the picture was sent to the production department.
- Whether the photo stands alone or accompanies a story.

Figure 9–4 Many editors would run the overall flooding shot (B) larger than the picture of the farmer laying sandbags in place (A). The pairing, however, has more impact if the close shot of the farmer is run larger than the scene-setting overall picture.

Columbia Missourian photos by Lee Meyer and Mike Asher.

A

B

When Photos Lie

"Photos never lie" is one of the oldest media industry axioms. It's doubtful whether this was ever true, and it certainly isn't today. Computerized processing of photos makes it easier than ever to manipulate pictures in ways that are totally unethical.

National Geographic magazine moved a pyramid closer to the Sphinx to improve the composition of a photo, then listened to cries of outrage from photographers and others who objected to the practice. *TV Guide* put Oprah Winfrey's head on another person's body and suffered a similar fate.

One can't help but wonder, though, how many similar things have occurred without someone noticing. The fact is that tampering with the content of a photo is just as wrong as printing a manufactured quotation and attributing it to a senator, the mayor or a police officer at the scene of a crime. It is unethical, and at many publications it is now grounds for dismissal.

Quality publications now limit computerized alteration of photographs to the equivalent of minor retouching, a process developed in the era of conventional photography. Editors and photographers are allowed to make a photo lighter or darker. They also are allowed to do electronic edge sharpening, the equivalent of improving the focus.

Most other forms of alteration are prohibited, although some publications allow the removal of distracting background elements. This might include removal of an electric wire dangling behind a subject in such a way as to appear the wire is emerging from the person's head. The best photographers eliminate such distractions the right way by making sure they aren't there in the original photo.

In computerized photo editing, this information is contained in metadata that accompanies the file.

Sometimes the photo may be deliberately separated from the story. A teaser picture may be used on Page One to entice readers to read the story on another page. If a long story has two illustrations, one illustration often is used on the page where the story begins and the other on the jump page. For major events, such as the death of a president, pictures may be scattered on several pages. In this case, readers are directed to these pages with a guideline such as "More pictures on Pages 5, 7 and 16."

Changing Photo Technology

Technology is changing the way photographs are processed at newspapers, magazines and Web sites. Today, most photographs are scanned into computers, where they are lightened or darkened, sharpened, cropped and sized using programs such as Adobe PhotoShop. More and more newspapers and magazines also are flowing photographs directly onto the page using personal computer programs such as Quark Xpress or Adobe InDesign. From there, entire pages, with all photos and graphics in place, are output to paper proofs, to film or even directly to the printing plate.

Scanning of photos is sometimes necessary because a few publications still prefer to use conventional photography to take pictures. Digital photography, in which photos are stored on miniature diskettes inside cameras rather than on film, is increasingly popular.

Now that digital photography is widely accepted, darkrooms and chemical photo processing are practically a thing of the past. Digital processing saves time, which is of paramount importance for publications, particularly newspapers and Web sites.

Taste in Picture Editing

It was a tragic fire in the Boston metropolitan area. A woman and a child took refuge on an ironwork balcony. As firefighters tried to rescue them, the balcony collapsed, sending the woman to her death and the child to a miraculous survival. Photographers took sequence shots of the action (see Figures 9–5 and 9–6 on Pages 274–275). Should a photo editor use the pictures?

Some readers would be incensed, accusing the papers of sensationalism, poor **taste,** invasion of privacy, insensitivity and a tasteless display of human tragedy to sell newspapers. Picture editors could reply that their duty is to present the news, whether of good things or bad, of the pleasant or the unpleasant. Defending the judgment to use the pictures on Page One, the editor of the *Battle Creek* (Mich.) *Enquirer and News* said, "The essential purpose of journalism is to help the reader understand what is happening in this world and thereby help him to appreciate those things he finds good and to try to correct those things he finds bad."

Of the flood of pictures depicting the war in Vietnam, surely among the most memorable were the Saigon chief of police executing a prisoner, terrified children fleeing a napalm attack and the flaming suicide of a Buddhist monk. Such scenes were part of the war record and deserved to be shown. More recently, the photograph of an airplane striking one of the towers of the World Trade Center in New York is similarly memorable.

Photos of fire deaths may tell more than the tragedy depicted in the burned and mangled bodies. Implicit could be the lessons of inadequate inspection, faulty construction, carelessness with matches, arson or antiquated firefighting equipment.

Picture editors have few criteria to guide them. Their news judgment and their own conscience tell them whether to order a picture for Page One showing a man in Australia mauled to death by polar bears after he fell into a pool in the bears' enclosure in a zoo. Of the hundreds of pictures available that day, surely a better one could have been found for Page One.

Caption Guidelines

Picture texts are known by many names—cutlines, captions, underlines (or overlines) and legends. *Caption* suggests a heading over a picture, but most editors now use the term to refer to the lines under the picture. **Legend** may refer either to the text or to the heading. If a heading or catchline is used, it should be under, not over the picture.

The editor "sells" the reporter's story by means of a compelling headline. By the same token, the picture editor can help control the photographic image with a caption. The primary purpose of the caption is to get the reader to respond to the photo in the manner intended by the photographer and the picture editor.

Readers first concentrate on the focal point of the picture, then glance at the other parts. Then, presumably, most turn to the caption to confirm what they have seen in the picture. The caption provides the answers to questions of who, what, where, when, why and how, unless some of these are apparent in the picture.

The caption interprets and expands on what the picture says to the reader. It may point out the inconspicuous but significant. It may comment on the revealing or amusing parts of the picture if these are not self-evident. The caption helps explain ambiguities, comments on what is not made clear in the picture and mentions what the picture fails to show if that is necessary.

The ideal caption is direct, brief and sometimes bright. It is a concise statement, not a news story. It immediately gets to the point and avoids the "go back to the beginning" of the background situation.

If the photo accompanies a story, the caption shouldn't duplicate the details readers can find in the story. It should, however, contain enough information to satisfy those who will not read the story. Ideally, the picture and the caption will induce readers to read the story. Normally, the caption of a picture with a story is limited to two or three lines. Even when the picture relates to the story, the caption should not go beyond what the picture reveals. Nor should the facts in the caption differ from those in the story.

Captions stand out in the sea of words and strike the reader with peculiar force. Every word should be weighed, especially for impact, emotional tone, impartiality and adherence to rules of grammar.

Any editor who tries to write or rewrite a caption without seeing the picture risks errors. The cropped photo should be examined, not the original. The caption has to confine itself to the portion of the picture the reader will see. If the caption says a woman is waving a handkerchief, the handkerchief must be in the picture. In a layout containing two or more photographs with a single caption, the editor should study the layout to make sure that left or right or top or bottom directions are correct.

Although no one should try to write a caption without first looking at the picture, pictures often have to move quickly to the production department. When dealing with a paper copy of the photo, the editor removes the captions (from wire service and syndicated pictures) and jots down the slug and size of the pictures and any revealing elements in the pictures that might be added to the cutlines. A photocopy of the picture may be made. When dealing with the photo

Figure 9–5 One of the controversial sequence shots of a fire tragedy in a Boston apartment. Scores of readers protested the use of these widely distributed photos.

Photo by Stanley Forman of the *Boston Herald-American*, distributed by UPI.

Figure 9–6 The second shot of the balcony collapsing in Boston. Most editors defended the use of the tragic photos.

Photo by Stanley Forman of the *Boston Herald-American,* distributed by UPI.

Writing the Caption

Here are some tips on caption writing:

- **Don't tell the obvious.** If the person in the photo is pretty or attractive, that fact will be obvious from the picture. The picture will tell whether a person is smiling. It may be necessary, however, to tell why he or she is smiling. An explanation need not go as far as the following: "Two women and a man stroll down the newly completed section of Rehoboth's boardwalk. They are, from left, Nancy Jackson, Dianne Johnson and Richard Bramble, all of West Chester." An editor remarked, "Even if some of the slower readers couldn't have figured out the sexes from the picture, the names are a dead giveaway."

- **Don't editorialize.** A writer doesn't know whether someone is happy, glum or troubled. The cutline that described a judge as "weary but ready" when he arrived at court must have made readers wonder how the writer knew the judge was weary.

- **Use specifics rather than generalities.** "A 10-pound book" is better than "a huge book."

- **Omit references to the photo.** Because the readers know you are referring to the photograph, omit phrases such as "is pictured," "is shown" and "the picture above shows."

- **Use "from left" rather than "from left to right."** The first means as much as the second and is shorter. Neither *left* nor *right* should be overworked. If one of two boys in a picture is wearing a white jersey, use that fact to identify him.

- **Avoid "looking on."** One of the worst things you can say about a person in a photo is that he or she is "looking on." If that is all the person is doing, the photo is superfluous.

- **Don't kid the readers.** They will know whether this is a "recent photo." Give the date the photo was taken if it is an old photo.

Also, let readers know where the picture was taken—but not how. Most readers don't care about all the sleet and snow the photographer had to go through to get the picture.

- **Write captions in the present tense.** This enhances the immediacy of the pictures they accompany. The past tense is used if the sentence contains the date or if it gives additional facts not described in the action in the picture. The caption may use both present and past tenses, but the past time element should not be used in the same sentence with a present-tense verb describing the action.

- **Make sure the caption is accurate.** Double-check the spelling of names. The paper, not the photographer, gets the blame for inaccuracies. Caption errors often occur because someone, the photographer or the reporter accompanying the photographer, failed to give the photo desk enough, or accurate, information from which to construct a caption.

- **Double-check the photo with the caption identification.** The wrong person pictured as "the most-wanted fugitive" is a sure way to invite libel.

- **Be careful.** Writing a caption requires as much care and skill as writing a story or a headline. The reader should not have to puzzle out the meaning of the description. Notice these jarring examples:

  Fearing new outbreaks of violence, the results of Sunday's election have been withheld.

  Also killed in the accident was the father of five children driving the other vehicle.

- **Don't hit the reader over the head with the obvious.** If the photo shows a firefighter dousing hot timbers after a warehouse fire and a firefighter already has been mentioned in the text, it is ridiculous to add in the caption that "firefighters were called."

- **Avoid last-line widows or hangers.** The last line of the caption should be a full line, or nearly so. When the lines are doubled (two two-columns for a four-column picture), write an even number of lines. Short last lines are known as **widows** or **hangers**.

- **Captions should be humorous if warranted by the picture.** Biting humor and sarcasm have no place in captions.

- **The caption should describe the event as shown in the picture, not the event itself.** Viewers will be puzzled if the caption describes action they do not see. Sometimes, however, an explanation of what is not shown is justified. If the photo shows a football player leaping high to catch a pass for a touchdown, viewers might like to know who threw the pass.

- **Update the information.** Because there is a lapse between the time a picture of an event is taken and the time a viewer sees the picture in the newspaper, care should be taken to update the information in the caption. If the first report was that three bodies were found in the wreckage, but subsequently two more bodies were found, the caption should contain the latest figure.

- **Be exact.** In local pictures, the addresses of the persons shown may be helpful. If youngsters appear in the photo, they should be identified by names, ages, names of parents and addresses.

- **Credit the photographer.** If the picture is exceptional, credit may be given to the photographer in the caption, perhaps with a brief description of how he or she achieved the creation. On picture pages containing text matter, the photographer's credit should be displayed as prominently as the writer's.

- **Pictures without captions.** Although photographs normally carry captions, mood or special-occasion pictures sometimes appear without them if the message is obvious from the picture itself. Not all who look at pictures will also read the captions. In fact, the decline is severe enough to suggest that many readers satisfy their curiosity merely by looking at the photo.

- **Know your style.** Some papers use one style for captions with a story and another style for captions without a story (called *standalone* or *no-story*). A picture with a story might call for one, two or three words in boldface caps to start the caption. In **standalones**, a small head or catchline might be placed over the caption.

- **Give the location.** If the dateline is knocked out in the caption, make sure that the location is mentioned. Example:

  GUARDING GOATS—Joe Fair, a 70-year-old pensioner, looks over his goats Rosebud and Tagalong, the subject of much furor in this northeastern Missouri community, boyhood home of Mark Twain.

- **Rewrite wire-service cutlines.** The same photos from news agencies and syndicates appear in smaller dailies as well as in metropolitan dailies. Some papers merely reset the caption supplied with the pictures. Most, if not all, such captions should be rewritten to add to the story told in the picture and to indicate some originality on the paper's part.

- **Watch the mood.** The mood of the caption should match the mood of the picture. The caption for a feature photo may stress light writing. Restraint is observed for photographs showing tragedy or dealing with a serious subject.

on a computer, simply copy the caption to a text field and edit as necessary. Time permitting, a proofsheet showing pictures and their captions should be given to the photo editor to make certain all the pieces have been put together properly and that the caption matches the content of the photo.

After the caption has been set in type or readied for the Web, the editor should compare the message with the picture. The number of people in the picture should be checked against the number of names in the caption. Everyone appearing prominently in the photo should be identified. If a person is obscured in the crowd, that person need not be brought to the reader's attention.

USING INFORMATION GRAPHICS

Photographs help the reader gain a visual appreciation of reality; **information graphics** help the reader understand the massive, the intangible or the hidden. A map of part of the city is usually a better locater than an aerial photo of the same area. A chart often helps the reader track trends over time. An artist's cutaway can show the undersea levels of a sinking ship.

In recent years, information graphics, as these illustrations are known, have appeared with increasing regularity in newspapers and magazines, large and small, and on Web sites. Personal computers are ideal for creating such graphics quickly and inexpensively, and newspapers rushed to embrace them in the 1980s. Suddenly, publications that once had only photographers and artists added graphic designers to create charts, graphs and maps. Contests added categories for graphic design, and the Society of Newspaper Design was formed.

Many believe this transformation was sparked by the arrival of *USA Today* in 1979, and there is no doubt that it set new standards for the use of color and graphics. Colorful charts, graphs and maps play a key role in *USA Today,* which the Gannett Co. designed for the busy reader. Charts, graphs and maps are a good way of communicating lots of information in a hurry, and *USA Today*'s editors were quick to embrace them. The newspaper's colorful weather map has been emulated by papers worldwide (see Figure 9–7).

USA Today is far from alone in adopting information graphics. *The New York Times* and other prestigious newspapers now publish full-page graphics on section fronts, *Time* magazine produces startling graphics, and syndicated services of graphics material proliferates. The Associated Press greatly increased the quality and quantity of the graphics it provided.

Like photographs, however, information graphics can be good or bad. Confusing charts, graphs and maps hinder readers rather than help them. Graphics that are too busy may confuse rather than enlighten.

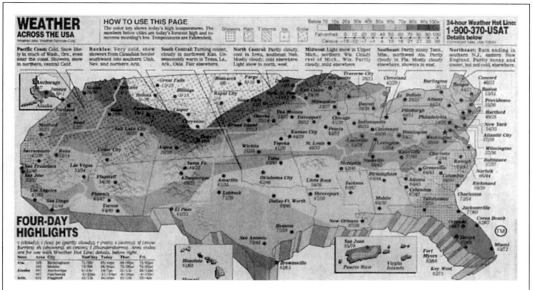

Figure 9–7 The *USA Today* weather map.

Courtesy of *USA Today*.

Types of Information Graphics

Illustrations help the reader understand complex things or concepts, including information that may be extremely difficult or impossible to describe in words. They take many forms, from the simple illustration to the complex diagram.

Maps, of course, help the reader locate things. Local maps help the reader locate places within the city. Maps of counties, states, regions or nations help readers locate sites with which they may not be familiar (see Figure 9–8). Good graphics departments maintain computerized base maps of various locales. When an event occurs, it is a simple matter to add specific locater information to the base map to create a helpful aid for the reader. Secondary windows within maps sometimes are used to pin down specific areas within geographic regions or to show the location of the specific region within a larger area.

Tables are used to graphically display numerical information (see Figure 9–9). They are useful when lots of numbers are involved, as in precinct-by-precinct election results.

All these devices are tools the editor uses to help convey information to readers. Some information is conveyed best in words, some in pictures and some in information graphics. The editor who knows when to choose each of these devices helps to create an easy-to-read publication.

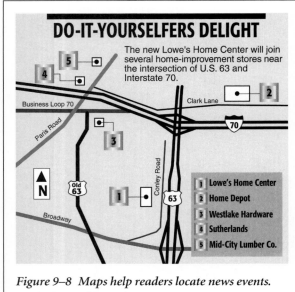

DO-IT-YOURSELFERS DELIGHT

The new Lowe's Home Center will join several home-improvement stores near the intersection of U.S. 63 and Interstate 70.

1. Lowe's Home Center
2. Home Depot
3. Westlake Hardware
4. Sutherlands
5. Mid-City Lumber Co.

Figure 9–8 Maps help readers locate news events.

Graphic by Satoshi Toyoshima.

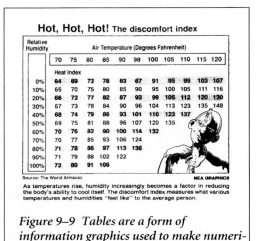

Hot, Hot, Hot! The discomfort index

Relative Humidity	Air Temperature (Degrees Fahrenheit)										
	70	75	80	85	90	98	100	105	110	115	120
	Heat Index										
0%	64	69	73	78	83	67	91	95	99	103	107
10%	65	70	75	80	85	90	95	100	105	111	116
20%	66	72	77	82	87	93	99	105	112	120	130
30%	67	73	78	84	90	96	104	113	123	135	148
40%	68	74	79	86	93	101	110	123	137		
50%	69	75	81	88	96	107	120	135			
60%	70	76	82	90	100	114	132				
70%	70	77	85	93	106	124					
80%	71	78	86	97	113	136					
90%	71	79	88	102	122						
100%	72	80	91	108							

Source: The World Almanac

NEA GRAPHICS

As temperatures rise, humidity increasingly becomes a factor in reducing the body's ability to cool itself. The discomfort index measures what various temperatures and humidities "feel like" to the average person.

Figure 9–9 Tables are a form of information graphics used to make numerical information easier to read.

Courtesy of Newspaper Enterprise Association.

Bar charts help the reader visualize quantities (see Figure 9–10), and **fever charts** show quantities over time (see Figure 9–11). **Pie charts** are used to show the division of the whole into components (see Figure 9–12). **Process drawings** help readers visualize detailed plans (see Figure 9–13).

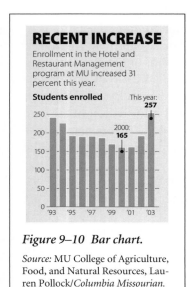

RECENT INCREASE

Enrollment in the Hotel and Restaurant Management program at MU increased 31 percent this year.

Students enrolled

This year: **257**

2000: **165**

Figure 9–10 Bar chart.

Source: MU College of Agriculture, Food, and Natural Resources, Lauren Pollock/*Columbia Missourian.*

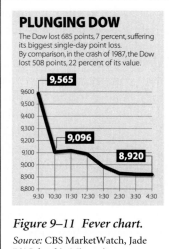
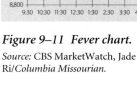

PLUNGING DOW

The Dow lost 685 points, 7 percent, suffering its biggest single-day point loss. By comparison, in the crash of 1987, the Dow lost 508 points, 22 percent of its value.

9,565

9,096

8,920

Figure 9–11 Fever chart.

Source: CBS MarketWatch, Jade Ri/*Columbia Missourian.*

SMITH'S SHARE

From 1988 to 1996, Jeffrey E. Smith Development Co. has received the lion's share of the $1,696,195 in federal and state low-income-housing tax credits given to Columbia developers.

$1,563,495
Smith Development

$132,700
Westin Financial Group

Figure 9–12 Pie chart.

Source: Missouri Housing Development Commission, *Columbia Missourian.*

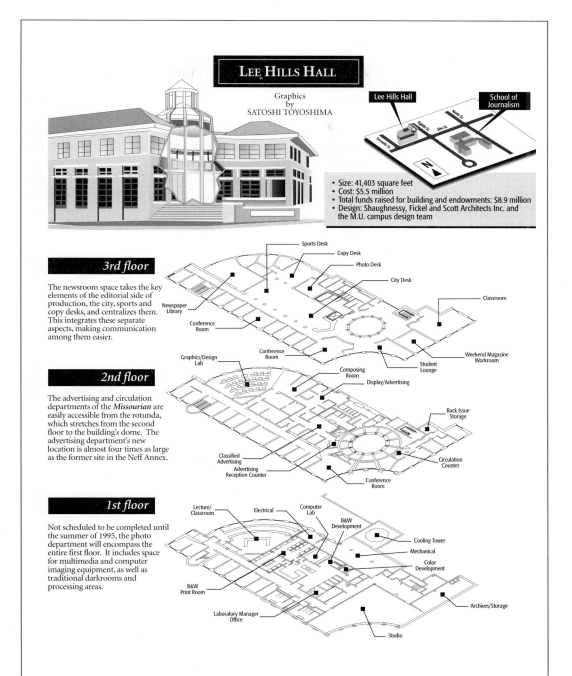

Figure 9–13 Process drawings help readers visualize progression of action or detailed plans.
Graphic by Satoshi Toyoshima.

USING TYPE

Photos and graphics have strong eye appeal and therefore rank as important elements in creating visually attractive newspaper, magazine and Web pages. Even television uses a fair amount of graphics, and wise selection of typefaces is important in all the media.

Type is used in the print media as both *body type* and *display type.* **Body type** is the primary typeface used for the text of a publication's stories. **Display type** is that used for headlines, blurbs, pull quotes and similar items that use large type. Although some magazines (and a few newspapers) switch body type styles with regularity, most stick with one basic typeface chosen for its legibility. **Legibility** refers to the ease with which a reader navigates a story. If a typeface is easy to read, it is legible. If it's difficult to read, it's not legible.

Here are examples of some typefaces considered to be legible:

This typeface is called Palatino.

This typeface is Baskerville.

This typeface is Times.

This typeface is Goudy.

It's obvious that some of those faces have a wider *set width* than others. Typefaces with wide sets require more space to print the same amount of copy (compare Palatino and Times in the example above). Newspapers often opt for more compact typefaces, such as Times, because they allow much more information to be printed in a given space than less compact faces such as Palatino. Magazines, often more concerned about overall appearance rather than space restrictions, often opt for the more attractive typefaces with wider sets.

Almost always, body typefaces are chosen for a combination of legibility and set width. (See Figure 9–14.) Here are other factors to consider, based on various legibility studies:

- Italic type is more difficult to read than roman, or upright, type.
- A line set in all capital letters is more difficult to read than a line set in caps and lowercase.

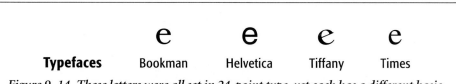

Figure 9–14 These letters were all set in 24-point type, yet each has a different basic design. The names of the typefaces are underneath the e's.

- Ornamental and cursive typefaces are more difficult to read than simple ones.
- **Serifs,** the small strokes at the ends of letters, aid legibility, particularly in body type. A serif is a relatively fine line at the bottom and top of letters such as *d, h, i, l, m, n, p, r, u, x* and *z*. Serifs also appear on capital letters of a serif typeface.
- Conversely, *sans serif* type is more difficult to read as body type.
- **Reverse** type, white letters on a dark background, is more difficult to read than black on white.

Generally, once a publication or Web site is designed, editors stick with the same body typeface all the time. Although the body type is an important part of the overall design of a publication, it has far less impact than display type on luring readers. Therefore, in this chapter we'll focus on the importance of display type—headlines, blurbs, pull quotes and similar devices that employ large type. First, however, let's review the basics of typography.

How Type is Measured

Most type measurements are carryovers from the old days of hot type and are identical to those used by traditional printers. Although desktop computers allow measurement in inches, many people retain the printers' practice of measuring in picas and points. Following are the basic traditional measurements:

- *Points.* 72 points equal 1 inch (a point is $\frac{1}{72}$ of an inch). The height of all type is measured in points. An editor can specify 12-point or 6-point type or any point size. Type may even be quite large, such as 120 points.
- *Picas.* 6 picas equal 1 inch (a pica is $\frac{1}{6}$ of an inch). 12 points equal 1 pica. The width of a line of type is usually expressed in picas—for example, 14 picas or 35 picas wide.
- *Page measurements.* The *trim size* is usually measured in inches. For example, a page may measure 7 by 10 inches. (Width is usually expressed first and length second.) But the *type area* (the trim size minus the margins) is usually measured in picas. A page 7 by 10 inches with a half inch margin all the way around has a type area of 36 by 54 picas.

Differentiating Typefaces (Fonts)

An editor or designer specifies a particular typeface, or font, when preparing copy to be set. Specifications for any particular type may vary in several ways, including point size (see above), typeface (also called a *font*), weight and width (light or bold, condensed or expanded, for example) and style (roman or italic), as shown in Figure 9–15.

Five Ways Typefaces Differ and Sample Specifications

How these could be specified:	(1) By Point Size	(2) By Type- face	(3) By Weight	(4) By Width	(5) By Style
Example 1	24 pt.	Bodoni	Lightface	Regular	Italic
Example 2	60 pt.	Century	Boldface	Condensed	Roman

Figure 9–15 Basic information that should be on type specification sheets.

DIFFERENCES IN TYPEFACE OR FONT

Just as members of the same human family tend to have similar facial characteristics, so do members of a type family. A type family includes all variations of a given type with common characteristics. Some type families have many variations; others have few. Figure 9–16 shows one of the large families of typefaces. Any one of the styles within that family may be referred to as a *typeface* or *font.* All of those in Figure 9–16 are sans serif typefaces, which means they do not have fine closing strokes at the ends of the letters. The body type in most newspapers has serifs, as does most of the the body type in this book. The three examples of large type in Figure 9–17 also has serifs. Research shows that typefaces with serifs are easier to read in large blocks of type, so most publications prefer a face with serifs for text. Headlines may be either serif or sans serif.

Type letters also differ in their use of thick and thin elements, which can be placed in slightly different positions on each letter. Figure 9–17 on Page 286 illustrates the differences among three typefaces. The type user, however, should not pay too much attention to slight variations of single letters but should concentrate on their appearance in mass form, as in a typical newspaper or magazine paragraph. A paragraph of about 50 words can show the overall look of a typeface.

DIFFERENCES IN TYPE WEIGHT AND WIDTH

Type may be differentiated by the weight or width of the letter. Most typefaces are created in regular and boldface. Some faces are also created in lightface medium, *demibold,* heavy and ultrabold as well. The terminology tends to be confusing. One type designer calls its medium-weight type *demibold,* whereas another calls a corresponding weight *medium.* The terms *heavy, bold* and *black* also may mean the same thing. Figure 9–18 on Page 287 shows common examples of type weights. Most typefaces are manufactured in normal (or regular) widths (see Figure 9–19 on Page 287). Regular widths are used in most reading matter, but wide and narrow widths also are available. Type manufacturers have created extra-condensed,

Futura Light

Futura Regular

Futura Bold

Futura Extrabold

Futura Regular Italic

Futura Bold Italic

Futura Light Condensed

Futura Regular Condensed

Futura Bold Condensed

Futura Extrabold Condensed

Futura Bold Outline

Figure 9–16 Some members of the Futura type family. Although each typeface is different, each also has family characteristics. When mixing different typefaces on the same page, use different members of the same type family.

Differences Among Typefaces

Shown below are three typefaces often used on desktop computers. Study the differences and read the comments.

Here is an example of 24 pt. Bookman

Here is an example of 24 pt. Times

Here is an example of 24 pt. Palatino

Comments

- The letters in one typeface are designed to be wider than others.
- Some letters in one face are taller than others.
- Compare the design of an "e" or "a" in each typeface. Note the differences.
- Each typeface has its own set of peculiar characteristics.
- Note the mass effect of each typeface below.

How Sample Typefaces Look in Paragraphs

10 pt. Bookman

Typefaces have been designed to have unique characteristics. In selecting typefaces for a story, think of the connotation (or feeling) of the typeface and its relationship to the story. Is one typeface better than another? Some typefaces are warmer, more legible, more powerful or more delicate. Some are more feminine or masculine.

10 pt. Times

Typefaces have been designed to have unique characteristics. In selecting typefaces for a story, think of the connotation (or feeling) of the typeface and its relationship to the story. Is one typeface better than another? Some typefaces are warmer, more legible, more powerful or more delicate. Some are more feminine or masculine.

10 pt. Palatino

Typefaces have been designed to have unique characteristics. In selecting typefaces for a story, think of the connotation (or feeling) of the typeface and its relationship to the story. Is one typeface better than another? Some typefaces are warmer, more legible, more powerful or more delicate. Some are more feminine or masculine.

Figure 9–17 Some of the more important ways typefaces differ.

LITHOS EXTRA LIGHT

LITHOS LIGHT

LITHOS REGULAR

LITHOS BOLD

LITHOS BLACK

Figure 9–18 Various weights of typefaces within the Lithos family.

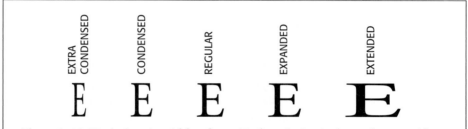

Figure 9–19 Variations in widths of type. Each variation is chosen for a specific purpose.

condensed, expanded and extended typefaces in addition to regular. These additional widths, however, are not manufactured in all type sizes or families.

DIFFERENCES IN TYPE STYLE

There are a number of ways to differentiate type by style. Each of them helps the editor find some unique quality in most typefaces. The most common classification divides type into broad categories termed *roman, italic* and *script*. It is best to think of these classifications as style characteristics that help in differentiating and identifying typefaces.

Roman Type. Roman type (see Figure 9–20) has a vertical shape and serifs. It usually has combinations of thick and thin elements in each letter. The body copy

A B C D E F G H I J K L M N O P Q R S T U V W X Y Z

Figure 9–20 A roman typeface (Bodoni) showing a vertical look with thick and thin elements.

is always set in a roman typeface with serifs. Some type experts consider all vertical letters to be roman, even those without serifs or with no variations in the width of letter elements. This form of classification, therefore, may be confusing to the beginner because the roman designation will have two purposes: one to distinguish it from sans serif and the other to distinguish it from italic.

Italic Type. Sometimes called *cursive,* italic types are characterized by their slanted letter shapes (see Figure 9–21). Although italic typefaces were originally designed to print many letters in relatively little space, their use today is limited to citations or words that must be emphasized. They are also used in headlines and body types. Italic types are designed to accompany roman types to provide consistency in the family of design.

Script Type. Script letters resemble handwriting. Although the type designers have tried to make it appear as if all the letters are joined, small spaces can be seen between them. Some script letters appear to have been written with a brush, others with a calligraphic pen. Script should never be set in all capital letters because it is hard to read in that form.

ELECTRONIC DISTORTION OF TYPE

Computers and computer design programs such as Adobe InDesign and Quark XPress have simplified typesetting and design. The software is so powerful that it permits distortions of type that can seriously damage the legibility of type.

When desktop publishing arrived in the early 1980s, default *letterspacing* (the space between letters in a word) was so loose that the resulting typography was often extremely unattractive. Designers with an eye for such things figured out ways to tighten the letterspacing but often with poor results. Applying the same

ABCDEFGHIJKLMNOP   *qrstuvwxyz*

Figure 9–21 Italic version of the Bodoni family.

space between each pair of letters produced varied results. As desktop publishing matured, default type settings improved dramatically. The problem now is that some designers can't resist the temptation to overdesign, sometimes resulting in horrid distortions of typefaces.

Some software makes it possible to take a roman typeface and artificially create an italic version by slanting the type. But as any good typographer knows, that's an abomination. Good italic fonts have the italicized sweep built right into the design of each letter. Publications that care about typography have set limits on the ability of designers to distort type electronically. Such distortion should be used rarely and then only in small doses as in a headline (or title) for a magazine feature story.

Finally, it's always a good idea to use only Postscript fonts in your designs. Mixing Adobe's Postscript fonts with TrueType fonts from Microsoft can have nasty consequences. TrueType fonts often don't translate correctly when outputting to PostScript printers or typesetting devices, and the results can be awful. Similarly, they probably will not translate correctly to a PDF file, used as a common transport for computer-designed pages.

How to Measure Type from a Printed Page

It's possible to measure type on a printed page but with less than complete accuracy. The height of type is measured from the top of the ascenders (the top stroke of a lowercase *d,* for example) to the bottom of the descenders (the bottom stroke of a lowercase *p* as an example).

Figure 9–22 shows imaginary lines by which letters are created. These lines are called the *base line,* on which all letters other than *g, j, p, q* and *y* rest; the *cap line,* to which most capital letters and tall letters rise; the *lowercase line,* where small letters align (called the *x-height* of letters); and the *descender line.* Each line helps in aligning letters.

For example, the ascender of the letter *h* rises above the lowercase line, but there is no descender below the base line. Thus, the shoulder underneath the letter must be included in the measurement. To accurately determine ascender space,

Figure 9–22 The dashed lines define ascenders, descenders and x-height.

Figure 9–23 Measure the distance between the top ascender and lowest descender to determine type size.

Figure 9–24 Why printed type is so difficult to measure. Each of these E's is 48 points high, but the shoulder space (or descender space) of each varies.

simply look for a capital letter or one with a high ascender. If it is necessary to measure the point size of a line of capital letters, take the space normally used for descenders into consideration (see Figures 9–23 and 9–24).

Still, measuring type this way is far from accurate. Most typefaces have built-in leading to ensure white space between lines of type that is set solid. Further, on occasion printers enlarge or reduce pages during the printing process, so the end result might not be quite the same size as the original. So, at best, measuring type on a page is an estimate. When it is attempted, those who work with type use a pica ruler, most of which measure inches, points and picas, or an acetate type guage. With today's computerized typesetting, there's seldom a need to use such devices. The computer does it for you.

An Introduction to Leading

The space between lines of type is called **leading** (pronounced "ledding"). Remember that leading for body type usually has been determined when a newspaper creates its basic design. Therefore, computerized typesetting systems may be preset to control the amount of line spacing that the designer recommended. The machine automatically provides the leading desired.

But do not assume that because the leading has been preset it never can or should vary. In most operations, provisions have been made for changing the leading to meet certain needs, most often in feature stories or other special kinds of stories. When editors want to feature a momentous story, they should use additional leading. Leading usually makes lines of type easier to read because it gives readers more white space between lines, which helps them focus their eyes on the type. Also, when lines of type are 20 picas or wider and the shoulders of typefaces are short, additional leading should be used.

LINE SPACING

The principle of making each line of type an easy eyeful can be aided by the generous (but not too generous) use of space between the lines. This provides a "right-of-way" for the eye along the top and bottom of each line. Types with short ascenders and descenders and large lowercase letters need more space between lines than faces with long ascenders and descenders and small lowercase letters. A fairly safe rule is to let the spacing between the lines approximately equal the space between words.

The above paragraph is set with generous spacing (3-point leads) between lines, while *this* paragraph is set with no leads and is consequently tougher ploughing for the eye. The type is the same size but looks smaller. Educated instinct will in time tell you the difference between jamming and scattering type lines.

Figure 9–25 The top paragraph has been leaded three points. The bottom has been set solid, meaning that there is no leading between lines. Leaded lines usually are easier to read than solid.

What, then, are the leading options? If a newspaper uses no leading at all beyond the height of the type itself, that practice is called setting type "solid." (Actually there is a tiny bit of space between lines of type when it is set solid, caused by the descender space at the bottom, or shoulder, of each letter.)

Options range from one-half–point to six-point leading for body type, and the range is extended from three to about 12 points of leading for headlines. The only way to know how type will look after it is leaded is to set a sample paragraph or two and study its readability. See Figure 9–25 for samples of alternative leading.

The Typography of Headlines

Type is most noticeable in publications and on Web sites when it is used in headlines. Indeed, one of the primary purposes of a headline is to attract the reader's attention. As noted earlier, a headline often does this best when used in conjunction with photos or information graphics. Nevertheless, the bold display type used in headlines can be effective in attracting attention even when used alone.

As noted in Chapter 8, most headlines are set in a downstyle in which editors use the same rules of capitalization as in sentences:

Bush defends decision to invade Iraq

Older forms of headline writing are increasingly out of style:

BUSH DEFENDS DECISION TO INVADE IRAQ
Bush Defends Decision to Invade Iraq

The all-cap style is out of vogue based largely on research that shows legibility is best, even in headlines, when normal rules of capitalization are followed.

Occasionally, however, the news demands a splashy headline that conveys the added drama of the moment:

UNTHINKABLE TRAGEDY
Thousands die as airliners hit World Trade Center

Designers now know that any headline-size type can help draw readers into a story. As a result, newspapers, magazines and even Web sites use devices such as blurbs or pull quotes to draw readers into a story:

**Eyewitness describes horror
of trapped victims leaping
to their deaths 100 stories below
'I thought I had seen everything,
but this was the pinnacle of hell.'**
—James Culligan,
New York firefighter

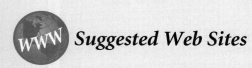

Suggested Web Sites

National Press Photographers Association   **www.nppa.org**
Pictures of the Year International   **www.poyi.org**
Society for News Design   **www.snd.org**

Suggested Readings

Baines, Phil, and Andrew Haslam. *Type and Typography.* New York: Watson-Guptill Publications, 2002.
Peck, Wendy. *Great Web Typography.* New York: John Wiley & Sons, 2003.
Zavoina, Susan C., and John H. Davidson. *Digital Photojournalism.* Upper Saddle River, N.J.: Pearson Education, 2001.

 **CHAPTER 10**

EDITING NEWSPAPERS

For more than 200 years, newspapers have been the most comprehensive news medium around. Although they have lost much of their immediacy to radio, television and the Web, newspapers still provide unparalleled depth of information, particularly in the area of local news. In almost every city on Earth, the largest news staff is that of the local newspaper, often exceeding the size of the staffs of all the local broadcast stations combined.

It's important to recognize the roles the various media play:

- Radio gets attention mostly when people are driving to and from work, although National Public Radio is the source of some of the highest-quality news produced each day in United States.

- Television is the medium of choice for developing news, and with the recent proliferation of channels, there is no shortage of choices. Radio and the Web offer the only real challenges to television's dominance in the realm of immediacy.

- Magazines, because they are issued less frequently than newspapers, must emphasize depth almost entirely. Immediacy is not a strength.

- Newspapers, usually only one per city, provide far more depth than any of the other traditional media and typically do the best job of explaining. They have more immediacy than magazines but less than the electronic media and the Web.

- The Web offers challenges to all the traditional media because of its ability to handle audio, video and depth that even newspapers and magazines can't match.

While it's conceivable that the Web will someday supplant the traditional media, or at least reduce their influence, for now we're a long way from seeing that happen. As noted in Chapter 1, newspapers are quite profitable and are terrific vehicles for conveying large volumes of information. From the perspective of the budding journalist, good jobs abound in the labor-intensive newspaper industry. If you have the misguided notion that newspapers are an old, dying medium, consider these facts from the Newspaper Association of America:

- Almost eight of 10 adults (77 percent) nationwide read a newspaper or a newspaper Web site during the course of a week.
- Newspapers reach 65 percent of young adults (aged 18 to 24) in a given week.
- Newspapers reach high-income earners. Eighty-one percent of consumers planning to spend $35,000 or more on a vehicle in the next six months read newspapers. Indeed, newspaper readership increases as income increases.
- Newspapers reach men and women almost equally. About 78 percent of men and 77 percent of women read newspapers or their Web sites regularly.
- People with significant investments read newspapers. More than 80 percent of those with investments in stocks, mutual funds, money-market funds and the like read newspapers regularly.
- When consumers look to buy things, they think of newspapers first. Fifty-five percent go to newspapers first compared to only 19 percent for the Internet and 8 percent for television.
- Consumers rank newspapers as the best place to prepare for shopping for any kind. Direct-mail advertising and the Internet are distant second- and third-place choices, and television lags far behind.
- Visitors to newspapers' Web sites say these sites are among their most-used media sources during the workday. Forty-nine percent spend time on these sites between the hours of 8 and 11 a.m.
- Eighty percent of newspaper Web site viewers cite these online destinations as their top Internet source for local news and information.
- Two-thirds (66 percent) of all online newspaper readers visit a newspaper Web site at least once a day. Half of these visit several times a day.

All of this is important information for the prospective newspaper editor. The statistics describe a vibrant, profitable medium that is critical in the lives of many Americans. The statistics also describe a medium that has become a major player in the emergence of the Web as a viable and important source of news.

The trick for editors in any medium is to have a strong grasp of the relative strengths and weaknesses of their medium. Clearly, the emergence of radio, television and the Web have forced newspaper editors to realize they must change. Fifty years ago, a newspaper could be written as if readers were learning about a news event for the first time. Often, they were. Today, however, most newspaper readers will already have learned about a breaking news event from radio, television or the Web. This forces editors to take a new approach.

In today's best newspapers, for example, fewer stories are written in the inverted-pyramid style that newspapers and wire services pioneered. Newspaper readers today are much more likely to be given stories written with techniques borrowed from magazines and even literary writing. An example is the *focus piece,* also known as *The Wall Street Journal* formula. In it, the writer starts the story with a person affected by an issue. The writer then transitions into the larger issue, explains it in detail and at the end refocuses on the individual about whom the story began. This personalization of an issue makes the story more readable because it is always more interesting to read about people rather than issues or institutions. *The Journal* made the technique famous in its classic Page One features.

Here, then, are some good descriptors of the typical U.S. newspaper of today:

- **Newspapers are well-designed and colorful.** Unquestionably, newspapers are better-designed than they were 30 or 40 years ago, and they are much more colorful as they attempt to compete with magazines and television for eye appeal.
- **Although printed on poorer stock than magazines, newspapers still have dramatic eye appeal.** The format alone, often an oversized **broadsheet,** commands attention.
- **Newspapers have lots of amplification and explanation not found on radio or television.** Only magazines and Web sites can equal newspapers here, and few magazines are available for the interpretation of local news.
- **A local newspaper has the best-trained and largest news staff in town.** A newspaper, because of the large staff it employs, covers news that simply cannot be found elsewhere.

These additional statistics help explain the size of the newspaper industry:

- In 2005, there were 1,452 daily newspapers in the United States (morning and evening).
- In the same year, there were 914 Sunday newspapers and more than 8,000 weeklies.
- Newspapers employed about 3.8 million people in 2003, making the industry a significant factor in total U.S. employment. It is, however, declining. Employment peaked at almost 4.6 million in 1990.

The newspaper industry is much, much larger than first meets the eye. In addition to the dailies and weeklies with which we all are familiar, the industry includes:

- Business publications.
- Industry-specific publications.
- Shoppers and throwaway publications, some of which have news content.

✎ EDITING THE WIRES

In Chapters 3 through 7, we explained in detail the role of the newspaper copy editor and the micro- and macro-editing that he or she must do. We also discussed legal and ethical issues that face the editor; grammar, usage and style; and how to put it all together. In this section, we address a facet of editing—editing wire copy—that is done almost exclusively at newspapers. To be sure, radio, television and Web sites also carry information from the wires, but much of it is run exactly as received. At newspapers, editors are encouraged to hone and improve that which comes from the Associated Press and other services. Only at newspapers are reports from various wire services regularly molded into an entirely new story.

News from the wire services plays different roles in the various media. For radio, television and the new online media, breaking news provided by the wires remains a staple of the daily news report. For newspapers, which usually get second crack at wire stories after the broadcast media have used them, interpretation has become more important.

To be sure, newspapers still contain plenty of inverted-pyramid stories provided by the wires. But, increasingly, these are short summaries confined to roundup columns. The wire stories favored by newspapers today are those that expand on the bare-bones reports provided by radio and television. The mission of newspapers is to interpret, to explain and to amplify. That's true of local news, too, but the trend is particularly noticeable in the wire report.

Today, most newspapers prefer what editors call *second-day leads* for second-day wire stories. For example, a broadcast report of an airplane crash might be written like this for radio, television and the online media:

> BOGOTA, Colombia (Reuters)—All 164 people aboard an American Airlines passenger jet en route from Miami died late Wednesday when it slammed into a mountain in southwest Colombia and burst into flames, authorities said Thursday.
>
> "All we know is that the plane was torn to pieces," said Alvaro Cala, the head of Colombia's Civil Aviation department.
>
> The accident involving a Boeing 757 was the most deadly involving a U.S. carrier since the 1988 bombing of a Pan Am flight over Lockerbie, Scotland, that killed 270 people. It was also the worst in Colombian history.
>
> The crash of American Flight 965, en route from Miami to Colombia's southwest city of Cali, took place within hours of the Dec. 21, 1988, anniversary of the Lockerbie crash.
>
> There is no evidence so far that the disasters are in any way related, but American Airlines spokesman Al Comeaux in Fort Worth, Texas, said the pilot, who was scheduled to touch down in Cali at 9:54 p.m. EST, apparently was unable to radio any distress call to local air traffic controllers.

This inverted-pyramid account serves the broadcast and online media well, but by the time the local newspaper is published tomorrow morning, a fresh approach is required:

From AP and Reuters

BOGOTA, Colombia—U.S. government agencies were working feverishly Thursday to determine if the crash of an American Airlines 757 in Colombia was caused by terrorists. The crash came on the anniversary of the worst disaster in U.S. aviation history, the 1988 terrorist explosion of a Pan Am flight over Lockerbie, Scotland.

The crash, which killed all 164 people bound for Cali from Miami aboard Flight 965, occurred when the plane slammed into a mountain in southwest Colombia and burst into flames, authorities said. It was the first-ever crash of a Boeing 757, and it came in good weather conditions. The pilot had issued no radio warning of mechanical difficulty, and all navigation aids in the area were working properly, Colombian officials said.

Newspapers, then, try to answer the question: Why or how did this happen? Seldom do they have the opportunity to beat the electronic media to a wire story. That reality leads to a different approach to writing the story. It also dictates a different approach to the headline. Headline writers are admonished to emphasize the new angle, not the old. For the plane crash story, tomorrow morning's newspaper headline might read like this:

U.S. suspects terrorist link to air crash

Taking this approach is tacit recognition of the fact that the various media have different strengths. The broadcast and online media excel at delivering the news with speed; newspapers have the time and space to provide analysis and insight.

Sources of Wire News

The dominant wire service in the United States is The Associated Press, a cooperative owned by member newspapers and broadcast stations. Privately owned United Press International, once a major competitor, shriveled into a minor player after going through a series of bankruptcies and ownership changes during the past 50 years. Today, owned by News World Communications, UPI's main presence is in radio newsrooms, where it provides a bare-bones news service at a relatively low price. Its news report is no longer adequate for newspapers to use as their only source of wire news, and few newspapers in today's tough market can afford two mainstream services.

The decline of UPI opened the door to the U.S. market for British-owned Reuters, French-owned Agence France-Presse and other foreign-based services. Major U.S. newspapers often subscribe to such services, which provide excellent alternatives to AP for international news at affordable rates. Increasingly, the major foreign services cover U.S. news as well.

Another source of wire news is the so-called supplemental wire services—syndicates and news services formed by major metropolitan newspapers, alliances of such papers or a newspaper group. Such services make it possible for a newspaper in Danville, Ill., to carry a major investigative piece from *The New York Times* on the same day the *Times* itself carries the story. Thus, even small newspapers have the opportunity to provide investigative accounts and in-depth reporting that radio and television rarely offer. Among the supplemental services are The New York Times News Service, the Los Angeles Times–Washington Post News Service, and the Copley, Gannett and Scripps-Howard news services. By syndicating their news, publishers participating in the supplemental services are able to recoup some of the costs of news gathering and, in fact, have been able to expand news coverage.

The services mentioned are among more than 200 syndicates offering news, features, photographs, illustrations and special services. In addition to giving spot and secondary news, these services provide news of sports, food and fashion, and bylined columns and features that cover everything from personal computing to zoo animals.

News is visual as well as written, so the wire services and syndicates often handle pictures and graphics in addition to text. The Associated Press has special networks for delivering both photos and graphics. Photos are transmitted into a special computer designed for that purpose or directly into the newspaper's computer system. Today, almost all wire photos are processed in digital form rather than with conventional photo-processing techniques. Information graphics—maps, charts and graphs—are delivered directly to Macintosh computers.

With UPI's decline, that service's once-powerful picture service also suffered. Consequently, UPI linked with the French news agency, AFP, to retransmit its photos in the United States. Reuters also has entered the picture business in the U.S., as have several syndicates.

How the Wires Operate

Stories delivered by a wire service come from several sources:

- Copy may be developed by the agency's own large staff of reporters, feature writers, analysts, columnists and photographers.
- Rewrites of stories may be developed by subscribers. Newspapers and broadcast stations contracting with a wire service agree to make their own news files available to the service, providing electronic versions of broadcasts or stories. Other wire service staffers rewrite from any source available—smaller papers, research reports and other publications.
- **Stringers** or **correspondents** in communities where there is no bureau can submit stories. These newspaper reporters are called *stringers* because of the old practice of paying correspondents by their strings of stories represented in column inches.
- Exchanges can be made with other news agencies, such as foreign agencies.

A reporter transmits a story to the state bureau of AP. If the story has statewide interest, AP files the story on its state wire. If the story has regional interest, the state bureau offers it to a regional bureau, or, in some cases, the state office may offer the story directly to the national desk.

The national desk thus becomes the nerve center for the entire operation of the news agency. This desk collects news from all the state, regional and foreign bureaus, culls the material, then returns it to the regional and state bureaus or to subscribers directly.

The operation sometimes is referred to as a *gatekeeping system*. A Dutch story, for example, would have to get by the Amsterdam office before it could be disseminated in Holland. The same story would have to clear the London bureau before being relayed to New York and the national desk. That desk then would decide whether the story should be distributed nationally. The desk could send the story directly to newspapers or route it through regional and state bureaus. In the latter cases, the regional bureau would judge whether to transmit the story to a state bureau, and a state bureau would have the option of relaying the story to subscribers. A wire editor then would accept or reject the story. Finally, the reader would become the ultimate gatekeeper by deciding which stories to read and which to ignore.

Traditionally, the wire service has opened the news cycle with a news **budget** or digest that indicates to editors the dozen or more top national and international stories that were in hand or were developing. Today's wire editors may get a four- or five-line abstract of the complete offering—foreign, national, regional and statedirectly to the newspaper's computer. From these abstracts or from computer directories, wire editors select the stories they think would interest their readers. Then they retrieve these stories directly from the newspaper's computer.

Budgets and Priorities

The wire services operate on 12-hour time cycles—PMs for afternoon papers, AMs for morning papers. The broadcast wire is separate, but major broadcast stations also take the newspaper wire, which is more complete. The cycles often overlap so that stories breaking near the cycle change are offered to both cycles, or stories early in one cycle are picked up as stories late in the other cycle.

For a morning paper, the wire news day begins about noon with the following:

```
a200
d lbylczzcczzc
Starting AMs Report, a201 Next
1202pED 03-07
```

Then follows the news digest (or budget), notifying editors of the dozen or more top news stories in sight (see Figure 10–1). An addition to the first budget

p9990
vb
AP-AP NEWS DIGEST

Tuesday AMS

The supervisor is Theasa Tuohy (212-621-1608). The photo desk supervisor is Susan Plageman (ext. 1900). The graphics desk supervisor is Kathryn Tam (ext. 1891).

All times EST.

HEADLINES:

- U.S. to require armed officers on some international flights
- Girl rescued from rubble in quake-devastated Iranian city
- Bush administration seeks to bolster confidence in beef supply
- Libya's nuclear program in early stage, U.N. nuclear chief says
- Settlers promise a fight if soldiers dismantle West Bank outpost
- Church scandal: Californians rush to sue before window closes

TOP STORIES:

Security stepped up for international airlines flying over U.S.

WASHINGTON - Heading into a New Year's holiday with terror threats high, the U.S. government says it will begin requiring international airlines to put armed law enforcement officers on certain passenger and cargo flights to, from and over the United States. Officials already are conducting checks on passenger and flight crews, as they worry about the threat of Sept. 11-style attacks using hijacked airliners as weapons.

BC-Airline Security. New material, latest PMs p0235.

By John J. Lumpkin.

Girl found alive in earthquake-devastated Iranian city

BAM, Iran - Rescuers pull a 12-year-old girl alive from the rubble of her home and gravediggers detect signs of life in three men they are preparing to bury three days after Iran's devastating earthquake. As the death toll rises above 25,000, Iran's president and supreme leader visit Bam and pledge to rebuild the ancient city.

BC-Iran-Earthquake. 900 words. New, developing.

By Ali Akbar Dareini. AP Photos VAH101, 106; GVW101, 104; MOSB113, MOSB114, VAH106.

Bush administration seeks to bolster confidence in beef supply

WASHINGTON - The Bush administration looks at ways to boost consumer confidence in beef as the list of countries rejecting American beef exports because of the mad cow scare grows to 30. Japan, the single biggest foreign market, dismisses U.S. pleas to consider lifting its ban.

BC-Mad Cow. Developing. Agriculture Department holds technical briefing at 2 p.m. EST.

By Mark Sherman. AP Photo.

Figure 10–1   This is the top of a typical Associated Press budget for newspapers. Information listed here helps editors plan their wire coverage.

Settlers promise a fight if soldiers dismantle West Bank outposts

GINNOT ARIEH, West Bank - Jewish settlers at this West Bank outpost vow they will not be taken from their homes alive despite an Israeli government decision to dismantle their unauthorized community. Settlers and some lawmakers say they hope to stop the evacuation, a required step under the U.S.-sponsored "road map" peace plan. Past declarations that outposts would be dismantled have fizzled.

BC-Israel-Defiant Settlers. 700 words.

By Laurie Copans. AP Photos JRL 103-107

Church scandal: Californians rush to sue before the window closes

LOS ANGELES - Californians are rushing to file hundreds of lawsuits against the Roman Catholic Church before a year-end deadline established under a state law that opened a window for old molestation allegations.

BC-Abuse Lawsuits. New for AMS. 700 words.

By Gillian Flaccus. AP Photo LA101. AP Graphic CALIFORNIA CHURCH ABUSE.

IRAQ & THE WAR ON TERRORISM:

Some leaders in Saddam's hometown want insurgency stopped

TIKRIT, Iraq - A group of influential spiritual leaders from Saddam Hussein's hometown - a center of anti-U.S. sentiment - work to persuade Iraquis to abandon the insurgency. Their efforts mark a shift in thinking for some leaders of Iraq's Sunni Muslim minority, a community that lost political dominance with the fall of Saddam and has largely formed the most outspoken and violent opposition to the occupation.

BC-Iraq-Reconciliation. 900 words. New, stands.

By Jason Keyser. AP Photos

WASHINGTON:

Gov't reimbursed $330 million in legal bills when contractors were sued

WASHINGTON - The Energy Department reimbursed its contractors for $330 million in legal bills over a five-year span, even for racial discrimination, sexual harassment and whistleblower lawsuits that companies lost, congressional investigators find. Footing legal costs provides little incentive for Energy Department contractors to act within the law, a congressman complains.

BC-Energy-Legal Fees. 700 words. Developing.

By Pete Yost.

BC-Energy-Legal Fees. 700 words. Developing.

By Pete Yost.

Figure 10–1 (continued)

WASHINGTON:

Gov't reimbursed $330 million in legal bills when contractors were sued

WASHINGTON - The Energy Department reimbursed its contractors for $330 million in legal bills over a five-year span, even for racial discrimination, sexual harassment and whistleblower lawsuits that companies lost, congressional investigators find. Footing legal costs provides little incentive for Energy Department contractors to act within the law, a congressman complains.

BC-Energy-Legal Fees. 700 words. Developing.

By Pete Yost.

BC-Energy-Legal Fees. 700 words. Developing.

By Pete Yost.

ELECTION 2004:

Clark shows himself with former President Clinton in new ad

WASHINGTON - Democratic presidential Wesley Clark releases a new television ad that includes a clip of him with Bill Clinton, another example of how the retired Army general is embracing his ties to and similarities with the former president.

BC-Clark-Ad. New material, 750.

By Liz Sidoti.

NATIONAL:

Inmate at center of landmark ruling could still face execution

ROANOKE, Va. - The Virginia inmate whose case persuaded the U.S. Supreme Court to bar the execution of mentally retarded killers remains on death row more than a year later, and prosecutors are determined to see him die. Daryl Renard Atkins, who has been reported to have an IQ of 59, might not even benefit from the landmark ruling that bears his name.

BC-Death Row-Retarded. New for AMS. 650 words.

By Chris Khan. AP Photo.

SCIENCE & MEDICINE:

New research describes how women can discontinue hormone therapy

WASHINGTON - About a quarter of women who stop taking hormone replacement therapy because of its risks wind up resuming the pills because of menopause misery, says the first research to explore how difficult it is to quit. Desperate for alternatives to alleviate hot flashes, many women now are turning to antidepressants.

BC-Hormone Therapy. New, 800. This is the HealthBeat column.

By Medical Writer Lauren Neergaard.

12/29/2003 12:44:16

Figure 10–1 This is the top of a typical Associated Press budget for newspapers. Information listed here helps editors plan their wire coverage. (continued)

may come a short time later. The budget gives wire editors a glimpse of the major stories forthcoming and aids them in planning space allocations.

FLASH: A two- or three-word statement alerting editors to a story of unusual importance: President shot. On the old teleprinter machines, a warning bell signifying a flash brought editors running to the machine. Today, a flash is seldom used because a bulletin serves the same purpose and is almost as fast.

BULLETIN: A short summary, usually no more than a lead, of a major story. Again, it is used primarily to alert editors and is not intended for publication unless the bulletin arrives at deadline. A bulletin also may be used to signal corrections, such as a mandatory "kill" on a portion of a story that could be libelous.

BULLETIN MATTER: Expands the bulletin with more, but brief, details. Unless the deadline is a factor, the wire editor holds up the story for a more detailed account.

URGENT: Calls editors' attention to new material or to corrections of stories sent previously.

Sorting the Pieces

Wire editors have two considerations in selecting wire copy for publication—the significance of the stories and the space allotted for wire copy. If space is tight, fewer wire stories are used, and heavier trims may be made on those that are used.

Budget stories usually, but not necessarily, get top priority. When stories listed on the budget arrive, they are so indicated by BUDGET, BJT or SKED, together with the length in words. If such stories are developing or are likely to have additional or new material, the editor places each story in a folder or computer holding queue and concentrates on stories that will stand.

Eventually, the stories in the folder or holding queue have to be formatted. The Associated Press has added a feature called DataRecaps to aid wire editors in handling a breaking story. Previously, editors had to assemble the pieces from multiple leads, inserts, subs (substitutes) and adds—or wait until space was cleared on the wire for a no-pickup lead. Now, the service notifies wire editors a recap is coming, then delivers a complete story at high speed.

Starts and stops occur even on copy apparently wrapped up. A story arriving early in the morning may describe a congressional appropriation of "$5.9 *billion*" to provide jobs for the unemployed. Fifty items later, editors are informed that the figure should be changed to "$6.4 *million*." Still later, New York sends a message that the original "$5.9 *million*" should stand. Eventually, the service again corrects the figure to the original "$5.9 *billion*." Such changes pose few problems for the editor if the story has not yet been formatted. The editor simply changes the copy in the electronic file.

Wire Stories versus Local Stories

Editing Wire Stories

- They usually take much less time to edit than local copy, but they still have errors. Don't trust them too much.
- You usually can cut more from them, and at least you don't get complaints from the reporter.
- Many newspapers don't use bylines for wire stories.
- Don't be afraid to call or e-mail the wire service with queries.
- Don't automatically assume that because you received a rewrite that you need to replace a story already on the page. Often, the rewrites contain only additional quotations or minor details. But you need to check them.
- Look for missed angles. Sometimes, the wires buy much more interesting angles than what they lead with, so move up the better ones, especially local angles.

Cutting Wire Stories

Given the limited space in many newspapers, editors usually try to run local stories fully and make cuts in wire stories. One thing you'll be called on to do is to cut wire-service stories—often to turn 18-inch stories into 3-inch briefs.

Remember, though, that if the story is written in an inverted pyramid, the most important 3 inches are at the top. If it's not in inverted pyramid form—if it's a feature, commentary of analysis—it should not be chopped. Don't even waste your time trying. Just point it out to the slot person, who probably was misled by a poorly written budget summary.

Here's what to do when told to chop a wire story to a brief:

- Scan it to make sure it's in the inverted pyramid form.
- Thoroughly edit the first four or five paragraphs, then ask yourself whether anything would be left up in the air if the remainder were cut.
- Scan the rest of the story to make sure a better detail is not buried, or that the first few paragraphs were not misleading.
- If necessary, move material up. If not, chop at that point.
- Measure the story, then tighten to the exact fit.

Editing Local Stories

- Even though you're working with professionals, local stories may have more problems than wire stories.
- Local stories should not be cut, if possible, by the time they reach the copy desk. That doesn't mean they aren't cut, just that you try to cut from wire stories first.
- The copy desk usually isn't as free to rewrite or reorganize local stories as it is wire copy, although editors hope they don't have to do much of either given the deadlines.
- Become familiar with the local stylebook and note how it handles these two categories of items: the few ways it differs from AP and those entries local to your paper, such as names of places in the area and ethics policies of your newspaper.

Selecting Wire Stories

On each news cycle, even the wire editors of large newspapers have more stories than they can use. On larger dailies using all the wires from the AP and several supplementals, the flow of copy is monumental. One way to handle this spate of copy is to categorize the news—one electronic folder for stories from Washington, another for New York and international, another for national, another for regional, another for area copy, and the like.

An advantage of the paper's subscribing to more than one news service is that the editor can use the story from one service to check facts against the same story from another service, such as casualty figures, proper names and spellings. If there is a serious discrepancy in facts, the editor asks the state or regional bureau for verification.

WIRES MAKE MISTAKES

Two points should be kept in mind as you edit wire copy:

- No wire service tailors copy for a particular newspaper. Abundant details are included, but most stories are constructed so that papers may use the full account or trim sharply and still have the gist of the report.

- The wire isn't sacred. The Associated Press has a deserved reputation for accuracy, impartiality and speed of delivery. It also makes errors, sometimes colossal ones. Other services do, too.

A source who turned out to be unreliable caused United Press to release a premature armistice story during World War I. A confused signal from a New Jersey courthouse caused AP to give the wrong penalty for Bruno Richard Hauptmann, convicted in the kidnapping and slaying of the Lindbergh child. The state wire, more often than not, is poorly written and poorly edited. Even the wire executives admit they still have bonehead editing and some stories that don't make sense. Stories abound with partial quotations, despite repeated protests from subscribers.

The Associated Press has an advisory committee, composed of managing editors who monitor writing performance. Here is one example from the Associated Press Managing Editors writing committee:

DETROIT (AP)–Two Detroit factory workers were killed Wednesday evening on their jobs, Detroit police said today. (Clearly an industrial accident.)

The two men, employees of the Hercules Forging Co., were identified as James H–, 51, the father of nine children, and M. C. Mc–, 37, both of Detroit. Mc– may have been struck accidentally, police reported. (Oh, somebody struck him accidentally but hit the other fellow on purpose.)

Police said they had a man in custody and added he would probably be charged in connection with the deaths. (Let's see, both of them were killed by the same man, but one death may have been an accident, but the suspect is charged with two murders?)

Police say they interviewed 15 workers at the plant who could give no reason for the shootings. (Now gunplay gets into this story.)

Witnesses told police the man confronted H– with a carbine and shot him when he tried to run. He fired a second shot after H– fell, they said.

The third shot, apparently aimed at another workman, hit Mc–, police said. (Now we are beginning to understand that what started out sounding like an industrial accident has become double murder.)

PECULIARITIES OF WIRE COPY

At most newspapers, wire copy is edited the same as local copy, but a few peculiarities apply to the editing of wire news. First, wire news, unlike local news, usually carries a *dateline,* which indicates the city of the story's origin:

> OVERLAND PARK, Kan. (AP)—An apparent good Samaritan who helped start a woman's car talked about how dangerous it was to be out at night, then pulled a gun and took her purse, police said.

Note that the city of origin is in capital letters, and the state or nation is in uppercase and lowercase letters. At most newspapers, style calls for the dateline to be followed by the wire service logotype in parentheses and a dash. The paragraph indention comes before the dateline, not at the start of the first paragraph.

Stories that contain material from more than one location are called **undated stories.** They carry no dateline but a credit line for the wire service:

> **By The Associated Press**
> Arab extremists said today they would blow up American installations throughout the Middle East unless all Americans leave Beirut immediately.

Stories compiled from accounts supplied by more than one wire service carry similar credit lines:

> **From our wire services**
> LA PAZ, Bolivia—Mountain climbers experienced in winter climbing tried today to reach the wreckage of a Ladeco Airlines Boeing 727, which crashed Monday while approaching La Paz in a snowstorm.

When editors combine stories, they must be sensitive to the fact that wire stories are copyrighted. If material in the story was supplied exclusively by one service, that service should be credited within the text. If the story comes from multiple agencies, all should be credited, usually at the end of the story. Combining the stories this way often provides a newspaper's readers with a better story than could be obtained from either of the major services alone. Good newspapers make a habit of doing this often.

Wire stories often use the word *here* to refer to the city included in the dateline. If the editor has removed the dateline during the editing process, the city must be inserted in the text. Otherwise, *here* is understood to be the city in which the newspaper is published.

The Associated Press uses Eastern time in its stories. Some newspapers outside the Eastern time zone prefer to convert these times by subtracting one hour for Central time, two for Mountain or three for Pacific. When this is done, if the dateline remains on the story, it will be necessary to use phrases such as "3 p.m. St. Louis time" or "1 p.m. PDT" in the text. The newspaper's local style will specify the form to be used.

Here are some additional wire-service eccentricities:

- AP doesn't know how to use semicolons in a series, almost always leaving out the last one before the final *and.*

- UPI doesn't use commas when it should before a conjunction and puts them in when it shouldn't. The People column often has backward apostrophes in it. UPI puts "D.C." after Washington and "City" after New York.

- *The New York Times* capitalizes *federal, government* and *administration,* contrary to AP style. The *Times* writes *3rd* rather than *III* behind a name. It's necessary to change these to your newspaper's style, which usually conforms to AP style.

LOCALIZING WIRE STORIES

Wire stories often become ideas for local stories. If Congress has reduced the amount of money it will provide for loans to college students, a newspaper in a college town may want to contact the college's financial aid officer to determine what effect the measure will have locally.

When the Soviet Union shot down a Korean Airlines plane, the *Columbia Missourian* learned that two people were aboard who had just completed their doctoral degrees at the University of Missouri. Their daughter was with them aboard the jet. Because members of the family had lived in Columbia for several years, many people knew them. As a result, a major international story became a local story:

> Recent University of Missouri graduates Somchai Pakaranodom and his wife, Wantanee, were on their way back to Thailand after living in Columbia for four years. They never made it.
>
> The couple, along with their 7-year-old daughter Pom, were among the 269 killed when a Soviet jet shot down Korean Air Lines Flight 007 north of Japan.
>
> "We had laughed about the flight schedule," education Professor Dorothy Watson recalled Friday, sitting in her living room where a week earlier she had thrown a going-away party for the Pakaranodoms.
>
> The couple left Columbia Saturday. They were traveling first to Chicago, then on to New York to catch the flight to Seoul and eventually on to Bangkok, Thailand.
>
> With the sound of news reports about the crash coming over the television from the next room, Mrs. Watson fought back the tears. "I kept thinking they couldn't possibly be on the plane," she said. "It is just such a waste, so stupid."
>
> At first, she didn't connect the crash with her friends.
>
> On Friday, another faculty member called to break the news to her. She said even then she refused to believe it, until Korean Air Lines confirmed the family was on the flight.
>
> Both Fulbright scholars, the Pakaranodoms received their doctoral degrees from the university Aug. 5. Somchai's degree was in agricultural engineering, Wantanee's in reading education.

Here are some tips for localizing wire stories:

- Convert time to local (EST becomes CST, for example).
- Adjust for local style.
- If you find a local name or place buried in a wire story, move that angle up or develop it into a sidebar or a story, using the wire service for background.
- Add the votes of local legislators to wire stories. These votes will often move on the wire as a sidebar to the story if the issue is important.
- Even if there is no local name in the story, ask yourself whether the story has local impact. If so, give a printout of it to the city desk and suggest a local sidebar.

➤ DESIGNING THE NEWSPAPER

Once material for the newspaper is gathered and edited, it's time to produce the final product. Although the most important part of a newspaper is unquestionably its content, a close second is the newspaper's design, which plays a critical role in selling it to readers.

A half century ago, newspaper design was an afterthought at most papers. When top editors felt pressed to compete with the eye appeal of television, however, that began to change. Now, design is considered a critical part of the newspaper's sales equation. A reflection of that reality was the creation of the Society for News Design, an organization that has led revolutionary change in design over the past 25 years.

How to Recognize a Well-Designed Newspaper

Although graphic designers may disagree about the precise criteria of good design, there is enough agreement to build a body of knowledge that can help people recognize good design. The general characteristics of a well-designed newspaper are given here, and ways to achieve them are included on the following pages.

- *Good organization.* Good design organizes the news to help readers easily find the news they want to read. Similar kinds of news ought to be in proximity, if possible. Readers dislike reading stories in one section of the paper and then having to look for additional stories of the same type in some distant part of the paper. Organization also covers the smooth transition of news from one column to the next.
- *Adequate white space.* There usually is a sense of agreement about what is attractive and what is not. Generally, an attractive newspaper has an adequate amount of space between lines of type, between stories and between columns. Avoid a tight page design, in which there is so little space between stories that

readers have difficulty concentrating their attention on any one item. Good design tends to have generous amounts of white space carefully distributed on a page, which aids legibility.

- *Attractive display of illustrations.* Photographs with a fine screen (above 100 lines to the square inch) are usually the ideal. This makes it easy to see the details. However, the quality of newsprint often determines screen sizes, and better-quality paper makes fine screens and reading somewhat easier. With the cost of newsprint rising, the better-quality paper may be too expensive. Photographs must be given adequate space, and enough of them should be used to illustrate at least the highlights of the news. They enhance the total page design if they are the right size and number. There are no rules that require a precise number of photographs be used each day or how large they should be. Artistic judgment is usually required to place illustrations on a page. Some designers like at least one dominant illustration on every page, accompanied by one or more smaller illustrations. The worst-designed pages tend to use illustrations that are all about the same size.

- *News that is easy to follow.* Pages should be arranged in a way that makes it easy to follow a story from column to column. It is not a simple matter to wrap stories from one column to the next right-hand column for an easy-to-read style. The art of wrapping stories requires good judgment as to *where* in the next right-hand column a story should be continued.

- *Pages with contrast.* Of all the basic principles of design, contrast is the most important for attractiveness. Pages should be designed to have some, but *not overwhelming,* contrast. Contrast generally provides attractive pages by offering readers a change of pace. The contrast may be large versus small photographs, dark versus light sections of the page, regularly versus irregularly shaped stories or illustrations and vertically versus horizontally shaped photographs.

- *Unity.* Attractive pages usually look unified, as if everything on the page were carefully placed just where it is.

- *Different typefaces kept to a minimum.* Editors may be tempted to use too many typefaces on the same page when they set type. They are used to having many type choices. The professional knows how many alternative faces are just right. Again, it takes artistic experience to decide.

- *Balanced pages.* The best pages usually are not top- or bottom-heavy. Although readers usually cannot discern balance in particular, they get the feeling that a page is or is not out of balance, one way or another.

- *Generous line spacing.* Good typography usually requires adequate to generous amounts of leading between lines. But there may be a point of diminishing returns on leading. In other words, leading can be too loose. Many designers use too much leading when they already have an adequate amount of space on a page. Newspapers are not trying to sell each story separately, but it takes a keen sensibility to know what leading is ideal. Wider column widths require more leading than shorter widths.

- *Placement of stories that is well thought out.* The top editors and writers review the content of each issue (before it is laid out) from the point of view of story importance. They decide where in the newspaper lead stories should be positioned. Smaller or less important stories usually don't require long discussions about positioning and may be placed after all important stories have been positioned.

Objectives of Newspaper Design

Five major objectives should guide an editor in working effectively with newspaper design:

- The design should organize the news.
- The design should create an attractive page.
- The design's connotations should complement the stories.
- The design should be interesting or dramatic.
- The design should appear contemporary.

The design should organize the news. Good design may be defined as a plan for bringing order to an entire newspaper or a specific page. Every design should show how the news has been organized for the day so readers know which stories are most and least important. Those who spend a great deal of time reading will have to spend less time searching for stories of interest if the organization of the paper is clear and simple.

One element of organization is story placement throughout the newspaper. The design staff should place stories adjacent to other, similar stories in certain sections of the paper.

Organization also covers each individual page, where stories often are graded in importance from the top down. This does not mean that important stories cannot occasionally be placed at the bottom, however, for variety's sake. Page designers have many ways of telling readers which stories are most important: by placing them at or near the top of a page, by placing them in boxes and by setting their headlines in large type.

The design should create an attractive page. Because attractiveness is a major cultural value, good design should be attractive to most readers. We all like things that look nice, and we use this principle in selecting beautiful clothes, furniture and cosmetics that enhance personal appearance. An attractive design invites readers to come into a page and read the news. An unattractive design could do the opposite.

Readers often skim a page before reading it. In other words, they may be looking for an interesting story, and a skim may save time in finding it. But pages that are too dark, or too light, may not be read. Of course, scintillating news of great importance may be strong enough to motivate a reader to read a page regardless of the impediments. Readers devoted to poorly designed newspapers often defend their paper's design with great fervor because they have become acclimated to it. They don't recognize poor design, and they perceive only their favorite paper. Even in this situation, readers will often approve of a new and easy-to-read layout if they can be persuaded that it is indeed better than the old one.

The design's connotations should complement the stories. Occasionally, a design can match the nature of a story. For example, various artistic devices can be used to surround stories for Thanksgiving Day, Christmas and dramatic political or sporting events.

The design should be interesting or dramatic. To avoid creating a monotonous page, a design editor can vary story shapes or design stories into strongly vertical or horizontal shapes. Stories can be boxed, run over colored tints or run with multiple photographs. All these are styling devices to avoid boredom. After many years of reading a newspaper, readers may simply wish for some variety, even though they may not write to the editor. Slight variations in design may be just what are needed to avoid dull-looking pages.

The design should appear contemporary. Some of the best graphic designers believe that design should reflect contemporary culture. For newspaper design, this is important because news is the essence of the contemporary scene. It seems illogical to place contemporary news in an old-fashioned format.

Newspapers and the Principles of Artistic Design

The application of artistic design principles can help design editors achieve their objectives and carry out their responsibilities. The newspaper is a graphic art form, using words, pictures, color, lines and masses subject to the same principles of artistic design as other art forms. The principles most applicable to newspapers are known as balance, contrast and unity.

BALANCE

Balance means equilibrium. In other words, a page should not be overwhelmingly heavy in one section or extremely light in another. An unbalanced page may give readers a vague feeling of uneasiness because of the concentration of weight in only one or two sections of the page. As mentioned earlier, most readers do not know whether a page is balanced or unbalanced. They are not artists and do not care about the principles of artistic design. Yet they often know that a certain page "feels" better to read than other pages. Top-heaviness is the most common form of imbalance in newspaper design, caused by placing large and bold headlines at the top while using almost insignificantly light headlines at the bottom. Another cause of imbalance is the practice of placing a large, dark picture at the top without having one of similar size or weight at the bottom. As a result, readers' eyes tend to gravitate toward the bolder sections of the page and away from the lighter portions. Assuming that every element on a page has value, an unbalanced page is more difficult to read than a balanced page.

Balance in newspaper design is achieved by visually weighing one element on a page with another on the opposite side of the page, using the optical center as a fulcrum. The optical center is a point where most people think the true mathematical center is located. It is a little above and to the left of the actual mathematical center (see Figure 10–2). This practice does not lead to precise balancing, but there is no need for that degree of precision. All that is required is a feeling of equilibrium on a page, not precise mathematical weighing.

Which elements need balancing? Any element on a page that has visual weight should be balanced. To determine which elements have visual weight, squint at a page and notice that much of the printed material disappears. What remains are pictures, headlines and black type of any kind. Although body type does have some weight, it isn't significant enough for consideration in visual weighing. The goal is to pleasantly distribute prominently weighted objects on the page.

Balance is most often done between top and bottom rather than side to side. The process is similar to balancing a heavy person with a light person on a seesaw. The heavy person must move closer to the fulcrum, whereas the lighter person must move farther away on the opposite side of the fulcrum.

To implement the principle of balance, weigh the most outstanding elements, such as bold or large headlines, at the top of a page against similar headlines at the bottom. If the bottom of the page has no bold or large headline, the page is probably top-heavy. Plans should be made to include such headlines at the bottom. Follow the same procedure with pictures. A headline or picture at the bottom need not be as large or bold as one at the top because it is farther away from the fulcrum.

Page balance may be formal or informal. *Formal balance* is achieved by placing headlines and pictures of the same size on each side of a page. It is sometimes called *symmetrical balance* because one side of the page tends to mirror the other. But symmetrical design may be unbalanced from top to bottom. Most newspapers employ an informal balance from top to bottom. The feeling of equilibrium is there even though it is not obvious.

CONTRAST

Contrast is the principle of using at least two or more elements on a page, each of which is dramatically different from the other. A light headline may contrast with

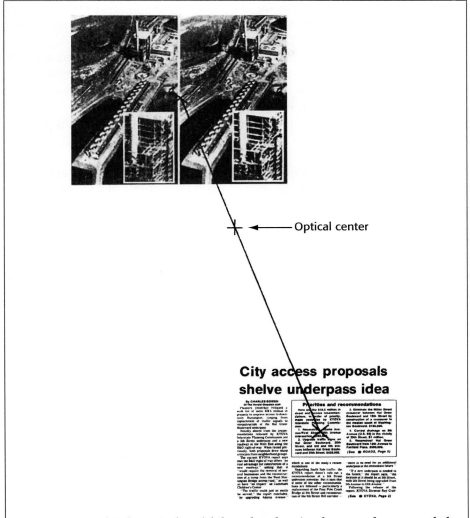

Figure 10–2   This theoretical model shows how heavier elements of a page are balanced against lighter elements. The fulcrum is the optical center. Heavier elements are placed closer to the optical center, and lighter ones are more distant.

a bold headline, a small picture with a larger one. Because one element is different from the other, the page appears lively and interesting.

Contrast, therefore, is a means of preventing artistic pieces from becoming dull. Almost all art forms have some contrast—especially musical compositions, theatrical plays and printed material. A symphony, for example, contrasts a fast and loud first movement with a soft and slow second movement. A play has a relatively quiet scene contrasting with a lively scene. A book or magazine may have most pages printed in black and white contrasting with full-color illustrations.

In page design, contrast prevents a page from appearing too gray, a problem that occurs when there is too much body copy and too many light headlines. Gray pages appear uninviting and forbidding.

Sometimes, when a page has been deliberately designed to feature balance, it may lack contrast and appear rather dull. The editor, therefore, may have to brighten that page by adding another picture or large, bolder headlines to bring about better contrast.

Contrast may be achieved in four general ways: by shape, size, weight and direction:

- *Shape contrast* may consist of a story set justified in opposition to another story set flush left, ragged right. Or a profile of a person may be used with a rectangular picture.

- *Size contrast* may be achieved by using a large illustration on the same page as a smaller one, or large type with smaller type.

- *Weight contrast* may employ a picture that appears black with a lighter picture, or a headline set in boldface type contrasted with one set in lighter typefaces.

- *Direction contrast* would show vertically shaped stories next to horizontally shaped stories.

These contrast alternatives are but a few of many that are possible on any given page. An objective of designing a page, however, is to achieve pleasant contrast.

UNITY

The principle of *unity* creates a single impression in a page design. Stories on a unified page each appear to contribute a significant share to the total page design. A page that does not have unity appears as a collection of stories, each fighting for the reader's attention to the detriment of a unified page appearance.

Lack of unity often results when stories are placed from the top of the page downward. The design editor is building a page piece by piece and cannot be sure how each story will contribute to the total page design until the design is complete. At that point, however, the designer may find that there is not enough time to shift stories to achieve unity. The result is that readers may find it difficult to concentrate on any one part of the page because of too many centers of interest. A unified page, on the other hand, appears as if everything is in its correct position, and the page is therefore interesting.

The editor plans for a unified page by keeping the design of the entire page in mind at all times while working on any part of it. Each story, therefore, must be visually weighed against all other stories in terms of the probable appearance of the entire page. In page design, the editor may have to shift some stories until a satisfactory arrangement has been found. As with the other principles of artistic design, an appreciation of unity ultimately aids legibility.

Quick Guide to Newspaper Design

The Basics

- Work in rectangles.
  - On inside pages, begin by squaring off rectangles that match the top of the ads.
  - Make the design primarily horizontal, but try to get at least one vertical element on each page.
  - It is not essential to avoid gutters all the way down a page, but try to do so anyway. Think of a brick wall or a Piet Mondrian painting.
- Avoid bumps (headlines beside headlines) unless ideally:
  - One is one column, one is multicolumn.
  - There is at least one standard point size difference between them (e.g., 24 against a 36, skipping 30).
  - The multicolumn head is only one line deep.
- Avoid boxes against boxes.
- Avoid placing photos and graphics next to unrelated art.
- Avoid placing boxes or art against ads if they could be confused with the ad stack.
- Balance opposite quadrants of the page.
  - Avoid formal balance. Asymmetrical design works better.
  - On inside pages, place graphic elements in the corner opposite the ad stack.
  - On the front page, the main story is usually either stripped across the top or put in the upper-right corner. The dominant art is usually placed in the upper-left quadrant of Page One and is often four-columns and boxed.

How to Add Flair

- Add second decks.
- Add read-out or read-in external (summary) blurbs.
- Add internal blurbs.
- Add a hammer or kicker.
- Set the story on a bastard measure (such as 5 on 6).
- Use art supplied with the story.
- Pull a mugshot from the morgue of someone prominent in the story.
- Create a summary box of bullet items from the story, such as key quotes from a speech or main items voted on at a City Council meeting.
- Create your own information graphic.

PROPORTION AND MOVEMENT

Two other principles of design less relevant in newspaper design are proportion and movement. *Proportion* is based on a cultural concept first delineated by the ancient Greeks, who felt that certain proportions are more interesting to look at than others. The ideal proportion is a ratio of approximately 3-to-5. You can see it most often in architecture, where one side of a rectangle is smaller than the other. The proportion of doors and windows is approximately 3-to-5, but square windows are not. In newspaper photographs, the more attractive shapes are about 3-to-5. Even story modules tend to be about 3-to-5. In graphic design, one may see square objects deliberately designed to be square. They often attract attention because of their unique shape. But books and magazines tend to be vertical and in pleasant-to-look-at shapes.

Movement is sometimes used on paintings, drawings, photographs and similar kinds of artwork. Advertising design often uses the concept of movement to get readers to move from the upper left-hand part of an advertisement, where the message usually begins, to the lower right-hand corner where the logotype often closes the ad. But for regular reading material, there is a natural movement in headlines and body type because we read from left to right. It isn't necessary to try to move readers' eyes in other directions. However, in devising photographs for news pages, strong vertically designed pictures tend to be a moderate force to move the readers' eyes down the picture to stories placed lower on a page. Boxed stories with type rules on all four sides are a modest eye movement motivation.

Visualizing Total Page Structure

Page design begins with some idea of general structure. Will pages be horizontally or vertically shaped? If the designer doesn't determine this early in the process, pages may have a circus design with little order to them. Modular designs, which are so widely used throughout the country today, tend to be distinctly vertical, horizontal or a mixture of the two.

In early U.S. newspapers, pages were all vertical. On a typical page with eight columns, the stories all started at the top, and readers read down and then up to the top of the next right-hand column. Reading down and up describes vertical designs.

Today, although there are some horizontally styled pages, most are designed to be a mixture of vertical and horizontal page divisions and not in equal proportions. Generally, newspapers are divided into 75 percent–25 percent or 67 percent–33 percent proportions of stories that are vertical to horizontal.

Do either of these proportions have clear-cut advantages? The answer is no, except that we know from preference tests among consumers that most dislike equal divisions of space. Figures 10–3, 10–4 and 10–5 show how a page divided into equal proportions tends to look dull, while papers with uneven proportions tend to look much more interesting.

Figure 10–3 Dividing a page into two equal divisions (either vertically or horizontally) tends to be dull or uninteresting.

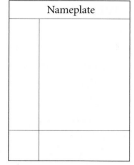

Figure 10–4 Dividing a page into unequal modules is far more interesting. This arrangement is particularly attractive.

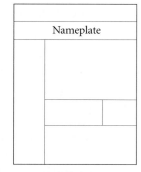

Figure 10–5 Additional page divisions also may be interesting, but may become too complex and hard to read.

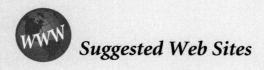

Suggested Web Sites

The Associated Press   **www.ap.org**
Los Angeles Times–Washington Post News Service   **www.newsservice.com**
Society for News Design   **www.snd.org**

Suggested Readings

The Associated Press Stylebook and Briefing on Media Law. New York: The
   Associated Press, 2007.
Moen, Daryl R. *Newspaper Layout and Design: A Team Approach*. Ames, Iowa: Iowa
   State University Press, 2000.

CHAPTER 11

EDITING MAGAZINES AND NEWSLETTERS

We said in Chapter 3 that copy editing offers job opportunities of which many journalism students are unaware. In this chapter, we look at another opportunity for those looking for a possible career niche: the world of magazines and newsletters.

In a nutshell, the opportunity stems from these facts:

- There are far more magazines and newsletters than you ever dreamed.

- Magazine and newsletter offices are located all over the country, so there are probably jobs near you that you have no idea are there.

- Magazines often pay more for opening positions than recent journalism grads would make at a first newspaper job—sometimes between half again as much to almost twice as much.

- Editing for a magazine or newsletter often offers a chance to make a living writing and editing about a field of specific interest to you, one you'll enjoy using your skills to cover.

- Because fewer journalism graduates know about these jobs, and because the jobs often favor candidates with specific interests that few people other than you may have in combination with your writing and editing skills, you often stand a better chance of being hired.

- Because many magazines use freelancers for much of their material, staff positions often are in editorial positions.

- Despite the popularity of the Internet, magazines seem to have a bright future.

WHAT IS A MAGAZINE?

In addition to the job opportunities, another thing may surprise you about magazines: No one can say for sure how many there are, or what the average pay is, partly because it's so hard to come up with a good definition of a *magazine*. Why would that be when we all think we know a magazine when we see it?

Try to come up with your own definition, then compare yours with the list of traits that follows. These are characteristics that people commonly associate with magazines, but each poses a problem when it comes to making a definition:

- **Magazines come out less often than daily newspapers.** True, but so do weekly newspapers, for example.

- **Magazines are printed on better-quality paper than newspapers and are bound.** But some magazines are published on lightweight nonglossy stock, as well, and aren't always bound. *Parade* magazine, for example, isn't bound, and its paper is only slightly better than newsprint.

- **Magazines appeal to a more specialized audience than newspapers.** But what about the general-interest magazines with broad appeal, like *Reader's Digest?*

- **Magazines use extensive color photography and special layouts.** But so do many newspapers these days, and meanwhile there are some magazines without color and with only mediocre graphics.

- **Magazines tend to have articles that are longer and less objective than newspaper stories.** Magazine writers take a more leisurely, feature approach to presenting information. But newspapers also offer features that match this description, and some magazines are full of straightforward news items.

- **Magazines tend to be held onto longer than newspapers.** But so are weekly TV listings and advertising supplements that regularly appear in newspapers.

In addition to the problems with these attempts at definition, there are questions about whether to classify certain categories of publications as magazines. Should one-shot publications that look like magazines but that focus on one subject of contemporary interest—like those that appeared after Sept. 11, 2001—be counted as magazines? Should supermarket tabloids be counted as magazines? How about scholarly journals? Should newsletters be counted as magazines? How about comic books? How about magazine supplements in Sunday newspapers? Should publications put out by trade groups and associations be called magazines (like the AARP's *Modern Maturity*)?

If we count these as magazines, how about regular public-relations materials such as airline magazines, corporate magazines and hospital newsletters? Church bulletins? Corporate quarterly reports?

The word *magazine* comes from the French, who adapted it from the Arabs, to whom it means a storehouse of ammunition. (But Arabic, oddly, has a different word for magazine as a publication.) Magazines probably developed in

17th-century France from bookseller catalogs and book publisher notices inserted in newspapers. Think, for example, of when you join a book or DVD club and you receive a monthly "club magazine," as they call it, that contains just a catalog of items for sale and perhaps a few glowing reviews.

Although the total number of magazines published in the United States depends on which you count, and with different sources reporting different counts, here are some figures that help give a picture:

- Some say there are 800 to 1,200 consumer magazines in the United States; others say there are as many as 2,000. Of these, only about 200 are seen on most newsstands.
- There are about 12,000 specialty magazines.
- There are about 13,000 PR magazines and newsletters.
- By the time you add in industry and association magazines, there are perhaps 50,000 magazines total, says one source, more than all other media combined.
- In addition, there are an estimated 50,000-plus **zines**—privately printed, small-run magazines—in print editions and another 50,000 or more **e-zines** on the Internet.
- In 2002, more than 1,000 magazines were started—about five times that of 15 years earlier—although fewer than 20 percent were estimated to still be publishing two years later.

The sheer number of magazines attests to their bright future, but so do these facts:

- More than 80 percent of U.S. households subscribe to at least one magazine, and the average household subscribes to six or more.
- The top 10 magazines in the United States, in terms of 2006 circulation, distribute more than 4 million copies per issue—the lowest being 4 million—and actual readership for magazines if often about four times the number circulated. Compare this to newspapers. As of 2006, only three newspapers in the country had circulations over 1 million: *USA Today* at 2.2 million, *The Wall Street Journal* at 2 million and *The New York Times* at 1.1 million.
- Even Internet providers and cable-TV channels are offering print magazines.
- TV broadcasters are hurt by cable, satellite, videotapes, DVDs, video games and commercial skipping, so advertisers who have been using television are looking again to print. Also, the move to 15-second commercials means broadcast ads can't get across the details a print ad can.

- Newspapers can't deliver target clientele as intensively as magazines. Specialty magazines offer the cheapest ad dollar cost per desired reader.

- People are getting tired of junk mail. Some magazines are now being delivered in a shrink-wrapped package with freestanding inserts. For advertisers, this is an alternative distribution system to direct mail. Although advertisers pay less to insert their material than they would for a full-page four-color ad, inserts may provide supplemental income. They may even work for specialty publications, which can deliver a more specific market to an advertiser. And inserts allow advertisers four colors even when the publication is a black-and-white offset newsletter.

What comes to mind when we think of the term *magazine* are the big consumer magazines found on newsstands. Examples include *Time, Newsweek, U.S. News and World Report, Cosmopolitan* and *O*. If the only magazines you know are those you see on the newsstands, look in the annual *Writer's Market,* easily found in library reference sections and even in mall bookstores, which lists 4,000 to 5,000 magazines. Other sources for names and addresses of magazines are *Bowker's Working Press of the Nation* and *Gale Directory of Publications and Broadcast Media.* In other words, don't just think of getting a job at a big consumer magazine. There are more specialty magazines, and they often make great places to start—or stay:

- *Corporate communications publications.* These are mainly internal, employee newsletters, but there are also business publications aimed at distributors and customers. These publications often hire people with degrees in journalism, public relations, technical writing or English, and they tend to pay much more than newspaper jobs at the same level.

- *Trade publications.* **Trade publications** are specialized publications aimed at people in a particular field, such as farming, automaking or plumbing.

- *Association publications.* **Association publications** are magazines published by associations of various kinds, such as trade groups. For example, members of the College Fraternity Editors Association (www.cfea.org) publish more than 100 titles.

- *Government and nonprofit organizations' publications.* Municipal, county, state and national governments all have their own publications, as do hospitals, colleges and various nonprofit organizations, such as churches. Examples include *Missouri Resources* and *Arizona Highways.*

- *Special-interest publications.* **Special-interest publications** range from *PC Computing* to *Golf,* from *Sewing* to *This Old House.* For almost any possible hobby, there is a magazine or two—sometimes more.

- *Newsletters of various kinds.* This is the fastest-growing category of all print publications. Schools, hospitals and public utilities often have their own. Credit unions have their own. Then there are the financial, political and other special-interest newsletters.

When you start thinking in these terms, you begin to see that there are far more writing and editing jobs available in far more places than you ever imagined—many of them at places you never thought of as media outlets, like auto companies, hospitals and professional associations. In addition, if you have special knowledge in some field—perhaps because you grew up on a farm or in a certain religion or you have certain hobbies or interests—you may have just the right combination, with your writing or editing talent, to fit into a niche publication—and face far less competition for the job.

Smaller publications are especially interested in people who have skills in several or all of these areas: writing, editing, photography and graphics, desktop publishing and Web editing. If you want to work eventually for a big consumer magazine in a city like New York, these small publications are where you get your experience. The big consumer magazines seldom hire students right out of college, except as a gofer. And the best bet for jobs in consumer magazines? You guessed it: copy editing.

Magazine Staffing

Like newspapers, commercial magazines have an editorial side and a business side. The editorial side consists of writers, editors, designers, photographers and artists, while the business side consists of people in marketing, advertising, circulation, and accounting. Most magazines use commercial printers.

The **publisher** of a commercial magazine has the job of making sure the magazine remains profitable. More often, the publisher has a background in ad sales rather than journalism, although this is starting to change. Magazines in a large publishing house may have a group publisher responsible for several magazines.

The **editor in chief** of a commercial magazine is in charge of the editorial content. This person guides the magazine along a certain vision and makes decisions about content and covers. The editor in chief also works with the publisher on the budget and increasingly works with marketing and advertising people.

The staff's access to the editor in chief tends to be primarily through the managing editor or executive editor. Some large magazines have both a managing editor and an executive editor, although most just have one or the other.

The **managing editor** hires, fires and promotes editorial staff, and makes sure they and freelancers stick to deadlines so the magazine gets out on time.

This person also directly assigns stories or works with department managers in doing that.

The **executive editor,** if a separate title, is often someone who balances the skills of the managing editor. If the managing editor is strong on editing but weak on managing or vice versa, the executive editor steps in to fill the gap.

Below these top positions at a consumer magazine are a number of other editorial positions:

The **art director** oversees the design of the magazine.

The **section editors,** sometimes called *senior editors,* overlook a particular section of the magazine, such as letters to the editor or reviews of new products.

Associate and assistant editors assign, write and edit articles for particular departments of the magazine.

Copy editors edit the articles and write titles, captions and pull quotes, just like copy editors at newspapers.

Online editors are in charge of editing content for the magazine's Web site.

Contributing editors are not staff members but regular freelancers who tend to be experts in the field about which they write.

The magazine may also have **staff writers** and **photographers**, but fewer do anymore, relying almost exclusively on freelancers.

As for nonconsumer magazines and newsletters—such as those published by corporate communications departments, associations and nonprofits—the chain of command is based more on each particular organization's job titles and duties.

For example, a corporate communications department at an automobile company may have a number of responsibilities, including writing speeches for executives, organizing participation in car shows, handling general PR and advertising duties, writing technical manuals, putting together sales brochures for dealers, and putting out an employee newsletter and magazines for distributors and customers. The department could be quite large with many people in many specialties.

By contrast, someone putting out an employee newsletter for a hospital might either be the hospital's sole PR representative or someone whose job is to handle all the reporting, picture taking, writing, editing, printing and distribution.

How Magazine Editing Differs From Newspaper Editing

Magazine editing doesn't differ that much from the work done in comparable positions in newspaper editing. The advice given earlier in this book—such as using the Three R's of copy editing; macro, micro and holistic editing; and working with big type and graphics—applies just as much to magazines and newsletters as to newspapers. But there are differences:

Magazines have fewer deadlines, so everyone has more time to work on an issue.

This means the contents should be interesting, well-written, carefully edited and accurate. Magazine articles are edited more than the average newspaper story. *Time*'s editors are notorious for rewriting and rewriting, then editing and re-editing. *The New Yorker,* known for its high literary content, is also famous for having the best fact-checking department in the business. This attention to detail often makes magazine writing more polished and refined than the average newspaper story.

Such high standards don't always exist, however, at small magazines and newsletters. When one editor does everything—writing, editing and design—there is little opportunity, if any, for additional sets of eyes to challenge and improve the content.

Magazines usually have longer and better-written articles that tend to be more featurish, more personal and more opinionated. How-to articles, top-10 lists and celebrity interviews are often key sellers touted on the cover, but what appeals to many writers about magazines is the chance to produce longer, more involved, more personal articles of high quality.

Editors should, however, beware of trying to make every article appeal to everyone—it can't be done. Nor is it a good idea to put all your best articles in one issue—it's better to spread them out. Otherwise, even avid readers won't read them all because few people read a magazine cover to cover.

Readers expect more from a magazine than a newspaper. Readers expect longer, more entertaining articles, better photos, better layout and higher-quality paper. They probably throw away the newspaper after one day, but they keep the magazine around the house, perusing it longer.

MAGAZINE DESIGN

It's particularly important that a magazine have a good art director. A publication's look should match the image it wants to offer its readers. It would probably be inappropriate, for example, for a religious institution or a large corporation to use a faddish, cutting-edge look.

A publication should be redesigned every five or six years to stay current and infuse new life into it. The trick is to attract new readers without alienating old ones who felt comfortable with the publication as it was. You especially want to be wary about making drastic changes to a publication's signature style. This can be done either by keeping the overall look but making minor improvements or by introducing changes gradually so longtime readers aren't suddenly shocked.

It's not usually a good idea to redesign a publication simply because the editor or ownership has changed. It makes more sense to redesign mainly to bring a publication's image more in line with its mission and appeal more to new read-

Translating Magazine Terms

MAGAZINE	NEWSPAPER	DEFINITION
article	story	nonfiction essay presenting information
cover line, cover blurb	cover blurb	a teaser headline on the cover
logo	flag, nameplate, banner	the design of the publication's name on the cover or top of Page One
title	headline	the title over an article
pull quote, insert	internal blurb	quotation from an article repeated in big type to break up the page
subtitle	second deck, drop head	a second headline between the main headline and the article

ers. This is especially true when sales have been slipping or there is a conscious effort to reach out to a broader demographic base.

As we've said, magazines are usually published on high-quality paper that allows better reproduction of photos and use of color. Magazines tend to use more white space in their layouts, allowing pages to breathe and not seem as cramped visually as newspapers. They also tend to vary their typefaces and layouts from one article to the next much more than newspapers.

Magazines provide great opportunities to enhance words with pictures, which in turn enhances both of their meanings. In general, what makes this possible is simply that there is more space available for that purpose than in newspapers. When space is limited, as in newsletters, there is little room left for design to affect readability.

Furthermore, because the editorial material of magazines is often emotional and dramatic, rather than simply a presentation of facts, good graphic design better fits the communication environment than elsewhere. A deeply moving story with full-color illustrations, printed on glossy paper, is a magazine's stock in trade. Such stories stand out and become desirable to a reading public. (See Figure 11–1.)

Newspapers, because they are published daily, are more restricted in using graphic design. In addition, newspapers use lower-grade paper stock than magazines and newsletters typically do.

The design of magazines, then, becomes a criterion for helping readers choose one magazine over another or over any other medium. A magazine that uses outstanding graphic design tends to attract advertisements that also are beautifully designed. Thus, most magazine advertisements harmonize with the basic idea of providing good design, making the entire publication consistently attractive.

Figure 11–1 *This article about a PET scan helped diagnose breast cancer and saved a woman's life is typical of magazines' human-interest approach to service journalism.*
Photo by Bill Aron/PhotoEdit.

Type and illustrations, or gray and black blocks, are the dominant elements in newspaper page design, although color has become more common in recent years. In magazine design, a third block—white—is used more often than in newspapers. To the magazine art editor, white space is not wasted space but rather a means of stressing other elements.

The editor may generously use space around headings, between text and illustrations, and around illustrations. The editor deliberately plans to get white space on the outside of the pages. To gain extra space, illustrations may **bleed** off—run into the margin of—the page.

Some stories are told effectively in text alone, but others are told more dramatically in pictures. The ideal is a combination of text and pictures, and the emphasis depends on the quality of the illustrations or the significance of the text. A picture's value, says one editor, is best exploited when it sweeps the reader rhythmically into the text. Too often, the story is adequate but good pictures are lack-

A Potpourri of Publication Design Tips

Ads   Some advertisers think a dull page of copy next to an ad helps the ad stand out, but research says the ad is actually helped by readers staying on the spread longer. This means go ahead and put a photo or blurb on a page with ads.

Blurbs   Read-in blurbs are less successful than read-out blurbs because a reader's eyes go to the big type first. An alternative to a read-out blurb is to boldface the lead. All-cap blurbs are hard to read.

Cover art   *People* magazine says a good cover should picture someone recognized by 85 percent of the audience. Of course, that's a celebrity magazine. Your cover should picture whatever or whomever you think will make your audience want to pick up and read your magazine.

Cover lines   *Psychology Today* says a good cover line can sell 50,000 copies. Generally, don't promote departments on the cover because people find those anyway. Cover lines are typically placed down the lefthand side or across the top, although many magazines do them on both sides of the cover art. Cover blurbs usually don't tell you the page because they're written far in advance of ad deadlines and layout of the inside of the magazine.

Departments   Departments build regular readership, so they're a good idea. One of the most read departments in most magazines is simply a letters-to-the-editor column.

Page breaks   Always end a page with either the end of a story or, if the article skips a page, a jump line (also called a *see-line*). The *jump line* tells readers where to turn for the rest of the story. If the article continues to the next page, a jump line is not necessary, but don't end the page with a hyphenated word.

Photos   Too many stories are told twice—once in the article and once in the pictures. Instead, the two should complement each other, each supplying additional information not in the other. The dominant photo should get the dominant caption. Don't tilt photos or cut into them, overlapping them. Photos cut out to stick out of a layout for a 3-D effect, however, can add drama, but be careful when cutting out the background or you may end up with a person with jagged hair. Use a variant of the cover photo with the main story so

the reader easily recognizes it. It's hard to go wrong with a photo of a cute kid or an animal, even though they are clichés.

Q-and-A articles   Run an article in the question-and-answer format when you think the reader will want to read every word of the interview. The Q-and-A format breaks up an article, too, and adds bold type (the "Q" and the "A") to a page, making it editorially and graphically more interesting than the gray text of a long article.

Sidebars   Break out sidebars or boxes whenever possible. This shortens articles, keeps them to a single point, makes them more inviting and gives the reader more big type to read, informing them more. When technical jargon is essential, pull out a glossary. When location may be unknown to readers or directions needed, provide a map. Use sidebars also for lists, pithy quotes from a speech, and times and costs for upcoming events.

Table of contents   It's frustrating for readers to be attracted by a great cover line, then be unable to find the story in the table of contents. Although short descriptions in a table of contents seldom simply repeat the cover lines, a reader should be able to match the two and find the article. The TOC description can be the same blurb accompanying the article. Even newsletters of four or more pages need a table of contents, so readers can see an overview of what's included and quickly find any given article or department.

Theme issues   *Sports Illustrated*'s swimsuit issue aside, theme issues aren't usually a good idea because readers who don't like the topic can skip the entire issue. For this reason, advertisers don't like theme issues. And what do you do with the departments in a theme issue? Extra editions with a timely or popular theme, however, are justified as additional revenue.

Type   Studies show a 30-pica line is the maximum for readability, other than with display type. Don't reverse serif type, running it white on a black background, because you tend to lose the serifs. Italic type tends to downplay something compared with bold type. Avoid the ransom-note look of mixing all kinds of typefaces in an attempt to be creative.

ing, thus robbing the story of its dramatic appeal and producing a dull page of straight text.

A magazine page usually has these elements:

- At least one dominant picture, usually in color.
- A title, preferably with a subtitle.
- A block of text, usually beginning with a typographical device that will compel the reader's attention to the opening of the story. The opening device may be a **dingbat**—a graphic character such as black square—followed by a few words in all capital letters. Or it may be a decorative capital letter, either a **drop cap** (its top lined up with the top of the indented small letter) or a raised, **stick-up initial** (the bottom of the initial base-aligned with the bottom of the other letters in the first line). (See Figure 11–2.)

Simplicity is the keynote in effective page design. An easy, modular arrangement is more likely to attract readers than a tricky makeup with oddly shaped art and a variety of typefaces. Illustrations need not be in the same dimensions, but they should be in pleasing geometric proportions.

Margins should be uniform or at least give the overall effect of uniformity. Usually, the widest margin is at the bottom of the page, the next widest at the side, the third at the top and the narrowest at the inside or gutter. The content of the page is thus shoved slightly upward, emphasizing the eye level or optical center of a rectangle. The outside margin is larger than the gutter because the latter, in effect, is a double margin.

Some designers feel it's important to touch each margin at least once, regardless of whether illustrations are used. Others contend that the eye is so accustomed to the regular margin that even when the margin is touched only once, an imaginary margin is defined clearly in the reader's mind. If the illustration bleeds off the page, the margin on the bleed side may be widened to give more impact to the item that bleeds.

A WILD Alaskan wolf yawns broadly as he lolls in the warm sun of the arctic spring. Trumpeter swans dabble in the cool

There aren't any weekend beer parties on campus. No pep rallies. No homecoming queen, no dormitories and no Saturday

Figure 11–2 Top: Two-line drop cap. Bottom: Raised cap.

The art director must know the position of each page—whether left, right or double spread—and whether the page contains advertising. It also helps if the art director knows the content and appearance of the advertising on the page to avoid embarrassing juxtaposition, as well as the content and appearance of the facing page.

One danger most art directors seek to avoid is cluttering. This occurs when too many illustrations are placed on the same page, when the pages are crowded because of lack of spacing or uneven spacing, or when too many elements—dingbats, subtitles, boldface type—make the page appear busy. The primary goals of magazine design, as for newspaper or Web page design, are to catch and direct the reader's attention and to make the pages easy to read.

Goals of Page Designers

Design is a means rather than an end. If the reader becomes aware of the design, the design is probably bad. The main goals of magazine page designers are:

- To create an environment where readers are likely to find an assembly of interesting stories.
- To attract readers to specific stories as readers casually thumb through pages of a magazine.
- To hold readers' attention in each story until they have finished.
- To use design devices that dramatize the key issues of each story. This is a matter of creating a competitive edge so that readers remember that the magazine is superior to others in the same category.
- To use design to make the most of the readability of each story or page.
- To avoid page designs so powerful that readers spend too much time admiring the design and lose their desire to read a particular story.

GRAPHIC STYLING ALTERNATIVES

There are so many ways to lay out a magazine page that it is difficult to define any one particularly outstanding style. But the easiest way is by a *columnar technique* in which each page is divided into a certain number of columns (usually three or four). The trend today is to vary column widths to make the most of readability.

The designer usually determines how many columns will typically be used unless there is some good reason for changing it. A 7-by-10-inch page (one of the standard sizes used in U.S. magazines) is usually divided into three columns. Four columns may be used occasionally.

The first page of any article usually has better design techniques on it to make it more interesting than ordinary pages. The technique used is the designer's choice. The following sections describe some of the more popular techniques.

Body and Headline Typeface Styles

If you examine the typefaces in major magazines, you will find a wide variety of styles. But there are some similarities, too. Most common is the use of **serif** as opposed to **sans serif** body type. Serif type is the most widely used typeface for body copy, even though the specific names of typefaces vary a great deal. But here, the variance is mostly unnoticeable by readers, who can't tell the difference among Baskerville, Caslon and Goudy fonts. Typographers who have developed a keen eye usually can tell the difference, and that is how they decide which typeface to use. (The body copy of this book is set in Minion.)

The differences are actually slight. The one thing readers agree on is that serif typefaces are all equally readable. Check the body typeface found in three different magazines. Even though each may be different, they look very much alike.

Headlines are also set in a wide variety of type styles, as graphic designers try to be innovative. Not only are digital typefaces used, but also some are designed especially for the main story using a computer program like Fontographer. The fonts used or headlines created tend to have connotations related to the action or concepts of a particular story (see Figure 11–3). These special typefaces are reserved for the first and presumably the most important headline (see Figure 11–4), while subheads or minor heads are usually selected from the many typefaces that the typesetter has available.

Initial Caps As Ornamentation

A bit of ornamentation can be added to a page through the use of a large initial letter for the first word on some paragraphs. This technique works well with serif typefaces but not sans serif ones (see Figures 11–2 and 11–5).

The first letter of the first word of a paragraph—usually the first letter of the article—is set typically two to four times the size of the rest of the text type, although in special cases, the initial cap may be up to 10 times the size. Sometimes, a designer will use an initial cap at intervals throughout the story—most logically to mark different parts like chapters.

Line Spacing or Leading

Line spacing, or *leading,* varies a great deal because research evidence shows that more space is needed between lines as the type size and line widths are increased.

Informal
Alexa

OUTRAGEOUS
Cinema Solid

OLD WEST
Birch

Inviting
Lydian Cursive

Fluency
Brush Script

Far East
Peking

SPONTANEOUS
Herculanum

PROPER
Blackfriar Normal

HIGH TECH
Modula Black

POSTER
Falstaff

Figure 11–3 Mood typefaces.

working together on the Job

Figure 11–4 Headline design.

Using Large Initial Letters

Here is an example of a page design that uses a raised cap that base aligns with the first line. Its purpose is to provide styling to a page that looks dull to the reader and to

Here is the same large initial letter base aligned with the third line of text. Its purpose is to provide ornamentation to a page that looks dull to

Here is an an example of an initial letter that is four times as large (48 points) as the body type (12 points). Its purpose is to provide ornamentation to a page that looks

Here is an example of the contemporary use of a drop cap. This "H" is 84 points high (or seven times as large as the body type, which is 12 points). The use of initial letters this large defeats the purpose of creating an attractive page. The purpose is *not* to attract attention to the letter; a reader may stop to study the unusual design and then move on to another story, thus missing the value of the

Figure 11–5 The large initial capital letter as ornamentation.

There are differences of opinion about how much line spacing is optimal, but the amount found in the most readable magazines is generous. Almost every magazine uses line spacing as a design technique, and almost all of it is excellent. If there are errors in line spacing, it's usually because some designers have used too much—using too little is typically more obvious.

Blurbs or Type Inserts

One of the most popular design techniques in magazine pages is the use of **blurbs,** sometimes called *type inserts* in the magazine world. As with newspapers, blurbs may be external blurbs or internal blurbs. **External blurbs** always help summarize the story and come above the story, either reading into (a **read-in blurb**) or out from (a **read-out blurb**) the article's title. **Internal blurbs** are placed inside the columns of type of the story and always provide a sample from the story, usually a **pull quote**—a quote taken from the story.

Placement of blurbs is up to the designer, but read-out blurbs make more sense than read-in blurbs because the readers' eyes are naturally drawn to the bigger type first, and a blurb would be smaller than the title's type. Also, internal blurbs are best placed above the point in the story from which they're drawn so that they will make the reader want to read on rather than thinking he or she has already read the best parts.

Rules

Rules are lines and can be used in varying widths and styles. Horizontal rules can be used to set portions of a story apart so readers will not miss them or to set off bylines, a writer's credentials or contact information. Vertical rules can be used between columns of type. Boxes can be used to set off sidebars.

The thinnest hairline to widths as large as 24 points can be used, in black or in color. If the designer wants a rule that is unique, the editor may have an artist create it using a program like Adobe Illustrator.

Sidebars or Boxes

Sidebars—also called *boxes*—are related stories or parts of stories set inside ruled frames to set them off on the page.

The size of the lines, or *rules,* of the frame may vary from hairline to six points in width. The key to using attractive boxes is to make sure the *inset*—the space between the text and the frame—is adequate. Some well-designed magazines have boxes with less than 12 points of space inside the box on each side, and that is unattractive. At least 12 points of space on all four sides looks best.

Background Screens or Tint Blocks

A *tint block* of some color is often used as a background for type. Tint blocks are most often prepared in a rectangle, but they may also be free-form.

Tint blocks may be used over internal blurbs from a story, but usually they're used around a sidebar or even an entire story, typically a shorter, brighter one.

Common colors for tint backgrounds are light red, tan and light blue, but they may be almost any color. A danger in using tint blocks is that the contrast between words and background is not sharp enough to be read easily. Good shades for a tint block are 10 to 20 percent. Anything above that may make the type too difficult to read.

Picture Styles and Uses

One of the key graphic techniques of magazine design is the use of pictures chosen, cropped, sized and placed for their dramatic impact.

Pictures may be photographs or illustrations. Each has its own value, but what is important is that they help tell the story that words alone cannot and that they also provide needed graphic contrast to the type to make the whole package interesting to the readers.

Some techniques that can provide impact in magazines, newspapers and Web pages are:

- Pictures are usually more dramatic the tighter the focus on the main part—whether by the photographer taking it as close as possible or by cropping it later—and the bigger they are run in the publication.

- Make one picture or illustration dominant—larger than the others—with the less important ones smaller and in clear support of the large one. When all illustrations in an article are the same size, there is usually a loss of dramatic impact.

- A *cutout* or *outline photo* is a good way to provide change from the typical rectangular look of photos. All of a picture's background is removed digitally or with a knife, thus concentrating on the subject in the foreground. This can be combined with the newest two techniques, the bleed and the wraparound.

- A *bleeding picture* can add drama by breaking outside the type block of the page into the margin, just as a cutout breaks out of the typical rectangular shape of a photo. A bleed will typically go into the top or outside margin of a page, but some pictures bleed on all four sides, with the inside gutter bleed disappearing into the binding.

The path of time that will lead us from today through the 2lst century will be lined with many bright new mechanical and electronic marvels, with better energy sources, and new construction mate-rials and methods. How we respond to these changes will tell us how well our society is

Figure 11–6 Wraparound type.

Bleeding pictures attract readers because they stand out from the other graphics in the magazine. Most pages have a white margin around the outer edge, so a bleed has eye-catching power.

- Type may be *wrapped around* a photo placed inside a column or overlapping part of two columns (see Figure 11–6).

It's important that every picture have a caption that explains who or what is being shown. And remember that the caption should not just say what's obvious in the picture but should convey more information to readers, especially those whose interest and knowledge of the story is confined to reading the big type.

Color

Magazines are usually ablaze in color because color has the ability to attract read-ers' attention. Magazines have long made more use of the **four-color process** than newspapers have, although they are catching up. The term means that when black, magenta, yellow and cyan inks are added to each other in different per-centages, almost any color can be reproduced.

Placement of Advertising

The usual newspaper practice is to pyramid the ads on the right of the page. In a magazine, the ads generally go to the outside of the pages or may appear on both outside and inside, leaving the *well* for editorial copy. The ads need not restrict edi-torial display, especially if the well is on a double spread.

At magazines where the advertising manager determines ad placement, there is usually a give and take between ad manager and editor. The editor may want to start an article in a certain part of the magazine, but there is a two-column ad on

---

10 Principles of Graphic Design for Magazines

1. Graphic design's function in magazines is to help people read more of what is written and to read faster, with more meaning.
2. Graphic design is not an end in itself: It is a mediator between the sender and receiver of messages.
3. Graphic design that is simply pretty to look at has not done enough. It hasn't facilitated reading.
4. Readers may say that they like or dislike the appearance of a magazine, but they do not buy or subscribe because of outstanding design.
5. The attempt to improve circulation by providing a more attractive design has never been a continuing success. Many good magazines have failed despite having an attractive design.
6. When readers notice design and not the contents, they have missed the essence of that publication.
7. Good design is unobtrusive. At times, however, a good article demands a strong, visible presence.
8. Good design is rarely found by casual observation. It requires research of readers, with data broken down by demographics and psychographics.
9. Research must be based on randomized samples to avoid bias. Occasional casual comments made to an editor may be biased.
10. When readers cannot remember what they read, the media they were exposed to probably did not have the type of content they prefer.

Figure 11–7 General principles of graphic design for magazines, with emphasis on making reading easier, faster and more meaningful.

---

the most likely page. The editor then asks the ad manager whether the ad can be moved to another page. Unless the ad was sold with position guaranteed, the ad manager usually tries to comply, especially if the editors is suggesting the ad move forward.

Figure 11–7 is a summary of 10 general principles of graphic design for magazines.

WHAT IS A NEWSLETTER?

Newsletters are published for every special interest you can think of—even a newsletter on newsletters. Although many newsletters are sent freely to a business's customers or an association's members, others sell for a yearly price comparable to a magazine's or even many times more. Some newsletters cost $800 to $1,000 a year, and some highly specialized financial newsletters have even been known to cost up to $25,000 a year.

Newsletters remain a successful medium in hard times despite the fact that if they are sold, they command a higher price per word than regular magazines. Why? Because people give up frills in recessions but see the information in newsletters as more specialized and more vital.

W. M. Kiplinger offered this advice, which is still sound for newsletter editors: "The secret of the newsletter business is to produce a product for a dime, sell it for a dollar and make it habit-forming."

Not only are newsletters good money makers, but they're also less costly to mail and cheaper to start than a magazine—especially since the rise of desktop publishing in the 1980s. All you need is a computer, a desktop-publishing program, a list of potential subscribers, postage and a good idea. You can even avoid postage and hard-copy publishing costs by publishing a Web-based newsletter or e-mailing your newsletter to your subscribers.

If you have a special interest you don't think is being served well in the mass media, check to see whether any newsletters currently serve it. If not, you might find fortune and fame by starting your own. Start the traditional way, in print form, and sell subscriptions, or create a Web site—your costs will be lower but probably so will your income.

Aside from money, starting a newsletter can give you instant credibility. It can catapult you to the forefront of your field because your credentials now include publishing your newsletter for that field. This can mean more recognition, a better résumé and more job offers outside the newsletter business.

Newsletters Then and Now

A **newsletter** is a short, newsy publication with a frequent publication cycle and a high degree of specialization. It's usually distributed exclusively through subscription to a limited circulation.

Newsletters are one of the oldest forms of written journalism. Cicero (ca. 106–43 B.C.), for example, hired a man named Coelius to send him, at his home in the country, a daily report of news from Rome. He paid enough that Coelius hired several reporters to do the writing for him.

The Kiplinger Letter, often called the first published in the United States (1923), reported on government doings to businessmen and is still the longest-published newsletter in America. Actually, however, the Continental Congress used newsletters earlier. *The Federalist Papers* can also be seen as a kind of newsletter.

Newsletters have had a healthy expansion since World War II. In 1977, a formal newsletter association was established: the Newsletter Association of America, now known as the Newsletter & Electronic Publishers Association

What Are Some Ways to Launch a Newsletter?

- Give the first issue away as a sample, and solicit subscriptions.
- Organize an association where one doesn't exist, charge membership fees, and give away the newsletter.
- Become a freelance newsletter publisher. Offer to do public-relations newsletters for companies, hospitals, churches and nonprofit organizations that don't have their own.
- Offer a personalized, executive news summary. This is becoming a hot, lucrative field.

- If you're publishing a magazine and want extra revenue, consider publishing a newsletter as an update between issues. Or add a newsletter that specializes in one or more of the especially popular subject areas of your magazine. Put a complimentary copy of the first issue of the newsletter in the magazine, and solicit subscriptions.

(www.newsletters.org). There are even directories of newsletters. Print directories of newsletters can be expensive. For example, *The Oxbridge Directory of Newsletters 2007* sells for $995. Bowker and the Gale Group have also offered newsletter directories costing in the hundreds of dollars. Obviously, at these prices you might prefer to check your local library.

One of the most convenient—and free—directories is online at Newsletter Access (www.newsletteraccess.com). It claims to be "the largest and most frequently visited newsletter directory anywhere," listing 9,549 newsletters at latest count and letting you read sample articles.

Another useful online directory is at http://ezine-universe.com. It lists e-zine newsletters—small newsletters published on the Web—8,749 of them before the end of 2007.

What is the Key to a Newsletter's Success?

Publishers of newsletters establish an intimate relationship with their readers—more intimate than usually achieved in other mass media. Norman King sums it up this way in *The Money Messiahs:*

> Newspapers employ a scattergun technique. They run stories appealing to the masses, to specific groups, and to isolated individuals: there is no attempt to address exclusively any particular segment of society. On the other hand, a newsletter can be selective and can be sent to specific readers interested in a particular subject. It can be expansive, detailed, and more precisely worded; it can be familiar, using special jargon, and doesn't have to assume the reader is an ignoramus. There is a feeling of intimacy, of confidentiality, a feeling of being on the inside that can be exploited in the writing style of the newsletter.

Newsletters make their readers believe:

- They get useful, personalized information found nowhere else—inside, expert, close-to-the-source stuff from an independent expert they can trust. Knowing these things admits them into an elite group of people in the real know of the larger context for the news others get.

- They find current topics of importance, often discussed here first. Newsletter promotion letters are always talking about all the times they scooped *The New York Times* or the TV networks or *Time* and *Newsweek*. (By the way, don't quote *The New York Times* and other mainstream media often in your newsletter. You are the expert. If readers can get this information somewhere else first, why should they buy your newsletter?)

- They will save time because the material is condensed and save money because of the accurate forecasts of the future. They have to feel they'll get their money's worth no matter how expensive the newsletter.

HOW TO MAKE MONEY WITH A NEWSLETTER

The single biggest mistake in starting any business is to expect to turn a profit right away. You need to have enough money available when you start to get you through the lean years before you become profitable. With newsletters, you need to allow yourself a two-year break-even point. To be successful, you want a 50 percent renewal rate your second year and a 70 to 80 percent rate your third. This is better than magazines, which should expect to lose money the first three to five years.

In the meantime, here are some things you can do to help tide you over:

- Consider selling ads, perhaps as inserts. These can, however, risk your credibility as an independent, unbiased source of information.

- Offer seminars. These can bring in big bucks, help sell yourself as an expert and help sell the newsletter.

- Sell in-person consultations and evaluations, or do independent surveys and studies.

- Offer telephone consultation—either for a price per minute or as an incentive to buy the newsletter.

- Offer related products for sale through your own mail-order store: reprints, collections of tips; CDs, DVDs or MP3s of lectures or courses; books in the field (especially your own); directories of the field, T-shirts with your logo;

related products in your specialty (such as ukulele strings, pickups and tuners, if you're offering a newsletter for uke players); and so on.

- Sell your subscription list. It's expensive to maintain a special-interest list in a mobile society, so some companies pay big money for addresses of people with a proven interest in the market they're trying to serve.

NEWSLETTER DESIGN

Whether you're putting out a newsletter as an independent entrepreneur or as part of your job for a business or association, consider not using the word *newsletter* in the title. Make it more fun sounding. For example, there used to be a dairy newsletter called "Udder Facts—No Bull."

But it should also be noted that sometimes editors make their newsletter titles so clever that readers don't have a clue what they're about or whom they serve. For example, a local library titled its newsletter "Read On." Clever, but what exactly does that mean? Come to the library and read lots of books, or keep reading this newsletter? In such a case, it might help to add a subtitle that clarifies the publication's purpose.

It's a good idea to have a designer create the newsletter nameplate for the title. This should match the typeface chosen with the style, subject and feel of the publication, and serve as a repeating, anchoring piece of art that gives the newsletter a memorable identity.

The standard page size for newsletters is $8\frac{1}{2}$ by 11 inches, with margins of at least one-half inch all around. Even though desktop publishing makes fancy design cheap and easy, some newsletter advisers counsel that it's a good idea to make a newsletter look like a typewritten letter—more urgent and personal. But increasingly, newsletters in the past 20 years have gone to a more designed, professional look. (See Figure 11–8.)

Opinions vary as to the ideal number of columns for a newsletter, but anything wider than three would be too narrow for a standard $8\frac{1}{2}$-by-11 page. Two or three columns are probably the most common, with the downside on two being a gutter down the middle of the page, on three being the narrowness of the columns. Some newsletter designers use only one column, with wider margins or sometimes with added white space on one side into which headlines, blurbs, photos and graphics are placed.

How long should a newsletter be? Some go as long as 32 pages and come out monthly. The answer depends on whom you're serving, the subject covered, the amount of news and the resources available. But remember, the idea of a newsletter is news. It's probably better to be timely than lengthy, meaning you should consider a shorter length but more frequent publication.

Massachusetts Coalition Newsletter

Reach Out and Read Massachusetts Coalition ■ 56 Roland Street ■ Suite 100D
Boston, MA 02129 ■ Tel: 617.455.0655

Fall 2007

A Coalition of 192 ROR Sites and Satellites

Reflections from the Road

What you're thinking: *Where did those lovely books come from?*

What you're feeling: *Wow. This is so unbelievably kind.*

What you're pondering: *The very last gently used book in the waiting room went home with a family just last night. This morning, a donation suddenly arrives! How does this happen? The minute we need something, it seems to magically appear!*

But of course, it's not magic. There's no wand being waved except the wand of good intention. And, like all good magic, the trick with generosity is that it's usually not meant to be seen, even though, off stage, someone has indeed juggled a rabbit or two – not to mention boxes! And whose sleight of hand makes the delivery of thousands of donated books to dozens of ROR programs look easy? Who initiates these book drives?

The magicians are sometimes businesses and sometimes teens; sometimes anonymous families and sometimes your own ROR program's staff who just wish to "help out". In a global sense, they are truly your brothers and sisters. In a more local sense, they are your neighbors.

NEW PROGRAMS: Welcome to ROR!

We are pleased to note the addition of the following practices since our last newsletter:

Pediatric Healthcare of Brockton, Brockton

Pleasant Hill Pediatrics, West Bridgewater

Quincy Pediatric Associates, Quincy

Monson Pediatrics and Family Practice, Monson

Pediatric Associates of Malden, PC, Malden

Westfield Pediatrics, Westfield

Riverbend Medical Group, Agawam

And in a very specific sense, they are your program's guardian angels. For this issue, I hope you'll flip through the pages and find a few of them.

Thank you, Reach Out and Read donors and volunteers, and thank you, ROR doctors and nurses, for always expressing your gratitude when the magic, indeed, happens.

– Gretchen Hunsberger
ROR-MA Programs Director

Spotlight on Staff...

Hello! My name is Nora Murphy and I am the new Massachusetts Programs Assistant. But I am also the new Boston Medical Center ROR Coordinator. Thus, my exposure to all aspects of ROR-in-action is certain to better help me help you, and that's what I'm here for.

It's wonderful to join the team here at Reach Out and Read.

> **Several months into it, ROR has been a big success at CCP! The word is even out in the community. I had a 9 year-old boy ask me if he would get a book like his baby cousin had at a past well child check. So, I told him, 'Maybe you could read your baby cousin's book aloud to him.' But now, with the donated books, I can give him one in the future!"**
>
> **– Dr. Rashna Irani, Cape Cod Pediatrics, Forestdale (a new ROR program)**

As an avid reader, I feel as though I am in splendid company! I hold a degree in Child Life Therapy from Wheelock College in Boston. Child Life is hospital based social and emotional care for children who are chronically or terminally ill and their families. My previous positions include internships on the acute care units of Children's Hospital 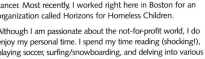 and Shriner's Hospital for Children with Burns. After college, I worked at Barretstown Gang Camp in County Kildare, Ireland. Barretstown is a camp which caters to children with cancer. Most recently, I worked right here in Boston for an organization called Horizons for Homeless Children.

Although I am passionate about the not-for-profit world, I do enjoy my personal time. I spend my time reading (shocking!), playing soccer, surfing/snowboarding, and delving into various artistic endeavors at which I am, at times, somewhat successful.

I would like to thank everyone for the warm welcome to ROR. I look forward to working with you!

Figure 11–8 Sample newsletter of a nonprofit program.

Source: Used by permission. Gretchen Hunsberger and Nancy Berman for Reach Out and Read.

Questions to Ask If You Want to Start Your Own Newsletter

- What is your target audience? (The smaller and richer the better if you want to make a profit.)
- What does you audience have in common? (Some possible answers include the desire to recognize themselves and their friends, to increase wealth or save money, to feel safe, to save time, to have fun or be entertained, or to learn about a subject.)
- What is the purpose of the newsletter? Teach, motivate, recruit, solicit, praise, promote, explain, inform, entertain, solidify, impress?
- What are the costs and marketing problems?
- What competition would you face?
- What should the price be if it's not freely distributed?
- What resources do you have (money, equipment and talents)?
- How often should it come out?
- What should its design be?

The article length, too, can be considered part of the design. Newsletters tend to work best when articles are short and clear, but written in highly condensed, even memo-like form. Some of the most successful newsletters are only one page front and back. Just pick a lead story, write a sidebar or factoid, and put in some regular departments.

As for photographs, try to avoid these typical mistakes of amateur newsletters and small-town papers:

- *The firing-squad shot,* where the photographer has lined up people and shot them.
- *The giant-check-passing photo,* when someone has made a donation.
- *The grip and grin,* when people meet or congratulate someone.
- *The phone in the ear,* where someone is talking on the phone.

In short, avoid stiff, posed, artificial photos. Try to use ones instead that are more natural, showing people doing what they normally do.

If there's only one photo to run on a page, usually it's a good idea to run it big, especially if it's a strong photo. (See Figure 11–9.) It can be dramatic to cut the background out of some photos so that the picture seems to pop out, such as a front shot of a marching band coming forward, with the drum major's hat coming out of the frame, into the top margin, as though the band were marching right out of the page toward the reader.

If there's more than one picture on a page, the pictures should usually be run different sizes, some horizontal, some vertical, with the strongest picture run the largest.

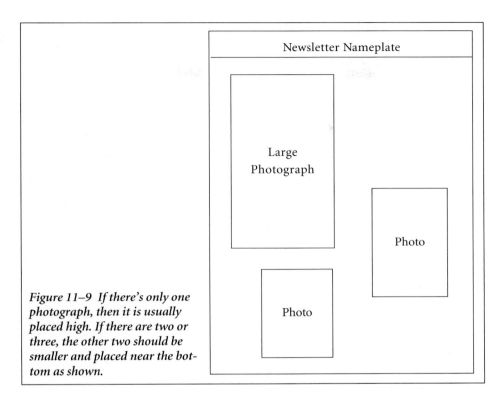

Newsletter Nameplate

Large
Photograph

Photo

Photo

Figure 11–9 If there's only one photograph, then it is usually placed high. If there are two or three, the other two should be smaller and placed near the bottom as shown.

If there are lots of **mugshots** (thumbnails 6 picas by 9 picas or 1-column headshots) for one page, group them into one large rectangle.

Be sure all photos are identified with their own caption or in a block caption referring to each photo. The captions should identify everyone by name and also by title where applicable.

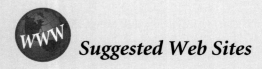

Suggested Web Sites

Ezine Universe   **http://ezine-universe.com**
Magazine Publishers of America   **www.magazine.org**
Newsletter Access   **www.newsletteraccess.com**
Newsletter & Electronic Publishers Association   **www.newsletters.org**

Suggested Readings

Bowker Staff. *2004 Working Press of the Nation: Newspaper Directory, Magazine and Newsletter Directory, TV and Radio Directory.* 3 vol. set. New Providence, N.J.: R. R. Bowker, 2004.

Brewer, Robert Lee, and Chuck Sambuchino. *2008 Writer's Market.* Cincinnati, Ohio: Writer's Digest Books, 2007.

Folio. The magazine about the magazine industry.

Johnson, Sammye, and Patricia Prijatel. *The Magazine From Cover to Cover.* 2nd edition. New York: Oxford University Press, 2006.

Ranly, Don, and Jennifer Moeller. *Publication Editing.* 3rd edition. Dubuque, Iowa: Kendall/Hunt, 2001.

Shaw, Eva. *The Successful Writer's Guide to Publishing Magazine Articles.* Loveland, Colo.: Rodgers & Nelsen, 1998.

Striplin, Deborah, Ed. *Oxbridge Directory of Newsletters 2003.* New York: Oxbridge Communications, 2003.

Williams, Robin. *The Non-Designer's Design Book.* 2nd edition. Berkeley, Calif.: Peachpit Press, 2003.

CHAPTER 12

EDITING FOR THE WEB

When the World Wide Web arrived in 1994, newspapers and broadcast stations began putting their content online. Their efforts reminded veteran journalists of the early days of television, when, absent knowledge of how to use the strengths of that medium, newscasts amounted to nothing more than a reporter reading the news on camera. Similarly, early efforts to put news online amounted to little more than making the text of stories available on the Web.

As the Internet has evolved, online journalism has become more and more sophisticated—so have editors' views of what they are doing. Explains Scott Whiteside, a vice president of Cox Enterprises:

> Newspaper editors are defining local Internet services, but, in a more subtle way, editors are being redefined by the services themselves. For example, they are finding that an electronic editor must segment readers and sometimes depart from the traditional approach to newspaper journalism.
>
> In addition, the services are growing up. Newspaper online services are approaching a new competitive phase that will paradoxically require them to:
>
> • Have their own organization, independent of the newspaper.
> • Have a close relationship with the newspaper in order to produce particular news-related services.
>
> Online services are redefining newspaper editing by forcing editors to become specialists rather than generalists. Most newspaper editors understand the groups and subgroups who make up the sprawling newspaper readership. In short, they know a little about a lot. And, although this fact makes them good dinner companions, they may be bad webmasters.

What online readers are seeking, Whiteside argues, is more detailed information about subjects of interest to them. On a parallel track, advertisers are learning to communicate directly with targeted electronic audiences. And, while small targeted audiences may be too small to sustain newspapers or magazines, they are large enough to warrant attention from news-oriented Web sites.

Online readers differ from those in the traditional news audience. They tend to be younger, and they are attracted by the Internet's informal language and the intimacy afforded by electronic mail and bulletin boards. Electronic readers feel more like participants in an online community than consumers of a printed product. With access to e-mail, blogs, bulletin boards and chat rooms, they form communities to argue about and discuss the issues of the day. In comparison, the traditional media, with their one-way form of communication, seem to be, in Whiteside's words, "preachy and arrogant." Today's news consumers want to talk back to the providers of their news, and they want to participate in discussions about the events of the day.

The objectivity and authoritative tone of the traditional newspaper, so valued by editors, clearly is not preferred by online consumers. Indeed, these consumers may value just as highly the opinion or approach of a fellow online consumer. Thus, if newspapers, broadcast stations and other traditional media are to succeed online, they must rethink the way they relate to their customers.

As Whiteside points out, there still is a need on the Internet for the authoritative services provided by the traditional media. But in Whiteside's view, much of the online business opportunity for newspapers and broadcast stations "may lie in providing informal, inclusive, community-of-interest services as well as services based primarily on commercial transactions such as classifieds and home shopping." Says Whiteside:

> Such services may need to exist under their own brand and editorial standards. For example, a dating service may be quite different in tone from the home-buying service and be promoted differently to its own audience. In addition, some services will have more "advertorial" than "editorial" content.
>
> In short, the different reader services now bundled in the newspaper product are likely to become unbundled over time as they eventually deepen into various electronic services with their own editorial missions.
>
> That evolution is virtually assured by the low cost of targeting interactive services at individual consumers and the same economic forces that have caused decades of media fragmentation.
>
> As a result, a traditional newspaper editor may wonder how "journalism" squares with:
>
> - Publishing massive amounts of information that has little to do with "news" or broad public issues.
> - Adopting the point of view of the groups being "covered."
> - Providing content for services dedicated solely to selling.
> - Editing numerous services independent of the newspaper brand, services that may appeal to people who hate newspapers.
> - Being so accountable to the interactive reader that a degree of editorial "control" is ceded to the readers themselves.

In the minds of traditional journalists, some of these issues are problematic because they challenge the norms of traditional newsroom values and ethics. A real journalist, they argue, would not be associated with "advertorial" copy. Nor would a real journalist adopt a point of view or cede a portion of editorial control to the reader. Yet, it is clear that online journalism demands that these norms be challenged. Notes one editor: "Alternative newspapers and topic-specific magazines have been doing some of those things for years, and in the process they have built loyal audiences. They also have built credibility with their audiences that the mainstream media too often lack."

Still, the idea of relaxing traditional newsroom standards to accommodate the demands and expectations of the online media makes some publishers uncomfortable. This has sparked a movement to divorce online operations from traditional newsrooms. Those who have done so understand that the values of the newspaper or broadcast newsroom may well clash with what's needed to succeed in the online marketplace. In their view, what the online marketplace needs, and demands, is smaller, focused organizations uninhibited by the agendas of their parent organizations. Rather than adhere to one set of norms throughout an entire organization, different sets of norms may be needed in the online world, each depending on the site and content. Still other media organizations have found this approach to be counterproductive. Online operations must become central to the organization's focus, and to separate online operations from the traditional newsroom is increasingly viewed as a mistake.

To many traditional journalists, adaptation to the online culture smacks of a major relaxation of journalistic standards and ethics. To others, it is nothing more than adaptation to the realities of a changing marketplace. But one thing is certain: In a medium that permits readers to become active participants, attempts to shut them out and retain the "we know best" attitude, so prevalent among newspapers, is doomed to failure.

Some innovative editors are adapting well to the new realities. Minnesota Public Radio embraced the concept of citizen participation in the news-gathering process by creating a huge database of experts on all sorts of topics. When something important happens, MPR finds it easy to tap the expertise of people willing to talk publicly about the event or problem.

Similarly, the *Milwaukee Journal Sentinel* has revamped its education coverage to create Web-based discussions with the public about what needs to be done to improve public education in its coverage area. Groups of school administrators, teachers and students serve as willing participants in discussions with the public about school reform.

WHO-TV in Des Moines uses its Web site to broaden the discussion of the important role of Iowa's caucuses in presidential politics. WHO political reporters now operate blogs and contribute significantly to the station's Web site in addition to their traditional role of producing television news stories. Editors roles similarly have changed.

Online media, then, require reporters and editors who are willing to engage the public in ways that promote interactivity rather than those who are deeply rooted in the traditions of one-way communication. Clearly, some individuals may be well-suited for online editing while others may be better-served by remaining in the traditional media. For the foreseeable future, both types of editors will be needed.

↗ LAYERS AND LINKS

Increasingly, journalists recognize that writing and editing for the online media differ from writing and editing for the traditional media. And, while space is virtually unlimited in the online media, there is an increasing awareness that long, unrelieved blocks of text inhibit reading rather than promote it. As a result, online editors typically work with *storyboards,* computerized blueprints that tell them whether the information they are compiling will fit in the prescribed space, often one screenful of information. From there, stories are layered, usually with these parts:

- The headline or title.
- A one-sentence tease, or lead.
- The first page or a quick summary of what happened, not unlike a short radio or television story.
- Accompanying visuals, usually photos or graphics.
- Accompanying audio and video, if any.
- The in-depth report, often broken with subheads.
- Links to related material.

It is layering and links that make editing for the online media different. **Layering** makes it simple for readers to consume as little, or as much, as they want. **Links** provide access to incredible depth that far exceeds what newspapers or magazines can offer. Indeed, rich links provide online consumers with all they could want to know about the subject at hand. As one pundit put it, the Internet is the world's largest library. Links enable the online editor to take advantage of that.

Editors have at their command all the necessary information to tell the story in the best way possible. But the online editor has to be a jack-of-all-trades. At a newspaper, magazine or broadcast station, the work of assembling the various parts usually is parceled out to reporters, graphic artists, photographers, videographers or editors. In an online newsroom, one person is likely to handle most or all of these functions. Thus, the online journalist is a converged journalist.

There is no single way to produce a story for online publication. Although traditional newspaper and magazine writing formulas often work in the online newsroom, there may be better ways. A quick story may lend itself to the classic newspaper inverted-pyramid writing style, a staple of quick-hitting news Web sites. A more complex one may require links to audio, video and still photos with multiple layers of text. Major projects may require complex forms of storytelling.

Online journalism is multimedia journalism. Thus, the journalist is required to select the best medium—text, graphics, photos, audio or video—in which the story should be told. Almost without exception, the best way to tell any story is with a combination of these.

ONLINE JOURNALISM AND CREDIBILITY

Like their print or broadcast counterparts, online editors must be careful to use information only from reliable sources. But an added danger of online journalism is providing Web links to unreliable sources. Stan Ketterer, a journalist and journalism educator, suggests that editors evaluate information on the Internet by following the same journalistic practices they use for assessing the credibility and accuracy of any information. He developed these guidelines:

- Before using information from a Web site, verify it with the source. There are exceptions to this rule. Information from a highly credible government site like the Census Bureau is probably OK. And perhaps one source must suffice on a breaking story because of time constraints. An editor must clear all exceptions.

- If you have any doubts about the accuracy of the information and you cannot reach the source, find a second source, such as a book or another contact person. When in doubt, omit the information.

- In most cases, information taken directly from the Web and used in a story must be attributed. You can use the name of the copyright holder or government agency in the attribution—for example, "according to the EPA" or "EPA figures show." If you cannot verify the information, attribute unverified information to the Web page, such as, "according to the Voice of America's site on the World Wide Web." Consult your editor before using unverified information.

- Check the extension on the site's Internet address to get clues as to the nature of the organization and the likely slant of the information. The most common extensions used in the United States are .gov (government), .edu (education), .com (commercial), .mil (military), .org (nonprofit organization) and .net (Internet service provider).

    Most of the government and military sites have credible and accurate information. In many cases, you can take the information directly from the site and attribute it to the organization.

    If college and university sites have source documents, such as the U.S. Constitution, attribute the information to the source document. But beware. Personal home pages of students often have .edu extensions, and the information on them is not always credible.

- Do not use information from a personal home page without contacting the person and without the permission of an editor.

- In almost all cases, do not use information from the home pages of commercial and nonprofit organizations without verification. Verify and attribute all information on these pages.

- Check the date when the page was last updated. The date generally appears at the bottom of the first page of the site. Although a recent date does not ensure that the information is current, it does indicate that the organization is paying close attention to the site. If no date appears, if the site has not been updated for a while or if it was created some time ago, do not use the information unless you verify it with the source.

As Ketterer notes, using the Internet as a source of information is no riskier than using books, magazines or other printed material, provided one uses common sense. He also cautions editors to remember that material on the Internet is subject to copyright laws. With some exceptions, there is no problem linking to an Internet site. But taking copyrighted material and placing it on your own site is clearly a copyright violation.

TYPES OF NEW MEDIA

The term **new media** has been used to refer to any number of different attempts to find innovative ways of distributing information electronically. Some include under that heading the **audiotext** services run by some newspapers. With audiotext, users dial a telephone number to connect, then press additional numbers to hear recorded information on a variety of subjects. More often, though, the term *new media* is used to refer to computer-based sources of information. Two have emerged as the most important:

- *The Internet.* The Internet has become the most prominent of all the online services. Thousands of newspapers, magazines and broadcast stations around the world have set up shop on the Internet. In addition, the Internet is a repository for massive amounts of information provided by universities, governments and private companies. It's an appealing place to those who have learned to navigate it; where else in the United States can you get today's news from a newspaper in St. Petersburg, Russia?

- *CD-ROMs and DVDs.* Interactive CD-ROMs and DVDs, while not suited for breaking news, are fast becoming the most intriguing magazines of the new-media world. *Time* magazine published an interactive CD-ROM on the war in Iraq, for example, and photojournalists publish the results of the annual Pictures of the Year competition on CD-ROM. There, consumers not only see the winning photos but also hear why the judges picked them.

For journalists, new-media operations in all those areas represent new places of employment. But while CD-ROM publishing is growing, online media represent the fastest growing sector of the media industry. Jobs by the thousands are being created each year.

SOURCES OF INFORMATION

Journalists have two primary interests in online media. As we've already discussed, online media are the newest medium for publishing text, graphics, audio and video. But they also are an invaluable source of information—online libraries, of sorts—that can be used to provide background information for stories or to check facts. Obviously, commercial databases and the Internet are great sources of information for journalists. But some additional sources merit attention as well:

- *Commercial database services.* These services are not intended for the general public but cater to journalists, lawyers and others who need to do background research. The commercial services provide archives of information from wire services, newspapers, magazines and other sources. LexisNexis is an example of a commercial database service. It has both its own proprietary interface and a Web-based interface.

- *Government databases.* All levels of government—federal, state, county and municipal—maintain extensive databases of information of use to journalists. Some of these are still maintained on mainframes, which makes them difficult to access. Organizations such as the National Institute of Computer-Assisted Reporting in Columbia, Mo., have led the way in showing journalists how to access government data for news stories. Increasingly, though, government agencies are recognizing the usefulness of making that data more readily available. Today, thousands of government databases are accessible through the Internet. For federal databases, start with Thomas, the service of the Library of Congress (http://thomas.loc.gov).

- *Special-interest group databases.* Many private groups maintain databases of information of use to journalists. Usually, these are maintained by nonprofit groups with a cause, such as Planned Parenthood (www.plannedparenthood.org). Journalists must exercise care in using such databases because of the potential for distortion as these groups champion their causes. Nonetheless, such databases can be quite useful. The journalist may find data there that are not available elsewhere.

- *Internet search engines.* Sites like Google and Yahoo! are terrific gateways to databases of all sorts. They will simplify your searches.

- *Other computerized databases.* These include the **electronic libraries** (or **morgues**) maintained by the various media and databases created by reporters themselves as they attempt to document stories.

THE ONLINE EDITOR

Editing for the online media has been likened to editing for a 24-hour news service. There are no set deadlines; more precisely, there is a deadline every minute. Online editors constantly face deadlines, and they must be skilled in the presentation of news in many formats—the written word, graphics, audio and video. That's because the online media increasingly use all these devices to transfer information to consumers. In a real sense, then, online media editors are **multimedia journalists.** Says John Callan, a founding senior editor at the Microsoft Network (later MSNBC), who was instrumental in assembling that service's news staff:

> We knew we needed to bring in people from all the existing media because it was unlikely we would find people who had all the skills we wanted. We brought in newspaper reporters, editors, magazine people, broadcast journalists, photojournalists, graphics artists, even computer programmers. Throwing all those people, with their varying skills, into the same operation was fascinating. We learned from each other every day.

It's unlikely that someone trained as a writer or editor will suddenly become an accomplished graphic artist or photojournalist. But, as Callan points out, in the online media it is essential to think in multimedia terms: What device is best to convey this particular bit of information? A story? An information graphic? A video clip? Audio? Or should they all be used? The online journalist must be able to think in visual concepts as well as in written ones.

Obviously, the online editor must be proficient in using computers, a key tool of the craft. But the medium itself also creates the need for new kinds of journalists. Microsoft coined the term **linkmeister** to describe the job of one individual in the newsroom. The linkmeister's job? To find sites on the Web to which MSNBC can link. For example, if a news story reports on census trends, it's a simple matter to link to the U.S. Census Bureau site on the Web, where the reader can find plenty of additional information. Doing so provides a service that none of the existing media can match.

Such **hypertext** links to other sites are one of the major advantages of the online media over traditional media. It takes just seconds to establish links to other Web sites that may be invaluable in helping the reader understand a story. And for those who are intensely interested in a subject, links are established that provide all the information they want.

Indeed, the online media offer many such advantages over the traditional media. It's even possible to provide the user with tools for exploring databases that reside on the Internet. The challenge for journalists is to think creatively about how computers can assist in the presentation of news. As they do so, they redefine the medium.

What Callan and others like him are doing is inventing a new medium, one rooted in the traditions of the existing media but one that rejects their shortcomings as unacceptable. Thus, the online media combine the depth of newspapers and magazines with the immediacy of radio and television. And they combine the eye appeal of television with the enduring quality of magazine reproduction. The multimedia journalists who work in the online media must use their existing skills while learning new ones. For those who like challenges and who view every day as a new opportunity to learn, online operations are exciting places to work.

THE WEB'S IMPORTANCE

The transformation of the Internet from a computer network for academics and the military into the world's newest news medium occurred almost overnight. It happened during the early 1990s with the widespread adoption of the World Wide Web, a user-friendly front-end for the notoriously unfriendly Internet.

The concept of the Web was developed by Tim Berners-Lee at a laboratory in Switzerland. What made it popular, however, was the development in 1993 of a computer program called *Mosaic* at the University of Illinois in Urbana-Champaign. Mosaic is known as a **browser** because it allows the user to browse the Internet's content using a point-and-click graphical interface. Mosaic, freely distributed on the Internet, spawned improved commercial versions of browsers, including Netscape, Microsoft's Internet Explorer, Apple's Safari and *Mozilla's* Firefox.

Today, it's fair to say that no one can be a serious journalist without a good working knowledge of the Web. There's simply too much information available there for anyone to ignore. It's important for journalists to use the Web as a source of information, and it's important for journalists to see what others are publishing on it.

Because of the importance of the Web in the new media, many journalists are learning how to create Web pages. They do so by learning HTML, or hypertext markup language, a simple coding scheme, or its newer version, XHTML. HTML and XTHML tags tell a computer how to display text and other items as headings, body text, photos or similar elements. Increasingly, tools are being developed that make it unnecessary to learn HTML or XTMHL for all but the more complex design chores. With such programs, a click of the mouse inserts the proper coding. Similarly, XML, extended markup language, is being designed into newer newspaper and magazine computer systems so that material may be output easilty for either print or the Web.

The real key to understanding the power of the Web is understanding hypertext. Within a Web document, links to related information are established. Linked words or phrases appear in a color different from the rest of the text. When a

Tips on Using HTML

Learning to use HTML, the language behind the World Wide Web, is not particularly difficult. Indeed, it's much simpler than learning a foreign language. Below is a simple, sample HTML source page with the code explained. But first understand this:

- All HTML code is written inside the angle brackets, located above the comma and period on the keyboard.
- HTML tags must appear in pairs, like opening and closing parentheses. The ending code is always the same as the opening one but with a forward slash after the first bracket.

Here's an explanation of the most common HTML codes:

- <html> All HTML documents must start with this.
- <head> This identifies the document in the source code only, not on the page.
- <title> This codes the title of the Web page in the browser bar.
- </title> This ends the title code in the browser bar.
- </head> This ends the head information.
- <h1> This codes your headline visible in the browser. You have up to six head sizes available, designated from 1 (the biggest) to 6 (the smallest). Main headlines are generally <h1>, subheads <h3>.
- </h1> This ends the head code.
- <body> This starts the body of your text.
- <p> This starts each new paragraph.
- <b> This turns on boldface.
- </b> This turns off boldface.
- <i> This turns on italics.

- </i> This turns off italics.
- </p> This ends each paragraph.
- <a href="http://www.msnbc.com"> This establishes a link to MSNBC's site.
- </a> End link coding.
- <hr> This draws a horizontal rule across the page and is an exception to the rule about always needing an ending tag to pair with it.
- </body> This ends the body of your text.
- </html> All HTML documents must end with this.

In addition to the above, you'll want to learn to do the following:

- Make the four kinds of lists available in HTML.
- Create internal links to places above or below on the page.

Meanwhile, here are a couple of goodies to know:

Image Insertion and Image Aligning

<img src="URL or folder and name of image with extension .gif or .jpg" align=left, middle or right>

This inserts an image from a URL or folder on your drive and then aligns it in your choice of three ways.

Inserting an E-Mail Address

<a href="mailto:your e-mail address">E-mail me</a>

This inserts an e-mail link that when clicked on will open the reader's e-mail program and address an e-mail to you.

mouse pointer is dragged across a hypertext link, the shape of the pointer changes. Clicking at that spot takes the user to the linked electronic file.

The linked file may not be on the same computer. Indeed, it may be located in another state or even in another country. With good links, the wide, wide world of the Internet is placed at the user's fingertips.

Users can navigate the Internet by inserting a URL, or **uniform resource locater,** in a space the browser provides. Each file on the Internet has a unique URL. Inserting that address and pressing the computer's ENTER key takes the user directly to that file. For example, to go to the Cable News Network home page on the Web, the user inserts this URL:

http://www.cnn.com

URLs begin with *http,* which stands for hypertext transmission protocol. This alerts the computer that the destination address is a World Wide Web site. Many URL addresses follow with *www,* which is the Web site on the provider's computer. In the preceding example, *cnn* stands for Cable News Network, and *com* indicates that the site is run by a commercial, or for-profit, corporation (see Figure 12–1).

A browser makes navigating the Internet a simple matter. Nothing, however, is perfect. Some users may have a slow connection to the Internet, which can make the downloading of images, in particular, painfully slow. Because the Internet is a collection of both high-speed and slow-speed computer networks around the world, responsiveness is often less than desirable.

Sites also come and go, so today's valid URL may be obsolete tomorrow. For this reason, in your Web citations it is important to include the date the information was accessed. Still, the Web is an exciting place for journalists to explore. Becoming familiar with it is essential to the practice of modern journalism.

DESIGNING FOR THE WEB

Here are some key tips on how to design Web pages:

- Design pages to be 640 pixels wide, the screen size most users have.
- Keep the design consistent among the pages on your site. For example, typefaces and backgrounds should be consistent, and recurring items should look the same and be in similar spots from page to page. Make this consistency easier to maintain with less effort by using a template.
- Put the best material near the top of the page, where it's visible before the reader has to scroll down.

Figure 12–1   Cable News Network is one of the Internet's most popular Web sites and is increasingly filled with Flash-based video.

Source: © 2008 by CNN. Used with permission.

- Break up the type with block quotes, subheads and bulleted lists.
- Limit the amount of scrolling a reader has to do by using internal links to take a reader to selective spots lower down on the same page or external links to take readers to sidebars.
- Use View Source to copy coding for elements of others' Web pages you like, and keep a library of special effects you can block-save and drop in.
- Just because you have lots of fonts doesn't mean you should use lots on a Web page.
- Flashing type is distracting and annoys viewers.
- Don't use color type against a background it will blend with. Yellow type seems especially hard to read.
- Stick to the 216-color palette both Netscape and Internet Explorer use. If you create others, they will distort.

- Don't use background colors that will make it harder for a user to get a readable printout.

- Lots of sound, animation and photos make the page slow to download and irk viewers who have a slow connection speed.

- Don't make photos too big, or they will be slow to download and may not be viewable without scrolling.

- Save photos in JPEG format, graphics in GIF format.

ONLINE MEDIA AND THE FUTURE

The phenomenal growth of the Web has fueled much speculation about the future of the existing media. Some even predict an eventual melding of television, radio, newspapers and magazines into a new information medium, or *infomedium*. Others think the new media already provide these services and that nothing stands in the way of achieving that goal but cables or telephone lines into homes with bandwidth sufficient for video. In most urban areas, such high-speed networks are already available, and Adobe's Flash technology, which underlies much of the video on the Web, makes television-like programming increasingly possible.

The existing media are betting heavily that a dominant new medium will evolve from the Internet. Major investments in Web sites by radio, television, newspapers and magazines are ample evidence that the existing media view the online media as both a threat and an opportunity. Instead of fighting the trend, they have chosen to participate.

It's clear to most that the Internet is almost surely the information super-highway that will carry the infomedium of the future, regardless of its eventual form. No serious new medium could exist without a close connection to the Internet. That's how powerful the Internet has become.

Cable television and telephone companies are battling it out to provide your connection to the superhighway. Already, cable modems that turn cable television lines into high-speed lines for Internet transmissions are common. Some cable companies are installing even faster fiber-optic links into people's homes. Not every cable system is well-prepared to do that, however, and in many ways the telephone companies are in the best position to succeed. They are rushing to provide those connections before the cable companies are ready.

Potentially even hotter is mobile phone technology. In Europe and Asia, and increasingly in North America as well, consumers have access to third-generation (3G) cell phones that permit news and other information—including video—to be delivered to the phone with ease. It's just a matter of time before all information providers begin delivering information this way, since for younger people, in particular, it's the way they want to consume news.

As usual, government will play a key role in how this develops. As government sets the rules for the Information Age, expect less regulation of the media than before. In recent years, Congress has moved to deregulate the communications industry. Still, control of the electronic media and common carriers (as the phone companies are known) is a governmental nightmare. The federal government regulates broadcasting, state governments regulate telephone companies, and local governments often regulate cable television companies. Who, then, will regulate this new medium and to what degree will it be regulated? The answers to these questions will have much to do with the speed of its spread into the marketplace.

Through it all, don't expect the existing media to disappear. Although it's likely that the number of newspapers will continue to decline, they won't just vanish—nor will broadcast radio and television, nor will magazines. For the foreseeable future, we're likely to see fierce competition among them all.

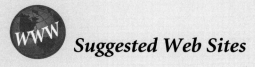

Suggested Web Sites

British Broadcasting Corporation **www.bbc.co.uk**
Cable News Network **www.cnn.com**
ESPN **www.espn.go.com**
MSNBC **www.msnbc.msn.com**
The New York Times **www.nytimes.com**

Suggested Readings

Eccher, Clint, Eric Hunley and Erik Simmons. *Professional Web Design: Techniques and Templates* (Internet Series). Hingham, Mass.: Charles River Media, 2004.
Jenkins, Sue. *Web Design: The L Line, The Express Line to Learning.* Indianapolis, Ind.: Wiley Publishing, 2007.

CHAPTER 13

EDITING FOR THE BROADCAST MEDIA

Most of the techniques for editing in newspapers and magazines apply as well to news on radio and television. Those responsible for news copy for any medium must have good news judgment, a feeling for the audience and the ability to handle the language. But because the broadcast newscaster must pack enough items into the newscast to give listeners and viewers the feeling they are getting a summary of the significant news of the moment, condensation is required.

A newspaper often offers its readers a 1,000-word story and lets them decide how much, if any, they want to read. The broadcast audience has no such choice. If the newscaster gives too much time to items in which listeners and viewers have only a mild interest, they grab the remote and go to another station.

Here are two wire-service accounts of the same story, the first one intended for newspapers, the second for radio and television stations:

> MASSENA, N.Y. (AP)—Unarmed Canadian police scuffled with some 100 Mohawk Indians today and broke their blockade of the international bridge that goes through Mohawk territory in linking the United States and Canada.
>
> The Mohawks put up the human and automobile blockade after Canadian government officials refused to stop levying customs duties on them—duties the Mohawks say are illegal under the Jay Treaty of 1794.
>
> The Mohawk Indians had brought 25 automobiles into line at the center of the bridge linking the United States and Canada, and Mohawk women had thrown themselves in front of police tow trucks to hinder the clearing of the roadway.
>
> There were no reports of serious injury. Forty-eight Mohawks were arrested—including most leaders of the protest—and taken into custody by police on Cornwall Island.
>
> A spokesman for the Mohawks called for the other five nations of the Iroquois Confederacy to join the protest Thursday.
>
> The Mohawks began the blockade after the Canadian government refused Tuesday to stop customs duties on Mohawks who live on the St. Regis Reservation, part of which is in the United States and part in Canada.
>
> Scattered fighting and shoving broke out among the Mohawks and police when officers tried to move in to clear away the automobile blockade. One automobile and two school buses were allowed over the international span around noon.

A newspaper copy editor might trim as many as 50 words from this lengthy story to make it tighter and to eliminate any repetition. The story was pared to about 70 words for the broadcast wire roundup item:

> Unarmed Canadian police have arrested 48 Mohawk Indians. Today, the Mohawks formed a human wall and blocked the international bridge linking Canada and the United States near Massena, New York.
>
> The Mohawks are up in arms about Canada's insistence on collecting customs duties from Mohawks traveling over the bridge to and from their reservation. They say it's a violation of the 1974 Jay Treaty.

As an item in the broadcast news summary, it was cut even more:

> Forty-eight Mohawk Indians have been arrested by Canadian police near the New York state border. The Mohawks blocked a bridge that links the U-S and Canada. They claim violation of a 1974 treaty. The Mohawks say they plan another blockade tomorrow.

News is written and edited so newscasters will have no trouble reading and understanding it. Broadcasters must write news they can read fluently and that sounds right to the listeners. Broadcast news style must be so simple that listeners can immediately grasp its meaning. The language must be so forceful that even casual listeners will feel compelled to give the story their full attention (see Figure 13–1).

A reader's eyes may on occasion deceive but not to the extent that the listener's ears deceive. A reader who misses a point can go over the material again. A listener who misses a point likely has lost it completely. All radio and television news manuals caution against inserting information that separates subject and predicate. For example, if the copy reads, "The Community of Christ, a break-off group from the Mormon Church, has ordained women for decades," many listeners will be left with the impression that the Mormon Church ordains women.

The broadcast message is warm and intimate. The tone is more personal than that of the newspaper story. It suggests, "Here is an item that should interest you."

The refreshing, conversational style of broadcast news writing has many virtues that all news writers might study. Broadcast writing stresses plain talk. The newspaper reporter may want to echo a speaker's words, even in an indirect quote: "The city manager said his plan will effect a cost reduction at the local government level." Broadcast style calls for simple words: "The city manager said his plan will save money for the city."

The newspaper headline is intended to capture the attention and interest of news readers. The lead on the broadcast news story has the same function. First, a capsule of the news item, then the details:

> The F-B-I says there was an overall 19 percent crime rate increase the first months of this year, and the crime that increased the most was purse-snatching, up 42 percent.

Figure 13–1 Katie Couric, anchor and managing editor of the "CBS Evening News with Katie Couric," makes her debut broadcast on Sept. 5, 2006.
Photo by JP Filo/CBS Photo Archive/Getty Images.

The New York stock market took a sharp loss after backing away from an early rise. Trading was active. Volume was 15-million-950-thousand shares compared with 16-million-740-thousand Friday.

The newscast is arranged so that the items fall into a unified pattern. This may be accomplished by placing related items together or by using transitions that help listeners shift gears. Such transitions are made with ideas and skillful organization of facts and not with crutch words or phrases. One editor said, "Perhaps the most overworked words in broadcast copy are *meanwhile, meantime* and *incidentally.* Forget them, especially *incidentally.* If something is only 'incidental' it has no place in a tight newscast."

Broadcast copy talks. It uses contractions and, often, sentence fragments. It is rhythmic because speech is rhythmic. The best broadcast copy teems with simple active verbs that produce images for the listener.

The present tense, when appropriate, or the present-perfect tense, creates immediacy and freshness in good broadcast copy and helps eliminate repetition of the word *today.* An example:

A winter storm has covered the Atlantic seaboard—from Virginia to Maine—with up to 20 inches of snow. Gale-force winds have piled up six-foot drifts in Virginia, bringing traffic there and in West Virginia to a virtual halt. The storm has closed schools in six states.

Trains and buses are running hours late. Pennsylvania and Massachusetts have called out huge snow-clearing forces.

SOURCES OF COPY

Copy for the broadcast newsroom comes from news-gathering associations and from local reporters. Some radio and television stations subscribe to a newspaper news service as well as to the broadcast newswire. This provides a greater number and variety of stories. The news agencies deliver the news package in these forms:

- *Spot summary.* A one-sentence item:

   (DENVER) F-B-I sharpshooters have shot and killed a gunman who held two hostages aboard a private plane at Stapleton International Airport in Denver.

- *Five-minute summary.*

   (DENVER) F-B-I agents fatally shot a gunman early today as he boarded an airline jet in Denver, which he thought was to fly him to Mexico. The F-B-I said the gunman had his two hostages with him at the time of the shooting. He had held them on a small private plane for seven hours. Before he left the first plane, the gunman had told authorities over the radio, "I'll tell you what. I'm still gonna have this gun right up the back of his [the hostage's] head, and it's gonna be cocked, and if anybody even budges me, it's gonna go off, you know that."

   The chief of the Denver office of the F-B-I, Ted Rosack, said 31-year-old Roger Lyle Lentz was killed shortly after midnight, ending an episode that began in Grand Island, Nebraska, and included two separate flights over Colorado aboard the commandeered private plane. Neither hostage was injured.

- *Takeout.* This is a detailed, datelined dispatch concerning one subject or event.
- *Spotlights and vignettes.* Both are detailed accounts, the latter usually in the form of a feature.
- *Flash.* This is seldom used and is restricted to news of the utmost urgency. A flash has no dateline and is limited to one or two lines. It is intended to alert the editor and is not intended to be broadcast. The flash is followed immediately by a bulletin intended for airing.
- *Bulletin.* Like the flash, the bulletin contains only one or two lines. A one-line bulletin is followed immediately by a standard bulletin giving details.
- *Special slugs.* These include AVAILABLE IMMEDIATELY (corresponds to the budget on the news wire), NEW TOP, WITH (or SIDEBAR), SPORTS, WOMEN, FARM, WEATHER, BUSINESS, CHANGE OF PACE, PRO-NUNCIATION GUIDE, EDITOR'S NOTE, ADVANCE, KILL, CORREC-TION, SUBS (or SUBS PREVIOUS).

Some local stations broadcast the news in the form they receive it from the news agency. But most broadcast news is edited by trained reporters who know how to tailor the news for a specific audience. Almost all wire copy is rewritten before it is assembled for broadcast and sometimes from newscast to newscast during a day to give the listener some variety in items that are repeated.

PREPARATION OF COPY

All local copy should be triple-spaced in capital and lowercase letters. If a letter correction is to be made in a word, the word should be scratched out and the correct word substituted in printed letters. If word changes are made within sentences, the editor should read aloud the edited version to make sure the revised form sounds right. If the copy requires excessive editing, corrections should be made and a new copy printed before it is submitted to a newscaster.

Most television newscasters read stories on the air using a script projection system called a TelePrompTer. The TelePrompTer works by beaming a picture of the script to a monitor mounted on the studio camera. The script image reflects in a two-way mirror mounted over the camera lens, so the newscaster actually can read the script while appearing conversational and pleasant. There is no need to refer to notes, but newscasters have them in case the TelePrompTer fails. Script copy averages only four words a line so the newscaster's eyes do not have to travel noticeable distances back and forth across the page as he or she reads from the Tele-PrompTer or from the script itself.

All editing of broadcast copy is done with the newscaster in mind. If a sentence breaks from one page to another, the newscaster will stumble. No hyphens should be used to break words from one line to the next.

News editors prefer to put each story on a separate sheet. This enables them to rearrange the items or to delete an item if time runs short. A few briefs tacked near the end of the newscast help fill leftover time.

Properly edited broadcast copy also should include pronunciation aids when necessary. The most common dilemma for newscasters is place names, many of which get different pronunciations in different regions. No newscaster should confuse the Palace of Versailles (vur-SIGH) in France with the town of Versailles (vur-SALES) in Missouri. The editor should add the phonetic spelling to the script, and the newscaster can underline the word on his or her copy as a reminder.

The wire services provide a pronunciation list of foreign words and names appearing in the day's report. The guide is given in phonetic spelling (Gabon—Gaboon) or by rhyme (Blough—rhymes with how).

Television Newsroom Organization

Television newsrooms are organized to assemble news rapidly and in multimedia format, one that encompasses the written (or spoken) word, graphics, sound and moving pictures. Combining all these into a coherent newscast is a challenging assignment. Typically, those in television news departments have these titles:

- *News director.* The top news executive manages newsroom personnel and resources and sets newsroom policies. An *assistant news director* or *managing editor* often directs the day-to-day news-gathering operation.
- *Executive producer.* The producer determines the overall look of the station's newscasts, including how video, graphics and live reports are handled, and how upcoming stories are teased before a commercial break. Most stations also have *show producers,* who are responsible for the various newscasts.
- *Reporters.* Like their print counterparts, broadcast reporters do the tough work of gathering the news in the field. But unlike print reporters, broadcast reporters must pay attention to the demands of the camera. Much of their work involves writing a story on the spot and recording it on tape. Sometimes, they work with videographers or field

producers to do live remotes from the field. In such cases, they must be exacting in their work; no editor corrects their mistakes.
- *Videographers.* Broadcast camera operators, or videographers, work with reporters to assemble news reports in the field.
- *Anchormen and anchorwomen.* These lead newscasters work in the studio to tie together the various parts of the newscast. They introduce reports from other reporters or read those that are text only.
- *Desk assistants, assignment editors and other support staff.* Back at the station, others help track the news. These include desk assistants, who assemble news from the wires and coordinate network material to be included in the local newscast, and assignment editors, who may be responsible for assigning news teams to breaking stories. Various technical support staffers are also there to handle live remote transmissions, camera repair and similar chores.

Networks often have additional levels of support. The *correspondents* you see regularly on network news may be backed up by *field producers* or *off-camera reporters* who do much of the work of gathering the news.

Phonetic Spelling System Used by Wire Services

A	like the *a* in cat	EW	like the *ew* in few
AH	like the *a* in arm	IGH	like the *i* in tin
AW	like the *a* in talk	IH	like the *i* in time
AY	like the *a* in ace	OH	like the *o* in go
EE	like the *ee* in feel	OO	like the *oo* in pool
EH	like the *ai* in air	OW	like the *ow* in cow

U	like the *u* in put	Z	like the *s* in disease
UH	like the *u* in but	ZH	like the *g* in rouge
K	like the *c* in cat	J	like the *g* in George
KH	guttural	SH	like the *ch* in machine
S	like the *c* in cease	CH	like the *ch* in catch

BROADCAST STYLE

ABBREVIATIONS

No abbreviations should be used in radio or television news copy with these exceptions:

- Common usage: *Dr. Smith, Mrs. Jones, St. Paul*
- Names or organizations widely known by their initials: *U-N, F-B-I, G-O-P (but AFL-CIO)*
- Acronyms: *NATO*
- Time designations: *A-M, P-M*
- Academic degrees: *P-H-D*

PUNCTUATION

To indicate a pause where the newscaster can catch a breath, the dash or a series of dots is preferable to a comma:

> The House plans to give the 11-billion-500-million dollar measure a final vote Tuesday . . . and the Senate is expected to follow suit–possibly on the same day.

The hyphen is used instead of the period in initials: F-B-I. The period is retained, however, in initials in a name: J. D. Smith. All combined words should have the hyphen: co-worker, semi-annual. (Spelling should also use the form easiest to pronounce: employee.)

Contractions are more widely used in broadcast copy than in other news copy to provide a conversational tone. Common contractions—*isn't, doesn't, it's, they're*—may be used in both direct and indirect quotes:

> Members of the Transport Workers Union in San Francisco say if the municipal strike doesn't begin looking like a general strike by this afternoon, they'll reconsider their support of the walk-out. The refusal by drivers to cross picket lines set up by striking craft unions has shut down most transportation in the city.

Good broadcast writers, however, avoid contractions when they want to stress verbs, especially the negative: "She does not choose to run" instead of "She doesn't choose to run."

QUOTATION MARKS

The listener cannot see quotation marks. If the reporter tries to read them into the script—"quote" and "end of quote"—the sentence sounds trite and stilted. It is easier and more natural to indicate the speaker's words by phrases such as "and these are his words," "what she called," "he put it in these words," "the speaker said."

FIGURES

Numbers are tricky in broadcast copy. "A million" may sound like "8 million." No confusion results if "one million" is used.

In most copy, round numbers or approximations mean as much as specific figures. "Almost a mile" rather than "5,200 feet," "about half" rather than "48.2 percent" and "just under two percent" rather than "1.9 percent" are clearer to the listener.

An exception is vote results, especially when the margin is close. And it should be "100-to-95 vote" rather than "100-95 vote." The writer or editor can help the listener follow statistics or vote tallies by inserting phrases such as "in the closest race" and "in a landslide victory."

Here are some additional style rules for figures:

- Fractions and decimals should be spelled out: *one and seven-eighths* (not $1\frac{7}{8}$), *five-tenths* (not 0.5).

- Numbers under 10 and over 999 are spelled out and hyphenated: *one, two, two-thousand, 11-billion-500-million, 15-hundred* (rather than one-thousand-500), *one-and-a-half million dollars* (never $1.5 million).

- When two numbers occur together in a sentence, the smaller number should be spelled out: *twelve 20-ton trucks.*

- Any figure beginning a sentence should be spelled out.

- Figures are used for time of day *(4:30 this afternoon)*, in all market stories and in sports scores and statistics *(65-to-59, 5-foot-5)*. If results of horse races or track meets appear in the body of the story, the winning times should be spelled out: *two minutes, nine and three-tenths seconds* (rather than 2:9.3).

- In dates and addresses the *-st, -rd, -th* and *-nd* are included: *June 22nd, West 83rd Street.* Figures are used for years: *1998.*

- On approximate figures, writers sometimes say, "Police are looking for a man 50 to 60 years of age." This sounds like "52" to the listener. It should read, "Police are looking for a man between 50 and 60 years old."

TITLES

The identification or **title** prepares the ear for the name. Therefore, the identification usually precedes the name: Secretary of State Condoleezza Rice. Some titles are impossible to place before the name, such as: The vice president of the Society for the Preservation and Encouragement of Barbershop Quartet Singing, Joe Doe. Use "Vice President Joe Doe of the Society for the Preservation and Encouragement of Barbershop Quartet Singing." Use "Police Chief Don Vendel" rather than "Chief of Police Don Vendel."

Some radio and television newsrooms insist that the president should never be referred to by his last name alone. It would be President Bush, the president or Mr. Bush.

Broadcast copy seldom includes middle initials and ages of persons in the news. Of course, some initials are well-known parts of names and should be included: Richard M. Nixon.

Ages may be omitted unless the age is significant to the story: "A 12-year-old boy—Mitchell Smith—was crowned winner." Ages usually appear in local copy to aid in identification. Place the age close to the name. Do not say, "A 24-year-old university student died in a two-car collision today. He was John Doe." Use "A university student died in a two-car collision today. He was 24-year-old John Doe."

Obscure names need not be used unless warranted by the story. In many cases the name of the office or title suffices: "Peoria's police chief said . . . ." The same applies to little-known place names or to obscure foreign place names. If the location is important, identify it by placing it in relation to a well-known place: "approximately 100 miles south of Chicago." In local copy, most names and places are important to listeners and viewers.

When several proper names appear in the same story, it is better to repeat the name than to rely on pronouns unless the antecedent is obvious. Also, repeat the names rather than use *the former, the latter* or *respectively*.

DATELINES

The site of the action should be included in broadcast copy. The dateline may be used as an introduction or a transition: "In Miami." Or the location may be noted elsewhere in the lead: "The Green Bay Packers and the Chicago Bears meet in Chicago tonight in the annual charity football game."

On the newspaper wire, *here* refers to the place where the listener is. Because radio and television may cover a wide geographical area, such words as *here* and *local* should be avoided. A radio news editor said, "If the listener is sitting in a friendly poker game in Ludowici, Ga., and hears a radio report of mass gambling raids 'here,' he may leap from the window before realizing the announcer is broadcasting from Picayune, Miss."

TIME ANGLE

In the newspaper wire story almost everything happens *today*. Radio copy breaks up the day into its parts: *this morning, early tonight, just a few hours ago, at noon today*. The technique gives the listener a feeling of urgency in the news. Specific time should be translated for the time zone of the station's location: "That will be 2:30 Mountain Time."

In television especially, use of the present and present-perfect tenses helps downplay the time element:

> Searchers have found the wreckage of a twin-engine Air Force plane in Puerto Rico and continue to look for the bodies of six of the aircraft's eight crewmen. Authorities confirm that the plane, missing since Saturday, crashed atop a peak 25 miles southeast of San Juan.

TASTE

Broadcast news editors should be aware of all members of their audience—the young, the aged and the sensitive. Accident stories can be reported without the sordid details of gore and horror.

On many stations, someone other than a news reporter gives the commercials. One reason for this practice is to disassociate the newsperson from the commercial plugger. Even so, the director or reporter should know the content of commercials sandwiched in news. If a news story concerns a car crash in which several are killed, the item would not be placed ahead of a commercial for an automobile dealer. Airlines generally insist that their commercials be canceled for 24 hours if the newscast contains a story of an airliner crash, a policy that is likewise applied to many metropolitan newspapers.

But the sponsor does not control or censor the news. The story of a bank scandal should never be omitted from a news program sponsored by a bank. Nor should a sponsor ever expect sponsorship to earn news stories publicizing the business.

Should identification of accident victims be made before relatives have been notified? Some stations insist on getting the coroner's approval before releasing names of victims. If the release is not available, the tag would be, "Police are withholding the name of the victim until relatives have been notified."

In stories containing condition reports on persons in hospitals, the report should not carry over the same condition from one newscast to another without checking with the hospital to find out whether there has been a change.

SOUNDBITES

All news copy for radio and television should show the date, the time block, the story slug, the writer's name or initials, the story source and an indication whether the story has a companion audio or video. If more than one **soundbite** accompanies a story, the slug should indicate the number.

If a soundbite is used, a cue line is inserted for each. Many stations print the *outcues* (the last few words of the soundbite) in red ink, or place red quotation marks around the cue line. After the soundbite has played, the newscaster should again identify the speaker.

If several soundbites are used in one newscast, they should be spaced so that the same voices, or series of voices, are not concentrated in one part. The control room needs time to get the soundbites ready for broadcast.

The outcues should be noted in the *exact* words of the person interviewed. That will ensure that the engineer will not cut off the soundbite until the message is concluded. The producer should provide the engineer or board operator with a list of soundbites to be used and the order in which the producer intends to use them.

TELEVISION NEWS

Newspapers communicate with printed words, radio with spoken words and television with spoken words and moving pictures. Editing a television news or special event show involves all three. Television news editing is the marriage of words to pictures, words to sound and pictures to sound (see Figure 13–2).

Reuven Frank, former president of NBC News, contended that the highest power of television is to produce an experience. Television cannot typically disseminate as much information as newspapers, magazines or even radio. But in many instances, it causes viewers to undergo an experience similar to what would happen if they were at the scene.

One can feel sympathy when reading about bombed civilians or the drowning of a child at a swimming pool. But watching the same thing on a television newscast is a wrenching personal experience that gets people worked up, even angry. Television is an instrument of power, not because of the facts it relates but because of the experience it conveys to viewers.

Words speak for themselves to the newspaper reader. In radio, a newscaster voices the words for the listener. In television, the newscaster is there, in the viewer's living room, talking directly, eye-to-eye to the viewer about the news. The newscaster is the key actor. Many a station has fallen behind in ratings for its news shows, not because the station did not have good reporters and camera operators or lacked a well-paced news format, but because competing stations had better on-air talent.

Figure 13–2   Interior of CNN control room.
Photo by Bob Krist/Bettman/Corbis.

In the early days of television, stations hired journalists to report and write the news, then handed over the polished manuscript to a good-looking announcer with mellifluous tones. Today, more and more newscasters are men and women who may not sound or look like movie stars but who know what they are talking about.

News editing, the sorting or processing of the news, requires more time for television than for radio. Producers and writers must spend hours reviewing, sifting and editing all the material available for a single half-hour newscast. They use these criteria in selecting items: how significant the item is, whether it is interesting either factually or visually, how long it is and how well its content complements the rest of the program.

Before local video is edited, it must be examined to determine how much to cut. Sometimes a video may have relatively little news value but is included because of its visual quality. A barn fire might not rate mention on a radio newscast, but the video could be spectacular.

Network tapes also are examined. Afternoon network news stories are reviewed to determine what can be lifted for the late-evening local news program. The networks provide their affiliates with an afternoon news feed for use as the affiliates see fit. This closed-circuit feed from New York consists of overset material not used on the network news. These feeds are recorded and usually include more than a dozen one- to two-minute video stories from the nation and the world. The producer has to monitor these feeds to decide which stories to use.

In addition to editing video reports, the producer must go over the vast number of news service stories and pictures, not to mention stories filed by local reporters. Having selected what to use, the producer's next job is to determine how and where it can be used within the time allotted the news show.

Video editing systems transformed television news production procedures following the heydey of film. The editor plays back on one recording machine the pictures shot in the field, selects the shots he or she wants, their length and order, and assembles the edited story by transfer-dubbing those shots to a second cassette in another recorder (see Figure 13–3). Today, digital editing is replacing videotape, making editing even easier and more precise.

Figure 13–3   A video editor takes direction
Photo by John Coletti/Photolibrary.com

In a typical newscast, the anchorman and anchorwoman, sitting in a brightly lighted studio set, read stories into studio cameras. They also introduce edited stories, which beam onto the air when the director instructs an engineer to start.

The minicam's portability has added a new dimension to local television newscasts. Lightweight transmitters allow a reporter and engineer to beam live reports back from remote locations—even from an airborne helicopter—straight to the station and onto the air. Portable editing rigs mean the remote reports can include packaged pieces, as well.

More and more broadcasts are also making use of video from the Web. Such video is often amateurishly produced and of inferior technical quality. But viewers don't seem to mind the pixilated images or digital noise, especially when it's footage otherwise unavailable. In fact, *citizen journalism*—where ordinary people who happen to be where news strikes gather sound and video, for example, with their cell phones and send it to a station or to the Web—has added a new dimension to journalism in recent years.

COPY FORMATS

There are almost as many copy formats and scripting styles as there are broadcast newsrooms. Terminology varies, as well. In one newsroom the script designation *voiceover,* or *VO,* might mean that a newscaster is reading over video; in another newsroom *voiceover* might mean that the reporter's recorded voice is running with video.

Figure 13–4 is a typical script from KOMU-TV in Columbia, Mo. It is from a 6 o'clock newscast devoted to local news. The robbery arrest story calls for the newscaster to read it all, but after a few lines the picture will change from the newscaster's face to video illustrating the story. The script instructions tell the director that the video source is ENG (electronic news gathering) videotape, to begin as the newscaster says "an eyewitness" and to last for 22 seconds. Other designations show the number of the cassette, the location of the story on the cassette ("Cut 1 cued") and whatever written information ("key") will be superimposed on the screen and when.

A good television script should not compete with the pictures. It should prepare viewers for what they are about to see or specify what may be difficult to see, but it should avoid repeating what viewers can see or hear. If the mayor has criticized the city's water supply and his statement is on video, the script merely sets up the statement with a brief introduction. Good scripts also direct the viewer's attention to significant details in the video, but they should avoid phrases such as "we're now looking" or "this picture shows."

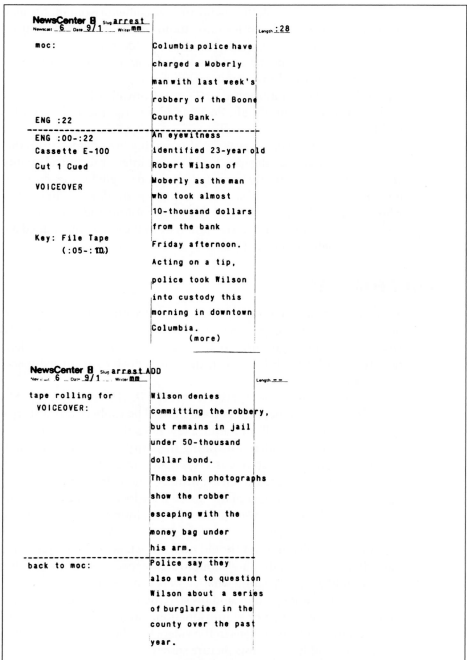

Figure 13–4   Television script indicating use of voiceover. The newscaster continues to read the script while videotape illustrates the story.
Courtesy of KOMU-TV, Columbia, Mo.

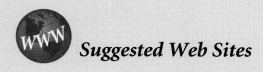 *Suggested Web Sites*

National Association of Broadcasters **www.nab.org**
Radio–Television News Directors Association and Foundation **www.rtnda.org**

Suggested Readings

Block, Mervin. *Rewriting Network News: Wordwatching Tips from 345 TV and Radio Scripts.* Chicago: Bonus Books, 1990.

Block, Mervin, Jr., and Joe Durso. *Writing News for TV and Radio: The Interactive CD and Handbook.* New York: Bonus Books, 1999.

Dotson, Bob, Matt Lauer, and Mervin Block. *Make It Memorable: Writing and Packaging TV News With Style.* New York: Bonus Books, 2000.

Kalbfeld, Brad. *Associated Press Broadcast News Handbook.* New York: McGraw-Hill, 2000.

Tompkins, Al. *Aim for the Heart, Write for the Ear, Shoot for the Eye: A Guide for TV Producers and Reporters.* New York: Bonus Books, 2002.

CHAPTER 14

EDITING IN OTHER FIELDS

Many students who take journalism classes are preparing for careers in fields other than newspapers, magazines, radio, TV or the Internet. Rather than writing or editing news, many of them will make a living writing public-relations press releases or advertising copy, and some will edit books. We'd like to take a brief look here at the role editing plays in three other career choices for journalism majors: public relations, advertising and book publishing.

JOB OPPORTUNITIES IN PUBLIC RELATIONS AND ADVERTISING

Public relations and advertising—unlike newspapers, magazines, newsletters, the Web, radio, television and books—aren't media but rather adjuncts closely connected to the media. Advertising is the major way American media are financed (except books, movies and music), and PR is one of the major sources of news in the United States (with about half of news stories originating from a press release).

Both advertising and PR try to influence our attitudes about businesses, groups, people and issues, but there are some distinctions between PR and advertising:

- Advertising has been described as overt persuasion, public relations as covert persuasion.
- Advertising sells products; public relations fosters good will for an organization, person or cause.
- Advertising works mainly through mass media, although it may be through smaller alternative media like fliers; public relations works through news releases, press conferences, publicity events, sponsorships—and sometimes advertisements.

- Mass media charge for advertising space or time, but they often give free publicity.
- Advertising is regulated by the government; PR isn't.
- The main difference is that advertising messages are controlled by those who put them out, but PR messages aren't—they're at the mercy of journalists.

Someone pays to have their advertising message placed in the media to sell you something. Public relations is a message someone wants to get out to the public, and it becomes news if a journalist agrees it's newsworthy.

There are more than 13,000 ad agencies and 2,200 PR firms in the United States, and many more work outside agencies. For example, the media themselves hire people to create their own advertisements. In fact, this is one place new advertising graduates get their first job. And many people who do public relations are employed directly within businesses, nonprofits or government agencies, or work as volunteers to help their church, school or fraternal organization with publicity.

Advertising and public-relations jobs, even starting ones, tend to pay much more than comparable media jobs—typically 20 percent more with an ad agency than doing comparable work in media. Some people who initially go into journalism take their experience and switch to public relations, in part for the higher salary.

Many of the best-paying introductory jobs in writing and editing are in communications departments of corporations—putting out employee newsletters, annual reports, and magazines and brochures for customers. Such a job can be a good high-pay alternative to a traditional media job, as well as a way of breaking into the magazine industry. And if you're a woman, as the majority of journalism graduates have been for the past 30 years, you may be interested to know that women tend to rise faster in advertising and PR than anywhere else in the media.

Public-relations jobs can be in industry, government agencies or nonprofit associations. These jobs involve a wide variety of activities: spoken, written or broadcast communication; speechwriting; writing and editing publications; preparing financial reports; writing proposals; researching and monitoring issues; fund-raising; dealing with the media; publicizing products and programs; promoting a corporate image; or lobbying of government.

The one thing people hiring for public-relations positions insist on is good writing skills. A survey of PR directors reported in 2002 in *Public Relations: Strategies and Tactics* said the most important traits they look for when hiring are, in this order:

1. Ability to write.
2. Verbal skills.
3. Professionalism.
4. Maturity.

5. Poise.

6. Appearance.

Bad traits, they said, are the inability to work with others rather than independently, having an inflated opinion of your own writing ability and an inability to compromise.

⤴ PUBLIC RELATIONS

Public-relations practitioners and corporate communications specialists are called on almost daily to write and edit news releases. In most cases, a news release is written in the inverted-pyramid format on the assumption that the person who reads it will skim the release quickly to see whether anything in it is of interest.

Typically, the audience for which news releases are intended is working journalists—newspaper city editors and broadcast station news directors. The release attempts to provide basic information about a topic. It's understood that the newspaper or broadcast station will not use the release verbatim. If the story is used at all, it likely will become the genesis of the media outlet's own story.

News releases usually come in three varieties:

- Announcement of a coming event or action (see Figure 14–1).
- Information promoting a cause.
- Information designed to build an image.

The best releases quickly and succinctly give the media the information they need. The releases also explain where to go for more information. In all cases, news releases must be accurate and truthful. Editors who feel misled by inflated or overstated releases soon learn to ignore the next one from the same organization.

It's important for the promotional writer to remember that the media are inundated with news releases. Releases with the best chance of attracting attention have a local news hook, are short and to the point, are clearly written and follow journalistic conventions of the medium for which they're aimed. Promotional writers will also find that it's much easier to get attention from editors with whom they have developed a working relationship. Like journalists, promotional writers must develop strong principles of professional ethics. Truthfulness is the foundation on which successful public relations careers are built.

Promotional writers and editors also produce corporate reports, manuals and other material that will be used both inside the company and by external audiences. In each case, the quality of the publication directly affects the improvement or deterioration of the corporate image. Audiences often judge institutions by the quality of the written materials they produce.

TUE 14:59 FAX 972 487 0655 GARLAND NEWS 002

Pastor co-hosts Internet luncheon

By Chris McGathey
The Garland News

In response to growing problems with Internet sites that produce hate, violence, and pornography, several Metroplex pastors, including Dr. Steve Davis of First Baptist Church, will co-host an Internet safety luncheon Thursday.

Life Way*online*, a new Internet filter service provided by LifeWay Christian Resources, is hosting the event at the Hilton DFW Lakes, 1800 Highway 23 E, Grapevine.

Dr. Mark Laaser, executive director of the Christian Alliance for Sexual Recovery and author of Faithful and True, will be the featured speaker. The book is part of a recovery series published by LifeWay Christian Resources. Dr. Mike Miller, director of LifeWay Church Leaderships is also scheduled to speak.

Davis' co-hosts are Dr. Claude Thomas of First Baptist Church, Euless; Steve Stroope of Lake Pointe Baptist Church, Rockwall; Dr. James McGlothlin of Lakeside Baptist Church, Dallas; Dr. Charles Cruce of Lamar Baptist Church; and Ken Sharp of Irving's Christian Counseling Centers.

The pastor's luncheon is the first of 28 luncheons LifeWay will sponsor throughout the nation. The conference theme is, "For Such A Time As This — Cyberspace Armor For the 21st Century Church," based on Bible passages.

"An Internet filter is a simple, common-sense solution to the problem of inappropriate Web sites," Davis said. "As church leaders, we need to help our congregations understand the enormity of the problem and the importance of protecting their family members from potential dangers on the Internet."

"As church leaders, we need to help our congregations understand the enormity of the problem and the importance of protecting their family members."

—Dr. Steve Davis
First Baptist Church

Davis said that over the last 3-5 years he has counseled married couples who have had mates addicted to inappropriate material on the Internet.

Pastors who attend the luncheon will have an opportunity for their congregations to participate in a seminar about sexual addictions and Internet safety through Laaser's organization.

"Sexual addiction is the fastest growing addiction in America and the Internet provides instant access to pornographic sites," said Laaser, a former pastor who said he lost his ministry due to sexual addiction. "It's an explosive combination with potentially devastating consequences."

Laasar underwent an extensive recovery process and now counsels pastors and others who have sexual addictions.

According to *Focus on The Families*, in Citizens magazine, an estimated 260 new pornographic sites are added to the Internet every day. A recent Associated Press story cited a college psychologists' study that found at least 200,000 Internet users are hooked on porn sites, X-rated chat rooms or other sexual materials online.

The study led researchers to conclude that Internet pornography, "is a hidden public health hazard, exploding because very few are recognizing it as such or taking it seriously."

According to Laaser, one of the reasons the Internet is so powerful is because it is so private.

"No responsible parent would want a pornographer teaching his or her children about sex, yet the Internet has the ability to bring an adult bookstore into the privacy of one's home," Laaser said. "We are bringing a message of warning to churches and families about the potential dangers of the Internet and a message of hope to those caught in the destructive cycle of inappropriate Internet use."

Figure 14–1** **Example of a story about an upcoming event, typically prompted by a press release received at the newspaper.
Source: The Garland News.

A good example is IBM, which won the Malcolm Baldridge Award for its high-quality products. But its image still suffered because the manuals that accompanied these products were "written backward," in the words of many critics. To find what you wanted in an IBM manual, the joke went, you turned to the back of the manual first.

In too many cases, there was truth in that criticism. As a result, the company launched an effort to streamline and simplify its product manuals based on time-tested principles of simplicity in writing and editing.

If you're going into public relations, the best tip is to write your press releases as much like a news stories as possible. Use *The AP Stylebook* for newspaper press releases and the AP's broadcast version for releases going to radio or television outlets. The more your press release resembles a news story, the easier it will be for the editor to recognize its potential and the more likely your message will get through.

Don't make the mistake common among amateurs of writing your press release like an ad. If editors run it at all, the first thing they'll do is take out all the nonobjective, self-serving language. They'll also refocus the story on what they think is news their audience will find useful or interesting—which may not be the message you were trying to get across.

So, in writing a press release, ask yourself the same question the editor would: Where is the news here? By focusing your press release on that angle and following regular journalistic style, you'll increase your chances of being heard.

PRINT ADVERTISING

The media depend on the professionals who create advertising to bring home the revenue that pays the bills. News departments inevitably are drains on company resources. Advertising departments, on the other hand, create the revenue to support news operations.

Print advertising specialists, in particular, borrow many techniques from the news department. Key among them is learning to write a headline that sells. Like the news headline writer who tries to lure the reader into the story, the ad headline writer lures the reader to the wares of a paying customer. In both cases, the headline is expected to be compelling.

Alastair Crompton, a British advertising expert, writes in *The Craft of Copywriting*:

> One point I cannot emphasize too strongly. There can be times when a headline [in an advertisement] does not need an illustration; but there can never be a time when an illustration doesn't need a headline. Of course you will see ads that go straight into the body copy from the picture: I call these ads "headless wonders." They are the occasions when the copywriter has copped out. Advice to art directors: Never let your writer make you run an ad without a headline. If he suggests it, tell him not to be so damned lazy. A great picture deserves a great line to back it up; even the painting of the Mona Lisa in the Louvre needs a small brass plate underneath reading "La Gioconda by Leonardo da Vinci."

The relationship between the photograph or illustration in a print ad and the headline is critical to an ad's success. The two must work together, not compete, Crompton says. He warns the beginning ad designer not to let a picture simply illustrate the headline. Instead, he urges, make sure the two key parts of the ad do their own half of the work.

Both the advertising illustration and the headline are designed to catch quickly the reader's attention. That's because most readers spend no more than a second or two scanning an ad. If it doesn't sell immediately, it's unlikely to sell at all. For that reason, the elaborate rules for writing news headlines are abandoned in advertising. Ad headlines often don't have verbs. Sometimes, they are prepositional phrases. Occasionally, there may be no complete thought at all. Some examples:

Ontario, Canada
We treat you royally.

The sound of fast relief. Plop, plop, fizz, fizz.

In each case, the ad's purpose is clear. Most readers will instantly recognize the first as a tourist ad for Ontario and the second as one for Alka Seltzer. One of the classic advertising headlines of all time was one simple word below a picture of a Volkswagen Beetle:

Lemon.

Readers were instantly drawn to the ad, wondering why Volkswagen would label one of its products with the most derogatory of all comments about cars. In the text block that followed, readers learned why: The car in the photograph, perfect on the outside, had been rejected by a Volkswagen inspector for a tiny blemish on the glove box. The ad highlighted Volkswagen's commitment to quality. Such eye-catching cleverness is what the advertising creative process is all about.

The lemon headline is a classic example of the *curiosity headline,* one of the three types used in advertisements. The others are news headlines and benefit headlines. *News headlines,* as the name implies, do much the same job as those in the news pages: They inform. *Benefit headlines* help the reader understand why he or she should be interested: **Earn money in your spare time.** Curiosity headlines, like the one for Volkswagen, can be fun to write but are risky. If the reader isn't curious, the ad fails.

Getting the reader's attention with a compelling headline and a quality illustration is merely the beginning of the creative process. Once the writer has the reader's attention, it's time to follow up with material to show the reader why he or she should be interested:

Headline: **Everything from A to Sea.**
Follow-up: With so much to do at Hilton beach resorts, the only hard part is deciding what to do first. Whether you want to stretch your legs with a game of tennis or just stretch out for a few winks. Come discover the ways to play that suit your style. For information and reservations, call your professional travel agent, Hilton's Resort Desk at 1-800-221-2424 or 1-800-HILTONS.

After the ad captures the reader's interest, it builds desire for the product—in this case a resort vacation—and tries to convince the reader to act. Here, the objective is to convince the reader to call Hilton for more information.

The four-step process used in the Hilton ad is one known to advertisers as AIDA:

1. Attract ATTENTION.
2. Build INTEREST.
3. Create DESIRE.
4. Compel ACTION.

Too often, though, ads fall victim to the same problems that plague the news—incorrect grammar, spelling errors and similar unforgivable mistakes. Protecting and polishing the language is just as important in ads as in news. Educated consumers find such mistakes irritating, and as a result they may vow never to buy the product. When that happens, the ad has the opposite result from the one intended.

BROADCAST ADVERTISING

Like online journalists, broadcast advertisers must learn to work with all forms of communication—the written word, graphics, audio and video. All combine to produce one of the most effective forms of communication ever devised: broadcast advertising.

With radio ads, it's relatively easy to play tricks on listeners with sound effects and simple devices like British accents because radio has only one dimension: sound. But too often, radio ad writers merely repeat trite approaches such as easy humor based on some person who doesn't use the product talking with someone who does. And radio ad readers and actors too often sound unnatural or phony.

Radio ads have only one dimension: audio. Television ads, on the other hand, become major productions. They are expensive to produce, and they must combine the effective use of audio, video and graphic design. Once produced, the television ad competes with dozens of others for the viewer's attention and often is sandwiched between them.

Writing and editing a compelling script is merely the beginning of the process of creating a successful television commercial. Creative video and audio production are critical to its success. Finally, editing it all together is a talent that is much in demand.

JOBS IN BOOK PUBLISHING

Books, like magazines, are actually doing better now than earlier in the previous century. Book publishing had trouble from 1910 to the 1950s but has been picking up in the past 60 years. In 1950, about 11,000 new book titles were published a year. By 2005, that was up to more than 172,000.

In dollar terms, book publishing in 1947 was a mere $435 million industry, but by 2005 it was a $36 billion industry.

If you'd like to go into book publishing as a career, English is a good major, but perhaps even better is journalism, partly because most books published are nonfiction. Also, journalism school is one of the best places to learn grammar, usage, tightening, adherence to a stylebook and copy-editing symbols. (Yes, editing symbols are still used in book publishing despite the rise of the computer.)

After you graduate, there are two main career paths into the book publishing world. One is to work for a university press or specialty press, such as Gale Publishing in the Detroit area, which caters especially to library reference-department sales. Specialty and university presses are found all over the country, meaning near you wherever you are right now.

A second approach is to attend a publishing institute, the most famous of which is the six-week summer one that used to be at Radcliffe until it moved to Columbia University in 2000. Here are the addresses for some:

University of Denver Publishing Institute
2075 S. University Blvd. D114
Denver, Colo. 80210

Columbia Publishing Course
(formerly Radcliffe Publishing Course)
Columbia University Graduate School of Journalism
2950 Broadway, MC 3801
New York, N.Y. 10027

Department of Professional Studies and Special Programs
Emerson College
120 Boylston St.
Boston, Mass. 02116

Summer Publishing Institute
New York University
School of Continuing and Professional Studies
Center for Publishing
11 West 42nd St., Room 400
New York, N.Y. 10036

To keep up on the book publishing business, read *Publishers Weekly* and *Retail Bookseller*. Also, follow the *New York Review of Books* and *The New York Times* best-seller lists.

In the interest of full disclosure, we should also mention the bad news in book publishing: Entry-level jobs with major publishers are among the most competitive, and editorial assistants typically make about the same as beginning journalists. Also, the jobs often aren't very stable. There's a rapid turnover, similar to broadcasting, with people often switching jobs. Adding to the turnover is the fact that mergers in recent years have tended to consolidate companies, close offices and lay off employees.

Also of interest is the fact that most publishers have only small staffs and use lots of freelancers. After the acquisitions editor scouts out and signs authors for book deals, an in-house editor works with the author in shaping the book. But at that point, the copy editing, design, production, proofreading and indexing may all be done by freelancers. This means you may be able to freelance from your home doing these editing tasks, and they often pay well.

Until recently, book publishers tended to ask authors for computer files of chapters but edited them on hardcopy manuscript pages using standard copy-editing symbols. More and more, however, editing is done online using tracking and comment features of Microsoft Word or e-mails referring to posted Adobe pdf files of pages. Copy editors suggest changes to the authors or ask questions about vague passages, and the authors accept or reject the changes and answer the questions.

After the edited manuscript is formatted, the author is sent proofs to approve. A second set of page proofs goes to a freelance proofreader, and, for most non-fiction titles, a third set goes to a freelance indexer. The final corrections are made, the index is formatted, and the book goes into print—usually about 18 months after the initial book deal was made.

If you go into book publishing, it will be useful to familiarize yourself with stylebooks other than *The AP Stylebook* so universal in journalism. More common in the book world are *The Chicago Manual of Style* and *Words Into Type,* but other stylebooks might be used depending on the field of the book. For example, the editor of a book of literary criticism will probably use Modern Language Association style, while the editor of a psychology book will probably use the style of the American Psychological Association.

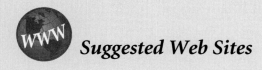

Suggested Web Sites

Advertising Age   **www.adage.com**
The Editorial Eye   **www.eeicommunications.com/eye**
New York Review of Books   **www.nybooks.com**
Publisher's Weekly   **http://publishersweekly.com**

Suggested Readings

Wilcox, Dennis L., and Glen T. Cameron. *Public Relations: Strategies and Tactics.* 8th edition. Boston: Allyn and Bacon, 2005.

Judd, Karen. *Copyediting: A Practical Guide.* 3rd edition. Menlo Park, Calif.: Crisp Publications, 2001.

New York Review of Books.

Publisher's Weekly.

Rabiner, Susan, and Alfred Fortunato. *Thinking Like Your Editor: How to Write Great Serious Nonfiction—and Get It Published.* New York: W. W. Norton, 2003.

Retail Bookseller.

Skillin, Marjorie E., and Robert M. Gay. *Words Into Type.* 3rd edition. Englewood Cliffs, N.J.: Prentice-Hall, 1974.

University of Chicago Press Staff. *The Chicago Manual of Style.* 15th edition. Chicago: University of Chicago Press, 2003.

CHAPTER 15

THE EDITOR AS COACH

People often enter the field of journalism because they enjoyed writing for their high school newspaper, delighted in editing the yearbook or worked part-time at a local radio station. Typically, they rank among the top graduates of their high school because they write well, a critical skill for succeeding in life.

Then they get to college and take a course in news writing. More often than not, in the first couple of weeks a professor unmercifully rips into something they have written with harsh criticism. Sound familiar? It probably does because this has happened to all of us. Here's a bit of advice: Get used to it.

The truth is that the print media are as good as they are because the coaching of writers and fixing of stories (some would less charitably call it second-guessing) never ends. Ideally, every point in a story should be checked, double-checked and checked again. Every phrase should be tuned and retuned to make certain it communicates as effectively as possible. Given the number of editors involved in producing a large newspaper or magazine, a story can be edited as many as a dozen times with each editor changing, adding or subtracting.

More often than not, the result of that process is an improved story. But it's undeniably true that one lousy editor—or teacher—can spoil the whole thing. When that occurs, you're likely to hear a reporter howling, "He butchered my story!" But it's also likely that you'll hear: "Oops. The copy desk saved me on that one!"

In the media environment, teamwork is essential. It's important not to take the criticism of your work personally, and it's important to understand that the whole process results in better newspapers, magazines, broadcasts and Web sites. When the process works best, the reporter reports and writes, the editor coaches and fixes, and the story gets better. With that in mind, let's take a look at some of the key relationships in the editing process.

THE ASSIGNMENT EDITOR AND THE REPORTER

In any medium, the relationship between a reporter and the *assignment editor* (this can be a city editor, a sports editor, a television news director, etc.) is critical. Story ideas come from any of these individuals. Assignment editors like reporters who come up with many of their own ideas because this eliminates the need for the editor to brainstorm for a whole staff of reporters.

Once the story idea is assigned, the reporter must understand how that editor wants it written or produced. It's useful, indeed almost essential, to have a good understanding of the editor's desires before leaving on assignment. What often happens, though, is that a story turns out to be something quite different from what the editor or reporter originally conceived.

Think of the reporting process as something quite similar to the process a researcher employs when using scientific investigation methods. A good reporter begins the fact-gathering process with a hypothesis and then determines whether this hypothesis is correct or incorrect. The reporter then returns to report the findings objectively.

When reporters return from reporting assignments, no matter the medium, they first sit down with the assignment editor to review what's there. Together, the two set the final direction for the story based on the facts the reporter uncovered.

"That's not the story I sent you out to get," says the assignment editor.

"That story doesn't exist," replies the reporter. "I'm giving you the story as I found it."

"OK, let's do it," the editor decides.

Or perhaps the editor is convinced that the reporter did a lousy reporting job and simply didn't get the information that's there. In this case, the reporter may be sent back into the field, and publication or broadcast of the story may be delayed.

When the story finally is ready for editing, the reporter and editor usually sit down together to review it. Words and video clips (yes, the writing process occurs in television, too) are added or deleted until both parties are satisfied with the product.

From there the story goes to other editors, who also may make changes. Regardless, the relationship between an assignment editor and a reporter is always one of the most critical in the news business.

The Assignment Editor As Coach and Fixer

Roy Peter Clark and Don Fry, in their landmark book *Coaching Writers: Editors and Reporters Working Together Across Media Platforms,* describe **coaching of writers** as a two-way process in which the coach asks good questions but also listens. They suggest that the process works best when reporters and editors share control of a story.

"All stories need some degree of editorial touch-up and repair," Clark and Fry write, "but the good editor prefers to leave control with the writer, even if significant changes are needed." Thus, a good editor helps a reporter fix a story while allowing the reporter, who is closest to the subject matter, to feel in full control. Editors who steal control and take a slash-and-burn approach to editing almost invariably introduce inaccuracies and distortions.

Clark and Fry point out that fixing a story is not the same as coaching. "Coaching is the human side of editing, fixing the literary side. In other words, the editor coaches the writer but fixes the story."

Editors who approach the process as coaches become valuable allies of reporters rather than antagonists. In the absence of coaching, what happens is that story-editing sessions breed ill will, verbal outbursts and occasionally even fisticuffs.

Good editors understand there is a delicate balance here. Coaching is all-important for a variety of reasons, but as deadline approaches, fixing the story becomes more important than coaching. Delicately handling both coaching and fixing is one mark of a first-rate editor.

The Assignment Editor As Coach and Mentor

As Clark and Fry suggest, the editing process works best when the editor assumes the role of coach and mentor rather than the role of adversary. Editors who treat reporters as they would like to be treated invariably are more successful than those who do not. The editor who has won the reporter's confidence as coach, ally and mentor is in much better position to fix what needs to be fixed because he or she has the confidence and respect of the writer.

Old-timers in the news business tell stories for hours on end about the cigar-chomping editors of the past who took belts from a bottle of booze on a regular basis and took delight in unmercifully chopping reporters' stories to shreds. In some cases, their managers even worsened such environments by pitting reporters against each other in a process they derisively called **creative tension.** In that system, two reporters often were sent out to get the same story. The one who produced the best story saw it published, and the other was chastised or even fired. One can imagine how well reporters reacted to that atmosphere.

Today, some editors are still inclined to do lots of fixing and little coaching, but mercifully they are increasingly rare. In today's world, most editors are smart enough to realize that a positive work environment in which reporters are encouraged and rewarded yields far better results than intimidation. Reporters who find themselves with editors who like to be adversaries quickly move to other jobs.

Good reporters simply will not put up with a stressful work environment in which top-down managers think they know it all.

Most editors understand that reporters are happier and more productive when they work in an environment that rewards and nourishes rather than one that denigrates and discourages. In the end, when reporters feel good about their relationships with their editors, job satisfaction is likely to be high. When that occurs, almost invariably the reporters get better and their productivity increases. Moreover, better journalism is produced.

THE ASSIGNMENT EDITOR AND THE PRODUCTION EDITORS

After the reporter has written or produced a story, and after it is edited into final form by the assignment editor, it goes to another editor for production. At a newspaper or magazine, it goes to the copy desk, where a copy-desk chief reviews it before assigning it to a copy editor for final edit. At a television station, the story goes from the assignment editor to the producer, who is responsible for putting together the newscast. At a Web site, the copy goes from an assignment editor to the **Web producer,** who reworks the story for that medium. All are **production editors** who review the original creation and prepare it for print, broadcast or the Web. Sometimes they are called **reviewing editors.** These editors are found in every medium and even in advertising, where an account executive or manager edits the copy of an advertising copywriter.

In all of these cases, the story goes from someone who considers it a finished product to someone who is reviewing it for the first time. Often, the production editor is not quite as satisfied with the story as the writer and assignment editor may have been. The production editor is reading or viewing the story as a reader or viewer would look at it. In that sense, the production editor becomes the reader's advocate, asking questions the typical reader is likely to ask.

At this point, problems often occur for the following reasons:

- **The reporter and assignment editor are so close to the story that they understand it, but they fail to explain it to the reader.**   In other words, the story is too fuzzy to comprehend.

- **The story leaves out essential background information.**   This occurs when the reporter and assignment editor are so familiar with the story that they assume everyone is. You cannot assume that the reader read the last story on the subject. In a sentence or two, you must explain the background.

- **The story contains internal inconsistencies.**   For example, when a total amount appropriated by the legislature appears in the lead, do the breakout numbers in the paragraphs below add up to the total? Does the spelling of a name change between paragraphs two and nine?

- **The story leaves out essential facts.**   If the story is a preview of the City Council meeting, are readers informed when and where it will be held?

Unfortunately, these problems are common and sometimes lead to awkward situations. Say, for example, that a newspaper copy editor detects a critical missing piece of information in a story. The story simply cannot run that way, yet it has already cleared the desk of the metropolitan editor, who outranks the copy editor. What happens?

Most newspapers and magazines, and some broadcast stations, have protocols for handling such situations. At some, the copy editor is encouraged to go straight to the reporter for the missing information. At others, protocol requires that the copy editor go back through the chain of command. The copy editor would call the problem to the attention of his boss, the copy-desk chief, who in turn would take up the matter with the metro editor, her equivalent in rank. The metro editor would then call the reporter to provide the answer.

Whatever the process, it's important to understand that the media industry relies heavily on collaboration and teamwork. No one should be offended by being questioned about a mistake. We all make them. The idea is to have several sets of eyes on each story so that mistakes are minimized.

THE PRODUCTION EDITORS AND THE SUPERVISOR

The newscast producer, the newspaper or magazine copy editor, and the Web producer are often the last editors to see or read a story before it is printed, broadcast or put online. Because of this responsibility, they exercise tremendous authority in the media hierarchy.

The newspaper copy editor, for example, is considered the rough equivalent of a reporter in seniority and pay but in some respects has just as much power as an assignment editor. Perhaps that's why some large newspapers historically have paid higher salaries to copy editors than reporters. At unionized newspapers, there often is a **copy-desk differential** that adds to a copy editor's weekly paycheck. Although the base pay of a reporter and a copy editor with similar experience may be the same, the differential means that the copy editor's take-home pay is higher.

Typically, production editors—copy editors and broadcast producers—are the beneficiaries of incredible respect in the office. Someone who tackles the responsibility of serving as the final editor for a story earns, and deserves, plenty of respect. Good production editors are difficult to find, so when supervisors do find them they offer plenty of support. Some of the closest relationships you'll find at a newspaper are among the copy-desk chief and his or her copy editors.

That trust and respect are earned, not given freely. Newcomers to the copy desk and new television producers can expect to receive close scrutiny in the early months of employment. As they earn the trust of their supervisors, their standing in the newsroom rises quickly and dramatically.

 ## EDITORS COACHING JUNIOR EDITORS

Editors learn by watching and emulating other editors. Good ones emulate the best editors, not those who vacillate and cut corners.

Too often, senior editors fail to coach junior editors as they develop their editing skills. In the rush of day-to-day production, they take the attitude that there simply isn't time. But the reality is that failure to coach junior editors leads to job dissatisfaction for the junior editor and frustration on the part of the senior editor with the junior editor's work. Because of that, failure to take the time to coach junior editors becomes a fatal flaw that invariably results in problems.

For more than 50 years, the Dow Jones Newspaper Fund has operated a copy-editing internship program for college students as a way of drawing students to editing careers. Too many students are enamored with bylines and fail to consider editing as a career. The Newspaper Fund seeks to increase the pool of copy editors—many of whom eventually become assignment editors, managing editors and executive editors—by providing good internship experiences and scholarships.

What is the biggest single complaint of those who participate in the program? When supervising editors fail to provide adequate feedback on how the intern is progressing. One student repeatedly sought a performance review from his copy-desk chief at the large Midwest newspaper where he was working. When it didn't occur after weeks and weeks of asking, he sought feedback from an executive editor and incurred the wrath of his supervising editor. The intern, the junior editor, was totally frustrated, and the copy-desk chief was furious, despite the fact that she caused the problem by not doing her job in the first place.

The Newspaper Fund, to its credit, dropped that newspaper from its lineup the next summer so another student would not have a similar experience. Over the years, it has dropped other papers when supervising editors shirked their responsibility to junior editors.

It doesn't have to work that way, and at good media operations, it doesn't. Some newspapers, for example, go to great lengths to have formal training programs for interns, away from the daily grind of the desk, and others insist that supervisors hold weekly critique sessions with interns and new hires.

As a junior editor, don't be afraid to:

- Ask your supervisor for regular updates on how you are performing.
- Inquire about your relative strengths and weaknesses. Understanding your weaknesses lets you know which areas of your work need improvement.

- Seek help from more experienced peers. You'll quickly determine who the best ones are. Ask for their help, and emulate their work habits.

And remember this: When you become a supervising editor, embrace the role of mentor, coach and teacher. You, your subordinate and your media outlet will improve as a direct result of your efforts.

SOME ADVICE FOR BEGINNERS

So much of practicing journalism involves learning to work as part of a newsroom team. Here are some tips for those entering the business:

- **Embrace the editing process.**   Understand that editing almost invariably makes the product better.

- **Embrace the coaching process.**   Take criticism of your work not as something personal but as an opportunity to improve.

- **Find peers to respect and emulate.**   Almost every newsroom has role models for you to follow. Watch what the pros do and how they do it. Similarly, avoid the bad habits of the worst.

- **Seek advice.**   Don't come across as a know-it-all. Show your editors that you are willing to grow professionally and improve your skills.

- **Don't be seen as a complainer.**   Remember that no workplace is perfect. Keep your complaints to yourself or complain directly to your supervisor, not to the entire newsroom.

- **Work hard.**   People advance to higher positions in the news business when they outwork and outperform their peers.

- **Adhere to the highest standards of ethics.**   If you see a co-worker take ethical shortcuts, quietly report that to your boss. Never, ever take an ethical shortcut yourself.

- **Adhere to the highest standards of excellence.**   Practice good journalism in every story, no matter how long or how short. There is no such thing as an unimportant news story.

- **Never be satisfied with your work.**   You can always get better.

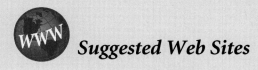 **Suggested Web Sites**

American Society of Newspaper Editors   **www.asne.org**
Radio–Television News Directors Association and Foundation   **www.rtnda.org**
The Poynter Institute   **www.poynter.org**

Suggested Readings

Clark, Roy Peter. *Free to Write: A Journalist Teaches Young Writers.* Portsmouth,
N.H.: Heinemann, 1995.

Clark, Roy Peter, and Don Fry. *Coaching Writers: Editors and Reporters Working
Together Across Media Platforms.* 2nd edition. Boston: Bedford/St. Martin's,
2003.

Kovach, Bill and Tom Rosenstiel. *The Elements of Journalism: What Newspeople
Should Know and the Public Should Expect.* (Revised and Updated). New York:
Three Rivers Press, 2007.

CHAPTER 16

THE EDITOR AS MANAGER AND LEADER

Editors aren't just editors; they also are managers, and the best ones are leaders. They have a concept of what their product should be, arrange financing, budget resources, hire staff and oversee production. The better ones also encourage and embrace change, recognizing that a stagnant organization isn't really stagnant but one in decline. The best editors do more: They inspire.

Too often in media work, you learn about good management mainly by seeing bad management. Jimmy Gentry, former dean of the William Allen White School of Journalism at the University of Kansas, has coined what he calls Gentry's Law, which states that any company whose main business is communicating to others is always terrible at communicating to its employees.

Think of all the movies and television shows you've seen about crusty old newspaper editors who slug down vast quantities of gin between editions. Even characters with hearts of gold—like Lou Grant on the old *Mary Tyler Moore Show*—are portrayed as feeling compelled to put up a mean front. But today's best managers know that intimidation is not the best way to lead people.

To be sure, this is not just a media problem. We've all worked for managers who don't know how to manage. Fast-food restaurant managers manage; they seldom lead. U.S. military officers manage, but they almost invariably lead. Indeed, our military could easily claim a copyright on leadership. Few institutions practice it better, and few go to greater lengths to preach its importance. But in all too many organizations, people are promoted to management for being good at other things. In the media, people often are promoted for being good writers or editors, not for being good managers or leaders. As a result, they enter management with no idea about how to do it well. They have only their own previous managers—good or bad—to emulate. It need not be that way.

The purpose of this chapter is to help you think about how you'll manage and lead when you become the boss. It's never too early to start preparing.

⚡ MANAGE OR LEAD?

It's extremely important to understand the distinction between management and leadership. And make no mistake about it, they are different.

Management is getting things done through other people. Managers focus on maintaining standards. They watch for declines in productivity and quality, and seek to move the organization back to the point of achieving standards. To some extent, it's fair to say that managers look backward and fix things that are broken.

Leadership results from people who are innovative, see the need to change, embrace change and implement change. Leaders look forward and plan for the future, all the while honoring and recognizing the organization's historic strengths. Leaders definitely manage, but they also lead.

The individual who manages or leads wants a certain level of performance from others. Media operations are businesses, and making a profit depends on performance, which in turn leads to a product that people want. Performance is based on three things:

- *Ability.* You must have good people to do the job. You achieve this through hiring talented people in the first place, and you enhance their skills through training

- *Motivation.* You must have the desire to do well. You try to buy a certain amount of motivation when you hire people by looking for those with can-do attitudes. You enhance motivation through rewarding people who do well with money or praise.

- *Role perception.* The employee must bring to the table a base level of ability and motivation, but role perception comes almost completely from the manager. Managers must explain what's expected of employees and set the standards by which they'll be judged.

Managers: What They Do

Managers, at the base level, must do five things—hire people, organize these people into a cohesive unit, communicate with these people, plan for the future through budgeting and other processes, and control the operation by maintaining standards. Leaders do more. They inspire a collective vision for the organization. Let's examine each of a manager's functions.

HIRE A STAFF

Talk with almost any manager, and he or she will tell you that good hiring is essential to good management. It's difficult to manage well if you have a staff that is incompetent, not focused on the mission of the organization or indifferent to the organization's success.

It's important to recruit and hire people carefully. If you do, you'll avoid lots of problems later. Check references and, perhaps more important, trust your instincts. If a person comes across as an arrogant know-it-all, he probably won't fit into the organization you're developing. If an individual seems to be short of knowledge needed for the position, she probably is.

Once you hire the staff, develop it. Seek ideas from the staff about how to make the product better. Recognize that good ideas come from almost any source, not just you.

Finally, take the time to evaluate employees at least once a year—formally and in private. Be honest. Evaluation allows employees to learn of your expectations and documents problems in case you must fire someone later.

ORGANIZE THE STAFF

Organization is the structure we put in place to achieve our plans. Good managers pay careful attention to organization because it's so critical to success. Traditionally, departments in U.S. newsrooms engage in an excessive amount of turf protection. To get a newsroom functioning properly, it's important to encourage department managers to work as a team.

The quality of the finished product, not the self-interest of any person or department, must be paramount. Organization is not about organization charts, although producing these to delineate responsibilities may be important. Instead, organization is about encouraging teamwork and cooperation. People who can't function well within a group make poor managers.

COMMUNICATE WITH THE STAFF

Internal communication is the area most lacking in most newsrooms. We're in the business of communicating with our audiences, but, as Gentry noted, we're often poor at communicating with our co-workers.

There's no excuse for this shortcoming. Managers are responsible for keeping open the lines of communication throughout the newsroom. With electronic mail, there's no justification for a staff member being uninformed about what's going on. Good managers don't let that happen.

It's also important that the manager be seen. One editor, after assuming control of his newsroom, decided to devote 30 minutes a day in the newsroom, mingling with reporters, photographers, editors and graphic designers. He later reported these became the most productive minutes of his day.

There also is a right way and a wrong way to communicate. When it's time to correct or reprimand an employee, do it in private, not in front of others. Humiliation may have an impact on the employee, but it won't be a positive one.

Performance Evaluation

The Seattle Times begins the annual employee review process by asking employees to fill out a self-evaluation. These are the questions asked:

1. List the top three priorities of your position.
2. Reflecting on the past year of your performance, what did you do well?
3. Reflecting on the past year of your performance, what could you have done better in your job?
4. What skills have you acquired or training have you taken in the past year, and how did that improve your work?
5. What will you achieve in your work in the next year? (For example: What actions will carry out the priorities in Question 1? What work-related skills will you develop and how do you intend to develop them? How will you become more effective in your job?)
6. Other comments:

PLAN FOR THE FUTURE

Without planning, a news department drifts from crisis to crisis. It's essential to have goals for each department, whether professional or financial. Planning reduces uncertainty and shows employees that there is a direction for the organization. Further, it provides an excellent opportunity for employees to provide suggestions. Today's best newsroom managers regularly review and update their organization's strategic plans, and they give employees ample opportunity to contribute.

It's also important to understand numbers. Journalists are notorious for trying to avoid math, but once you become a manager, you'll have to know about, create and manage budgets. The newsroom budget of a medium-sized newspaper or magazine, or even a small-market television station, is substantial.

CONTROL THE OPERATION

Control is a word with negative connotations, but for a manager, control is important. Managers control by setting minimum standards and ensuring that employees meet them. Standards may range from ethical principles to the number of stories a television reporter is expected to complete each week. Whatever is being measured, the goal must be clearly outlined, and the means of measurement must be clear. Further, minimum standards must be reachable and not so high that they cause morale problems. Minimum standards means just that.

The tough part of managing comes when an employee consistently fails to meet minimum expectations. The good manager ensures that the employee is first given the opportunity to correct the problem. Then, if the employee fails to do so, the manager must act. Is the employee in the right job? Is there another job in which the employee would have a better chance of success? If all that fails, suspension should be considered before the act of last resort, termination. It's never fun to terminate an employee, but occasionally it is necessary.

Leaders: What They Do

Leaders inspire. They show the way. They lead by example. They empower others.

One of the most important lessons to learn before you enter management is that managers push, but leaders pull. Managers drive people to perform, much like slave masters of the past. They cajole, and, if necessary, they punish to get results. Leaders create an environment in which employees feel pulled to greatness—inspired, empowered to make change and do great things.

People enjoy being led; they merely tolerate being managed. Managers demand and insist. They treat employees like essential parts of a machine. Leaders show respect for the employee's opinions. They show interest in the employee's family. They are good at being human.

Managers accept minimum standards. Leaders praise accomplishment. Managers enforce standards. Leaders have and share a vision.

Employees of those who manage may dread visiting with the boss. Those same employees always enjoy visiting with the leader. The leader, then, pulls from the bottom up while the manager pushes from the top down.

Finally, leaders have one other significant characteristic: They don't profess to know it all. They often provide all or most of the vision, but they seek advice from those closest to the situation—those in the trenches performing daily journalism.

Few choose to be managed; most desire to be led.

If all this sounds a bit hokey, think again. The reality is that leaders must manage, too, but by leading they create a more pleasant atmosphere in which to perform essential management functions. The great leaders in American history understood that. In the early 1960s, President John F. Kennedy set a goal of placing a man on the moon "before the decade is out," and on July 21, 1969, that goal was accomplished. Kennedy had long since been assassinated, but his goal was shared so strongly by others that it was accomplished on schedule. Leaders get results.

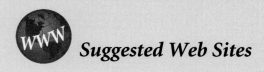 *Suggested Web Sites*

American Society of Newspaper Editors   **www.asne.org**
The Poynter Institute   **www.poynter.org**

Suggested Readings

Herrick, Dennis F. *Media Management in the Age of Giants: Business Dynamics of Journalism.* Ames, Iowa: Iowa State University Press, 2003.

Underwood, Doug. *When MBAs Rule the Newsroom.* New York: Columbia University Press, 1995.

Warner, Charles. *Media Management Review.* Mahwah, N.J.: Lawrence Erlbaum Associates, 1997.

GLOSSARY

active voice a verb is said to be in active voice when the subject is doing the action of the verb rather than being acted on by something else

adjective a word that modifies a noun or pronoun

adverb a word that modifies a verb, adjective or another adverb

agenda setter an editor who calls attention of the public to important issues

all-cap head a headline in which all letters are capitalized

antecedent the noun that a pronoun names

art director oversees the design of the newspaper or magazine

assignment editor an editor who assigns a writer or reporter to a story

associate and assistant editors those who assign, write and edit articles for particular departments of a magazine

association publications magazines put out by associations of various kinds, such as trade- or hobby-related groups

audiotext recorded information available to consumers through telephone calls

backshop part of a newspaper's production department where pages are pasted up

bank see *deck*

banner a headline that spans the width of the page and is placed at the top

bar chart a chart that helps readers identify quantities

barker see *hammer*

bleed a design technique that pushes illustrations or background screens outside the margin to the trimmed edge of the paper

blog a Web log discussion on the Internet

blurb display-sized type pulled from the text to attract the reader's attention; sometimes called a *pullout* or a *pull-quote* (if a quotation)

body type the type used in the text of a story

bottom-line lead a story introduction that tells the reader the essence of the news in the first paragraph

broadsheet a full-sized newspaper; contrast with *tabloid*

browser a computer program used for navigating the Web

budget a list of stories being readied for publication

caption the words that accompany and explain a photograph; sometimes called a *cutline*

catchline a headline-sized word or words placed over a caption and designed to help attract attention to a photo, usually a standalone

censorship   when government forces the media to publish or broadcast, or not to publish or broadcast, certain information; the opposite of editorial discretion

chat room   an online interactive discussion room on the Internet

city editor   the assignment editor in charge of assigning and editing all locally written stories other than sports and editorials and, depending on the newspaper, perhaps lifestyle-section stories

civic journalism   see *public journalism*

clause   a group of related words containing a subject and a verb

cloze procedure   a readability formula that factors in context or story structure

coaching of writers   a term used for dealing with the human aspects of editor-reporter relationships

collective noun   a noun that is singular in form but that names a group, such as *media, committee* or *council*

color piece   a story, often a sidebar or follow, that mainly tries to make the reader feel what it was like to be there

comma splice   something punctuated to look like a sentence but that really consists of two sentences joined with only a comma between them

comparative form of a modifier   the form of a modifier used when comparing two things; comparative adjectives, for example, end in *er* or have the word *more* or *less* in front of the positive form

compound modifiers   two modifiers in a row, with the first modifying the second, and together the two modifying another word; compound modifiers usually have a hyphen between them

copy-editing symbols   the symbols used in the copy-editing stage before the stories have been set in type on the page

conditional mood   a verb that expresses not what's true now but what could, might, should or would be true if a certain condition were met

conjunction   a word that connects other words, phrases, clauses or sentences

conjunctive adverb   an adverb like *although* that can join two clauses

contributing editor   a regular freelancer that a magazine often employs who tends to be an expert in the field on which he or she writes

convergence   the practice of sharing and cross-promoting content from a variety of media through newsroom collaborations and outside partnerships

conversational deck   a blurb written in sentence style

coordinate modifiers   two modifiers in a row that are equal (they can be reversed with *and* between them); coordinate modifiers should have a comma between them

coordinating conjunction   a conjunction that introduces an independent clause, such as *and, or,* and *but*

copy desk   the place on a publication where final editing of a story takes place

copy-desk chief   the copy editor in charge of the copy desk

copy-desk differential   the amount of extra compensation some publications provide to copy editors above what they pay reporters

copy editor   a person who edits the articles and writes the titles, captions and pull-quotes

copy flow   the steps through which a story moves from reporter to various editors on its way to production

correlative conjunctions   words that must appear together when connecting words, phrases or clauses, such as "not only" with "but also"

correspondent a writer who writes from a distance for a publication; sometimes a staff member but often a freelancer

cover line a teaser headline on the cover of a magazine; also known as *cover blurb*

creative tension a discredited management technique in which reporters are pitted against each other

crossline a horizontal headline that covers multiple columns

cub reporter a beginning, or novice, reporter

cutline see *caption*

Dale-Chall formula a readability formula that measures word familiarity

dangling participle a participial phrase that has not been placed next to what it modifies, resulting in confusion

dateline the city—and sometimes, the state or country—written before the first line of a story's lead (city in all capital letters but the state or country, if present, in upper and lowercase); datelines used to contain the date of the story, but with modern electronic transmission, is virtually never included now

deck a section of a multiple-bank headline

defamation slander or libel that damages someone's reputation or business

delayed-ID lead a brief description of the *who* of a story in the first paragraph rather than the person's name (the name often appears at the beginning of the second paragraph); used when the *who* of a story is not famous or does not appear often in the paper

dependent clause a clause that cannot stand alone as a complete sentence

developing story a story that is followed each day for awhile

dingbat a decorative font mark

display type headline-sized type

downstyle a headline writing style that follows sentence-style rules for capitalization

drop cap a large capital letter at the start of a paragraph, whose top is lined up with the top of the smaller letter to its right

drop head a second headline between the main headline and the article; also known as *second deck* or *subtitle*

editor anyone who assigns, selects, edits or arranges stories, images or sounds

editor in chief an editor in the chain of command below the publisher but above the managing editor

editorial-page editor the editor in charge of writing editorials for the editorial page and selecting columns, cartoons, letters and op-ed pieces for the opinion section; he or she typically reports to the publisher rather than the managing editor

electronic library a reference library for a media operation

electronic media broadcast media (radio and television) and the Internet

ethics morality, a code of behavior, principles of right and wrong, doing what's right even when what's wrong is legal

executive editor at a newspaper, an editor above the managing editor but below the publisher; at a magazine, often someone who balances the skills of the managing editor

external blurb a blurb that helps summarize the story and is printed in big type above or below the title or headline

e-zine a small, personal magazine published on the Internet

feature a story with a feature lead and a story structure with a dramatic beginning and end

feature lead   a story introduction that tries to dramatically introduce the news rather than telling the news immediately in the first paragraph

feature obit   an obituary written with a feature-story approach focusing on what the deceased's achievements were or what kind of person he or she was

fever chart   a chart that shows quantities over time

flag   a publication's nameplate (usually a newspaper term)

Flesch formula   a fomula used to determine the readability of text

flow   smooth movement in a story from point to point, making it easy for the reader to follow

focus group   a representative group of readers or viewers used to evaluate or suggest changes in news content

focus piece   a feature story taking *The Wall Street Journal* approach of focusing in the lead, and often the ending, on a person whose story exemplifies a particular issue

fog index   a readability formula that measures sentence length and number of syllables in words

follow   a follow-up story; a story that updates a previous story

formula obit   an obituary written to a formula a newspaper uses for all obituaries except its feature ones

four-color process   the method of printing photos or graphics of any colors from four basic inks: black, magenta, yellow and cyan

fragment   a group of words that does not have both a subject and verb or present a complete thought

freedom of the press   the idea that the media should be able to publish or broadcast without censorship

fused sentence   a group of words punctuated to look like one sentence but which really consists of two joined sentences without punctuation between them

futures file   a file a reporter or editor keeps of upcoming events and story ideas

gatekeeper   an editor who controls the flow of information to the public

gerund   a form of a verb, usually ending in *ing,* used in a sentence as a noun

gingerbread   decorative borders and the like that detract from modern design

graphics editor   the editor in charge of designing graphics for stories and, at some papers, especially larger ones, in charge of laying out the paper

hammer   a headline with a large word or two designed to attract quick attention

hanging indention   a typesetting style in which the first line is flush left and all subsequent lines are indented

hard-news stories   typically written with a bottom-line lead and an inverted-pyramid structure

headline   the display type designed to attract readers to a story

hoax   a fraud perpetrated as a practical joke; after a while, though, as with many widely circulated e-mails, people circulate them honestly thinking they are true.

holistic editing   recognizing the various journalism formulas that apply to a particular story and noticing when the story differs from them in nonintelligent ways, helping an editor spot at once various macro and micro problems in a story

hook   anything in any medium that serves to grab attention and hook in the audience's mind

human-interest story   a story that focuses on an emotionally involving or unusual situation; more broadly, used synonymously with *feature*

hypertext   a system of coding text that links electronic documents with each other

idiom   common expression in a language

illustration   a graphic artist's effort to explain something, often a process that normally cannot be visualized

immediate-ID lead   putting the name of the *who* of a story in the first paragraph; used when the *who* is famous or appears in the paper often

indefinite pronoun   a pronoun that has no expressed antecedent (*all, any, each, everybody, few, nobody*), so it is sometimes difficult to tell whether it is singular or plural

independent clause   a clause that can stand alone as a complete sentence

infomedium   a coined term for *information medium*

information graphics   charts, maps, graphs, and other illustrations used to convey relationships, statistics and trends

intensity density   the degree to which striking facts, wordings, quotes and graphic elements are packed tightly into a given space or time

interjection   a word that expresses an emotional outburst

internal blurb   a sample of the story, usually a pull quote, printed in large type inside a story

invasion of privacy   publishing or broadcasting personal information that is embarrassing, trespassing on someone's property, presenting someone in a false light or using someone's image or voice for commercial purposes without approval

inverted pyramid   a news-writing style used to tell simple stories

irregular verb   a verb that doesn't follow the normal forms for verbs, such as adding *ed* to the end of the main present-tense form to make the past tense

keyword method   a headline-writing technique in which the writer seeks to determine which words are most important to include

kicker   a headline style in which a smaller subhead appears above the main headline

layering   a technique for leading readers through a story on a Web site

lead   the introduction to a story; often the first sentence or first paragraph of a story, but a long lead may sometimes run for several paragraphs

leadership   the process of inspiring employees

leading   the amount of space between lines of type

leg   a column of type under a story

legend   the text or heading that accompanies a photograph

legibility   the ease with which a typeface can be read

libel   a published (or in many states, broadcast) statement that conveys an unjustly unfavorable impression of someone's reputation or business

line art   a drawing or graphic with little or no shading made up primarily of solid strokes of a pen

linking verb   a verb that draws an equation between the subject of the clause and a noun, pronoun or adjective following the verb

linkmeister   a term coined by Microsoft for a person designated to search for links to place on a Web site

links   uniform resource locator ties to other pages within a Web site or outside to other Web sites

lottery   any situation in which someone pays to be considered for a prize that is decided by chance; legally, raffles are considered lotteries

macro editing   looking for big problems in stories, such as accuracy, objectivity, legality, ethics and propriety

main head   the primary headline as opposed to secondary decks

"a man" technique   a writing technique used to avoid libel by using a generic term like "a man" to describe a perpetrator of a crime rather than a real name

management   the process of directing employees

managing editor   the editor directly in charge of the newsroom as a whole; reports directly to either the publisher or an editor above him or her with a title such as "executive editor" or "editor in chief"

map   a locator, usually used to locate news events

metropolitan (or metro) editor   the assignment editor in charge of assigning and editing stories relating to the city in which the paper is published

micro editing   looking for small things in stories, such as grammar, usage, spelling and style

misplaced modifier   a modifier not placed next to the word it modifies, resulting in confusion as to what's being referred to

mixed approach   the use of a feature lead on a news story

modifier   a word that describes another one; adjectives, adverbs and interjections are modifiers

morgue   a term used for a publication's or broadcast station's library

most-important-element-what lead   a lead that focuses on the most important news out of several things that happened related to the story

mugshot   a photo of a person's head and neck, usually one-column or one-half column wide

multimedia journalist   a person capable of functioning in more than one medium, usually print and broadcast

multiple-element-what lead   a lead that lists several things that happened related to the story

nameline   a one-line caption under a mugshot

negligence   failure to show enough caution or care in a situation that results in damage or injury to another

new media   publishing on a CD-Rom or a Web site

news editor   the copy-desk chief

news peg   a timely, newsworthy event on which to base a feature story

newsletter   a short, newsy publication with a frequent publication cycle and a high degree of specialization; usually distributed exclusively through subscription to a limited circulation

Nielsen Ratings   the results of surveys used to determine levels of television viewership

noun   a word that names a person, place, thing, idea or quality

nut graf   a paragraph that summarizes the bottom line of a feature story, usually after the lead paragraph

object   a noun, pronoun or other substantive that receives the action of a verb, verbal or preposition

objectivity   being factual, neutral, fair and, in a hard-news story, impersonal in style

obscenity   legally defined in the United States as something that appeals to the "prurient interest" of (would arouse) the average person, applying contemporary community standards to the work as a whole; that depicts or describes sexual conduct in a patently offensive way; and that lacks, as a whole, serious literary, artistic, political or scientific value

online editor   an editor in charge of content for a publication's Web site

outside-expert approach   a how-to story based on advice from a knowledgeable source who is not the writer

parenthetical   in common grammatical terms, "nonrestrictive," or in AP style terms, "non-essential"; parenthetical, though, more clearly expresses the idea that something is an aside or an afterthought and could be put in parentheses, but since journalists don't normally use parentheses, they set off parenthetical items with commas instead.

participle   a form of a verb, usually ending in *ing,* that's used in a sentence as an adjective

passive voice   the subject is not doing the action of the verb but is being acted on by something else

personality profile   a story focusing on a person rather than an event

photo editor   the editor in charge of choosing photos for the paper and recommending their cropping and sizing, as well as designing the photo-story packages

photojournalist   a master of graphic aesthetics as well as a journalist who happens to work with a camera

pie chart   a chart used to show division of the whole

play   the location of a newspaper story

positive form modifier   modifiers have three forms, the positive being the one about which no comparison is made to anything else—for example, one person is *tall* (the "positive" form) but that person is *taller* than another (the "comparative" form) or the *tallest* of three or more (the "superlative" form)

possessive   one of the three cases of nouns and pronouns, the one showing ownership

predicate nominative   a noun or pronoun following a linking verb that renames the subject

preposition   a connecting word that combined with its object acts as a modifier; in the sentence "He ran toward the trees," *toward* is a preposition, *trees* is its object, and the phrase *toward the trees* is a prepositional phrase that modifies "ran"

principal parts of verbs   the main present-tense, past-tense and past-participle forms of a verb

process drawing   an artist's drawing that helps readers visualize detailed plans

production editor   an editor who follows the work of the assigning editor

pronoun   a word that takes the place of a noun

proof   a copy of a completed page, ready to print except for any last-minute changes you may be able to make

proofreading   reading the proofs of a page after it's been formatted but before it goes to press, to check one last time for errors

proofreading symbols   the symbols used in the proofreading stage after the stories have already been copy edited and laid out on the page

propriety   the selection and presentation of material that is appropriate for a specific audience

public journalism   journalism that seeks citizen participation in key issues involving a community

publisher   the person appointed by the owner to be the chief executive officer of a newspaper or magazine, ultimately the person locally in charge of both the news and business operations

pull quote   a quotation from an article repeated in big type as an internal blurb to break up the page

pullout   see *blurb*

push poll   a propraganda technique sometimes used by people trying to promote a cause or candidate in which people posing as pollsters tell people "polled" some negative information about their opposition under the guise of simply asking people their opinions about it

pyramid   a headline style in which lines get progressively wider, emulating the appearance of a pyramid

Q-and-A interview   an interview written not as an article but in the form of a transcript of the questions and answers

race   a broad category of type

ragged right   type that is not justified (not lined up on the right side of the column as on the left)

readership studies   measure of the relative popularity of features in a publication

read-in blurb   a conversational headline element that reads directly into the main headline

read-out blurb   a subhead that comes between the headline and the text; often conversational and sometimes called a *conversational blurb*

relative pronouns   the pronouns *who, whom, whose, whoever, whomever, what, which* and *that* used to connect a subordinate clause to the main clause of a sentence

release date   a date on a press release before which time the information should not be made public

retouching   correcting imperfections in a photograph, usually done with a computer program like PhotoShop

reverse   white letters on a black background, also called *reverse type*

reverse kicker   see *hammer*

reverse plate   a headline with white type on a dark background

reviewing editor   see *production editor*

ribbon   see *banner*

right to know   the idea that the government must provide certain information to the public

rim editor   a copy editor who edits stories and writes headlines and blurbs

run-on sentence   a group of words punctuated to look like a sentence but that really consists of several run together

sans serif   type without the ending strokes called serifs

second-cycle story   a story appearing for the first time in your newspaper but that follows the publication of the same story in an evening paper if you're working for a morning paper, or vice versa

second-day story   a follow story to one appearing earlier in your paper

second deck   a second headline between the main headline and the article; also known as *subtitle* or *drop head*

section editor   an editor who looks over a particular section of the magazine, such as letters to the editor, reviews of new products, etc.; also known as *senior editor*

seesaw technique   the common story structure of seesawing back and forth between presenting information or paraphrasing and backing that up with a quotation

sensitivity   awareness about and concern for how others might perceive something

sentence   a group of related words with a subject and verb, and that expresses a complete thought

serifs   the ending strokes that appear on the ends of letters in some typefaces

service journalism   articles of practical use to a reader in more than a merely informative way; often used synonymously with *how-to article*

shield laws   laws that shield a person from revealing certain information due to a client relationship (for doctors, priests, and lawyers), but that rarely protect a journalist's relationship with a source of information

single-element-what lead   a lead that focuses on the only thing that happened, such as the one topic discussed at a meeting

skyline   a banner headline placed above the flag

slander   spoken defamation that damages someone's reputation or business

slot person   the copy-desk chief; the person in charge of the copy desk

soft lead   an introduction typical of a feature story or the mixed-approach story in which the writer does not reveal the bottom line in the lead but instead introduces the story dramatically before turning to the bottom line several or more paragraphs later in the story

soft news   another name for features

special-interest publications   magazines devoted to a particular, specialized subject

spread head   a multiple-column headline

staff writers   at a newspaper or magazine, the salaried writers as opposed to freelance contributors

standalone   a photo that stands by itself without an accompanying story

stepline   a headline in which the first line is flush left, the second is centered and the third is flush right; considered outdated

stet head   a standing headline

stick-up initial   a capital letter at the start of a paragraph, whose base is lined up with the base of the smaller letter to its right

story count   the number of articles per page, per issue or per writer

streamer   see *banner*

stringer   a writer paid by the column inch for contributing to a publication

style   the rules of such things as abbreviation, capitalization, numbers and punctuation

subject of a clause   the noun, pronoun or other substantive that the verb says is doing or being something

subject of an infinitive   a noun or pronoun immediately preceding an infinitive; in the sentence "They mistook her to be Joan," *her* is the subject of the infinitive *to be*

subjunctive mood   the form of a verb used when the speaker or writer of a sentence means to imply that something being expressed is contrary to fact or is a wish, doubt or prayer

subordinating conjunction   a conjunction that introduces a dependent clause, such as *because* or *since*

subtitle   a second headline between the main headline and the article; also known as *second deck* or *drop head*

summary-what lead   a lead that summarizes several things that happened related to a story

superlative form of a modifier   the form of an adjective or adverb when comparing three or more items; superlative adjectives, for example, end in *est* or have *least* or *most* in front of the positive form of the adjective

table   an information graphic composed of rows and columns of numbers

tabloid   a half-size newspaper format

talk radio   a radio station featuring discussion rather than entertainment

taste   judgment in matters of esthetics; sensitivity to how your audience is likely to regard something

tie-back paragraph   a paragraph in a follow-up story that transitions from the latest news back to previous developments to update readers who might have missed them or forgotten

timeliness   one of the main characteristics of news; to be news, something must have happened recently or have been recently revealed

title a term used for headlines, usually in magazines

trade publications specialized publications aimed at people in a particular field, such as farming, automaking or plumbing

uncountable nouns nouns with no different singular and plural forms

undated story a story with no place of origin at the start of the first paragraph; often used for roundups from multiple locations

underline a one-line caption

uniform resource locator the location of a site on the Web; also called *URL*

update a follow story looking back weeks, months or years later at what happened since the original story was in the news

upstyle a headline style in which the first letter of all words except short conjunctions and prepositions is capitalized

urban legend a tale that is actually modern folklore, although it masquerades as a news story

usage the use of the correct word; mainly a matter of the meaning of commonly misused words

vague pronoun reference a pronoun whose antecedent is unclear

verb a word that expresses action or state of being

videographer one who operates a video camera

visual literacy understanding the importance of visually conveying information with photographs and information graphics

Web editor an editor in charge of a Web site or who works on one.

Web producer someone who edits for the World Wide Web

writer-as-expert approach a how-to story based on the knowledge of the writer

zine a privately printed, small-run magazine

INDEX

Note: Boldface numbers indicate illustrations or boxed material.

"A Man" technique, 100
Abbreviations:
  in headlines, 239
  used in broadcast, 366
  style and, 164–165
Accident and disaster
    stories, 185–187, 369
Accuracy:
  in headlines, 244
  of news story, 69–81
  of photo captions, **276**
Active voice vs. passive
    voice, 146
Adams, Eddie, 130
Addresses, style of, 171–172
Addresses of deceased,
    printing, 207
Adjectives vs. adverbs, 151
Ads in magazines, **327**
Advance pieces, 187–188
Adverbs, 151, 155–157
Advertising:
  audience fragmentation
    and, 14–15
  job opportunities,
    376–378
  placement in magazines,
    335–336
Advertising dollars, media
    share of, **17**
Agence France-Presse, 297
Airwaves, ownership of, 114
*American Journalism
    Review,* 242
Analysis pieces, 188
Anchors, news, **365,** 373
Anonymous sources, 90,
    108–109, 122
AP Stylebook, The, 384
Apostrophes, 142
"Arrested for" as legal term,
    106
Art director, 323, 329

Assignment editor, 34, 57
  as coach, 387–389
  and production editors,
    relationship of,
    389–390
  and reporter
    relationship, 387–389
Associate and assistant
    editors, 323
Associated Press, 297
Associated Press Managing
    Editors writing
    committee, 305
*Associated Press Stylebook
    and Briefing on Media
    Law, The,* 164
Association publications,
    321
Attributions (*see* Crediting)
Audiences, 7, 15
  advertising, 14–15
  changing needs of, 26
  connecting with, 23, 57
  disconnection of, 13–16
  fragmentation, 14–15
  interaction with, 16–17
  measuring reaction of, **22**
  online media, **22**
  stories focusing on needs
    and wants of, 20, 57
  studies of, 21–23
Audiotext services of
    newspapers, 350
Averages and number
    editing, **79**

Backshop, 38
Balance:
  and contrast in
    headlines, 249
  in newspaper design,
    309, 311–312, **313**
Banks in headlines, **229**

Banner headline, **230**
Bar charts, 280
Barker, **230**
Battle Creek (Mich.) *Enquirer
    and News,* 272
Beginners, advice for, 392
Berners-Lee, Tim, 353
Bernstein, Carl, 25, 115
Bias, 123
  in news, 8, 75–76
  in political stories, 211
  in sports writing, 221
  in TV, 24
Black, Hugo, 86
Blair, Jayson, 25
Bleeds, 326, 334
Blogs, 3, **9**
Blurbs, 254–255, **327,** 333
Boating and shipping
    stories, 188–189
Boldface type, 284, **287**
Book publishing, jobs in,
    382–384
Bradlee, Ben, 18
Brand names vs. generic
    alternatives, **110,** 111
Brief, 188
  Broadcast media (*see also*
    specific medium)
  abbreviations, 366
  advertising, 383
  bulletin, 363
  copy formats, 373, **374**
  copy preparation,
    364–366
  copy sources, 363–364
  datelines, 368–369
  five-minute summary,
    363
  freedom of the press, 89
  numbers, 367
  phonetic spelling,
    365–366

punctuation, 366
quotations, 367
regulation of, 116–118
restrictions on, 91
soundbites, 370
special rules for, 116–118
special slugs, 363
spotlights, 363
spot summary, 363
style used by, 366–369
takeout, 363
TelePrompTer, 364
television news, 370–373
time angle, 369
titles, 368
vignettes, 363
vs. print regulations,
    114–118
voiceovers, 373
Browser, 353, 356
Brunvand, Jan Harold, 204
Bulletins, 363
Burger, Warren E. (Chief
    Justice), 117–118
Bush, George W., 76
Business stories, 189–191
Business terms, 190
Byline of analysis piece, 188

Cable modems, 357
Cable News Network, **355**
Cable-news networks, 8
Cable-television news
    channel, 1, 4
Calendar items, 188,
    212–213
Callan, John, 352
Capitalization, 165
  of foods, 202
  of government terms, 207
  in quotations, 170–171
Casey, Robert J., 178
Catchline, 256, **53**

Cause-promoting releases, 214
CBS Inc. v. Democratic National Committee, 117–118
CD-ROMs, 350–351
Celebrity news, 192
Censorship, 87–89
and freedom of the press, 89
on the Internet, 119
of school newspaper, 111–113
Chall, Jeanne S., **177**
Chat rooms, 9
Chicago Daily News, 178
Chicago Manual of Style, The, 384
Chronological stories, 193
Citizen journalism, 2–3, 373
City editor, described, 34, **37**
Civic journalism, **23**
Civil vs. criminal cases, **92**
Clarity of news story, 67
Clark, Roy Peter, 387–388
Clichés, 62, 64, 180–182
Cliches to avoid:
in accident stories, 187
in business stories, 191
in celebrity news, 192
in crime stories, 199
in entertainment stories, 200
in political stories, 211
in sports stories, 220
in travel pieces, 221
in war stories, 221
in weather stories, 223
Clinton, Bill, 89
Cloze procedure, **177**
Coaching of writers, 387–388
Code of ethics, 127–129
Colons, 167
Color pieces, 193, 335
Columbia Journalism Review, 242
Columbia Missourian, 3, 264, 307
Columns, 193–194
Comma splice, 136
Commas, 155, 166–167, 202–203
Commemorative features, 202

Commercial database services, 351
Commercial speech and the First Amendment, 91
"Common law," **92**
Communicating with staff, 396
Conciseness of story, 45
Confessions:
and ethical issues, 120
publishing, 124
Conflict as element of news, 7
Conflict of interest and ethical issues, 122
Confused words, list of, 157–163
Conjunctions, 148
Conjunctive adverbs, 155–157
Connecting words, 154–157
Constitutional law, **93**
Consumer-controlled information, 1, 2
Consumers defining news for themselves, 7
Contrast in newspaper design, 309, 312
Contributing editors, 323
Convergence between news and consumers, 17
Converging media, 5–6
Conversational deck, **253**
Cooke, Janet, 25
Coordinating conjunctions, 155
Copley, Gannett and Scripps-Howard news services, 298
Copy for broadcast media:
flow through news department, 37–38
formats, 373, **374**
in the newsroom, 363–364
preparation of, 364–366
Copy desk, **38**
Copy-desk chief, 34–36, **37, 47,** 389
Copy-desk differential, 390
Copy editing:
internship program, 391
sample of, **40, 48**
symbols used, **49**
three R's 43–46, 48
vs. proofreading, 53–54

Copy editors, 323
described, 36, **37**
importance of, 28, 29–32
improvement, suggestions for, 29–30, 31–32
internship, 47
and retractions, 105
skills of, 28–29, 30–31
symbols used by, 49
team system of editing and, **35**
writing headlines, 234–236
Copyright infringement, 91
Copyrighted works, 109–111
Corporate communications publications, 321
Corrections, printing, 104–105
Correlative conjunctions, 157
Correspondents, 298
Couric, Katie, **362**
Court stories, 194–197
Courtesy titles, 131, 172, 208, 368
Creative tension, 388
Credibility and the media, 23–26
of online journalism, 349–350
Crediting:
photographer, **277**
quotations, 168–170, 201
sources, 109, 111
Web stories, 349, 350
wire stories, 306
Crime stories, 197–199
Criminal vs. civil cases, **92**
Crompton, Alistair, 380
Cronkite, Walter, 5
Cropping (*see* Photos)
Crossover reporting, 5
Cub reporter, 211
Cultural differences among media, 5
Cutline, 228, 256
Cutout photo, 334
Cutting stories, 54, **304**

Daily Herald (Chicago), 257
Dale, Edgar, **177**
Dale-Chall formula, **177**
Dangling participles, 152

Dashes, 167
Datelines, 172–173, 368–369
Deadline pressure, 39
Deceptive information, publishing, 121
Decks in headlines, **229**
Delayed-ID lead, 59, 66, 186, 198
Denver Post, **230**
Dependent clauses, 155, 156
Design of magazines, 324–336
advertising placement, 335–336
bleed pages, 326
boxes, 333
color usage, 335
headline design, 330, **331**
initial caps as ornamentation, **328,** 330, **332**
principles of, **336**
rules, 333
tint blocks, 334
type inserts, 333
typefaces, 330, **331**
wrapping text, **335**
Design of newspapers, 308–316
attractiveness of page, 310–311
balance, 311–312, **313**
balanced pages, 309
complement to stories, 311
contemporary appearance, 311
contrast, 309, 312–314
easy-to-follow news, 309
flair, adding, **315**
illustrations, display of, 309
line spacing, 309–310
movement, 315–316
objectives of, 310–311
organization, 308, 310
proportion, 315
story placement, 310
structure of page, 316
typefaces, 309
unity, 309, 314
white space, 308–309
Designations preferred by groups, 133
Desktop publishing, 2–3

Developing story, 201
Digital editing, 372
Digital-imaging software, 262, 263
Digital Millenium Copyright Act, 119
Digital photography, 271–272
Dingbats, 328
Directions, writing, 203
Disconnection of audience, 13–16
Display type, 282
District courts, **94–95**
Dow Jones Newspaper Fund, 9, 391
Drawings, 261
Drop cap, 328
DVDs, 350–351

Eavesdropping and ethical issues, 122
Editing (*see also* Holistic editing; Macro editing; Micro editing):
for accuracy, 69–81
for broadcast media (*see* Broadcast media)
copy editor, value of, 28, 29–32
editor's role in, 28–29
for graphic appeal, 260–261
local stories, **304**
newspapers (*see* Newspapers)
numbers, 78–80
process, 38–43
quotations, 72
skills, 28–29, 30–31
in teams, **35**
for the Web (*see* Online journalism)
wire stories, **304**
Editor in chief, 32, 322
Editorial judgment and freedom of the press, 89
Editorializing:
in headlines, 240, 247
in photo captions, **276**
Editors:
as agenda setters, 2
changing role of, 1–2, 8–11

coaching junior editors, 391–392
described, 32
earning trust of public, 2
as gatekeepers, 1, 2
jobs for, 9–10
as managers and leaders, 394–398
and mistakes, 80–81
power of, 2
rewriting by, 81
role of, 3–4
Education stories, 199
Electronic distortion of type, 288–289
Electronic libraries, 351
Electronic media, 13–14
reasons against, **115**
regulation of, 113–119
Ellipsis, 171
ENG (electronic news gathering), 373
Entertainment stories, 200
Equity law, **92–93**
Errors in newspapers, 24, 25
Ethical issues:
anonymous sources, 122
confessions, 120, 124
conflict of interest, 122
deceptive information, 121–122
described, 119
harmful information, publishing, 123–124
help in deciding, 125–127
illegally obtained information, 122–123
individuals, information potentially harmful to, 123–124
juvenile offenders, 124
macro editing, 119–129
names and addresses, printing, 120, 123–124
off-the-record statements, 122
plagiarism, 123
politics or causes, involvement in, 123
privacy,. 123
restraints, acceptance of, 125
society, information potentially harmful to, 124

Society of Professional Journalists code of ethics, 127–129
special privileges, 122–123
sting operations, 122
warning signs of violations, 120–125
Executive editor, 32, 323
Executive orders, **93**
Executive producer, **365**
External blurbs, 254, 333
E-zines, 320

Fact checking, 9, 69–70
"Facts," common errors in, 72–73
Facts, objectivity of story and, 81–82
Fairness, objectivity of story and, 82
Fairness Doctrine, 89, 117–118
False connections in sentences, 138–139
Favorable treatment to obtain information, 122
Favre, Gregory, 16
Features, 59–65
body of, 63
commemorative, 202
endings, 62
on food, 202–203
leads, 60–62, 63–65
trimming, 62
vs. hard-news story, 66
vs. news, **61**
Feature-story lead, 60–62
Federal Communications Commission, 6, 89, **93**, 117–118
Federal courts, **93–94**
Federalist Papers, The, 337
Fever charts, 280
Fiber-optic links, 357
First Amendment, 86–91
applied in schools, 111–112
First-day lead, 201
First-person stories, 200
Five-minute summary, 363
Flash, 363
Flesch, Rudolph, **176**
Flesch formula, **176–177**
Focus groups, **22**

Focus pieces, 189, 200–201, 295
Fog index, **176**
Follows, 201–202
Fonts, 282–288
Food features, 202–203
Four-color process, 335
Fragments, 136
Frank, Reuven, 370
Freedom of the press:
broadcast media and, 87, 91
described, 87–88
editorial judgment and, 89
Internet and, 89
journalists' rights and, 90–91
responsibility and, 90
as a right, not as an entitlement, 89–90
vs. right to know, 90
Fry, Don, 387–388

Gatekeepers, editors as, 1, 2
Gatekeeping system of news agency, 299
Gentry, Jimmy, 394
Gingerbread, **231**
Glass, Stephen, 24
Government databases, 351
Government news stories, 207
Government publications, 321
Grammar, 136–157
connecting words, 154–157
guides, 135–136
in headlines, 238–239
interjections, 153
mistakes in news, 24
modifiers, 151–153
nouns and pronouns, 139–144
possessives and plurals, 142–144
sentence problems, 136–139
verbs, 144–151
Graphic appeal, 260–261
Graphic designer, 36
Graphic devices in headlines, 250
Graphic styling of magazines, 329–336

Graphics editor, described, 36
Grief and propriety, 130
Guilt, implying, 186–187, 194, 197, 245–246
Gunning, Robert, **176**

Hammer, **230,** 237
Hammer head, **253**
Hangers, **277**
Hanging indentation of headlines, **229**
Hard-news story, 58–59
 vs. feature, 66
Harmful information, publishing, 123–124
Hazelwood School District v. Kuhlmeier, 112
Headlines:
 abbreviations, 239, 240
 accuracy, 240, 244
 alliteration in, 249
 as all that is read of story, 228, 231–233
 in analysis pieces, 188
 balance and contrast in, 249
 in court stories, 194–195
 double entendres in, 242–244
 editorializing in, 240, 247
 evolution of, **229–231**
 fun with writing, **235**
 grammar, 238–239
 hammer, 237
 how to write, 240–252
 informative, 240–242
 for the Internet, 256–257
 keyword method, 235–236
 kicker, 237–238, 230
 libel, 245–246
 line breaks, 239
 in magazines, 330, **331**
 main heads, 237
 mechanics in, 238–239
 newspaper readership and, 227–228
 old news, rehashing, 245
 order, 236
 overstating, 246
 in print advertising, 380–381
 process of writing, 234–239

punctuation, 238
punch line, 248–249
 puns in, 250
 rhymes in, 250
 second deck, 237
 sensationalizing in, 247–248
 sidebar, 260–261
 terminology, 237–238
 type, **230,** 233
 typography, of 291–292
 typos in, 242
 vague, 242
 writer's block and, 251–252
Health stories, 216
Hiring staff, 395–396
History pieces, 203
Hoaxes, 73–75
Holistic editing, 184–225
 accident and disaster stories, 185–187
 advance pieces, 187–188
 analysis pieces, 188, 189
 boating and shipping stories, 188–189
 business stories, 189–191
 celebrity news, 192
 chronological stories, 193
 color pieces, 193
 columns, 193–194
 court stories, 194–197
 crime stories, 197–199
 education stories, 199
 entertainment stories, 199
 first-person stories, 199
 focus pieces, 189, 200–201
 follows, 201–202
 food features, 202–203
 government news, 207
 history pieces, 203
 how-to articles, 203
 human-interest stories, 203–204
 labor disputes, 204–205
 medical news, 205
 meeting stories, 206
 obituaries, 207–210
 personality profiles, 188, 189, 210–211
 political stories, 211
 press-release stories, 107–108, 212–214

question-and-answer interviews, 214–215
 religion stories, 215–216
 reviews, 216
 science and health stories, 215–216
 seasonal features, 217
 service journalism, 203
 speech stories, 217–219
 sport stories, 219–221
 travel pieces, 221
 war stories, 222
 weather stories, 222–224
Holmes, Oliver Wendell, **115**
Hooking the audience, 63, **65**
How-to articles, 203
HTML (hypertext markup language), 20, 353, **354**
Human-interest stories, 203–204 (*see also* Features)
Hypertext links, 352
Hyphens, 167

Idioms, 163
Illustrations, 279
 attractive display of, 309
Image-building releases, 214
Immediate-ID lead, 58–59, 66
Impact as element of news, 7
Imprecise words in news story, 77–78
Inconsistencies within story, 70–71
Indecency, FCC regulation of, 118
Indefinite pronouns, 149
Independent clauses, 155, 202–203
Infomedium, 20
Information, leaving out, 121
Information graphics, 278–281
Initial cap as ornamentation in magazines, 330, **332**
Intellectual property rights, 109–111
Intensity density, **65**
Interactivity between news and consumers, 17
Interjections, 153
Internal blurbs, 255, 333

Internet:
 as fact verifier, 69, **71**
 headlines and titles, 256–257
 law, 118–119
 magazines, 320
 news (*see* Online journalism)
 and online services, 350
 as provider of news, 1
 search engines, 351
Invasion of privacy, 106–108
 and celebrities, 192
 photos as, 106–108
Inverted-pyramid style story, 54, 219, 295, 296
 in headlines, **229**
Irregular verbs, 144–145, **147**
Italic type, 288

Jobs and sexist labeling, 132
Joint Credibility Project, 24
Jump line in magazines, **327**
Juvenile offenders, naming, 124

Kennedy, John F., 107
Ketterer, Stan, 349–350
Kicker, **230,** 237–238
Kilpatrick, James J., 29, 30
King, Norman, 338
Kiplinger, W. M., 337
Kiplinger Letter, The, 337
KOMU-TV (Columbia, Mo.), 373, **374**

Labor disputes, 204–205
Language precision (*see* Grammar; Style mechanics; Tightening stories and words; Vocabulary usage)
Lawrence (Kan.) *Journal-World,* 6
Lawsuits, 98
 and printing corrections, 104–105
Layering and online media, 348–349
Laying out pages, 35
Leaders, describing, 398
Leadership, describing, 395

Leading, 290–291
  in magazines, 330, 333
Leads, 58–65
  burying, 64–65
  clichéd, 62, 64
  delayed-ID, 66
  features, 59–65
  hard-news stories, 58–59,
    63–65, 66
  immediate-ID, 58, 66
  misleading, 64–66
  missing "real" story,
    64–65
  old news as, 65–66
  organization and flow of
    stories, 66–67
  quotes, 66–67
  rules for, 63–65
  short and simple, 63–64
  soft leads, 61
Leg, **53**
Legal problems (*see* Media
  law)
Legal terms, 196–197, **106**
Legends, 273
Leibling, A. J., **115**
Letterspacing, 288
Levinson, Suzanne, 256
Libel, 87, 90, 91
  and celebrities, 192
  common situations,
    96–98
  corrections, printing,
    104–105
  described, 95
  guidelines on avoiding,
    98–101
  in headlines, 97–98, 245
  lawsuits and, 98, 101–104
  protections against
    lawsuits, 101–104
  macro editing, 95–104
  media law, 95–104
  overview, 95–96
  questions about, 98–101
  quotations and, 98–99
  words to avoid, 97,
    99–100
Licensing by FCC, 88–89,
  91, 118
Limbaugh, Rush, 76–77
Line art, 261
Line spacing, 309–310, 330,
  333
Linkmeister, 352

Links and online media,
  348–349
Loaded terms, 204
Localizing wire stories,
  307–308
Los Angeles
  Times–Washington
  Post News Service, 298

Macro editing:
  accuracy, 69–81
  anonymous sources and,
    108–109
  described, 56
  electronic media,
    regulation of, 113–119
  flow of story, 66–67
  integrating with micro
    editing, 184–225
  intellectual property and,
    109–111
  invasion of privacy and,
    106–108
  leads, 58–65
  for legality, 85–119
  libel and. 95
  negligence and, 105
  objectivity of stories,
    81–83
  obscenity and, 109
  organization of story,
    66–67
  propriety and, 129–133
  raffles and, 109
  unanswered questions,
    68–69
  worthiness of story,
    56–58
Micro editing, 56–84
  described, 56
  grammar, 137–157
  style, 164–176
  tightening stories and
    words, 176–182
  vocabulary usage,
    157–163
Magazines:
  advertising, **327,** 335–336
  association publications,
    321
  bleed pages, 326
  blurbs, **327,** 333
  boxes, 333
  color usage, 335
  cover art, **327**

cover lines, **327**
definitions of, 319–320
departments, **327**
design, 324–336 (*see also*
  Design of magazines)
editing vs. newspaper
  editing, 323–324
government and
  nonprofits'
  publications, 321, **341**
graphic appeal, 329
page breaks, **327**
page designers' goals, 329
photos, **327,** 334–335
principles of, **336**
question-and-answer
  articles, **327**
role of, 293
rules, 333
sidebars, **327,** 333
special-interest
  organizations'
  publications, 321
specialty magazines, 320
staffing, 322–323
table of contents, **327**
terms used by, **325**
theme issues, **327**
tint blocks, 334
title heads in, 252–254
trade publications, 321
type, **327**
type inserts, 333
typefaces, 330, **331**
wrapping type, **335**
Main head, 237
Malcolm Baldridge Award,
  379
Mallasch, K. Paul, **9**
Management, describing,
  395
Managing editor, 322–323
  described, 32, 34
Maps, 279, 280
Marketing media products,
  15–16
Marketing plans, 20–21
Math errors in news story,
  78–**80**
Maugham, Somerset, **235**
McPhilips, Dorothy, 112
Media:
  cross-ownership of, 6
  environment, changing,
    108

Media attorneys, 101
Media General, 5
Media law, **92–95**
"Media watchdog" groups,
  76
Medical news, 205
Meeting stories, 206
Metropolitan or metro
  editor, 34
Miami Herald, 257
Micro editing, integrating
  with macro editing,
  184–225
Miklasz, Bernie, 17
Mill, John Stuart, **88**
Milton, John, **88**
Milwaukee Journal Sentinel,
  347
Minnesota Public Radio,
  347
Misinformation, publishing,
  121
Misplaced modifiers, 152
  in headlines, 244
Mistakes by editors, 80–81
Mixed approach for news
  stories, **61,** 62
Mixed metaphors, 139
Mobile phone technology,
  357
Modifiers, 151–153, 193
  in sports stories, 220
Moses, Monica L., 259
Most-important-element-
  what lead, 206
Mugshots, 255, 343
Multimedia journalists, 352
Multiple-element-what
  lead, 206
Murder as legal term, **106**
Murrow, Edward R., 5

Name titles (*see* Courtesy
  titles)
Nameline, 255
Names and addresses,
  printing, 120,
  123–124, 194
National Association of
  Broadcasters v. FCC,
  118
National Geographic, **271**
National Lampoon, 242
National Public Radio, 4, 293
Negligence, 105

Network news stories, 371–372

Neutrality, objectivity of story and, 82

New media, definition of, 350

New York Times, The, 25, 30, 71, 86, 124, **176,** 233, 234, 278

New York Times News Service, The, 298

New Yorker, The, 70, 324

News:
 biased, 8
 changing nature of, 1–8
 organization and flow of story, 66–67
 public's need for discussion with reporters, 3
 radio, 4
 24–hour TV channels, 4
 vs. features, **61**
 on Web sites, 6–7

News director, **365**

News editor, 34

News peg, **61**

News World Communications, 297

Newsletter & Electronic Publishers Association, 337

Newsletters, 322, 336–343
 described, 337–338
 design, 340–343
 directories of, 338
 launching, **338, 342**
 photos, 342
 profits made, 337, 339–340
 renewal rates, 339
 success, key to, 338–339
 sample of, **341**

News-oriented Web sites (*see* Online journalism)

Newspaper Association of America, 13, 294

Newspapers:
 advantages of, 19
 advertising share of, **18**
 advice for beginners, 392
 audience perception of, 21–23
 circulation of, 3, 4, 17

copy editors, 10

copy flow through news department, 37–38
 credibility of, according to public, 23–26
 decline in readership, 3, 13–14
 descriptors of, 295
 design (*see* Design of newspapers)
 digital newspapers, 13–14
 editors coaching junior editors, 391–392
 focus piece, 295
 graphic appeal, 260–261
 industry of, 295
 inaccuracy in, 24
 marketing and, 15, 20–21
 organizational chart, **33**
 profit margins, 4
 reader-produced news, 3
 readership and headlines, 227–228
 role of, 293
 sensationalism in, 24–25
 spelling and grammar mistakes in, 24
 staff organization of, 32–36
 target audiences and, 15
 terms used by, **325**
 wire services and (*see* Wire services)

Newsroom, organization of, 32–36

News-talk radio, 117

Newsweek, 75–76

Nielsen Ratings, **22**

Nixon, Richard, 25, 115

Nouns and pronouns, 139–141
 collective, 149
 possessives and plurals, 142–144
 pronoun-antecedent agreement, 139

Novelty as element of news, 7

Nudity and propriety, 130

Numbers:
 in broadcast copy, 367
 errors made in news story, 78–**80**
 in recipes, 202
 and style, 166

Nut graf, 62, 66, 193, 201

O'Reilly, Bill, 76–77

Obituaries, 207–210

Objectivity of news stories, 81–83

Obscenity:
 and lawsuits, 109
 and propriety, 130

Offensive language and propriety, 130–132

Off-the-record statements, using, 122

Online editors, 323, 352–353

Online journalism:
 audience for, **22**
 credibility, 349–350
 designing for the Web, 356–357
 future of, 357–358
 HTML, using, 353, **354**
 layers and links, 348–349
 online editors, 323, 352–353
 sources of information, 351
 types of new media, 350–351
 Web's importance, 353, 355–356

Online media (*see* Online journalism)

Organization:
 of news story, 66–67
 of newsroom, 32–36
 of staff, 396
 of TV newsroom, **365**

Outline photo, 334

Outside-expert approach, 203

Overediting, **42**

Pace of news story, 67

Page design of news, 316

Page designers, goals of, 329

Page measurements, 283

Page proofs, 52–53, 54
 marking, **51, 52**

Passive voice, 185
 vs. active voice, 146

People magazine, **327**

Performance criteria, 395

Performance evaluation, **397**

Personality profiles, 188, 189, 210–211

Phonetic spelling system used by wire services, 365–366

Photo editor, 262–263, 265
 described, 36

Photographers, 323
 relationship with editors, 263–264

Photos, 261–278
 captions for, 255–256, 272–273, 276–278
 as copy, 269, 271
 changing technology, 271–272
 cropping, 265–266, **267, 268**
 in magazines, **327,** 334–335
 photographer-editor relationship, 263–264
 present tense in captions, **276**
 retouching, 269, 270
 scanning, 271
 selecting, 264–265, 272
 showing taste, 272, 274–275
 sizing, 266, 268–269
 staging, 121
 that lie, **271**

Picas and points, 236, 283

Pictures (*see* Photos)

Pie charts, 280

Plagiarism, 123

Podcasting, 3

Political stories, 211

Pool, Ithiel de Sola, **115**

Possessive pronouns, 140

Possessives and plurals, 142–144

Pound, Ezra, 60

Poynter Institute, 259

Prepositions, 154–155

Press releases, 378–380
 stories, 187–188, 212–214

Prime Time Access Rule, 118

Print:
 advertising, 382 (*see also* Advertising)
 vs. broadcasting regulations, 114–118

Privacy (*see* Invasion of privacy)
Process drawings, 280, **281**
Production editors:
  and assignment editor, relationship of, 3889–390
  and supervisor, 390–391
Profanity and propriety, 130
Prominence as element of news, 7
Promotional writers, 378
Pronouns (*see* Nouns and pronouns)
Pronunciation aids, 364
Proofreading, 52–54
  checklist, **53**
  symbols, 50
Proofs (*see* Page proofs)
Proportion in newspaper design, 315
Propriety:
  described, 129
  designations for groups, 133
  gore and, 130
  gratuitous references and, 131
  grief and, 130, 369
  macro editing, 129–133
  nudity and, 130
  obscenities and profanities, 130
  offensive language and, 131, 132
  prejudicial passages and, 131
  racism, 130, 131
  sexism, 131, 132, 133
  stereotyping, 132
  tragedy and, 130
  sensitivity and, 130–133
Proximity as element of news, 7
Pseudo event, creating, 121
Psychology Today, **327**
Public interest, serving, 118
Public journalism, **23**
Public relations, 378–380
  job opportunities, 376–378
Publisher, 322
  described, 32
Pull quotes, 254, 333
Pullouts, 254

Punctuation and style, 166–167
  in headlines, 238
  of quotations, 170–171
  used in copy read by newscaster, 366
Push polls, 75
Pyramid style in headlines, **229**

Question-and-answer interviews and articles, 214–215, **327**
Questions arising from news story, 68–69
Quotations, 80–81, 168–171
  attributing, 168–170
  changing, 168
  common errors in, 72
  and libel, 98–99
  in news story, 66–67
  out of context, 121
  punctuating, 170–171

Radio:
  ads, 382
  and censorship, 89
  news, 4
  role of, 293
Rand, Ayn, 114
Ranly, Don, 43, 250
Rather, Dan, 24–25, 76
Readability of story, 44–45, **176–177**
Reader-centered writing, 43–44
Reader-produced news, 3
Reader's Digest, **176**
Readership:
  decline in, 13, 14
  studies, **22**
Read-in blurbs, 255, 333
Read-out blurbs, 254, 333
Reagan, Ronald, 117
Relative pronouns, 140–141
Religion stories, 215–216
Religion terms, 215
Reporters, **365**
  described, **37**
  relationship with assignment editor, 387–389
Restraints on the press, 125
Reuters, 71, 297
Reverse kicker, **230**

Reverse plate, **230**
Reverse type, 283
Reviewing editors, 389
Reviews, 216
Rewriting:
  by editors, 81
  wire stories, 298
Ribbon headline, **230**
Richmond (Va.) *Times-Dispatch,* 31
Right in all ways, making sure a story is, 46, 48
Right to know vs. freedom of the press, 90
Rim editors, 34, 36, 101
Roanoke (Va.) *Times,* 21
Robbery as legal term, **106**
Roman type, 287–288
Ruder, Bill, 115
Run-on sentences, 137

Sacramento Bee, The, 16
Samuelson, Robert J., 76
Satellite broadcast law, 118
Savitch, Jessica, 44, 57
Scandal and newspapers, 25
Schmedding, Teresa, 257
Science and health stories, 216
Script type, 288
Search engines, 351
Season features, 217
Second head, 237
Second-cycle story, 201
Second-day leads, 296
Section editors, 34, 323
Seesaw technique, 67
Semicolons, 167
Senior editors coaching junior editors, 391–392
Sensationalism, 121
  in headlines, 247–248
  in news, 24
  in photos, 272
Sensitivity of journalists, 130–133
Sentence problems:
  comma splices, 136
  false connections, 138–139
  fragments, 136
  fused sentences, 136
  mixed metaphors, 139
  run-on sentences, 137

unclear sentences, 137–138
Service journalism, 203
Shield laws, 91, 108
Sidebars, 260
  in magazines, 333, **327**
Single-element-what lead, 206
Skyline head, **230**
Slot person, 34
Society of Professional Journalists Code of Ethics, 127–129
Soft leads, 62–63
Soft-news stories, 59
Soundbites, 370
Special-interest group databases, 351
Special-interest publications, 321
Special privileges or gifts, accepting, 122–123
Special slugs, 363
Speech stories, 217–219
Spelling, 173–175
  mistakes in news, 24
Sports Illustrated, **253, 327**
Sports stories, 219–221
Spot summary, 363
Spotlights, 363
Spread heads, **231**
St. Louis Post-Dispatch, 17
Staff writers, 323
Standalone photos, 256, **277**
Star Tribune (Minneapolis and St. Paul), 73
State court systems, **93, 95**
Statutory law, **93**
Stepline of headlines, **229**
Stet head, **230**
Stick-up initial, 328
Stolen information, using, 122
Story, mechanics of, 46, 48
Story edit, example of, **41**
Streamer headline, **230**
Stringers, 298
Style mechanics, 164–177
  abbreviations, 164–165
  addresses, 171–172
  broadcast media, 366–369
  capitalization, 165
  datelines, 172–173
  numbers, 166

Style mechanics (*cont.*)
  punctuation, 166–167
  quotations, 168–171
  spelling, 173–175
  symbols, 165
  time-day-place, 171
  titles, 172
Stylebooks for newspapers, 164
Subjective pronouns, 140
Subject-verb agreement, 148–151
Subordinating
  conjunctions, 156
Summary-what lead, 206
Superlatives:
  for simple modifiers, 152
  unwarranted, 71–72
Supervisor and production
  editors, 390–391
"Sweeps" periods, **22**
Symbols, style and, 165

Table of contents, **327**
Tables, 279, 280
Tabloids, 192
Takeout, 363
Talk radio, 16
Tammen, Harry, **230**
Tampa Bay Online, 5
Tampa Tribune, 5
Taste:
  in broadcast news, 369
  in photo editing, 272, **274–275**
Taylor, Wilson L., **177**
Team system of editing, **35**
TelePrompTer, 364
Television:
  and censorship, 89
  news, 370–373
  newsroom organization, **365**
  role of, 293
Thelen, Gil, 5
Theme issues of magazines, **327**
Thomas, Richard L., 73
Tie-back paragraph, 202
Tightening:
  accident stories, 187
  business stories, 191
  court stories, 196
  crime stories, 199

education stories, 199
medical stories, 205
the story, **42,** 176–182
words, 176–182
Time magazine, **176,** 278, 324, 350
Time-day-place order, 59, 171, 213
Timeliness:
  as element of news, 7
  of stories and features, 60
Tint blocks, 334
Title heads in magazines, 252–254
Titles:
  for the Internet, 256–257
  of people (*see* Courtesy titles)
Trade publications, 321
Trademark infringement, **110,** 111
Traditional media,
  audience of, **18**
Tragedy and propriety, 130
Travel pieces, 221
Trim size, 283
Trimming stories, 58
  feature stories, 62
  hard-news stories, 59
TV Guide, **271**
Type, 282–292
  headlines, 291–292
  inserts, 333
  leading, 290–291
  in magazines, **327**
  measuring, 289–290
  typefaces, 282–288
Typefaces, 282–288, 309
  in magazines, 330, **331**

Unanswered questions,
  checklist for, **69**
Unclear sentences, 137–138
  (*see also* Sentence problems)
Undated stories, 306
Undercover investigations
  and ethical issues, 122
Underline, 228, 255
United Press International, 71, 297
Urban, Christine, 23
Urban & Associates, 23
Urban legends, 73–75

URL (uniform resource
  locater), 355
U.S. Supreme Court, **94**
USA Today, 233. 234, 278

Van Anda, Carr, 30
Verbs:
  irregular, 144–145, **147**
  parallel construction, 144
  passive voice, 146
  subjective mood, 146–148
  subject-verb agreement, 148–151
  tenses, 144–146
Video:
  editing systems, 372
  from Web, 373
Videographers, 260, **365**
Violation of privacy, 87
  and ethical issues, 123
Visual literacy, 262
Vocabulary usage, 157–163
  accident stories, 187
  boating stories, 189
  business stories, 190–191
  celebrity news, 192
  court stories, 195
  crime stories, 198
  labor stories, 204–205
  medical news, 205
  obituaries, 207
Voiceover, 373

Wall Street Journal, The, 98
Wall Street Journal
  formula, 295
War stories, 222
Washington Post, The, 25, 76, 115
Weather maps, 278, **279**
Weather stories, 222–224
Web:
  chat rooms, 9
  designing for, 356–357
  headlines, 256–257
  importance of, 353, 355–356
  role of, 293
  video, 373
Web editor, described, 36
Web producer, described, 389
Web sites, 20
  and news, 6–8

of newspapers, 17
verifying facts, 69, **71,** 76
Web-first model, 27
Web-first strategies, 21
Werner, Larry, 73
WFLA, 5
White, Byron (Justice), 112
White, E. B., 200
Whiteside, Scott, 345, 346
WHO-TV (Des Moines), 347
Widows, **277**
Wire services, 296–308
  budget of, 299–303
  cutting, **304**
  editing, **304**
  localizing, 307–308
  mistakes, 305
  operation of, 298–299
  peculiarities of, 306–307
  phonetic spelling system
    used by, 365–366
  priorities of, 299, 303
  selecting, 304–308
  sources, 297–298
  vs. local stories, **304**
Woodward, Bob, 25, 115
Words:
  to avoid libel, 97, 99–100
  betraying opinion, 82
  clichés, 180–182
  common vs. less
    common, 180
  confusing, list of, 157–163
  connecting, 154–157
  correct spellings to
    know, **174–175**
  imprecise, 77–78
  legal terminology, 196–197
  magazine terminology, **325**
  offensive, 131–132
  and phrases to avoid, **179–180**
  preferred by groups, 133
  tightening, 176–182
  traditionally outlawed, 118
Words into Type, 384
Wraparound type, 335
Writer-as-expert approach, 203